Philosophy of Mind: The Key Thinkers

BLOOMSBURY KEY THINKERS

The *Key Thinkers* series is aimed at undergraduate students and offers clear, concise and accessible edited guides to the key thinkers in each of the central topics in philosophy. Each book offers a comprehensive overview of the major thinkers who have contributed to the historical development of a key area of philosophy, providing a survey of their major works and the evolution of the central ideas in that area.

Key Thinkers in Philosophy available now from Bloomsbury:

Aesthetics, Edited by Alessandro Giovannelli
Epistemology, Edited by Stephen Hetherington
Ethics, Edited by Tom Angier
Philosophy of Language, Edited by Barry Lee
Philosophy of Religion, Edited by Jeffrey J. Jordan
Philosophy of Science, Edited by James Robert Brown

KEY THINKERS

Philosophy of Mind: The Key Thinkers

EDITED BY
ANDREW BAILEY

BLOOMSBURY
LONDON • NEW DELHI • NEW YORK • SYDNEY

Bloomsbury Academic
An imprint of Bloomsbury Publishing Plc

50 Bedford Square	1385 Broadway
London	New York
WC1B 3DP	NY 10018
UK	USA

www.bloomsbury.com

Bloomsbury is a registered trade mark of Bloomsbury Publishing Plc

First published 2014

© Andrew Bailey and Contributors, 2014

Andrew Bailey has asserted his right under the Copyright, Designs and Patents Act, 1988, to be identified as Editor of this work.

All rights reserved. No part of this publication may be reproduced or transmitted in any form or by any means, electronic or mechanical, including photocopying, recording, or any information storage or retrieval system, without prior permission in writing from the publishers.

No responsibility for loss caused to any individual or organization acting on or refraining from action as a result of the material in this publication can be accepted by Bloomsbury Academic or the author.

British Library Cataloguing-in-Publication Data
A catalogue record for this book is available from the British Library.

ISBN: HB: 978-1-4411-9537-1
PB: 978-1-4411-4276-4
ePDF: 978-1-4411-9096-3
ePub: 978-1-4411-6631-9

Library of Congress Cataloging-in-Publication Data
Philosophy of mind: the key thinkers/edited by Andrew Bailey.
pages cm. – (Key thinkers)
Includes bibliographical references and index.
ISBN 978-1-4411-4276-4 (pbk.) – ISBN 978-1-4411-9537-1 (hardcover) – ISBN 978-1-4411-9096-3 (ebook (pdf)) 1. Philosophy of mind–History. 2. Philosophers. I. Bailey, Andrew, 1969–
BD418.3.P49 2014
128'.209–dc23
2013016926

Typeset by Deanta Global Publishing Services, Chennai, India

CONTENTS

Notes on Contributors vii

1 Introduction: 90 years of philosophy of mind *Andrew Bailey* 1
2 Decoding Descartes' 'myth' of mind *Patricia Easton* 17
3 Edmund Husserl and phenomenology *Dermot Moran* 37
4 Merleau-Ponty: A phenomenological philosophy of mind and body *Sara Heinämaa* 59
5 Gilbert Ryle and logical behaviourism *William Lyons* 85
6 The contributions of U. T. Place, H. Feigl and J. J. C. Smart to the identity theory of consciousness *Brian P. McLaughlin and Ronald Planer* 103
7 David Lewis, David Armstrong and the causal theory of the mind *David Braddon-Mitchell* 129
8 Hilary Putnam and computational functionalism *Oron Shagrir* 147
9 Jerry Fodor and the representational theory of mind *Matthew Katz* 169

10 Donald Davidson, Daniel Dennett and the origins of the normative model of the mind *Andrew Brook* 189

11 Tracking representationalism: William Lycan, Fred Dretske and Michael Tye *David Bourget and Angela Mendelovici* 209

12 The neurophilosophies of Patricia and Paul Churchland *John Bickle* 237

13 Andy Clark, Antonio Damasio and embodied cognition *Monica Cowart* 259

14 David Chalmers on mind and consciousness *Richard Brown* 283

15 Postscript: Philosophy of mind – the next ten years *Andrew Bailey* 303

Index 315

NOTES ON CONTRIBUTORS

Andrew Bailey is associate professor of philosophy at the University of Guelph, in Ontario. His research deals with the problem of consciousness, embodied cognition and the thought of William James. He is the editor of three books and author of several papers on zombies and physicalism.

John Bickle is Professor and Head of the Department of Philosophy and Religion, Adjunct Professor in the Department of Psychology, and Fellow, Institute for Imaging and Analytical Technologies, at Mississippi State University. His research focuses on the philosophy of neuroscience, philosophy of science (especially scientific reductionism), and cellular and molecular mechanisms of cognition and consciousness. He is the editor of the *Oxford Handbook of Philosophy and Neuroscience* (Oxford University Press 2009) and author of *Psychoneural Reduction: The New Wave* (MIT Press 1998) and *Philosophy and Neuroscience: A Ruthlessly Reductive Approach* (Kluwer 2003) as well as two other books and more than 50 papers.

David Bourget was until recently a research fellow at the Institute of Philosophy, School of Advanced Study, University of London, but he has now taken up a position at Western University, Ontario. His research focuses on philosophical questions about consciousness; he is also the co-creator of PhilPapers (http://philpapers.org).

David Braddon-Mitchell is Professor and Head of the Department of Philosophy at the University of Sydney. His research deals with philosophy of mind and metaphysics, as well as meta-ethics, philosophy of science, philosophy of biology and epistemology. He is the author, with Frank Jackson, of *The Philosophy of Mind and Cognition* (Blackwell 2006) and of many papers.

Andrew Brook is Chancellor's Professor of Philosophy and Cognitive Science at Carleton University in Ottawa. He is a former President of the Canadian Philosophical Association and former Director of the Institute of Cognitive Science (ICS) at Carleton University. His research focuses on the project of interdisciplinary cognitive research, Kant, consciousness, and psychological and psychoanalytic explanation; he is the author or editor of seven books (two of which deal with the work of Daniel Dennett) and over 100 papers and book chapters.

Richard Brown is an associate professor at the City University of New York – in the philosophy program at LaGuardia Community College – and a member of the NYU Project on Space, Time and Consciousness. His work is focused on the philosophy of mind, consciousness studies and the foundations of cognitive science. He is also a rock drummer and organizer of Qualia Fest, which annually brings together in New York City bands featuring neuroscientists and philosophers, including David Chalmers.

Monica Cowart is chairperson and associate professor in the Department of Philosophy, Merrimack College, Massachusetts. Her research deals with philosophy of cognitive science and psychology, and applied ethics, and includes investigating the role of metaphor in mindfulness-based clinical treatments.

Patricia Easton is Professor and Chair of Philosophy, and Associate Provost for Academic Planning, at Claremont Graduate University. She specializes in the history of modern philosophy, particularly the philosophy of René Descartes and the Cartesians of the seventeenth century. She directed and edited *The Descartes Web Site*, which features seventeenth-century French and English editions of Descartes' work *The Passions of the Soul*, and is the author or editor of three books and several articles and chapters.

Sara Heinämaa is university lecturer in theoretical philosophy at University of Helsinki. Presently, she works as Academy Research

Fellow at the Helsinki Collegium for Advanced Studies, UH. She works on phenomenology, the mind-body relation, history of philosophy and philosophical women's studies, and is the author of *Toward a Phenomenology of Sexual Difference: Husserl, Merleau-Ponty, Beauvoir* (Rowman & Littlefield, 2003). She is the author or editor of a further 15 books and many papers.

Matthew Katz is a member of the Department of Philosophy and Religion at Central Michigan University. His research defends and elaborates the claim that human adults possess (at least) two systems for representing numbers, one of which employs a language-like format of representation and the other employing a system of mental magnitudes that is not language-like in format. He has published on the Language of Thought Hypothesis and also works on the philosophy of mind and psychology, and epistemology.

William Lyons is an emeritus fellow of Trinity College Dublin and a member of the Royal Irish Academy. He was formerly Head of the Department of Philosophy (1985–1995) and Professor of Moral Philosophy (1985–2004) in the School of Mental and Moral Science, Trinity College Dublin, and is the author of several books, including *Emotion* (1980), *Gilbert Ryle* (1980) and *Matters of the Mind* (2001). He has also written award-winning plays about Wittgenstein, Heidegger and Socrates.

Brian P. McLaughlin is Distinguished Professor of Philosophy and Cognitive Science at Rutgers University. He works on the mind-body problem and various metaphysical and epistemological problems concerning the mind. He is the author of numerous articles and editor or co-editor of several books, including *The Oxford Handbook of Philosophy of Mind* (2011).

Angela Mendelovici is an assistant professor of philosophy at Western University, Ontario, and her research focuses on the philosophy of mind, specifically the problem of mental representation. She received her PhD from Princeton in 2010 and was a postdoctoral fellow at the Australian National University.

Dermot Moran has held the professorship of philosophy (metaphysics and logic) at University College Dublin since 1989, and in 2003 was elected member of the Royal Irish Academy. He has published widely on mediaeval philosophy (especially Christian Neoplatonism) and contemporary European philosophy (especially phenomenology). He is the author of two books on Husserl, an *Introduction to Phenomenology* (Routledge 2000), and author or editor of a further 11 books, as well as many papers and book chapters. Prof Moran was awarded the Royal Irish Academy Gold Medal in the Humanities in 2012.

Ronald Planer is a doctoral student in philosophy at Rutgers University, New Brunswick. His research focuses on issues in the philosophy of biology, philosophy of mind and foundations of cognitive science. His dissertation examines the application of information-related concepts to low-level biological phenomena, in particular, gene expression and regulation.

Oron Shagrir is professor of philosophy, former chair of the Cognitive Science department and a member of the Centre for Language, Logic and Cognition, at the Hebrew University of Jerusalem. His current research aims at understanding the claim that the brain computes. He is the editor, with Jack Copeland and Carl Posy, of *Computability: Turing, Gödel, Church, and Beyond* (MIT Press 2013), and the author of many articles and book chapters on computation and supervenience.

CHAPTER ONE

Introduction: 90 years of philosophy of mind

Andrew Bailey

Among the many millions of cells making up the normal human retina, there are about 126 million specialist photosensitive cells. All of our visual sensation is, normally, the result of light striking these cells. About 120 million of them are photoreceptors called 'rods', which are sensitive to low levels of light; the rest are cones,[1] which require much higher levels of light to be activated but which are capable of detecting, not merely brightness and movement in the scene, but different wavelengths of light. It is the relative differences between light wavelengths that are the basis for colour vision, and in most human beings (as in most primates, but unlike the majority of the rest of the animal kingdom) this information is recorded using three different types of cone, sensitive to three different, overlapping, ranges of wavelength. Because of this, most humans are what is called *trichromats*: roughly, every colour we see is determined by the mix of red, blue and green light that makes it up.

Some humans, however, do not have three different kinds of cones; they have two (and are thus *dichromats*). These people cannot see as many colours because they rely upon the interaction of only two types of cone instead of three. They therefore have different colour sensations, and, in the case of *unilateral dichromats* (a rare situation where the subject is 'colour blind' in only one eye and so can compare trichromatic experience with dichromatic experience), we can ask what their colour sensations are like: it is, apparently, like being able to see all the shades on a normal colour line except with a 'grey point', often somewhere between blue and yellow, in which colours are indistinguishable from white or grey of equivalent brightness.

Now, some other humans, as well as most birds and some fish, amphibians, reptiles and insects, are *tetrachromats*.[2] That is, they have four different types of cone cell, and as a consequence can see colours that trichromatic organisms cannot distinguish. The question is: what will their colour experience be like? This is not a case of 'missing' colours but of *new* colours: colours that are simply not visible to trichromatic human beings. As far as I know, no cases of unilateral tetrachromacy have been confirmed, but even if we encountered one, what could we (assuming we are trichromats) find out about their colour experience? We could quite easily discover what discriminations they are able to make that we cannot make (e.g. between two samples that look identically coloured to us) – but how could we come to understand what it was *like* to see a colour we had never seen and never could see?

Bees are trichromats. However, unlike primates, cone cells in bees are sensitive to ultraviolet, blue and green, instead of blue, green and red. Furthermore, recent research suggests that bumblebees not only can sense the colour hues – from green to the ultraviolet regions of the spectrum – patterns, texture and fragrance of the plants they pollinate, but also can sense the tiny electrical fields generated by flowers (Clarke et al. 2013). Indeed, the researchers hypothesize, '[b]ecause floral electric fields can change within seconds, this sensory modality may facilitate rapid and dynamic communication between flowers and their pollinators'. What is it like to be a bee? We might be capable of some appreciation of what it is like to be a human tetrachromat, even without being one, insofar as the shades they see that are undetectable to us nevertheless putatively resemble the hues we can see; but in the case of bees, they see wavelengths that are not even on the spectrum that is visible to humans, and in addition have at least one sensory modality that is completely alien to us.

What are these qualities – the hues, the bee-feel of a minute electrical field – and similar sensory qualities such as smells, tickles, dizziness or toothache? Even the brief discussion thus far seems, provisionally, to suggest

   a that they are not naively 'in' the objects we experience, since one and the same object can produce very different experiences in different perceivers;
   b that they are distinct from the capacity to make particular perceptual distinctions, since we can understand the perceptual capacities of tetrachromats without grasping the additional colour sensations they undergo and indeed can experimentally determine the abilities of bees to detect electrical fields without even being sure that it is like *anything* to be a bee at all;
   c and most worrying of all, that the relationship between physiological perceptual machinery and first-personal experience is deeply opaque – we can study how different perceptual instruments allow for different suites of discriminative ability, but, on the face of it, we have no idea how it is that particular kinds of perceptual ability give rise to particular qualitative sensations; indeed, the qualitative sensations in question seem not even to be empirically visible.

This is one starting point for the philosophy of mind (one of several). It is a way of coming to feel – perhaps crystallizing existing half-felt intuitions – that the mind may be a quite different domain than the physical, and hence that it raises uniquely difficult problems for the scientific study of living things, perhaps even for a naturalistic, physicalist worldview in general. This is not what most philosophers of mind and cognitive scientists in fact do think: the large majority of philosophers of mind are working to develop naturalistic, empirically robust theories of our mental life. But it introduces a *problem*, arguably one facet of the key problem, that contemporary philosophers of mind set out to solve: our conscious colour experience (or our feeling of free will, or our ability to think and behave in accordance with what is rational or right, or our capacity to produce an apparently open-ended number of propositions, or our nature as passionate and emotional beings . . .) can easily come to seem disjoint from the physical world in such a way that it is apparently inexplicable how these mental phenomena could possibly arise from mere material mechanism. The problem for the philosopher of mind is to show how this is not so or otherwise to say something useful about just what is going on.

There is an inviting, and deceptively linear, story to be told about modern philosophy of mind, one that can even seem to have a certain kind of intellectual inevitability. Unlike some other areas of philosophy, which recognize a longer history as being of contemporary relevance, philosophy of mind – it is often assumed – focuses on the period from about 1950 onwards.[3] The story typically beings with what Gilbert Ryle called, in 1949, the 'official doctrine', a view of the mind that is usually thought of as inherited from Descartes and his early modern successors such as John Locke and Thomas Reid and then, to some extent, filtered through Kant.[4] Certainly there were philosophers of mind before Descartes, including such towering figures as Plato, Aristotle, Aquinas and William of Ockham, but Descartes' introduction of substance dualism is traditionally held to mark a decisive break from earlier theories of mentality and to be the view of the mind to which modern theorists are reacting.

In large part this is because Descartes was one of those ushering in the modern scientific understanding of the world, exemplified in mathematical physics, and rejecting the scholastic, teleological worldview that went before. Thinkers before Descartes may be suggestive of, or for, modern developments – as Aristotle is often said to be a forerunner of functionalism, for example – but (it is often assumed) the pre-Cartesians were playing on a quite different field than we moderns, a field where the distinctions between mind and matter, between the biological and the merely physical, between active intelligence and passive causation, is quite different – and much more blurry – than those we presuppose today. (Although, interestingly, a move back in the direction of re-blurring these boundaries is part of the trajectory of philosophy of mind in the past couple of decades, as we shall see.)

At any rate, the standard line on the mind in, say, 1940, for philosophers (at least Anglophone philosophers), scientists and even the person on the Clapham omnibus, was, crudely, as follows: The world consists of physical entities – mountains, streams, tables, table salt, sodium chloride molecules, photons – which are spatial, material (or energetic) and governed by the mechanical, often deterministic, laws elucidated by science. In addition, there exist entities of a quite different type: minds. Some but not all physical bodies – human bodies, but not tables – are somehow conjoined with individual minds (and in addition it is possible that some minds exist without bodies). Minds are unlike physical objects in every way: they are not spatial, they are not governed by laws of motion (though they may be governed by other, psychological laws, often held to be rational rather than causal), they are private rather than public – minds are directly accessible only by their possessors – and they instantiate qualities that are not present in the material world (such as colour, smell, sound, fear, hunger and the sensation of heat). The Cartesian background to modern philosophy of mind, a period that occupied some 300 years of active and diverse philosophy, is addressed by Patricia Easton in Chapter 2.

The standard narrative of contemporary philosophy of mind unfurls from this point in intellectual history. First comes behaviourism: instead of postulating essentially private, metaphysically mysterious, 'inner' episodes, the behaviourist builds her theory of mind exclusively upon overt behaviours. After all, overt behaviour (i.e. behaviour reasonably visible to the normal human observer, such as speech acts, limb movements, or blushes) is all that has ever been available to us when we come to form judgements about the mental lives of others – and of other species – and yet we are perfectly comfortable in applying predicates such as 'intelligent', 'irascible' or 'idealistic' to the people we meet. Why assume that these psychological judgements outrun – indeed, hopelessly outrun, without hope of empirical correction – the evidence available for them when we can, more reasonably, treat them as judgements *about that evidence* (i.e. about past and future behaviour)? The thought of Gilbert Ryle, arguably the figure most associated with philosophical behaviourism, is engagingly and sympathetically laid out by William Lyons in Chapter 5.

But wait, that can't be quite right can it? If we identify mental characteristics with overt behaviour, then what can we say about the *causes* of that behaviour (which, after all, are not themselves typically overt behaviours)? Must we deny that our actions are caused by our minds? Furthermore, a central element of the Cartesian legacy has a strong hold over our intuitions: we do seem to have an 'inner mental life' that we access introspectively, and that is not reducible to any of our propensities to behave. Our dreams are more than simply our dream reports, our pain is more than our pain behaviour and my pain is something I experience in a way quite different than the way I become acquainted with your pain.

So let's fix this by a partial return to the 'inner event' model of Cartesianism, but let us not throw out the naturalistic baby with the behaviourist bathwater. Let's suppose that our mental states and events are inner states in us, which when properly connected cause our deliberate actions, but which are not metaphysically different from the states and events we are used to dealing with in science. That is, they are not states of a mental substance but states of physical substance – brain states. This is the theory variously called 'central state materialism', mind/brain type-type identity theory, or reductive physicalism. What is pain? It is some kind of neural event – in the heyday of identity theory postulated to be 'c-fibres[5] firing' – that is the typical effect of painful stimuli and the typical cause of pain behaviour. Key figures behind this philosophical turn, in the 1950s and 1960s – Place, Smart and Feigl – are expertly explained by Brian McLaughlin and Ronald Planer in Chapter 6.

But wait a minute. We know that humans feel pain and have c-fibres. But other species, with different brain anatomies than ours, feel pain as well: some of these creatures might have no (or relevantly physiologically different) c-fibres. The standard philosopher's example, owing to an influential article by Hilary Putnam (1967), is the octopus, since octopuses are intelligent creatures to which we are strongly inclined to attribute a conscious mental life, yet they are – along with slugs and bivalves – members of the phylum *Mollusca* and physiologically quite different from us mammals.[6] And what about robots? Or aliens? Or angels? We can be quite sure that none of these three categories of being have c-fibres and yet, if they exist, it seems perfectly possible that they might feel pain.

What these kinds of examples – examples of a phenomenon called *multiple realizability* – seem to demonstrate is that pain cannot be *the same thing* as the firing of c-fibres, in the following sense: though c-fibre firing may be sufficient for pain (i.e. pain in humans might be nothing over and above c-fibre firings), it is not necessary for pain – pain in octopuses might not involve c-fibres at all, and in, say, aliens it might not even be realized by anything carbon based. Analogously, money is not *the same thing* as US dollar bills, and this would be true even if, by some historical quirk, US dollar bills happened to be the only monetary instrument in existence. So, if money is not some particular set of pieces of paper, metal, stone or shell, what is it? It is anything that can be used as a medium for the exchange of goods and services – anything that *functions* in that way to enable trade. Similarly, we can think of pain not as the particular physiological event (c-fibre firing in humans) typically caused by pain stimuli and causing pain behaviour, but as the *function* (crudely) of taking a certain kind of stimulus as an input and producing a certain set of characteristic outputs. Pain is not the occupant of, as it were, the pain role – it is the role itself.[7]

This is the theory called 'functionalism', a very broad church and, it is often thought, the latest stop for the philosophy of mind train (or, perhaps better, the sea into which the river of twentieth-century philosophy of mind empties). Functionalism is attractive for the way it seems to combine much of what was best about the theories that came before, and leave behind much of what was dubious. Like dualism, functionalism typically treats mental events as inner causes of behaviour (and is able to understand 'inner' a good deal less metaphorically than the dualist must). Furthermore, it seems to have the resources to distinguish those causes that are mental from those that are not, in a reasonably satisfying way: although human beings are physical objects in a physical world, as enmeshed in the bonds of causality as any physical object, we possess inner states that are meaningful – that have contents – and that are connected together by causal laws that mirror logic or reason, and it is these states that cause our deliberate behaviour.[8] Our confidence that this might be so comes from the rapid rise to salience of the computer, and of theories of computation, in the mid-twentieth century, a development that was itself a major factor in the growth of functionalism as a dominant theory of the mind. Computers are exactly that type of object: physical objects whose inner states can be interpreted as having symbolic content and whose operations are describable according to logical, rather than merely electro-mechanical, principles. Both the careful chapter by Oron Shagrir on Hilary Putnam's Turing machine functionalism, Chapter 8, and Matthew Katz's discussion of the influential work of Jerry Fodor, Chapter 9, pick up key elements of this story.

Also like dualism, functionalism is able to countenance the possibility of as yet unknown, possibly alien or non-biological or even (in principle) non-physical minds. This seems right, or at least desirable: no matter how confident we are in our physicalism, it seems rash to commit to the view that non-physical minds are incoherent – are not even a metaphysical possibility – because of the very nature of the mental. This is something that mind/brain identity theory apparently got wrong. But what it got right (perhaps) was the anti-dualist commitment to minds, in the actual world, being as a matter of fact nothing over and above the physical. And this is something the functionalist can say too. Just as earthly money is always physical (even if, these days, often electrical), even though someone could tell an internally coherent fictional story involving, say, ectoplasmic ghost currency, without doing violence to the very notion of 'money'; and just as there is nothing to a dollar bill beyond the printed piece of paper and cloth that realizes it; similarly, human minds are nothing over and above brains even though mental state types are not simply *the same thing* as types of neural activity. David Braddon-Mitchell's discussion of the important work of David Lewis and David Armstrong, Chapter 7, deals with this theme among others.

Functionalism, then, is defined by its focus on causal roles (rather than lumps of physical or mental substance, phenomenal properties, or patterns of overt behaviour) as constitutive of the mental. But the world is full of complex causal structure: which roles within that vast structure are specifically *mental*? And once we have identified those roles, is there really nothing to mentality over and above the playing out of those causal relations?

Functionalists have provided a range of answers to the first of these questions. Some, often called 'common sense' or 'analytic' functionalists, have postulated that mental causal roles are defined by natural language or 'folk psychology' – for example, *love* is the causal role specified by the (analysis of the) word 'love' ('amour', 'Liebe', 'kærlighed', 'cinta' and so on) in natural languages such as English. (See, again, Chapter 7). Others, often called 'scientific' functionalists or 'psychofunctionalists', take the relevant causal roles to be those fixed by scientific psychology and are open to the possibility that the categories of folk psychology might turn out to be empty – there might be no such literal thing as *love*, as we usually understand it – and have to be replaced by new categories driven by empirical discoveries. The energetic discussion of the work of Paul and Patricia Churchland by John Bickle, in Chapter 12, picks up on this theme.

Another debate, which to some extent cross-cuts the analytic versus scientific functionalism disagreement, is the extent to which some sort of evolutionary or learning *history* is required to individuate mental causal roles: for example, some functionalists hold that causal roles can be identified as mental only in terms of their biological purposes (their teleology). Analogously, a heart is defined functionally, but genuine hearts are only hearts because it is their evolved, biological purpose to pump blood – something may play a relevantly similar causal role in some system but not really be a heart because it does not have that biological purpose. (See, e.g. Sober 1985.) This amendment, often called 'teleological' functionalism, is often thought especially important for a proper account of mental representation – of what makes mental states intentional, or directed at the world. David Bourget and Angela Mendelovici's beautifully clear chapter on Dretske, Lycan and Tye, Chapter 11, discusses, among other things, the benefits and pitfalls of a teleological account of function.

A third important arena of disagreement within functionalism is the causal architecture to which it applies. 'Classical' functionalists hold that the mind can fruitfully be understood as a computer: as an organ that transduces information from the environment, operates upon it in combination with stored representations of the world, and produces new representations and overt behaviours. That is, the language of computation is literally true of the mind, and mental states are to be understood as input-output operations within these massively complex computations. Of course, some physical structure (the brain) is required to realize these computations, but the details of that realization are unimportant to what makes mentality mental (see, e.g. van Gelder 1995).

By contrast, other philosophers and cognitive scientists have argued that the brain's information processing cannot properly be described as classical computation, or at least that the level of description that best captures the mental is not at the level of classical computation but of 'connectionist' or 'parallel distributed' processing. Connectionist computation involves large networks of nodes joined together by connections of different strengths, or 'weights'; inputs produce shifting patterns of activation in the nodes, and adjustments of weights among the connections, and outputs consist in the network as a whole 'settling' into a stable pattern (see, e.g. Bechtel 1993). Structurally, this seems very different than the classical, serial manipulation of symbols in accordance with logical operations, and it is a disputed question whether connectionist networks even contain, or can realize, systematically related symbolic representations or syntactic laws (see, e.g. Fodor and Pylyshyn 1988; Bickle's chapter on the Churchlands is very relevant again here).

The history – even the summary, streamlined history being presented here – of late twentieth-century philosophy of mind is not made up solely of the proliferation of variants of functionalism, however. While functionalism was, and arguably is, the dominant paradigm for the explanation of cognition, it nevertheless faces serious criticisms.[9]

A central worry, from the very earliest days of functionalism, was the extent to which it suffices as a theory of *conscious* mental states, especially qualitative sensations such as colour perceptions, pains or emotions (mental states with properties that are usually called *qualia*). This is the second of the two questions raised above: is there really nothing to mentality over and above the playing out of whatever causal relations are spotlighted by the best-available functionalist theory? (Functionalism is committed to the position that there is not: it is a form of identity theory, *identifying* mental states with functional roles.) Of course, the question of which causal structures are the best candidates to be realizers of consciousness is still open, and the functionalist can claim that future empirical discoveries (e.g. neurophysiological advances) will answer the qualia objection. But the worry persists that no amount of detailed specification of functional relationships will ever make the jump from cognitive psychology to phenomenal consciousness – that the subjective sensation of pain, for example, has an intrinsic quality that is simply not reducible to any amount of physical structure and function. This species of objection to functionalism – and to physicalist theories of consciousness generally – arguably reached its acme in the work of David Chalmers in the 1990s, work that is ably introduced by Richard Brown in Chapter 14.

One particularly important variety of response to this kind of worry sets out explicitly to understand the phenomenal – qualia – wholly in terms of the functional, and in particular in terms of broadly functionalist accounts of *representation*. Thus, phenomenal mental states are nothing over and above states with a certain kind of representational content, and this content in turn is fully naturalistically accountable (e.g. as a certain sophisticated kind of tracking relation). David Bourget and Angela Mendelovici's chapter, Chapter 11, explains the key streams in this line of thought.

A second kind of objection to functionalism arises from the apparent *normativity* and *holism* of the attribution of mental states. There is a bundle of issues here. For one thing, mental states are interdefined in such complex ways that it seems plausible that two people could differ in their functional organization but have mental states in common, or alternatively have components of their functional organization be the same while their mental states are different. The causal role that constitutes the belief that, for example, water is thirst-quenching will involve an indefinite number of connections to other beliefs, desires, perceptual judgements and so on; yet two people could, presumably, have substantially different sets of beliefs, desires and experiences while both having the *same* belief that water quenches thirst. (See, e.g. Stich 1983; Shagrir also deals with this issue in his chapter on Putnam.)

Another aspect of this set of issues is the following worry for functionalism: while functionalists focus on the causal role of mental states in producing behaviour, another natural approach is to understand mental states in terms of their role in *making sense of* behaviour. Critics of this sort urge that this latter approach is both more fundamental than the functionalist approach, since our only avenue for the ascription of mental states is through the interpretation of behaviour, but also strictly *incompatible* with standard functionalism because the normative standards by which we attribute mental states – standards of rationality – invoke a form of explanation that is quite different from appeals to empirical relations among our internal states. Andrew Brook explores and assesses two key forms of this normative model of the mind, Davidson's anomalous monism and Dennett's type intentionalism, in Chapter 10.

Finally, there is a third influential species of objection to functionalism, and to non-reductive varieties of physicalism in general, which turns on the problem of mental causation. I will mention this problem again in the Postscript (Chapter 15).

This potted history of the philosophy of mind is, up to a point, helpful and even, as far as it goes, accurate: it is a decent starting point. But there is lots that is oversimple about it, and I will conclude this introductory chapter with some key caveats.

As one might expect, it is incomplete in various ways. Its focus is on the mind-body problem: on the nature of mental states and their (metaphysical, epistemic, causal) relation to the body and brain. However, there is more to the philosophy of mind than this – albeit, arguably, always premised on one approach to the mind-body problem (typically some variant of functionalism) or another – such as work on introspection, emotion, agency, personal identity, action, artificial intelligence, evolutionary and developmental psychology, innateness, psychopathology and our capacity to understand the minds of others. (Bechtel and Graham 1998, gives a good sense of some of this range.)

A particularly rich and diverse area of the philosophy of mind is the nature of mental content, and this includes much that is not strictly tied up with the mind-body problem, such as questions about the extent to which mental content is 'externalist' – that is, determined by elements of the world that are outside the head – the degree to which mental content must be conceptual, and the special role of indexical mental content (i.e. contents involving concepts such as 'I', 'now', 'this' and 'here'). I will have a little more to say about these matters in the Postscript (and see also Chapter 3).

Secondly, the philosophical positions that were 'succeeded' by functionalism never really died out and – analogously to the way the dinosaurs are still with us in the shape of the birds into which they evolved – they are still live options today. The interpretationism of Davidson and Dennett, which is explored in Andrew Brook's chapter, can be seen as a development of behaviourism; the reductivist neurophilosophies of the Churchlands, described by John Bickle, are related to mind-brain identity theory; and the anti-physicalist arguments of Chalmers, which are explained in Richard Brown's chapter, have been at the forefront of a re-examination of the prospects for some form of dualism (though more likely a dualism of properties, or of 'aspects', than of substances).

Furthermore, the boundaries between the positions sketched above are often more ill-defined and contested than a historical gloss can make them seem, as, for example, Brian McLaughlin and Ronald Planer's chapter on the identity theorists and Braddon-Mitchell's account of the causal theory of the mind make clear.

Thirdly, the narrative followed above entirely, and invidiously, excludes the important developments in philosophy of mind that were occurring in non–English-speaking philosophy, especially early twentieth-century German philosophy and post-war French philosophy. The seminal work of Edmund Husserl and Maurice Merleau-Ponty is lucidly laid out in the chapters by Dermot Moran (Chapter 3) and Sara Heinämaa (Chapter 4).[10] It is probably more or less true to say that so-called continental philosophy had relatively little direct influence on what could be considered the mainstream of philosophy of mind for much of the latter part of the twentieth century.[11] However, that is no longer the case, and one key feature of philosophy of mind in the past decade – as Moran and Heinämaa show – has been a new, very fruitful dialogue between the phenomenological tradition and cognitive science (see, e.g. Gallagher and Zahavi 2012).

Finally, and in part connected to the resurgent influence of phenomenology (and also to developments in, for example, robotics), there is a relatively recent movement in cognitive science and the philosophy of mind that calls into question the hitherto dominant paradigm of the mind as a kind of 'central processing unit' for the body that takes in data from the environment, manipulates that information in the form of contentful inner states and, on the basis of stored and occurrent representations of reality, plans and executes intelligent behaviour. The new paradigm, which is to some extent in tension with this classical computational/cognitive model of the mind (though it is a vexed question how much in dispute, and exactly how deeply the points of divergence go), is one on which the subject is treated as an embodied organism, thoroughly embedded in a biological, physical and social context. The basic idea is that the mindedness of the agent – the appropriateness of its actions – is scaffolded by its body and its environment in such a way that intelligent behaviours, such as walking a route through town or making a perceptual judgement that a piece of fruit is ripe, emerge from, or are constituted by, subtle interactions between that body and environment. Monica Cowart, in Chapter 13, describes two important figures in this movement: Andy Clark, who, with David Chalmers, originated a model known as the *extended mind* approach; and Antonio Damasio who is known for his work on what he takes to be the dependence of rationality (and hence what we classically think of as cognition) on emotions and other bodily feelings.[12]

The philosophy of mind is a very active area of philosophy, and for some decades now it has been repeatedly refreshed and reshaped, in productive ways, by streams of influence from the various areas of psychology, from neuroscience, computer science, linguistics, robotics, even Buddhism, and from other regions of philosophy itself such as philosophy of science and phenomenology. I hope this book will provide an engaging insight into some of the main tendencies in modern philosophy of mind and some of the fascinating figures who have shaped its progress.

Notes

1. There are also about 20,000 photosensitive ganglion cells in the retina, which probably support circadian rhythms and pupillary reflex though they do not contribute to vision.
2. One study (Jameson et al. 2001) suggests as many as half of women may be undetected tetrachromats, though this is disputed.
3. As Dermot Moran notes wryly in Chapter 3, where he delivers an important corrective, 'most analytic philosophers of mind . . . see themselves as having invented that discipline in the mid-twentieth century'.
4. Among various important simplifications here, I am setting aside the absolute idealism deriving from Hegel, such as that of F. H. Bradley (1846–1924), which was dominant in nineteenth-century Europe, though this was another important movement against which both the early analytic philosophers of mind and phenomenologists were reacting. Another important late nineteenth-/early twentieth-century stream of thought that stood in opposition to Cartesian dualism was 'American' pragmatism (associated with William James (1842–1910) and C. S. Peirce (1839–1914)) and this more or less directly influenced some important twentieth-century philosophers of mind such as Hilary Putnam (see Chapter 8) and Donald Davidson (see Chapter 10).
5. C-fibres are unmyelinated afferent nerve fibres of the autonomic nervous system, which respond to thermal, mechanical and chemical stimuli.
6. *Do* octopuses in fact have c-fibres? Octopus nociception (pain detection) has not been much studied and it is unclear whether and how they feel pain, though likely that they do. See Crook and Walters 2011.
7. Brian McLaughlin calls this 'role functionalism' in his Chapter 6, and distinguishes it from 'filler functionalism'. See also David Braddon-Mitchell's Chapter 7.
8. The notion that intentionality – the mind's 'direction upon its objects' – is the 'mark of the mental' is an old one and is especially associated with Brentano 1874. See Chapter 3.
9. Block 1980, continues to be a valuable starting point for these issues.
10. This is the reason why this introduction is called '90 years of philosophy of mind' rather than '70 years'.

11 There were of course some notable exceptions, such as Chisholm (1957) and Dreyfus (1972).
12 Noë 2004, is a good example of another stream within the embodiment approach, known as enactivism.

References

Bechtel, W. (1993), 'The case for connectionism'. *Philosophical Studies* 71: 119–54.
Bechtel, W. and Graham G. (1998), *A Companion to Cognitive Science*. Malden, MA: Blackwell.
Block, N (1980), 'Troubles with functionalism'. In N. Block (ed.), *Readings in Philosophy of Psychology*, Vol. 1. Cambridge. MA: Harvard University Press, pp. 268–305.
— (1981), 'Psychologism and behaviourism'. *Philosophical Review* 90: 5–43.
— (2011), 'Perceptual consciousness overflows cognitive access'. *Trends in Cognitive Sciences* 12: 567–75.
Brentano, F. (1874), *Psychology from an Empirical Standpoint*, transl. by A. C. Rancurello, D. B. Terrell, and L. McAlister. London: Routledge (second edition), 1995.
Carruthers, P. (2011), *The Opacity of Mind: An Integrative Theory of Self-Knowledge*. New York: Oxford University Press.
Chisholm, R. (1957), *Perceiving: A Philosophical Study*. Ithaca, NY: Cornell University Press.
Clarke, D., Whitney, H., Sutton, G., and Robert, D. (2013), 'Detection and learning of floral electric fields by bumblebees.' *Science*, Feb 21 (DOI: 10.1126/science.1230883).
Crook, R. J. and Walters, E. T. (2011), 'Nociceptive behavior and physiology of molluscs: animal welfare implications'. *Institute of Laboratory Animal Resources (ILAR) Journal* 52: 185–95.
Dennett, D. C. (1978), 'Beliefs about Beliefs'. *Behavioral and Brain Sciences* 4: 568–70.
Dreyfus, H. (1972). *What Computers Can't Do*. Cambridge, MA: MIT Press.
Fodor, J. A. (1983), *The Modularity of Mind: An Essay on Faculty Psychology*. Cambridge, MA: MIT Press.
Fodor, J. A. and Pylyshyn, Z. W. (1988), 'Connectionism and cognitive architecture: A critical analysis'. *Cognition* 28: 3–71.
Gallagher, S. and Zahavi, D. (2012), *The Phenomenological Mind*, second edition. New York: Routledge.

Jameson, K. A., Highnote, S. M., and Wasserman, L. M. (2001), 'Richer color experience in observers with multiple photopigment opsin genes'. *Psychonomic Bulletin & Review* 8: 244–61.

Nichols, S. and Stich, S. (2003), *Mindreading: An Integrated Account of Pretence, Self- Awareness and Understanding Other Minds*. New York: Oxford University Press.

Noë, A. (2004), *Action in Perception*. Cambridge, MA: MIT Press.

Prinz, J. (2012), *The Conscious Brain: How Attention Engenders Experience*. Oxford: Oxford University Press.

Putnam, H. (1967), 'The nature of mental states' (originally published as 'Psychological predicates'). In W. H. Captain and D. D. Merrill (eds), *Art, Mind and Religion*. Pittsburgh: University of Pittsburgh Press, pp. 37–48. Reprinted in H. Putnam, *Mind, Language and Reality, Philosophical Papers, Volume 2*. Cambridge: Cambridge University Press, pp. 429–40.

Sober, E. (1985), 'Panglossian functionalism and the philosophy of mind.' *Synthese* 64: 165–93.

Stich, S. (1983), *From Folk Psychology to Cognitive Science: The Case Against Belief*. Cambridge, MA: MIT Press.

van Gelder, T. (1995), 'What might cognition be, if not computation?' *Journal of Philosophy* 92: 345–81.

CHAPTER TWO

Decoding Descartes' 'myth' of mind

Patricia Easton

Such in outline is the official theory. I shall often speak of it, with deliberate abusiveness, as "the dogma of the Ghost in the Machine." I hope to prove that it is entirely false, and false not in detail but in principle. It is not merely an assemblage of particular mistakes. It is one big mistake and a mistake of a special kind. It is, namely, a category mistake. (Ryle 1949, pp. 15–16)

1 Introduction

It has been over sixty years since Gilbert Ryle declared that the time had come to explode Descartes' myth about the nature of mind (see Chapter 5). According to Ryle, the Cartesian mind is private and has privileged access to its own contents, it is non-spatial, its laws are not mechanical or deterministic, it is separate from the body and its interactions with it are mysterious. 'The mind is its own place and in his inner life each of us lives the life of a ghostly Robinson Crusoe' (Ryle 1949, p. 13).

The ensuing years have witnessed a succession of critiques of the Cartesian conception of mind from an array of distinguished scholars. Daniel Dennett laments the 'Cartesian Theatre' (1991; see Chapter 10), Patricia Churchland likens animal spirits to crystalline spheres (2005; see Chapter 12) and Antonio Damasio denounces Descartes' 'abyssal' error of separating the mind from body and reason from emotion (1994; see Chapter 13). Stephen Yablo, in his assessment of Descartes' account of mental causation, argues that Descartes' dualism '. . . breeds epiphenomenalism: the theory that our mental lives exercise no causal influence whatever over the progress of physical events' (1992, p. 245). And the pairing problem, raised against Cartesian mind-body interaction, asks how two similar minds attached to different bodies can be said to be causally paired with the appropriate body (Kim 1973, Sosa 1984). In the light of such negative assessments, one might ask why there has been so much attention given to an evidently erroneous model of the human mind. According to these and other commentators, Descartes' conception of the human mind has become part of the very fabric of our thinking about ourselves, and it has prevented us from making progress in understanding the nature of mind. Thus, from this point of view there is value in dissecting the Cartesian model as a corrective to our common non-scientific conceptions.

Not all commentary has been negative, however. Beyond the almost universal rejection of substance dualism, philosophers of mind have found valuable insights in Descartes' discussions of the nature and operations of the mind. Jerry Fodor's postulation of the Language of Thought Hypothesis draws on the Cartesian idea that ideas are representations in part constructed out of innate structures and conceptions (Fodor 1975; see Chapter 9). Descartes' idea that thoughts need not resemble or be like their objects in order to represent them supports the contemporary functionalist notion that we need not worry about the physical realization of representations in our analysis of their meaning (Putnam 1988; see Chapter 8). And, Descartes' language and action tests for the presence of mind in Part V of his *Discourse on Method* (1637; vol. 2, 1984–91)[1] which serve to demarcate human intelligence from animal and machine capabilities is not so different from John Searle's Chinese Room Argument, aimed at showing the implausibility of artificial intelligence (Searle 1980).² Moreover, contemporary philosophers are raising questions about the physicalist model of causation and are reconsidering what Descartes had to say on the matter of mind-body causation (Foster 1968, 1991, Audi 2011). Finally, contemporary neuroscientists, when not critiquing Descartes' rationalism and dualism, generally applaud his mechanistic model of the body and the advances he made in our understanding of optics, reflex actions and the motor cortex.³ In medicine, Westfall (1977, p. 94) has noted that Descartes' body-machine model lent itself well to the mechanical school of biology that developed during the seventeenth century, what has come to be known as iatromechanics or iatrophysics.⁴ The body-machine metaphor reached its zenith in the eighteenth-century materialism of Julien Offray de la Mettrie (1746, 1996) and has affinities with contemporary materialism.⁵ Thus, perhaps the lessons from studying Descartes' conception of mind are not merely negative but offer us some food for thought and critical reflection.

After more than sixty years of fighting the ghost in the machine, and the lessening of its perceived hold on our imaginations, we have begun to appreciate the positive lessons to be learned from Descartes' thinking on the mind. There is a growing body of scholarship challenging the strongly rationalist and dualist interpretation of Descartes on mind and body, reason and emotion.⁶ The long-standing neglect of Descartes' assertion that the mind and body in humans are closely united and intermingled is also beginning to receive attention.⁷ And finally, there is a growing sense of the importance for Descartes of the body, the passions, and the soul as 'embodied', in recent studies.⁸

As philosophers interested in what past thinkers have to offer us in the search after truth, it is not about finding agreement but, rather, ideas and arguments that expand our philosophical considerations. As an historian of philosophy interested in the rich and intrinsically interesting ideas and arguments of past thinkers, the guiding precept is that the rational reconstructions we make warrant the most charitable interpretation we can muster.⁹ In what follows, the emphasis is on getting at what Descartes thought about the nature of the human mind and how we might make sense of what Ryle has called the problems of the mind's privileged access to its own contents, its non-spatial aspects, its non-mechanical operations and the sense in which the mind is separable from yet interactive with the body. The hope is that we might dissipate the ghost in the machine while making progress in our understanding of the nature of the human mind.

2 Descartes' dualism of mind and body

Scarcely any discussion of the mind-body problem, or the relation of mind to brain, fails to mention Descartes's provocative thesis that the mind and body exist as separate substances: Descartes famously argues in the Sixth Meditation that 'I am really distinct from my body, and can exist without it' (CSM II: 54). Fewer discussions mention Descartes's thesis, also argued for in the Sixth Meditation, that the mind and body are intimately united, not merely as 'a sailor is present in a ship', but 'intermingled with it, so that I and the body form a unit' (CSM II: 56). Finally, that a mind can set a body in motion is known, according to Descartes, '. . . by the surest and plainest everyday experience' (CSMK: 358).

A number of problems arise when we try to make sense of these doctrines. Substance dualism seems to have the unhappy result that we, who are essentially thinking entities, can exist separately from our body. It is difficult to imagine any empirical grounds for holding to such an idea, and Descartes doesn't offer us any. I refer to this as the ontological problem of substance dualism. Moreover, when Descartes finally does appeal to experience, he tells us that nature teaches us that we are closely joined and intermingled with our bodies. But how can we, who are essentially non-material, be intermingled with bodies that are essentially extended in nature? I refer to this as the problem of unity. And finally the related causal question, how can minds produce effects in bodies, and bodies in minds, if they are separate substances sharing nothing in common? This is what Bernard Williams has called 'the scandal of Cartesian interactionism' (1978, p. 287; see Chapter 15).

One response to these difficulties is that Descartes's substance dualism is and ought to remain intractable and his mind-body union and interaction theses are just plain inconsistent with his dualism, and so can be discounted as irrelevant to Descartes's core philosophy. While criticisms of the plausibility of substance dualism are easy to come by and difficult not to concede, I think better sense can be made of it than is typically offered. As to the claim that Descartes was just inconsistent when he proposed the mind-body union and interaction theses, I find it highly implausible. Descartes valued consistency elsewhere in his philosophy, and to have made the inconsistent claims within a few pages of one another would be remarkable indeed. Moreover, Descartes argues explicitly in his last and most mature work, *The Passions of the Soul* (1649), that the passions of the soul are caused by motions in the body (Article 27), that the soul is united to all the parts of the body jointly (Article 30), that the will can move the body (Article 41), that the mind-body unity is responsible for pursuit of useful things in life (Article 52 and 74) and that human morality depends upon the wise employment of the passions (Article 212). The challenge, therefore, is to explain how Descartes could have maintained his substance dualism alongside and in concert with his union and interaction theses.

Perhaps more important than a defence of the coherence of Descartes's philosophy is the possibility that there is something to be learned from Descartes about the relation between mind and body. I conclude that there is something interesting that Descartes tells us about the nature and role of the passions in human life, and we will overlook these insights unless we can get beyond the obvious problems of substance dualism and its incompatibility with Descartes's view of the human being as a union of mind and body.

2.1 The ontological problem of substance dualism

Here is an abbreviated but, I think, fair version of Descartes's argument for mind-body substance dualism:

P1: Everything I clearly and distinctly perceive (cdp) is true.
P2: If I cdp x apart from y, then they are really distinct and capable of separation (at least by God).
P3: I cdp myself as a thinking, non-extended thing apart from body, an extended, non-thinking thing.
Conclusion: I am really distinct from my body, and can exist without it.

The usual interpretation of this argument is that Descartes is claiming that we *are* separate from our bodies, that is, that we actually *do* exist without our bodies as a kind of immortal ghost in a machine. As such, the thesis is interpreted as primarily an ontological one about the dual nature of individual human beings. There is some evidence for this reading, especially if we turn to Meditation Two, in which Descartes claims that the 'I' is identical to the thinking thing, not to such bodily functions as nutrition, locomotion or sensation (CSM II: 17–18). However, in the Fourth Replies, Descartes makes it clear that in the Second Meditation he concludes that attributes of body do not belong to the essence of mind, but does *not* conclude that the mind is the complete essence of *man*: 'And although mind is *part* of the essence of man, being united to a human body is not strictly speaking part of the essence of mind' (CSM II: 155, my emphasis).

It should also be noted that in all the places wherein Descartes makes the claim for the real distinction between mind and body, he never says we *do* so exist separately, only that we *can* so exist. I take it as significant that Descartes is careful never to claim that we, as living humans, exist separately from our body. Rather, what he claims is that because we clearly *understand* mind apart from body and body apart from mind, then this is evidence that mind and body are *capable* of existing apart, at least by the power of God.

Although Descartes believed that particular bodies *actually* exist apart from minds – whether they be stones, or clocks, or free-falling bodies; and although he believed that minds *actually* exist apart from bodies – whether they be angels or God; and although he seems even to have believed that human minds *actually* exist apart from bodies after death, I do not think he believed, and he certainly never says, that living human beings *actually* exist as minds apart from their bodies. To the contrary, in the Fourth Set of Replies he says:

> For the fact that one thing can be separated from another by the power of God is the very least that can be asserted in order to establish that there is a real distinction between the two. Also, I thought I was careful to guard against anyone inferring from this that man was simply "a soul which makes use of a body." For in the Sixth Meditation, where I dealt with the distinction between the mind and the body, I also proved at the same time that the mind is substantially united with the body. (CSM II: 160)

If Descartes only wanted to make a weaker and more general claim – that some bodies exist independently of minds, and some minds exist independently of bodies – then why did he frame his real distinction argument in first-person terms and refer to *my* body as being really distinct from me? Was he not indeed trying to show that we, as thinking entities, in fact exist independently from our bodies?

Two epistemological considerations may explain why Descartes frames the argument in first-person terms while not implying that the 'I' actually exists disembodied. The first consideration is Descartes's cognitive individualism, and the order of reasons followed in the *Meditations*. Descartes held that although the advancement of knowledge depends on the efforts of many, the search after truth is an ordered and individual cognitive process. The project of the *Meditations* is to clear away prejudices and to arrive at the first principles of knowledge by the natural powers of the mind. The meditator herself must uncover and possess each clear and distinct perception only on the basis of previous such conceptions. At the point of the Sixth Meditation proof for the real distinction between mind and body Descartes has not yet arrived at the truth that bodies exist (only that they possibly or probably exist). So, when he proves the real distinction between mind and body, he does so on the basis of his clear and distinct perception of mind apart from his distinct understanding of body. In other words, he proves the general claim from his own case. In the order of his reasoning, he cannot prove the certainty of the existence of body until he has proved the distinction between mind and body; furthermore, he cannot prove the union of mind and body until he has proved the existence of body.

The second consideration is a methodological one. Descartes believed that failure to distinguish our conception of mind from our conception of body leads to errors in physics. Unless we carefully distinguish the two conceptions in our understanding, we will erroneously attribute to the body qualities that actually belong to the mind. In the Sixth Replies, he remarks:

> But what makes it especially clear that my idea of gravity was taken largely from the idea I had of the mind is the fact that I thought that gravity carried bodies towards the centre of the earth as if it had some knowledge of the centre within itself. For this surely could not happen without knowledge, and there can

> be no knowledge except in the mind. Nevertheless I continued to apply to gravity various other attributes which cannot be understood to apply to a mind in this way – for example its being divisible, measurable and so on.
> But later on I made the observations which led me to make a careful distinction between the idea of the mind and the ideas of body and corporeal motion. . . . (Sixth Set of Replies, CSM II: 298)

Descartes goes on in the Sixth Replies to describe how making the real distinction between mind and body freed him from belief in real qualities and substantial forms. These previous beliefs were, he claimed, what had left him susceptible to erroneous conclusions and sceptical doubts. By discovering that the proper modes of body include shape, size, motion, but not tastes, sounds, or colours, scientific explanation of physical phenomena would appeal to only those properties belonging to body.

The upshot of Descartes's real distinction argument is that I take the grounds underlying the argument for substance dualism to be primarily epistemological and methodological, not ontological, and so the doctrine as an epistemological thesis loses some of its intractability. Descartes' essential point is that the search for truth requires that we keep conceptually distinct things that we conceive clearly and distinctly. As for things that we experience as united, we must be careful not to conclude that they are in fact the same thing. For example, the fact that we feel pain from the strike of a sword does not entail that the pain is *in the sword*; or that we taste bitterness or sweetness in a piece of fruit that the 'selfsame taste' I experience is *in the fruit*, etc.[10]

Thus, it is an epistemological principle for Descartes that if something is clearly and distinctly perceived apart from something else, then it is justified to exclude that thing from the other. Good science requires that we are clear about which properties belong to our object of study and which ones do not.

I am not the first to suggest that Descartes's main goal in the *Meditations* was to establish a solid foundation for his physics. Daniel Garber, among others, has argued this point in detail (Garber 1992). But one may rightly object that Descartes claims in the Synopsis of the *Meditations* that he lays the foundation for a proof of the immortality of the soul, and that this is what the real distinction argument of the Sixth Meditation is aimed at. But if we read the argument this way, it has, as Amélie Rorty puts it, 'dark consequences' (1986, p. 515). For any idea or function that is separable from the essence of mind is not part of its immortal being. An immortality that is assured by indivisible indestructibility, as this is, is not very interesting, for any mathematical point can have it. Descartes admits in the Synopsis that he doesn't pursue the topic of immortality in the *Meditations* and provides only 'enough to give mortals the hope of an afterlife, ... because the premises which lead to the conclusion that the soul is immortal depend on an account of the whole of physics' (CSM II: 10).

With some of the intractability of substance dualism put aside, I turn to the apparent inconsistencies of the doctrines of mind-body union and interaction.

2.2 Mind-body union and the problem of unity

Descartes first announces his theory of the mind-body union in the Sixth Meditation, four paragraphs after he has offered his demonstration of the real distinction between mind and body:

> Nature also teaches me, by these sensations of pain, hunger, thirst and so on, that I am not merely present in my body as a sailor is present in a ship, but that I am very closely joined and, as it were, intermingled with it, so that I and the body form a unit. (CSM II: 56)

However, it is not until later, in Descartes's correspondence with Princess Elizabeth, that he attempts to spell out this theory. We learn that Descartes put off the study of the union that is essential for medicine and ethics – the fruits of first philosophy – because he believed that the distinction between mind and body was more important to the foundation of the principles of knowledge and science and would have been obscured had he treated mind-body union at any length:

> There are two facts about the human soul on which depend all the knowledge we can have of its nature. The first is that it thinks, the second is that, being united to the body, it can act and be acted upon along with it. About the second I have said hardly

anything; I have tried only to make the first well understood. For my principal aim was to prove the distinction between the soul and the body, and to this end only the first was useful, and the second might have been harmful. (Letter to Elizabeth, 21 May 1643, CSMK: 217–18)

What sort of unity can the mind-body union be said to possess? For if mind and body are really distinct substances, and as such share no modes or qualities in common, then how is it that the mind and body can said to be united? How can a non-extended thinking thing become essentially conjoined to an extended thing?

Various solutions can be and have been proposed for the problem of unity. One solution is to argue that the mind-body union is a special third kind of substance. The result is a kind of trialism – a system of three rather than two substances – and hence a compromise of substance dualism.[11] Another solution also compromises substance dualism and is suggested by *Principles* I, 60, where Descartes says that we can make a real distinction between ourselves and every other thinking substance and from every corporeal substance. Hence, each human individual is a substance in her own right, permitting the multiplication of substances beyond necessity, amounting to metaphysical pluralism. No clear case has been made for this position, however, and it requires we ascribe an incoherence to Descartes' philosophy that militates against adopting it as a solution.

If we are to maintain the consistency of Descartes's dualism without marginalizing, ignoring or dismissing his doctrine of mind-body union, we need to understand what kind of thing a union of mind and body is. If the kind of unity possessed by a mind-body composite is not that of a substance, what is it like? Is it like that had by a heap of sand, a watch, a plant or a non-human animal? How are we to reconcile a metaphysics of dualism with the union of mind and body?

A promising solution comes from a successor of Descartes, Dom Robert Desgabets (1983).[12] He argued that humans – as individual mind-body unions – are *modal* beings, not substances, and the kind of unity they possess is extrinsic rather than intrinsic. On Desgabets' view, human beings are contingent beings that possess ways/modes of being that are common to both mental things and extended things; humans are not substances in any strict sense of the term.

The unity we possess is like that of a watch; so long as the parts of a watch are functioning properly to tell time, the unity is preserved; likewise, so long as the various modes of thinking and body are functioning to preserve the life of a person, the unity is preserved. This unity is essential for the preservation of the human being, but its unity is extrinsic, which is to say, corruptible and perishable. This speaks in favour of a functional rather than ontological unity.

The notion that human beings are a composite of mental and material modes is odd at first glance; one has to imagine oneself as a bundle of modes moving together through space, only to dissipate at death. However, consider what Descartes says in his *Fourth Replies* to Arnauld (CSM II: 157ff.):

> It is also possible to call a substance incomplete in the sense that, although it has nothing incomplete about it qua substance, it is incomplete in so far as it is referred to some other substance in conjunction with which it forms something which is a unity in its own right.
>
> Thus a hand is an incomplete substance when it is referred to the whole body of which it is a part; but it is a complete substance when it is considered on its own. And in just the same way the mind and the body are incomplete substances when they are referred to a human being which together they make up. But if they are considered on their own, they are complete. (CSM II: 157)

From this passage, we see that mind and body, when *referred* to some other substance – in this case a human being – form a unity. In much the same way, a hand, when referred to a whole body of which it is a part, together with the body constitutes a unity. Although Descartes plays fast and loose with the term 'substance' here, this is not unusual when his interlocutors are well versed in Scholastic terminology. What it highlights is that the relation of mind and body to a human being is not unlike that of the relation of a hand to the rest of a human body. The relation Descartes seems to appeal to here is mereological, that is, that of part to whole. In relation to a human being, mind and body only constitute parts of the whole, which is itself a composite.

In *Comments on a Certain Broadsheet*, Descartes reiterates his example of man as a composite entity: 'But that which we regard as having at the same time both extension and thought is a composite entity, namely a man – an entity consisting of a soul and a body' (CSM I: 299).

It is clear from this passage that the mind-body union is neither a substance in the sense that mind and body, which form unities of nature, are, nor is it an accidental unity, like that of a sailor in a ship. It remains to be shown that Descartes saw *functional* unity of mind and body as the key to the nature of the human being.

In the *Passions of the Soul* (1649), Descartes begins by carefully distinguishing the functions of the body from those of the soul and explains what the difference is between a living human body and a dead one, that is, how death results from the decomposition of the body, not the soul:

> And let us recognize that the difference between the body of a living man and that of a dead man is just like the difference between, on the one hand, a watch or other automaton (that is a self-moving machine) when it is wound up and contains in itself the corporeal principle of movements for which it is designed, together with everything else required for its operation; and on the other hand the same watch or machine when it is broken and the principle of its movement ceases to be active. [Part I, article 6; CSM I: 329–30]

The soul depends upon not only the proper functioning of the body – because the body provides not only nutrition, locomotion, respiration, etc., which are essential to the preservation of the mind-body union – but also properly disposed emotions that 'move and dispose the soul to want the things for which they prepare the body' (CSM I: 343). Likewise, the human body depends upon the proper functioning of the soul. The human mind is responsible for attention, perception, judgement, knowledge and volition. Perceiving, attending to, judging and desiring objects that are beneficial to us and avoiding those that are harmful, are essential for our preservation, and certainly the preservation of the body. A typical example of this that Descartes offers is the case of dropsy. Dropsy patients suffer from oedema or excessive swelling of the connective tissues. This condition also causes extreme thirst in the patient. However, drinking can worsen and even kill the patient. Knowledge of this fact is important to avoiding this fate, because the signals from the body tell the patient to drink, and normally such signals provide good guidance. Hence, here is a case wherein knowledge and judgement preserve the mind-body union against the advice of the body.

Thus, on Descartes' account, humans are a composite of mind and body, a unity of composition, not of nature, whose glue is the set of mutual functions that preserve the composite.

By way of conclusion to the ontological problem of dualism, and the problem of unity, I have argued that the typical picture of Descartes's substance dualism as an ontological thesis applied to human beings is an incorrect portrayal of Descartes's theory of the human being. An epistemological reading of the argument for the real distinction supports this view and reduces the intractability of substance dualism. In addition, I have argued that the problem of unity in Descartes' account of the doctrine of mind-body union is best resolved if we view humans not as substances but as contingent, modal, composite beings whose mental and physical functions are mutually dependent.

We are almost ready to address the concerns presented by Ryle's Ghost in the Machine conception of the mind. The final piece to the Cartesian puzzle of mind is the problem of interaction – how it is that the mind exerts causal control over the body and vice versa.

2.3 Interaction of the mind and body: Mental and physical causation

Having put aside some of the intractable problems presented by an ontological reading of dualism, we are now faced with how Descartes accounted for the genuine and mutual causal dependence of the mind on the body. Against his Scholastic predecessors, Descartes believed that there was no need for secondary causes, occult qualities or final causes in nature or in explanation. Nonetheless, Descartes' view on causation caused much confusion and criticism in his own day, as it does in ours, and some of his successors such as Nicolas Malebranche adopted the view of 'occasionalism' in response. Occasionalism is the view that the motions in the body occasion thoughts in the mind and vice versa, but there is no genuine causal interaction between the two. In contemporary terms, occasionalism applied to mental events amounts to 'epiphenomenalism', the position that mental events occur but have no effects upon physical events.[13]

However, there is good reason to believe that Descartes saw genuine causation in all three types of Cartesian interaction, namely body-body, mind-body and body-mind.[14] In Descartes' response to Princess Elizabeth in May 1643, we learn that he did not regard conceiving of mind-body interaction as a true problem but one that derives from a confusion. The confusion derives from attempts to 'conceive the way in which the soul moves the body by conceiving the way in which one body is moved by another' (CSM III: 219). In other words, if we think about mind-body causation as just like body-body causation we wrongly conclude that it is incoherent: 'If we try to solve a problem by means of a notion that does not pertain to it, we cannot help going wrong' (CSM III: 219). The Scholastics make a similar mistake when they ascribe mental powers to physical things and think that the heaviness of a stone is a real quality that impels a stone towards the earth. Descartes concludes, 'So it is no harder for us to understand how the mind moves the body than it is for them to understand how such heaviness moves a stone downwards' (Letter to Arnauld, 29 July 1648; CSMK: 358). In other words, by confusing our conceptions of how bodies move bodies with how minds move bodies there is the illusion of a problem of interaction. Descartes thinks that mind-body interaction or psychophysical causation is as self-evident as physical causation, and that two distinct kinds of causation and explanation are required.[15]

For example, suppose we explain a soldier's movements in battle by appeal to the laws of motion – that he (his body) changes only in response to the state of the other bodies around him. Such an explanation fails to account for the effects of the soldier's training through habit and for the effects of the soldier's determination through courage.[16] Appeal only to a physical cause and principle is inadequate to the case.[17]

As R. C. Richardson argues, the problem of interaction is illusory and depends upon (1) 'the presumption that psychophysical interaction must be similar in kind to physical interaction' and (2) 'the conviction that psychophysical dualism must lead to a naive attempt to attain an exhaustive segregation of properties into those that are attributable to the purely physical and those that are attributable to the purely mental'.[18] I have offered reasons why Descartes rejected both the analogy to physical causation in (1) and the strict ontological dualism in (2).

Conclusion

A few concluding remarks are in order in response to Ryle's critique of Descartes' alleged 'dogma of the Ghost in the Machine'. Recall that, according to Ryle, the Cartesian mind is private and has privileged access to its own contents, it is non-spatial, its laws are not mechanical or deterministic, it is separate from the body and its interactions with it are mysterious.

First, based on what Descartes writes about the union and dependence of mind and body in the living, human being, the Cartesian mind is a good deal less private and privileged than Ryle and others have thought. The embodied human being is subject to passions, sensations and emotions, which require training through habit in the coordination of the determinations of the will and the movements of the body. Modes of the union, such as pain, fear and love, are passions of the soul *and* motions of the body. Thus, they are both private and public in important respects.

Secondly, if the functional unity of the human being is correct, then there is no pairing problem for Descartes. It is the modes of the composite union that are mutually dependent and interact and as such they are always specifically united to a particular body. The dissolution of the functional unity, as in the case of the broken watch, is death itself.

Thirdly, although Descartes thought that we are conceptually capable of separating mental phenomena from physical phenomena, and that this is methodologically desirable in science, the study of the living human being requires examination of both.

Fourthly, the embodied human mind is spatial and subject to mechanical laws. Likewise, the human body is subject to the actions of the human will. There is psycho-physical causation, not epiphenomenalism on the Cartesian view.

I hope that I have offered enough to the reader to critically question both the ghost and the machine of Ryle's metaphor. Descartes' conception of man, and of the human mind, is far more complex in its characterization than a simple dualism, or mechanism, would suggest. Descartes' human mind is embodied, it is passionate, sensitive and physically efficacious. Perhaps the Descartes of the history books might be reconsidered in a more positive light as a contributor to our ongoing study of the human mind.

Notes

1. All references to Descartes' writings are to the English translation (1984–91). Citations will be to CSM, Roman numeral volume number, Arabic page number.
2. Gillot (2010) argues that despite Searle's attempts to reject Cartesian dualism, there are important linkages to Descartes through Searle's internalism and mentalism that make Searle out to be a friend rather than foe to the Cartesian conception of mind.
3. See, for example, Bennett et al. (2008), pp. 208–18; and Flanagan (1991). However, it should be noted that such attributions, particularly that Descartes discovered the reflex action, have been contested. For example, Georges Canguilhem (1955) has argued that it was Thomas Willis, not Descartes, whose work identified the reflex action.
4. 'Iatromechanics' or 'iatrophysics' are terms that refer to a medical philosophy that developed during the seventeenth century that offered physiological explanations in mechanical terms, an approach often attributed to Giovanni Borelli (1608–79) and Jan Baptist Van Helmont (1579–1644).
5. For an introduction to contemporary materialism, see Paul M. Churchland (1988).
6. For example, see Rodis-Lewis (1964), Marshall (1998), Brown (2006), Cottingham (1985 and 2008, esp. chapters 9, 12), Shapiro (2003), Alanen (2003) and Schmitter (2002 and 2005).
7. Shapiro (2003) and Brown (2003) make good progress on reconciling Descartes' dualism and union theses.
8. See Brown (2006), Shapiro (2003), Garber (2001), Cottingham (2008), Schmitter (2002) and Clarke (2003).
9. Donald Davidson identifies the 'Principle of Charity' as a methodological precept made to understand a view in its strongest, most persuasive form before evaluation. See Davidson (1974).
10. Descartes gives a number of such examples in the Sixth Meditation (CSM II: 56–7).
11. Many commentators have found strict readings of Descartes' dualism, especially in the case of the human being and mind-body interaction, problematic. Martial Gueroult (1968, 1985), Janet Broughton and Ruth Mattern (1978), Paul Hoffman (1986, 1999), William Seager (1988), and Lilli Alanen (1989) in particular have argued in diverse ways that Descartes was driven to a metaphysical

trialism. John Cottingham (1985) posits 'trialism' in response to Descartes' treatment of sensory awareness, which did not fit tidily into the dualism schema.

12 Robert Desgabets (1610–78) offered his views in two works, *Treatise on the Indefectibility of Created Substances*, and *Of the Union of Soul and Body*. His philosophical works were not published until 1983; see Desgabets (1983).

13 See Robinson (2012) for a discussion of this position.

14 It is worth mentioning that some commentators think that Descartes can't escape the consequences of dualism in an attempt to explain the interaction of mind and body. See Daisie Radner (1971), Margaret Wilson (1978a, 1978b).

15 What has made struck modern readers as especially implausible about Descartes' account of mind-body interaction is that the pineal gland serves as the seat of mind-body interaction. But the pineal gland, the only singular structure Descartes observed in the brain, was an empirical postulate about the site of interaction, not the explanation of interaction.

16 See Descartes' *Passions of the Soul* on habit (Article 44) and on determination of the will (Article 48).

17 I argue that Descartes provides the basis for an account of psychosomatic causation and explanation, which was developed by the seventeenth-century Cartesian medical doctor, François Bayle (Easton 2011).

18 R. C. Richardson 1982, p. 36.

References

Alanen, L. (1989), 'Descartes's dualism and the philosophy of mind'. *Revue de Métaphysique et de Morale* 94e Année (3): 391–413.
— (2003), *Descartes's Concept of Mind*. Cambridge, MA: Harvard University Press.
Audi, P. (2011), 'Primitive causal relations and the pairing problem'. *Ratio* 24: 1–16.
Bennett, M. R. and Hacker, P. M. S. (2008), *The History of Neuroscience*. Malden, MA: Wiley-Blackwell.
Broughton, J. and Mattern, R. (1978), 'Reinterpreting Descartes on the notion of the union of mind and body'. *Journal of the History of Philosophy* 16: 23–32.
Brown, D. (2006), *Descartes and the Passionate Mind*. Cambridge: Cambridge University Press.

Canguilhem, G. (1955), *La formation du concept de réflexe aux XVII et XVIII siècles*. Paris: PUF.
Churchland, P. S. (2005), 'A neurophilosophical slant on consciousness research'. *Progress in Brain Research* 149: 285–93.
Churchland, P. M. (1988), *Matter and Consciousness: A Contemporary Introduction to the Philosophy of Mind*. Revised edition. Cambridge, MA: MIT Press.
Clarke, D. (2003), *Descartes's Theory of Mind*. Oxford: Oxford University Press.
Cottingham, J. (1985), 'Cartesian trialism'. *Mind* 94: 218–30.
— (2008), *Cartesian Reflections*. Oxford: Oxford University Press.
Davidson, D. (1984; 2001), 'On the very idea of a conceptual scheme'. In Davidson, D. (ed.), *Inquiries into Truth and Interpretation*. Oxford: Clarendon Press.
Desgabets, R. (1983), *Oeuvres philosophiques inédites*. Analecta Cartesiana 2, ed., J. Beaude with introduction by G. Rodis-Lewis, Amsterdam: Quadratures.
Descartes, R. (1984–91), *The Philosophical Writings Of Descartes*, 3 vols., translated by John Cottingham, Robert Stoothoff, and Dugald Murdoch (Volume 3 including Anthony Kenny). Cambridge: Cambridge University Press.
Damasio, A. (1994), *Descartes' Error: Emotion, Reason, and the Human Brain*. New York: Putnam Publishing.
Dennett, D. (1991), *Consciousness Explained*. Boston: Little, Brown & Co.
Easton, P. (2011), 'The Cartesian doctor, François Bayle (1622–1709), on psychosomatic explanation.' *Studies in History and Philosophy of Biological and Biomedical Sciences*. doi:10.1016/j.shpsc.2010.12.004.
Flanagan, O. (1991), *The Science of Mind*. 2nd edition. Cambridge, MA: MIT Press.
Fodor, J. A. (1975), *The Language Of Thought*. New York: Crowell Press.
Foster, J. (1968), 'Psychophysical causal relations'. *American Philosophical Quarterly* 5: 64–70.
— (1991), *The Immaterial Self: A Defence of the Cartesian Dualist Conception of the Mind*. London: Routledge.
Garber, D. (1992), *Descartes' Metaphysical Physics*. Chicago: University of Chicago Press.
Garber, D. (2001), *Descartes Embodied*. Cambridge University Press: Cambridge.
Gueroult, M. (1968; 1985). *Descartes selon l'ordre des raisons*. Aubier-Editions Montaigne, Paris, vol. II. Translated into English by Roger Ariew, 1985, as *Descartes' philosophy interpreted according to the order of reasons: Vol. 2*. Minneapolis: University of Minnesota Press.

Gillot, P. (2010), 'Cartesian echoes in the philosophy of mind: The case of John Searle'. In J. Reynolds, J. Chase, and J. Williams (eds), *Postanalytic and Metacontinental: Crossing Philosophical Divides*. London: Continuum, pp. 107–24.

Hoffman, P. (1986), 'The unity of Descartes's man'. *Philosophical Review* 95: 339–70.

— (1999), 'Cartesian composites'. *Journal of the History of Philosophy* 37: 251–70.

Kim, J. (1973), 'Causation, nomic subsumption, and the concept of event'. *Journal of Philosophy* 70: 217–36.

— (1998), *Mind in a Physical World: An Essay on the Mind-Body Problem and Mental Causation*. Cambridge, MA: MIT Press.

La Mettrie, J. O. de (1996), *Man Machine and Other Writings*. A. Thomson (ed.). Cambridge: Cambridge University Press. (First published in French in Leiden 1747).

Marshall, J. (1998), *Descartes's Moral Theory*. Ithaca and London: Cornell University Press.

Putnam, H. (1988), *Representation and Reality*. Cambridge, MA: MIT Press.

Radner, D. (1971), 'Descartes' notion of the union of mind and body'. *Journal of the History of Philosophy* 9: 159–71.

Richardson, R. C. (1982), 'The 'scandal' of Cartesian interactionism'. *Mind* 91: 20–37.

Robinson, W. (2012), 'Epiphenomenalism.' *The Stanford Encyclopedia of Philosophy*. Edward N. Zalta (ed.), URL = http://plato.stanford.edu/archives/sum2012/entries/epiphenomenalism/

Rodis-Lewis, G. (1964), 'Le domaine propre de l'homme chez les Cartésiens'. *Journal of the History of Philosophy* 2 (2): 157–88.

Rorty, A. O. (1986), 'Cartesian passions and the union of mind and body'. In her *Essays on Descartes' Meditations*. Berkeley: University of California Press, pp. 513–34.

Rozemond, M. (1998), *Descartes's Dualism*. Cambridge, MA: Harvard University Press.

Ryle, G. (1949), *The Concept of Mind*. London: Hutchinson's University Library.

Schmitter, A. M. (2002), 'Descartes and the Primacy of Practice: The Role of the Passions in the Search for Truth.' *Philosophical Studies: An International Journal for Philosophy in the Analytic Tradition* 108 (1-2): 99–108.

— (2005), 'The Passionate Intellect: Reading the (Non-)Opposition of Intellect and Emotion in Descartes.' In J. Whiting, C. Williams, and J. Jenkins (eds), *Persons and Passions: Essays in Honor of Annette Baier*. Indiana: Notre Dame University Press, pp. 48–82.

Searle, J. (1980), 'Minds, brains and programs'. *Behavioral and Brain Sciences* 3: 417–57.
Shapiro, L. (2003), 'Descartes' passions of the soul and the union of mind and body'. *Archiv für Geschichte der Philosophie* 85: 211–48.
Sosa, E. (1984), 'Mind-body interaction and supervenient causation'. *Midwest Studies in Philosophy* 9: 271–81.
Seager, W. E. (1988), 'Descartes on the union of mind and body'. *History of Philosophy Quarterly* 5: 119–32.
Westfall, R. (1977), *The Construction of Modern Science: Mechanism and Mechanics*. Cambridge: Cambridge University Press.
Wilson, M. (1978a), *Descartes*. London: Routledge and Kegan Paul.
— (1978b), 'Cartesian dualism'. In Hooker, 1978, pp. 197–211.
Yablo, S. (1992), 'Mental causation'. *Philosophical Review* 101: 245–80.
Yandell, D. (1999), 'Did Descartes abandon dualism? The nature of the union of mind and body'. *British Journal for History of Philosophy* 7: 199–217.

CHAPTER THREE

Edmund Husserl and phenomenology

Dermot Moran

The Moravian-born mathematician and philosopher Edmund Husserl (1859–1938) devoted his life to exhaustive phenomenological investigations – employing a method that he essentially invented – that offer some of the most sustained and radical discussions of central topics in the philosophy of mind that can be found in twentieth-century philosophy.[1] Yet, it is still the case that most analytic philosophers of mind (who see themselves as having invented that discipline in the mid-twentieth century (see Chapter 1)) proceed to discuss the very same topics with no inkling of Husserl's extraordinary and enduring contribution.[2] In this chapter, I want to outline some of Husserl's major contributions to the philosophy of mind. I should also add that Husserl's work on consciousness is now being carefully studied especially by those interested in the cognitive sciences.[3]

Phenomenology, understood as the careful description of experiences in the manner in which they are experienced by the subject, proposes to study, in Husserl's words, the whole of our 'life of consciousness' (*Bewusstseinsleben*, Hua XIV 46)[4]; that is to say, it includes not just explicit cognitive states and acts, such as judgements, but all the myriad acts and states of consciousness such as sensory awareness, perception, memory, imagination, feeling, emotion, mood, free will, time-consciousness,[5] judgement, reasoning, symbolic thought, self-conscious awareness, as well as subconscious drives and desires, and I am by no means giving an exhaustive list here. Husserl also thought that psychology (due to its inherent naturalistic outlook) could not be the true science of subjectivity. The new science of subjectivity has to put aside all natural scientific and 'folk' concepts of the psychic and aims to confront genuine concrete experience. As Husserl writes:

> The first thing we must do, and first of all in immediate reflective self-experience, is to take the conscious life, completely without prejudice, just as what it quite immediately gives itself, as itself, to be.[6]

Husserl, moreover, not only analysed the structures of individual 'self-experience' (*Selbsterfahrung*), one's experience of one's own conscious states, but also offered groundbreaking discussions of the experience of others or of the other (*Fremderfahrung*) which following the psychology of his day (e.g. Theodor Lipps) he called 'empathy' (*Einfühlung*). He discussed the nature of the individual 'ego' (*das Ich*) as well as how egoic experiences are melded together into a single whole of a personal life. He also discussed, in *Ideas II*, for instance, the special level of relations between persons where they relate to one another as persons in 'the personalistic attitude' (*die personalistische Einstellung*).[7] Indeed, especially in his mature research, he was deeply interested in the manner in which humans relate to one another in what he called generally 'intersubjectivity' (*Intersubjektivität*), including the experience of belonging-together in a community and sharing a common world.

In his main publications, for example, *Logical Investigations*,[8] *Ideas I*[9] and *Cartesian Meditations*,[10] Husserl's approach is predominantly individualist or 'egological', describing conscious life primarily in the context of the individual self. This has led to Husserl being described as a Cartesian or as a 'methodological solipsist'. He was, on the other hand, always aware – and certainly from 1910/1911 this is a distinctive theme – that this egological approach *abstracts* from the fuller more concrete domain of intersubjective, communal, social consciousness. Indeed, Husserl was one of the first philosophers of mind to talk about specifically 'social acts', 'we-intentions' and collective intentionality generally.[11] A comprehensive phenomenology must aim to describe subjective and intersubjective life in its wholeness, including the large cultural and spiritual forms, leading to what Husserl calls a complete 'eidetics of the spirit' (*Ideas* II, Hua IV 314).

Husserl begins with his recognition of individual, subjective, personal consciousness, that is, consciousness in its full, living, concrete, dynamic richness, in what he called the 'Heraclitean flux' or 'stream of conscious life' (*Strom des Bewusstseinslebens*, Hua VII 251). Normally, we simply live, as Henri Bergson and William James would also have said, in the stream or flow of conscious 'experiences' (*Erlebnisse*) – a term he probably borrowed from Wilhelm Dilthey – that is, individual mental events or processes. Husserl himself recognized that the metaphor of a *stream* was in some respects quite misleading. These experiences form the seamless whole of our conscious, waking states and indeed we have to extend the concept of consciousness to include states of sleep, dreaming, hypnotic states, narcotic states, states of anaesthesia, meditative states and so on. To live, Husserl says, is to experience (*leben ist erleben*). Initially at least, Husserl's interest was primarily, but not exclusively, in what current philosophy now refers to as *occurrent* (rather than dispositional) acts of consciousness, their contents and their objective reference; that is, he primarily focused on conscious *episodes* as such. In his earlier years, he had nothing at all to say, at least in print, about 'the unconscious' and very little to say, at least in his earlier years, about our dispositional or emotional states, although he later, especially in his *Passive Synthesis* lectures[12] and in the *Crisis of European Sciences*, came to discuss the complex layerings of our 'pre-predicative' life, our drives, our being affected and being drawn towards certain things, our 'habits', 'convictions', our 'attitudes' and other 'sedimentations'. In his later years, Husserl was aware of what he called 'depth psychology' (*Tiefenpsychologie*) by which he meant the various forms of psychoanalysis being practiced at the time by Freud, Jung, Adler and others.

Conscious lived experiences are, as Descartes and Kant also recognized, primarily *temporal* events (they are not primarily spatial, but Husserl came more and more to see how the experience of spatiality comes to be constituted out of embodied experiences especially touch sensations).[13] Conscious experiences do not simply follow one another in a chain (as Hume sometimes suggests), but augment, modify and distort one another, as well as weaving together into the whole that we experience as one's life. In his early work – including the massive two-volume *Logical Investigations* (1900–01), Husserl, following his mentor Franz Brentano (himself influenced by Hume) tried to focus exclusively on the individual experiences that make up the stream, but fairly quickly (and influenced by his reading of Kant and of Neo-Kantians such as Paul Natorp) Husserl recognized that one had to address the issue of the ego and of the 'ego-pol' (*Ichpol*) that runs through all experiences. Husserl recognizes that this 'stream' is experienced as belonging to an individual ego or 'I' (*Ich*), and appears as a seamless, streaming whole, which at the same time can be divided into a multiform yet unified, and constantly unifying, temporal flow of individual *Erlebnisse*.

In his early work in particular, Husserl speaks of psychic 'states' (*Zustände*) and of 'acts' (while explicitly excluding the meaning of 'activity'; see the Fifth Logical Investigation). The term 'act' was used extensively in German psychology and is to be found in Brentano, Wundt, Stumpf and others. Gradually, Husserl became dissatisfied with the existing psychological terminology for psychic or cognitive states, and, borrowing from Descartes (see Chapter 2), he began to employ the Latin term *cogitatio* (literally 'thought'; plural: *cogitationes*) as his general term for a psychic state, to be understood in the widest sense to include all identifiable parts of the flow, that is, individual states and contents of consciousness that are immediately apprehended.

To clarify what is meant by the phenomenological approach, it is important to recognize that Husserl was not attempting any form of *explanation* in the sense of a naturalistic, causal (or what he would term 'genetic') account of the composition of human lives as conscious cognitive beings. Husserl offers no explanatory account of *how* it is that our embodied minds are able to function. To put it crudely, the 'brain' as an organ is not experienced directly in a first-person way by the subject (science tells us we have brains) and so it falls outside the purview of phenomenology. Husserl wants to begin by describing what is involved in conscious experiences, their contents and objects. He speaks of seeking the 'fundamental composition' (*Grundverfassung*, Hua XIII 111) and 'fundamental forms' (*Grundgestalten*) of consciousness. He wants to identify the essential structures and the a priori laws governing conscious acts, their objects and contents, their modes of givenness, their 'modes of validation' (*Geltungsmodi*), their confirmations and modifications, and so on. Phenomenology is an eidetic science.[14] Husserl is interested in the *essences* of diverse cognitive or epistemic attitudes (perceiving, remembering, imagining, judging, surmising and so on) that constitute the building blocks of our rational lives as knowers and doers (agents). He is also interested in the laws of transformation according to which one state or attitude turns into another or is modified by another (uncertainty becomes belief, perception turns to memory and so on) and also in the *internal*, that is necessary, *relations* between these cognitive attitudes themselves.

The fundamental key to unlock conscious experience is the understanding of intentionality.[15] Husserl's begins from the Brentanian insight that psychic states are essentially structured as intentional states. Intentionality is understood by Husserl generally as 'having something in mind' (*etwas 'im Sinne' zu haben*, Ideas I, Hua III/1 185). Every perception, memory, thought, feeling or emotion is about something, it is directed at some object. It is 'about' something. Husserl sees intentionality as 'the fundamental characteristic of all consciousness' (*Ideas* I §90). It is the 'name of the problem encompassed by the whole of phenomenology' (*Ideas* I, §146, p. 349; Hua III/1 303). As we have seen, Husserl prefers to use the Cartesian language of *cogitatio* and *cogitatum* (CM §14; Crisis §50). Every *cogitatio* intends a *cogitatum*. But, in his published work, *Ideas* I §§87–96, Husserl also introduces new terms borrowed from the Greek *noesis* and *noema* which he had been developing in his lectures from 1908. In his mature writings (see *Crisis* §48), he speaks of the 'noetic-noematic correlation' or the 'noetic-noematic structure [*Aufbau*]' (CM, Hua I 78).[16] The structural features of the intended object can be studied independent of its existence. I can be seeking the perfect partner (whom I may never find) but I can be quite sure of the specific traits of that person. Cultural products, art objects, religious artefacts and so on are all intentional objects. They are invested with meaning that comes to light depending on the noetic attitude adopted towards them. To study them as they present or disclose themselves is to study them noematically.

Studying the intentional correlation between act and object is a way of gaining access to the essences of mental states. As Husserl writes in his *Passive Syntheses* lectures:

> But if one has learned to see phenomenologically and has learned to grasp the essence of intentional analysis . . . then one will initially make the quite astounding discovery that those types of lived experience are not a matter of arbitrary special features of an accidental life of consciousness, but rather that terms like "perception," "memory," "expectation," etc., express universal, essential structures, that is, strictly necessary structures of every conceivable stream of consciousness, thus, so to speak, formal structures of a life of consciousness as such whose profound study and exact conceptual circumscription, whose systematic graduated levels of foundation and genetic development, is the first great task of a transcendental phenomenology. It is precisely nothing less that the science of the essential shapes [*Gestalten*] of consciousness as such, as the science of maternal origins. (APS 365–6; Hua XI 233)

It is not, therefore, just a matter of the enumeration or 'uncovering' (*Enthüllung*) of the layers of our intentional life. Husserl also wants to examine their interlocking interconnection into the single, unified framework which enables not just the unity and identity of a single consciousness but also participation in the shared, universal rational life, our cognitive life (*Erkenntnisleben*).

Husserl is a holist. Intentional life is an interconnected *whole*, a coherent, integrated 'complex' or 'nexus' (*Zusammenhang*). Attitudes, beliefs, modifications, 'sedimentations' (beliefs that have settled down into convictions and habits) are bound together or synthesized into one harmonious life in a continuously existing world. Husserl wants to uncover the basic forms of our conscious life in terms of their essential features and necessary structural interconnections. He often speaks of the different layers or 'strata' involved in an act of consciousness. He also points out that (in perception) these strata do not just sit on top of one another but 'interpenetrate or intersaturate' (*sie durchdringen sich oder durchtränken sich*, DR, p. 62; Hua XVI 75).

Following the psychology of his day (which ultimately derived from Descartes), and especially his teachers Franz Brentano

(1838–1917) and Wilhelm Wundt (1832–1920), Husserl initially accepted the distinction between external or 'outer' perception (*aussere Wahrnhemung*) and 'inner' perception (*innere Wahrnehmung*). Broadly speaking, we perceive objects outside of us in outer perception but we perceive the flow of our own conscious sensations, thoughts and feelings, in inner perception. In his mature phenomenology, Husserl maintained that whatever is occurrent in consciousness can be recovered by a specific act of reflection involving a change of attitude or stance (*Einstellungänderung*). In such a shift, we can go from seeing the tree to seeing that our seeing of the tree involves temporally changing profiles with differing sensory contents. It is this freedom to change stance – essential to our freedom as rational beings – that allows for the possibility of phenomenology. Just as when watching a film, I can go from being absorbed in the plot to reflectively examining how the camera shots are set up, the use of tracking and so on, I can vary my conscious attention from my doings in the world to my own manner of attending. It is the systematic description of what is uncovered in the reflective attitude that yields phenomenological information about how our conscious states are experienced. This is most complex. For Husserl, for instance, external perceptions are always partial and internally indicate they are never complete, whereas he thought that the information received in inner perception was complete and reliable and in this case, *esse est percipi*. In later years, he realized this was not completely true. I may be sure of my own grief or anger but it also (just like an external object) appears in profiles and I may reflectively come to the conclusion that my experienced anger was in fact a feeling of being hurt or whatever.

In *Ideas* I (1913), Husserl came to clear awareness of the relation between the naïve certainty of perception and the overall belief-structure of what he came to describe as 'the natural attitude' (*die natürliche Einstellung, Ideas* I §27). One of the greatest discoveries of Edmund Husserl's phenomenology is that the ordinary, everyday world of experience, the world of things, plants, animals, people and places, the pre-theoretical, pre-scientific world, is not just simply *there*, in itself, but is the correlate of a very specific attitude, namely, the *natural attitude*. Husserl's early descriptive phenomenology was realist but he moved in a transcendental direction in his mature works when he introduced the idea of the methodological suspension of the thetic or existence-positing commitments of the natural, normal attitude to allow the shape of perception to come fully into view, in an undistorted fashion, uncovering the role of the ego in this process. Phenomenology reveals the natural attitude, which is unaware of itself as an attitude, by adopting the transcendental attitude, an attitude which sees objectivity as produced by the achievements of cooperating subjects. Thus, for instance, a play is only constituted as a play if all participants (actors, directors, writers, audience, stagehands and so on) involve themselves in what they are doing with the belief that they are creating and staging a play, and, similarly, for all cultural products (religious rituals, artistic events, legal gatherings such as trials and juries, and so on). But Husserl went further to claim that nature (especially as understood in the modern scientific worldview) is itself the product of the natural attitude. Natural sciences function within the natural attitude and do not question it. But philosophy cannot live in this naïveté. This is essentially what *transcendental* as opposed to *eidetic* phenomenology is all about. According to the mature Husserl, the original, naïve acceptance of the world in the natural attitude must be treated as giving only the kind of evidence appropriate to it and be treated under the reduction as merely 'an acceptance phenomenon' (CM §7). Husserl believes we can abstain from the 'natural existence-positing' of the original perception (CM §15); we can actually abstain from commitment to 'every believing involved in or founded on sensuous experiencing' (CM §8, p. 19; Hua I 59). There raises, of course, the perennial problem of relating his eidetic account of perception with his unwavering commitment to transcendental idealism.

In this chapter, I shall steer clear of this knotty problem of transcendental idealism. But, one element is important: if we suspend the belief-moment of the perception are we not altering or modifying the original perception itself? Husserl answers this question affirmatively, but maintains we do not thereby misunderstand what is essential to perception as such. For this reason, I think we can largely ignore the role of the phenomenological-transcendental reduction in describing views relevant to his philosophy of mind.

Husserl's overall aim was to gain insight into the nature of cognition and especially into judgements and into the life of reason. As a committed, even radical, empiricist (he was an admirer of William James), Husserl begins his account of cognition with direct, immediate perceptual experience, which for him, as for Aristotle, Aquinas, and modern Empiricism, forms the basis of all consciousness.

The bedrock mental act is perception and therefore any study of knowledge and consciousness must begin with perception, although it clearly does not stop there. Perception offers a paradigm of a kind of consciousness where intention finds fulfilment, where the activity of perceiving receives immediate and constant confirmation and collaboration, and hence is a paradigm of the evidence, the 'primordial form' (*Urmodus*) of intuitiveness (APS 110; Hua XI 68; see also *Crisis* §28, p. 105; Hua VI 107). In *Ideas* I §39, Husserl writes:

> I shall look for the ultimate source which feeds the general positing of the world effected by me in the natural attitude, the source which therefore makes it possible that I consciously find a factually existing world of physical things confronting me and that I ascribe to myself a body in that world. . . . Obviously this ultimate source is sensuous experience. For our purposes, however, it will be sufficient if we consider sensuous perception which plays the role among experiencing acts of what may be called, in a certain legitimate sense a primal experience from which all other experiencing acts derive a major part of their grounding force. (*Ideas* I §39, pp. 82–3; Hua III/1 70)

It is perceptual consciousness that gives us our first sense of objectivity, physicality and the experience of 'world':

> [Perception] is what originally makes us conscious of the realities existing for us and "the" world as actually existing. To cancel out all such perception, actual and possible, means, for our total life of consciousness, to cancel out the world as objective sense and as reality accepted by us; it means to remove from all thought about the world (in every signification of this word) the original basis of sense and legitimacy.[17]

Perception of transcendent objects gives us the *sense* of an abiding world, of a world that is our disposal in so far as we can revisit and re-perform earlier perceptions, and so have an abiding knowledge:

> The fact that a re-perception, a renewed perception of the same thing, is possible for transcendence characterizes the fundamental

trait of transcendent perception, alone through which an abiding world is there for us, a reality than can be pregiven for us and can be freely at our disposal. (APS §3, p. 47; Hua XI 10)

Perception is much more than visual perception, of course, and Husserl did spend a lot of time analysing the relation between sight and touch (he has much less to say about the senses of hearing, smell and taste). With regard to vision, Husserl gives extensive, detailed descriptions of just *what* we see and *how* we see it (involving the nature of the act of perception, the nature of the perceived object, the sense of perception, the role of temporal awareness in the structure of perceiving, the dynamic nature of perceptual content, the nature of the indeterminate accompanying horizons and so on).

While phenomenologists (e.g. Maurice Merleau-Ponty and Aron Gurwitsch) have always been advocates of Husserl's direct realist account of perception, recently, analytically trained philosophers have begun to recognize its importance.[18] Many aspects of Husserl's discussion of perception are of interest to contemporary philosophers, for instance, his commitment to direct realism; his rejection of representationalism, and any view that would substitute a sign or picture for the perceptual object itself (see *Ideas* I §43); his rejection of 'sensualism' and causal accounts of perception; his rejection of *conceptualism*, that is, the claim that every sensory element in perceptual consciousness involves exercise of a concept;[19] and his account of the specific essence of perception as distinct from judgement. In the *Logical Investigations*, for instance, there is a sustained critique of the representationalist accounts of perception found in Locke, Berkeley, Hume, Mill and others. In *Ideas* I, he criticizes the atomism and representationalism of the Gestalt psychologists, Koffka, Köhler and others). Husserl (and Merleau-Ponty follows him in this regard; see Chapter 4) is a virulent critic of empiricist accounts of the sense datum or 'idea'. We do not see patches of colour or hear noises, but see the multicoloured landscape and listen to the sounds of traffic, birds or refrigerators. Husserl also rejects phenomenalist accounts, whereby the object simply consists of a series of appearances or sense data. His appreciation of the nature of the stream of consciousness led him to reject all 'sensualist' accounts of it as a stream of contents 'without sense in themselves'; rather consciousness always involves intending of objects, sense and constitution. As he would write in *Ideas* I:

> Consciousness is not the name for "psychic complexes," for "contents" fused together, for "bundles" or streams of "sensations" which, without sense in themselves, also cannot lend any "sense" to whatever mixture; it is rather through and through "consciousness," the source of all reason and unreason, all legitimacy and illegitimacy, all reality and fiction, all value and disvalue, all deed and misdeed. Consciousness is therefore toto caelo different from what sensualism alone will see, from what in fact is irrational stuff without sense—but which is accessible to rationalization. (*Ideas* I §86, pp. 207–8; Hua III/1 176)

Husserl repeats this critique of 'sensualism' and 'atomism' over and over (see CM, Hua I §16). It is just not true that we see our own sensations or that objects are bundles or collections of sense data. Phenomenology tells us otherwise. As Martin Heidegger puts it in *The Origin of the Work of Art* essay: 'much closer than any sensations are the things themselves' [the wind rustling in the chimney, and so on].[20]

Husserl also rejects various versions of the causal account of perception. For instance, T. H. Green maintained that 'the reference of a sensation to a sensible thing means its reference to a cause'.[21] But Husserl is clear that perceiving does not involve an awareness of causal connection, rather there is conscious sense of unmediated presence of the object. As Fred Dretske puts it, to hear the doorbell ringing is not to hear the button being depressed even if the button being depressed initiates the causal chain that results in us hearing the doorbell.[22] Dretske claims that the reason we hear the bell and not the button is that the bell is 'primarily represented' while the button is not:

> The reason we hear the bell, not the button, is because, although our auditory experience carries information about the properties of both the bell (that it is ringing) and the button (that it is depressed), the ringing (of the bell) is represented in a primary way while the depression (of the button) is not.[23]

However, I think Husserl's analysis is more to the point. We don't hear the *button* at all; we hear the *door bell ringing*. We only know that the button is being depressed because we assume a certain scientific and causal view already. We read causation into the perceptual scene as it were, we don't find it there.

Two main traits of perceiving that Husserl constantly stresses are that perception presents an object directly and immediately, and that the act of perceiving involves unquestioned *acceptance*. Or, as Husserl puts it, there are two characteristics of perception: one noetic, the other noematic. On the noetic side, the perceiving is straightforward and has the character of certainty; on the noematic or object side, the object perceived has the character of existing actuality (CM Hua I §15). In perception, the object is experienced as given in the manner of 'itself there' (*selbst da*). We have the immediate certainty of being in the perceptual presence of the perceived thing. Perception holds out, as it were, the promise of offering us the thing itself as it actually is, 'it itself' (*es selbst*). According to Husserl, it belongs to the very sense of a perceptual act to involve the self-appearance of the object (Hua XIX/2 589). The object is given 'itself' (*selbst*), 'there' (*da*), 'in the flesh', 'bodily' (*leibhaftig*), *in propria persona*, in the actual temporal present, in its own being and 'being so' (*Sosein*, Hua VII 251):

> . . . the object stands in perception as there in the flesh, it stands, to speak still more precisely, as actually present, as self-given there in the current now. (DR §4, p. 12; Hua XVI 14)

Perception is essentially 'simple' or 'straightforward' (*schlicht*, LU §46); for Husserl, this means there is no reasoning involved in perception:

> What this means is this: that the object is also an *immediately given object* in the sense that, as *this object perceived with this definite objective content*, it is not *constituted* in relational, connective, or otherwise articulated acts, acts founded on other acts which bring other acts to perception. (LU VI §46; vol. II, p. 282; Hua XIX/2 674).

We receive the object 'in one blow' (*in einem Schlage*), as he puts it. The fact that perception is straightforward means that it delivers the object at once, in the modes of actuality and certainty. But, of course, it does not mean that we see only a single object. We can have simple straightforward perception of complex objects (a pile of books, a book on the table, etc.). In his classic work *Perception*, H. H. Price believes that Husserl gets it right when he refers to the experience of the presence of the object in actual perception as being a *'leibhaftig' in propria persona* experience.[24] In this sense, for Price, perception resembles an intuition in its holistic or 'totalistic' nature and lack of discursiveness.

A second crucial component of perception is that it involves 'perceptual belief' and 'perceptual certainty', as Husserl says in *Ideas* I (1913) §103. Husserl often comments on the fact that *Wahrnehmung* in German means literally taking-for-true. An important structural feature of perception, for Husserl, is that it is normally accompanied by a kind of certainty, a *'primal belief* or *protodoxa'* (*Ideas* I §104, p. 252; Hua III/1 216) that he describes as 'unmodalised' (*Ideas* I §104). Husserl often emphasizes this naïve certainty (something one finds also in G. E. Moore). Thus, Husserl writes: 'One speaks of a believing inherent in perceiving' (APS 66; Hua XI 28) and: 'Every normal perception is a consciousness of validity' (APS 71; Hua XI 33). This *Urdoxa* is a bedrock certainty not amenable to doubt: 'The primordial mode is certainty but in the form of the most straightforward certainty' (APS 76; Hua XI 37). A belief, for Husserl, can become modified into an uncertainty, a deeming likely or maybe into something questionable (*Ideas* I §103), but the 'unmodified' or 'unmodalized' form of certainty has a privileged role. As Thomas Reid had already recognized in his *Essay on the Intellectual Powers of Man*, in perception there is, as he puts it, 'a strong and irresistible conviction and belief of its [the perceived object] present existence'.[25]

A third claim for which Husserl is also well known is that, in perception, the object is given as it is in itself, while at the same time it is given in profiles. Although we see the object from one side, somehow the *whole* object is given (see also Chapters 4 and 13). External perception has the 'sense' (*Sinn*) whole object, even if only one side is 'properly' seen. As Husserl makes clear, even if it is the case that the perception is only of one side under one aspect, nevertheless, it is clear that *the whole* object is intended and 'meant' in the act of perceiving:

> Let us begin by noting that the aspect, the perspectival adumbration through which every spatial object invariably

appears, only manifests the spatial object from one side. No matter how completely we may perceive a thing, it is never given in perception with the characteristics that qualify it and make it up as a sensible thing from all sides at once. (APS §1, p. 39; Hua XI 3)

As Gareth Evans has argued, to say that we see an object from one side is not to deny that we actually see the object itself. Husserl makes this clear in *Ideas* I §138. Despite the inadequacy of each one-sided perception, what 'properly' appears cannot be separated from the perception of the thing as a whole. The side that properly appears is really a non–self-sufficient part of the whole that is the 'sense' of the perception (*Ideas* I, p. 331; Hua III/1 286–7). In terms of his analysis of the essence of perception, Husserl maintains that what we think of as peculiarities particular to us are actually eidetic insights that belong to the Idea of a physical thing as such. A material thing unveils itself in endless spatial profiles. Even God can only grasp a physical thing in profiles (*Ideas* I §149, p. 362; Hua III/1 315). Similarly, a material thing also reveals itself in perception in a series of temporal moments. Not even God can alter this eidetic truth (DR, Hua XVI 65). Unrolling in spatial and temporal profiles pertains to the essence of a material thing (DR, Hua XVI 66). In part, this is why Husserl is convinced that what he is doing is not *psychology*.

Perception for Husserl is the bedrock of consciousness. All other forms of conscious experience are in one way or another *founded* on perceptual, sensory consciousness. Husserl contrasts the 'self-givenness' (*Selbstgegebenheit*) of perception with a very large class of conscious forms that he characterizes as 'representational' (*vergegenwärtig*) in one way or another. Representation, or more accurately 'presentification', 'presentation' or 'calling to mind' (*Vergegenwärtigung*), includes memory, fantasy, wishing and symbolic thinking – all forms that do not have the sense of the immediate presence of the object. When one remembers, imagines or fantasizes about an object, there is not the same sense of the immediate, actual, bodily and temporal presence of the object. Indeed, in memory and in expectation, the object is experienced as not presently there, but there is some kind of reference to its being, it is still being posited (as future or past) in a specific way. Unlike imagination, memory posits the real 'having-been' of something. Imagination entails no such positing of the real existence of its object in any temporal mode. Memory is not 'picture-consciousness' (*Bildbewusstsein*). It is a *thetic* or positing act, but the object is presented as 'being-past', 'having been' (Hua XIII 164) and as 'having-been-perceived-by-me' (Hua VII 252) and having been originally experienced *in a mode other than memory*. In other words, in an act of remembering, the experience remembered is presented as one originally experienced by me, but now with a *temporal distance* separating it from my current experience. This temporal distantiation is characteristic of memory:

> Recollection is not simply the being-conscious once again of the object; rather, just as the perception of a temporal object carries with it its temporal horizon, so too the recollection repeats the consciousness of this horizon. (ZB, p. 113; Hua X 108)

The object experienced in a fantasy (which includes reverie, daydream, act of deliberate imagining, fictional creation, etc.) is not necessarily past, present or future, but is presented 'as-if' (DR §4), and is not an actual perception. This is a structural feature of fantasy itself: it has the character of 'depicting'. In fantasy, there is no positing of the object. Moreover, the object of the fantasy is not located precisely as it would be in a perception. It 'hovers' or floats before the fantasist; it is not continuous with the objects or the space around it. Secondly, there is no temporal distance or gap experienced as there is in the case of memory. The fantasized image is apprehended in the present tense although that present is not itself experienced as perceptual present tense. On the other hand, the fantasized image can reappear and be recovered in memory.

Picture consciousness or 'depicting consciousness' (*Bildbewusstsein*) is another *sui generis* form of representative consciousness for which Husserl offers a very complex and challenging analysis – that received a recent reformulation on the concept of 'seeing-in' as developed by Richard Wollheim (1923–2003).[26] According to Husserl, a photograph or a postcard of a bridge is a complex object with multiple modes of givenness. There is a perceived physical object (postcard) and also a represented picture (bridge). There is involved a blend of perceiving and imaging. The postcard is a genuine object that can be seen, touched, tasted, etc. But it is also a 'picture-thing' (*Bildding*, Hua XXIII 489) hosting an image – the bridge – that floats somewhat free of the physical object. We can see past the brush-strokes to the face presented in the painting. This is a seeing-in. It is different from fantasy. The image in fantasy needs no physical substrate and belongs within consciousness itself and does not survive the act of fantasizing, whereas a depicted object based on a physical object does survive.

Another important form of 'representation' or 'presentiation' (*Vergegenwärtigung*) is our experience of other's conscious experiences. Husserl, following the psychological tradition of his day, calls this 'empathy' (*Einfühlung*).[27] Husserl's phenomenology has often been caricatured as solipsistic, either metaphysically or methodologically. He is seen as the last proponent of an essentially Cartesian 'philosophy of consciousness' that prioritizes phenomena as given to the individual ego as well as privileging the ego's self-presence to itself as the highest form of being understood as presence. But Husserl did devote considerable attention to the discussion of *empathy*, to *intersubjectivity* and to the experience of what is 'other', 'foreign' or 'strange' (*das Fremde, das Andere*), what he calls generally 'other-experience' (*Fremderfahrung*). He contrasts this 'originary' (*originär*) or 'primordial' manner of self-givenness in self-experience with 'other experience', which he regards as 'non-originary' (*nicht originär*). In the sense that I can never do more than *reproduce* the first-person life of the other which he or she experiences in a first-person, originary way, I cannot directly experience the other's first-person experiences. We can of course share experiences. Two siblings can *share* the grief of the death of their father; but both have individual griefs, and the analysis of the intentional structure of their griefs may differ even if they have the same intentional object, intensity and so on. Moreover, each is conscious not just of his or her grief but also of the other's grief as a distinct object. A sister can sympathize with a brother's grief but still find it cloying, and so on.

Husserl explores different ways in which the empathic understanding of the other can be achieved. One way is through the analogical pairing between my lived body and that of the other. In a handshake – each feels the other intending to make the contact. Of course, this is possible in many different ways – I can feel the reluctance of the other, the forced familiarity, the limp lifeless hand contact and so on, but in these cases my body is responding to the living bodily intentionality of the other. Another way Husserl explores empathy is through various modalizations of my self-experience. Husserl believes that the 'I' is primarily experienced in the present tense, in its immediate self-presence, and that, through a peculiar kind of synthesis, it identifies itself with the ego that intrinsically belongs to past experiences. I consciously take myself to be the same person as the child I am now remembering that I once was. This occurs through a kind of 'modalization' or 'variation' of myself that is governed by a priori essential laws that it is the business of phenomenology to identify. This *self-identification* over time gives Husserl a clue to how the other person is also constituted within my experience. Just as I identify with my earlier self in a memory, so also I can identify with the other in various forms of social experience. Husserl always sees empathy as the bridge to the other: 'Empathy creates the first true transcendence (thus transcendence in a unique sense)' (Hua XIV 8). In fact, the solipsistic way of approaching oneself is a one-sided abstraction for Husserl. The self is *never* experienced without the other. Self and other are always 'interwoven' and have an intimate 'belonging-together' (*Ineinandersein*). As Husserl makes clear in the *Crisis*, the presence of other persons is a necessary condition of the experience of objectivity. The first other experienced is the other living body (*Leib*). The recognition of the body *as lived body* is the first step towards objectivation (Hua XIV 110).

Husserl's phenomenology has much to say about the experience of the self and the manner in which time-consciousness is constituted. But he also recognizes that the truly human life is lived out at the level of the person. As we saw above, Husserl maintains that persons only come into view *as* persons from a particular standpoint which he calls the 'personalistic attitude' (*die personalistische Einstellung*). This is not to deny that persons are real entities of a unique kind; it is just that they are disclosed only when we view them from a certain dimension. The specifically personalistic attitude is

> . . . the attitude we are always in when we live with one another, talk to one another, shake hands with another in greeting, or are related to another in love and aversion, in disposition and action, in discourse and discussion. (*Ideas* II §49, p.192; Hua IV 183)

Husserl contrasts the personalistic attitude with the 'naturalistic attitude' (which is a specifically scientific attitude as developed in modernity and a subdomain of the more universal natural attitude). Husserl thinks that, while it may be necessary to view the human body as a physical body in order to highlight certain kinds of property (e.g. the body as a physical object in causal interconnection with other physical objects), it is a gross distortion to the human being if it is treated solely in a purely naturalistic manner:

> He who sees everywhere only nature, nature in the sense of, as it were, through the eyes of, natural science, is precisely blind to the spiritual sphere, the special domain of the human sciences. (*Ideas* II §51, p. 201; Hua IV 191)

The *person* is primarily an individual with an identity through changing states (infancy, childhood, maturity), who exercises freedom and is capable of rational actions and responsibilities. The person is oriented to values. Persons in the Kantian tradition are understood as irreducible ends in themselves, deserving of being treated with dignity and respect. The mature Husserl was undoubtedly influenced by the Kantian (and Neo-Kantian) conceptions of the self as person understood as an autonomous (giving the law to itself), rational agent. At the centre of the person, for Husserl, is a *drive* for reason, but it is a drive sitting upon many other affective and embodied elements (see Chapter 13). In 'its full concretion' (Hua XIV 26), it is a *self* with convictions, values, an outlook, a history, a style and so on. As Husserl writes in *Cartesian Meditations*: 'The ego constitutes itself *for itself* in, so to speak, the unity of a history' (CM, p. 75; Hua I 109). Furthermore, I come to understand myself as person precisely through apprehending others as persons within the wider enabling context of the personal world of 'co-humanity' (*Mitmenschheit*). We actually live in personal relations with one another, in community with others whom we understand as 'companions, not as opposed subjects but as counter subjects who live "with" one another' (*Ideas* II §51, p. 204; Hua IV 194). As he writes in 1925:

> I direct my interest purely toward the personal, that means, purely toward how persons behave as persons and behave toward one another, how they define themselves and others, how they form friendships, marriages, unions, etc. . . . If I do this, nature as nature is never my theme in all that, neither the physical nor the psychophysical.[28]

I am in the personalistic attitude in thinking about my relations to my families, to parents and children, in my experience as servant and master, in 'I-thou' (*Ich-Du*) relations (an expression Husserl uses – possibly inherited from Hermann Cohen), and so on. Moreover, social life is constituted by specifically social, communicative acts. Husserl has a great deal to say about 'social acts' and about 'we-subjectivity' (*Wir-Subjektivität*) and 'I-we' relations (e.g. Hua XIV 166). In fact, for Husserl, the personal arises out of the social rather than the other way around (Hua XIV 175). There are also communal selves, 'personalities of a higher order' (XIV 192). We belong in an open-ended, many-layered 'communicative sociality' (*Kommunicationsgemeinschaft*, Hua XIV 194), a term Husserl uses long before it was taken up by Habermas. 'Communication creates unity' (XIV 199); one consciousness 'coincides' with another consciousness to form a unity of understanding, of purpose, of shared interests, common 'in-group' jokes or whatever. This communal consciousness extends into the past. For instance, in the community of philosophers, I can argue with Plato, agree or disagree with his views, admire Aristotle as a person, and so on.

The objective world experienced as such through some kind of a priori harmony between myself and other subjectivities in their perception of it. It is co-presence of other subjects perceiving the same object from different sides and in different profiles that allows me to think of the world as common, shared, 'there for all' (*für Jedermann da*) and so on. Without the mediation of foreign subjectivities, the 'transcendent' object of my experience would remain merely 'transcendent for me', with the possibility that it remained something merely intended as opposed to absolutely transcendent (i.e. apprehended with 'being in itself').

Husserl's phenomenology is an extraordinarily rich resource for philosophy of mind. Analytic philosophy of mind – especially as stimulated by philosophers such as Tom Nagel[29] and Wilfrid Sellars, who themselves were influenced by Husserl – has reawakened issues such as the nature of the first-person perspective, individual and collective intentionality, the question as to whether emotions have objects, the nature of empathy, the understanding of free will, the nature of imagination, seeing-in and the entire constitution of the social and cultural world (e.g. in the work of John Searle[30]). It would indeed be a pity if analytic philosophers continued to 'reinvent the wheel' without going back to gain some knowledge of the enormous contribution of Edmund Husserl's phenomenological investigations.

Notes

1. For a study of Husserl's life and works, see Dermot Moran, *Edmund Husserl. Founder of Phenomenology* (Cambridge and Malden, MA: Polity Press, 2005). For Husserl's early mathematical studies, see *Edmund Husserl, Early Writings in the Philosophy of Logic and Mathematics*, trans. Dallas Willard, Husserl Collected Works V (Dordrecht: Kluwer, 1994).

2. On Husserl's philosophy of mind, see David Woodruff Smith and Ronald McIntyre, *Husserl and Intentionality. A Study of Mind, Meaning and Language* (Dordrecht: Reidel, 1982); Richard Cobb-Stevens, *Husserl and Analytic Philosophy* (Dordrecht: Kluwer, 1990); and Hubert L. Dreyfus, (ed.), *Husserl, Intentionality and Cognitive Science* (Cambridge, MA: MIT Press, 1982).

3. See for instance, Shaun Gallagher and Dan Zahavi, *The Phenomenological Mind: An Introduction to Philosophy of Mind and Cognitive Science* (London: Routledge, 2008).

4. The complete works of Husserl have now been edited in the Husserliana series, Dordrecht: Springer (originally Nijhoff and then Kluwer) 1950–. The full list of titles can be found on the Springer website at http://www.springer.com/series/6062. In this chapter, I shall cite works, where possible, by giving the title, section number and page number of the English translation and then the Husserliana [= Hua] volume, in Roman numbers and page number of the German edition.

5. See Edmund Husserl, *On the Phenomenology of the Consciousness of Internal Time* [1928], trans. J. B. Brough, Dordrecht: Kluwer, 1990.

6. Edmund Husserl, *The Crisis of European Sciences and Transcendental Phenomenology. An Introduction to Phenomenological Philosophy*, trans. David Carr (Evanston, IL: Northwestern University Press, 1970). Hereafter '*Crisis*'. The reference here is *Crisis* §68, p. 233; Hua VI 236.

7. Edmund Husserl, *Ideas pertaining to a Pure Phenomenology and to a Phenomenological Philosophy, Second Book*, trans. R. Rojcewicz and A. Schuwer, Husserl Collected Works III (Dordrecht: Kluwer, 1989). This work is usually referred to as '*Ideas II*'. It was edited for publication by Edith Stein and eventually published posthumously.

8. Edmund Husserl, *Logical Investigations*, trans. J. N. Findlay, ed. with a New Introduction by Dermot Moran and New Preface by Michael Dummett, 2 Vols. (London and New York: Routledge, 2001). This work was originally published in German in 2 volumes in 1900

and 1901. Hereafter 'LU' followed by the section, volume and page number of the English translation and the Husserliana volume and page number.

9 Edmund Husserl, *Ideas. A General Introduction to Pure Phenomenology*. trans. W. R. Boyce Gibson (London: Allen and Unwin, 1931; reprinted with a new Preface by Dermot Moran, London: Routledge Classics 2012). This work originally was published in German in 1913 and is usually referred to as '*Ideas I*'. See also E. Husserl, *Ideas pertaining to a Pure Phenomenology and to a Phenomenological Philosophy, First Book*, trans. F. Kersten (Dordrecht: Kluwer, 1983). Hereafter the pagination will be given for the Kersten translation.

10 Edmund Husserl, *Cartesian Meditations*, trans. D. Cairns (The Hague: Nijhoff, 1967). Hereafter 'CM'.

11 Thomas Szanto, *Bewusstsein, Intentionalität und mentale Repräsentation. Husserl und die analytische Philosophie des Geistes* (Berlin/Boston: De Gruyter, 2012).

12 Edmund Husserl, *Analyses Concerning Passive and Active Synthesis. Lectures on Transcendental Logic*, trans. Anthony J. Steinbock, Husserl Collected Works Volume IX (Dordrecht: Kluwer, 2001). Hereafter 'APS'.

13 Edmund Husserl, *Thing and Space: Lectures of 1907*, trans. R. Rojcewicz, Husserl Collected Works VII (Dordrecht: Kluwer, 1997). Hereafter 'DR'.

14 For a fuller discussion of phenomenology, see Dermot Moran, *Introduction to Phenomenology* (London and New York: Routledge, 2000).

15 John J. Drummond, *Husserlian Intentionality and Non-Foundational Realism. Noema and Object* (Dordrecht: Kluwer, 1990). See also Dermot Moran 'Heidegger's Critique of Husserl's and Brentano's Accounts of Intentionality', *Inquiry* 43 (March 2000), 39–65; and idem, 'Husserl's Critique of Brentano in the *Logical Investigations*,'*Manuscrito*, Special Husserl Issue, 23 (2000), 163–205.

16 Noesis and noema are referred to briefly in Husserl's *Amsterdam Lectures* (Hua IX 327) and in the *Encyclopedia Britannica* article (Hua IX 283).

17 Edmund Husserl, 'Kant and the Idea of Transcendental Philosophy', trans. Ted E. Klein and William E. Pohl, *Southwestern Journal of Philosophy* 5 (Fall 1974), 9–56, see p. 26; Hua VII 251.

18 See, *inter alia*, A. D. Smith in his *The Problem of Perception* (Cambridge, MA: Harvard University Press, 2002), who uses Husserl to critique Sellarsian accounts, and Kevin Mulligan's article 'Perception', in Barry Smith and David Woodruff Smith, (eds), *The Cambridge Companion to Husserl* (Cambridge: Cambridge University Press, 1995). See also Kevin Mulligan, 'Perception, Particulars, and Predicates,' in Denis Fisette, (ed.), *Consciousness and Intentionality. Models and Modalities of Attribution*, The Western Ontario Series in Philosophy of Science (Dordrecht: Kluwer, 1999), pp. 163–94. Mulligan links Husserl to Fred Dretske's account of perception in *Knowledge and the Flow of Information* (Cambridge, MA: MIT Press, 1983) – see Chapter 11).

19 A. D. Smith, *The Problem of Perception*, op. cit., p. 94.

20 M. Heidegger, 'The Origin of the Work of Art', Martin Heidegger, *Basic Writings*, 1st edition, p. 156.

21 A. D. Smith, *Problem of Perception*, op. cit., p. 68.

22 F. Dretske, *Knowledge and the Flow of Information*, op. cit., p. 162.

23 Ibid.

24 See H. H. Price, *Perception* (London: Methuen, 1932, Revised ed. 1950; reprinted Westwood, CT: Greenwood, 1981), p. 152.

25 See Thomas Reid, *Essay on the Intellectual Powers of Man*, ed. Baruch Brody (Cambridge, MA: MIT Press, 1969), Book 2 Ch. 5, pp. 111–12.

26 Richard Wollheim, *Art and Its Objects: An Introduction to Aesthetics* (New York: Harper & Row, 1968).

27 On Husserl's concept of empathy, see Dermot Moran, 'The Problem of Empathy: Lipps, Scheler, Husserl and Stein,' in *Amor Amicitiae: On the Love that is Friendship. Essays in Medieval Thought and Beyond in Honor of the Rev Professor James McEvoy*, ed. Thomas A. Kelly and Phillip W. Rosemann (Leuven/Paris/Dudley, MA: Peeters, 2004), pp. 269–312. See also Edith Stein, *On the Problem of Empathy*, trans. Waltraut Stein, Collected Works of Edith Stein, Vol. 3 (Washington, DC: ICS Publications, 1989).

28 Edmund Husserl, *Phenomenological Psychology. Lectures, Summer Semester 1925*, trans. John Scanlon (The Hague: Nijhoff, 1977), p. 168; Hua IX 220.

29 Thomas Nagel, *The View from Nowhere* (New York: Oxford University Press, 1986).

30 John R. Searle, *The Construction of Social Reality* (New York: The Free Press, 1995).

CHAPTER FOUR

Merleau-Ponty: A phenomenological philosophy of mind and body

Sara Heinämaa

Maurice Merleau-Ponty's phenomenology is nowadays celebrated as a forerunner of several important developments in philosophy of mind.[1] His phenomenological account of perception is taken as an antecedent to enactivist and externalist theories of perception and as a precursor of inquiries into preconceptual content. His work is cited by neuroscientists who work on mirror neurons as well as by connectionists who challenge the cognitivist paradigm of cognitive science.[2] More generally, he is seen as the initiator of the whole theoretical discourse on embodied consciousness with all its practical implications ranging from the treatment of psychopathologies to debates concerning bodily identities.[3]

These discussions highlight important aspects in Merleau-Ponty's works but, on the other hand, they give a one-sided view of his contribution to philosophical investigations of the human mind. Merleau-Ponty did not just come up with a set of ideas that proved crucial to later theory construction but developed a systematic and influential philosophy which includes a complete account of perception and cognition and their dependencies on our bodily motor relations with the environing world. This philosophy is phenomenological in nature and its methods include the methods of reduction, first-person reflection and eidetic analysis.[4] This means that Merleau-Ponty's philosophy has deep roots in the phenomenological tradition of the twentieth century that began with Franz Brentano's philosophical psychology and received its first full articulation in Edmund Husserl's works in the 1910s–1930s.[5]

Thus, if we want to avoid simplifications and misunderstandings and want to capture the core ideas of Merleau-Ponty's thinking in all their strength, the best way to approach his work is not to focus on its results merely – however relevant or useful these results may be to our own inquiries – but to start with a clarification of the philosophical questions, goals and method that lead to these results. Moreover, we also need to study Merleau-Ponty's original conception of the relationship between philosophy and the special sciences in order to see what relevance, if any, philosophical reflection may have to special scientific theoretization and what assistance special sciences, on the other hand, can give to philosophy.

For these reasons, I will begin this essay with an exploration of the main conceptual and methodological starting points of Merleau-Ponty's phenomenological of mind and body, and only after this proceed to discuss the results of his inquiries into perception, embodiment and intercorporeality as the foundation of intersubjectivity.

1 Behaviour, intentionality, presentation: Conceptual starting points

The main question of Merleau-Ponty's lifelong philosophical investigations concerns the proper objects of the behavioural sciences, that is, the sciences that study living organisms and their significant behaviours (*comportment*) in their proper environments (*milieu*). We can track the development of this questioning from Merleau-Ponty's first study *The Structure of Behaviour* (*La structure du comportment*, 1942) to his seminal work *Phenomenology of Perception* (*Phénoménologie de la perception*, 1945) and finally to the posthumous *The Visible and the Invisible* (*Le visible et l'invisible*, 1964) which was planned to become a multi-part volume but only includes four preliminary chapters because of Merleau-Ponty's unexpected death. From the very first publications to the last manuscripts and lecture notes, Merleau-Ponty worked to clarify the relationship between consciousness and the world in its different modalities: perceptual and cognitive, personal and intersubjective, individual and social, human and pre-human, static and genetic.

The first thing to notice is that in the context of Merleau-Ponty's oeuvre, the term 'behaviour' must be understood in the phenomenological sense of practical intentionality that covers meaningful action and interaction as well as reactive comportment towards experienced things and events, both human and animal, both normal and abnormal. What is at issue are not the stimulus-response correlations theoretized by behaviouristic psychologists and philosophers but the ways in which humans and animals intend environing things,[6] act on them and react to them. The relevant correlation is thus between the living organism and its environment as it discloses itself to the organism.

The aim is to provide a philosophical foundation for the sciences that deal with such subjects and such objects. These sciences include psychological sciences and life sciences, but this foundational project also has important implications for biosciences, medical sciences, psychiatry, social sciences and the humanities (e.g. Merleau-Ponty [1960] 1987, pp. 98–113; 1964, pp. 43–95).

Thus, there is a foundationalist undercurrent in Merleau-Ponty's philosophical project. However, we must not associate phenomenological foundationalism with any reductivistic doctrines of subjectivism or idealism criticized by Richard Rorty (1979) and other neo-pragmatists. The aim is to provide an explication of the core phenomena presupposed or taken for granted in the psychological sciences and the life sciences, not to reduce these sciences, their main concept or results, to some metaphysical principle or idea.

This kind of analytical foundationalism has roots in Edmund Husserl's phenomenological epistemology (see Chapter 3). Husserl argued that one of the main tasks of epistemology is to provide a clarification of the different regions of being that the sciences presuppose.[7] The objects that the geologists study, for example, are very different from the ones that the biologists investigate. Still both sciences deal with concrete material objects and thus both sciences differ from the sciences that work on ideal abstract objects, such as geometry, logics or generative grammar. To be sure, all these objects share certain formal features, and these formal features must be clarified philosophically in formal ontology, but the sciences also differ in crucial respects and the differences too need a philosophical illumination if scientific thinking is to be a rational enterprise and not just a useful or productive project.

In the case of the science of geometry, for example, the task is to give an account of geometrical objects (geometrical points, triangles, circles, etc.), their ways of being and their ways of relating to other types of objects, empirical shapes, on the one hand, and other mathematical objects, numbers and functions, on the other hand (Husserl Hua6: 365–86; cf. Merleau-Ponty [1945] 1995, pp. 243ff., 385–8). In the case of psychology and the life sciences, the task is to give an account of ensouled beings or 'minded beings', to use contemporary vocabulary, that is, beings that have intentional relations to their environments and to other similar beings and that act on their environing objects on the basis of their intendings.

The psychological sciences are in a central role in Merleau-Ponty's philosophical enterprise since they thematize the very relation between the organism and its environment that is presupposed in the other sciences that deal with minded beings, for example in social scientific discussions of human action, in medical discussions of pain behaviour and in zoological discussion of the mating behaviours and communicative relations of animals.

In the philosophical framework of Merleau-Ponty's investigations, the mind is essentially, that is, necessarily, embodied.[8] So we are not dealing here with mental contents, immaterial substances, ideal spirits or dimensionless egos but with living bodies that operate and orient themselves in the environing world in significant ways.[9] In the preface to *Phenomenology of Perception*, Merleau-Ponty famously writes: 'Truth does not "inhabit" only the "inner man", or more accurately, there is no inner man, man is in the world, and only in the world does he know himself. When I return to myself from an excursion into the realm of dogmatic common sense or of science, I find, not a source of intrinsic truth, but a subject destined to the world' ([1945] 1995, p. xi, cf. p. 407).[10]

The other remark that needs to be made concerns the concept of *intentionality* or *intentional relating*. The reference here is to what is usually called 'directedness' or 'aboutness' in analytical philosophy of mind and attributed to mental states. However, in Merleau-Ponty's case the concept of intentionality has to be understood in the broad phenomenological sense that questions three central tendencies of traditional analytical philosophy of mind: one-sided focus on judgements or judgemental acts, predominance of representational relations, and the mind-body opposition.[11]

Merleau-Ponty's intentional analyses proceed from perceptual experiences and their directionality to lived bodily movement, sensibility and affection, that is, preconceptual modalities of consciousness that all have their own forms of directedness or aboutness different from the intentionality of judgements, cognitions and decisions. These are not mental states in the abstract sense of lacking all bodily dimensions but involve the lived body of the perceiver, that is, her sensing moving body and its perceptual organs which are constantly co-intended in all perceptions directed at environing things and events (Merleau-Ponty [1945] 1995, pp. 77–9).

One must also bear in mind that intentionality in this context does not merely mean goal-directed action. As pointed out above, the phenomenological framework in which Merleau-Ponty operates, goal-directedness is called 'practical intentionality'. It covers all goals and all means to goals, human and non-human, explicit and tacit, precise and obscure. This type of intentionality is central in our actions, individual actions, joint actions and common human projects, and the understanding of its structures is crucial to the development of ethics and political theory. However, practical intentionality is not the only way in which we intend objects. We can perceive environing things, for example scenery, as beautiful (or ugly), and we can also study and describe entities in a disinterested manner without subjecting them or their ways of being to any human practices. These non-practical axiological and theoretical ways of intending are crucial to arts and sciences which, to be sure, are human practices but very particular kinds of practices since they essentially include *non-practical ways of intending the world* (Husserl Hua6: 325ff.). The aim of Merleau-Ponty is to clarify the relations between these different modalities of intentionality and to explicate, in particular, their functions in our perceptual lives.

The last thing that must be emphasized in respect to intentionality is that Merleau-Ponty's phenomenological analyses show that perception is not a *representation* of the perceived thing.[12] The perceived thing is *present* in perception in full flesh, so to say. It is not re-presented by any other entity, be it a mental state, a neural state or a component of some such state, or a picture, an image, an indicative sign or a linguistic item. Already in *The Structure of Behaviour* Merleau-Ponty states: 'the possession of a representation or the exercise of judgement is not co-extensive with the life of consciousness. Rather consciousness is a network of significative intentions which are sometimes very clear to themselves and sometimes, on the contrary, lived [*vévues*] rather than known' (Merleau-Ponty [1942] 2006, p. 173).

To be sure, the perceived thing only shows itself partly, it is not completely or fully present in perception. It gives some of its sides and profiles and hides others, and these vary depending on where we position ourselves and how we move in respect to the object. When I study my house from the porch, for example, the southern wall and the main door are there in front of my eyes, but the roof only shows its eaves. However, the roof too is intended in the perception of the house; I expect the roof to be there in so far as the object in front of me is a house. I do not merely *think* or *judge* that there is a roof, I approach the perceived object expecting to see a roof if I position myself in a certain way in respect to the building. In other words, intending an object as a house implies precisely this expectation or anticipation. If I climb up a tree next to the building, or fly above it in a helicopter, and see that the roof and the back side are missing, then I judge that the house that I saw is actually a ruin, an unfinished construction or a piece of stage scenery.

This dynamic presence–absence structure is essential to all perception. When new sides of the object reveal themselves and when new aspects come to the fore, the prior ones sink to the margins of the perceptual field, are covered by new aspects and finally disappear.[13]

The sides and profiles with which the perceived thing shows itself should not be theoretized as intermediate entities that stand between the perceiver and the perceived. Rather these factors must be understood and conceptualized as the object's very way of disclosing itself. They belong to the perceptual field as its structural elements.

2 On the method

In *The Structure of Behaviour*, Merleau-Ponty proceeded by way of dialectical-critical analyses of the then available accounts of consciousness in order to clarify its relations to the natural world. While struggling with the deep anomalies of his contemporary empiricist and intellectualist philosophies[14] and psychologies, he realized that he needed a new philosophical method that would be powerful enough to counter their reductionistic tendencies and their oppositional conceptions of sensibility and understanding. He found this method in twentieth-century phenomenology, that is, in the philosophies of Husserl and Heidegger: 'The suspension (epoche) of the natural movement which carries consciousness toward the world toward spatio-temporal existence, and which encloses it—this phenomenological reduction does not merely tend to a more faithful introspection: it is truly an introduction to a new mode of knowledge which moreover manifests the world as well as the self' (Merleau-Ponty [1935] 1996, p. 91; cf. [1945] 1995, p. xxx).

What these authors shared was a specific methodology designed for the purpose of illuminating, describing and analysing our intentional relations to the world in all its modalities, practical, axiological and theoretical. While studying Husserl's manuscripts in Leuven, Belgium, in 1939 and discussing his findings with Husserl's former assistant Eugen Fink,[15] Merleau-Ponty had already realized that phenomenological methods would allow him to reformulate the question of consciousness in a radical new way, to pierce into the structures of perception and the perceived thing and to investigate how these structures emerge in the process of experiencing (cf. Merleau-Ponty [1945] 1995, pp. vii–viii, 124–6).[16]

The phenomenological method is composed of a series of reductions. These however are not ontological steps that reduce areas of reality into other areas of reality, supposedly more fundamental or more primitive – steps, for example, that reduce chemical components into physical particles, or steps that reduce the ideal objects of the sciences into historical practices or into the psyche of human beings. The phenomenological reduction is not a reduction of reality but is a reduction of our preconceptions of reality and the pre-established significations of the real involved in these conceptions. In it, we put into brackets or out of action all our habitual conceptions of reality – practical, theoretical, metaphysical and scientific – and study our experiences of things and events as they give themselves to us.[17] The aim is not to question or reject any preconceptions but to dispense with them in the description of experiences and the phenomena that they involve.

> It is because we are through and through compounded of relationships with the world that for us the only way to become aware of the facts is to suspend the resultant activity, to refuse our complicity (to look at it *ohne mitzumachen*, as Husserl often says), or yet again, to put it "out of play." Not because we reject the certainties of common sense and a natural attitude to things ... but because, being the presupposed basis of any thought, they are taken for granted, and go unnoticed, and because in order to arouse them and bring them to view, we have to suspend for a moment our recognition of them. (Merleau-Ponty [1945] 1995, p. xiii, cf. pp. 395–8)

Thus conceived the phenomenological reduction is only a temporary suspension, not a permanent exclusion. After the clarifications that it makes possible, we can return to our cognitive and significative routines and continue our practical and theoretical lives as before. Phenomenology, like any self-responsible philosophy, leaves everything as it is, to use Wittgenstein's words (Wittgenstein [1953], 2009, §124, 55^e). It must not proceed to suggest theoretical hypotheses or practical improvements since its task is to investigate the foundations on which such suggestions rest, and must rest.

Many of the other reductions that Husserl uses, for example, the notorious 'reduction to the sphere of owness' (Hua1: 124ff.), are designed to help distinguishing between the different factors of experiencing and to illuminate their mutual dependences. The so-called eidetic reductions do not postulate essences, as is often assumed, but, by way of imaginary variations, distinguish between the dependent and the independent, the obvious and the hidden, the surfacing and the deeper factors of experiencing. In *Phenomenology of Perception*, Merleau-Ponty characterizes the task of eidetic variation in an illuminative and colourful way: 'Husserl's essences are destined to bring back all the living relationships of experience, as the fisherman's net draws up from the depths of the ocean quivering fish and seaweed' ([1945] 1995, p. xv; cf. 1964, pp. 49–50).

For Merleau-Ponty, the most crucial of the phenomenological methods is the reduction of the objective sciences. His critique of objectivism in *Phenomenology of Perception* and his critique of reflective philosophy in *The Visible and Invisible* are both grounded on this critical idea. Merleau-Ponty found the reduction of the objective sciences described in Husserl's manuscript *The Crisis of*

European Sciences and Transcendental Phenomenology (Hua6: 138ff.). In this last of his works, Husserl argued that if we proceed to the phenomenological suspension immediately, that is, if we proceed by a single enormous step, so to speak, then we easily neglect or disregard important relations of dependency between our various worldly dealings. Husserl called this way of proceeding 'the Cartesian way', since it resembled Descartes' radical doubt in its equalizing approach: all preconceptions, both scientific assumptions and practical convictions, both natural scientific theories and human scientific interpretations, are evened up and put out of action in one unitary critical gesture (Hua6: 157–8). Such a reflective philosophical leap, Husserl argued, could only be performed successfully by rare well-trained individuals or else by an ideal thinker, a God perhaps or an idealized version of ourselves. For concrete persons, phenomenology has to proceed by way of several steps. We must, so to speak, peel away layers of signification, and layers after layers, in order to reach the core experiences on which other experiences depend.

Husserl's *The Crisis of European Sciences* demonstrates that the entities of the objective world thematized, explained and conceptually articulated by the sciences are rational abstractions and idealizations resting on our direct experiences of the world (Hua6: 123ff., cf. Hua4: 191ff.). Husserl calls 'life-world' (*Lebenswelt*) the world of direct experience that is not given to us by theoretical methods and concepts but is composed of everyday practical and affective things and the persons that intend such things. The main argument of his work is that the philosophical delineation of the senses of science and scientific rationality demands that we make clear how, by what constitutive steps, the abstract entities of the objective sciences emerge from the things and the events of the life-world and from the intersubjective practices between persons operating in this world.

As I said, the life-world is a world occupied by practical things, for example, utensils, tools and instruments of different sorts, and affective things, that is, the things that attract and repulse our sensing moving bodies. Also scientific instruments of measurement and modelling belong here as practical tools, as well as scientific results as achievements of human persons and communities of human persons. In a series of manuscripts on intersubjectivity (Hua15), Husserl introduces the concepts of *home-world* (*Heimwelt*) and *alien-world* (*Fremdwelt*) to argue that the common life-world of pre-scientific experience organizes itself along the lines of familiarity and foreignness so that what we actually have are multiple layers of more or less homely practical environments.[18]

In *Phenomenology of Perception*, Merleau-Ponty undertakes to explicate the structures of the life-world ([1945] 1995, p. xviiff., pp. 299ff.). This requires the reduction of the objective sciences. At the very beginning of the work, he writes: 'To return to things themselves is to return to that world which precedes knowledge, of which knowledge always *speaks*, and in relation to which every scientific schematization is an abstract and derivative sign-language, as is geography in relation to the country-side in which we have learnt beforehand what a forest, a prairie or a river is' ([1945] 1995, p. ix; cf. p. 23).

Merleau-Ponty's main interest, however, is in the most basic layer or stratum of the life-world. This is the perceptual world, the world that is accessible to us simply as perceivers, independently of our cultural and historical practices and homely and alien interests. The objects of this world are not pieces of inert matter but are affective things that motivate us in different ways. The philosophical questions that Merleau-Ponty poses in *Phenomenology of Perception* concern the intentional structures of the perceptual world and its genetic constitution in experience:

> The perceiving subject ceases to be an "acosmic" thinking subject, and action, feeling and will remain to be explored as original ways of positing an object, since "an object looks attractive and repulsive before it looks black or blue, circular or square." (Merleau-Ponty [1945] 1995, p. 24, cf. pp. 395–8).[19]

3 Intercorporeality

'Intercorporeality' (*intercorporéité*) is a general heading for one of the most important and influential results of Merleau-Ponty's intentional analyses. To put it simply, this term refers to the basic corporeal connection that we have to one another as bodily subjects, a connection that lays the ground for and makes possible other ways of intending. Several conceptual points must however be made in order to clarify this result and to dispose of possible misunderstandings. The most important of these concerns the concept of *corporeality* or *embodiment*.

In Merleau-Ponty's phenomenological framing, 'corporeality' does not refer to the causal-functional processes that are observed, hypothesized or discovered by physiologists or neurophysiologists (Merleau-Ponty [1945] 1995, pp. 72ff., 105–6). What is at issue is a specific type of phenomenon in which our own operating body takes part in the disclosure of the perceptual object and at the same time appears itself at the margins of the perceptual field.[20] For example, when a goalkeeper in an ice hockey match notices an approaching puck, the thematic object of his perceptual experience is this threatening moving entity, this black and round thing that flies towards him with great speed, but at the same time his experience also involves several marginal factors, for example, his ice hockey stick, the goal, the teammates and the opponents. But this is not all. In addition to the thematic object and the marginal objects, the goalkeeper also experiences his own living and operating body in a specific way. The body is not at the centre of his attention, as it may be when he is learning a new bodily skill or is being treated by a dentist. Rather than being the object of thematic attention, his body is his fundamental grasp upon the world and the zero-point of orientation from which all his perceptions issue. It is permanently with him and never completely disappears from his perceptual field, but it constantly gives itself in a peculiarly fixed perspective: 'It is neither tangible nor visible in so far as it is that which sees and touches. The body therefore is not one more among external objects, with the peculiarity of always being there. If it is permanent, the permanence is absolute and is the ground for the relative permanence of disappearing objects, real objects' (Merleau-Ponty [1945] 1995, p. 92, pp. 278–9).[21]

Following Husserl, Merleau-Ponty argues that each perceptual experience involves a marginally given functioning body, a set of operating organs and a general gestalt of bodily operating (Merleau-Ponty [1945] 1995, pp. 316–17, cf. pp. 101–3). Thus understood, our bodies are not things or entities encountered in the world but are our means of experiencing things and acting on them. To be sure, we can objectify our operating bodies, study and treat them as things among other things, and we do this in multiple situations and for many different purposes, practical, theoretical and political. This possibility of objectification belongs essentially to our bodily existence. However, the phenomenologist argues that the objectification of our operating bodies is not a free possibility but is grounded in and motivated by experiences in which external objects are given to us by means of our own operating bodies. Thus, the objectifying attitude is not self-supporting or independent but rests on a more fundamental attitude in which bodies are given to us as our means of having thingly objects (Merleau-Ponty [1945] 1995, pp. 360–1).

The body as a power of having things is not bound or limited to any particular entities or groups of entities. Rather it is a general potential that allows us to relate to all things, actual or possible, real or imaginable. It is 'our general power of inhabiting all the environments that the world contains' (Merleau-Ponty [1945] 1995, p. 311). We may imagine and picture things that are beyond our reach, experienced merely by animals or extra-terrestrial intelligences, but each such imagination and picturing draws its sense from the experiential relation that is established between our own operating bodies and the things (cf. Hua4: 56–7).

In *Phenomenology*, Merleau-Ponty argues that the phenomenological tradition – as all post-Kantian philosophy – has been preoccupied with practical and cognitive relations to the extent that it has neglected the analysis of a more fundamental type of bodily relating. Our bodies are not merely tools or instruments for the uncovering and manipulation of objects; they are also communicative expressive gestures by which we address one another and respond to the addresses of other minded beings (Merleau-Ponty [1945] 1995, pp. 145ff.).

Merleau-Ponty calls 'intercorporeality' the *immediate* communicative and expressive connection that prevails between living bodies of humans and animals independently of their social roles and cultural circumstances. The best-known example that he gives of this fundamental phenomenon is a young infant who is able to recognize the bodily intentions of an adult by merely looking at his facial movements:

> A baby of fifteen months opens its mouth if I playfully take one of its fingers between my teeth and pretend to bite. And yet it has scarcely looked at its face in the glass, and its teeth are not in any case like mine. The fact is that its own mouth and teeth, as it feels them from the inside, are immediately, for it, an apparatus

to bite with, and my jaw, as the baby sees it from the outside, is immediately for it, capable of the same intentions. (Merleau-Ponty [1945] 1995, p. 352, cf. 1964, pp. 117–8).

Intercorporeality is a direct recognition of the other body as similar to one's own body. The similarity at issue is not merely that of visual and tactile form but also, and more importantly, that of intentional movement, that is, directional movement in respect to one's own body and directional movement in respect to other bodies, towards them, away from them, along with them and in line with them (Merleau-Ponty [1945] 1995, p. 354, cf. Hua1: 142–4).

The connection is direct in the sense that it is not mediated by any thought-processes or inferences, such as introjection, projection, simulation, analogical inference, conceptual subsumption or theoretical or practical reasoning.[22] The link between the two bodies is constituted simply on the basis of the similarity of their manners of moving:

> It is imperative to recognize that we have here neither comparison, nor analogy, nor projection or "introjection." The reason why I have evidence of the other man's being-there when I shake his hand is that his hand is substituted for my left hand, and my body annexes the body of another person in that "sort of reflection" it is paradoxically the seat of. My two hands "coexist" or are "compresent" because they are one single body's hands. The other person appears through an extension of that compresence; he and I are like organs of one single intercorporeality. (Merleau-Ponty [1960] 1987, p. 168)

This immediate recognition of similarity is possible because neither body 'coincides' exactly with itself. Neither is a self-enclosed unitary system but both are internally divided or differentiated in a specific way: In each living body, each performed movement is given, so to speak, both from 'inside', that is, kinaesthetically, and from 'outside', that is, tactually or visually.[23] I raise my arm, and I see the arm moving at the same time as I feel its movement kinaesthetically. The body is thus a dual system, a dynamic intertwinement of interiority and exteriority. Its duality is constituted in the fundamental process in which our movements are localized in different parts of our bodies, in the tongue, in the lips, in the face, in the fingers, in the legs, etc. This means that intercorporeality and intersubjectivity are grounded in the experiential structures of our own bodies. Husserl argues very strongly and consistently for this constitutive fact (e.g. Hua1: 127ff.; Hua4: 164–75, 197–200; Hua6: 106–8, 220–1), but we find the same insight defended by Merleau-Ponty in *Phenomenology*:

> Through phenomenological reflection I discover vision, not as a "thinking about seeing," to use Descartes' expression, but as a gaze at grips with a visible world, and *that is why* for me there can be another gaze; that expressive instrument called a face can carry an existence [conscious subject], as my own existence is carried by my body, that knowledge-acquiring apparatus. (Merleau-Ponty [1945] 1995, p. 351, emphasis added; cf. pp. 92–3; cf. 1964, pp. 120–1, [1964] 1975, pp. 80–2, 123–5, 192)[24]

Thus, intercorporeality does not mean that separate bodies or bodily functions blend or merge to form one unified super-body, as is sometimes suggested. What it means is an immediate corporeal correspondence between individual bodily subjects or 'minded bodies', grounded on the kinaesthetic, proprioceptive and sensory capacities of the bodies in question. On the basis of this basic correspondence, human and animal bodies can spontaneously operate in concert, that is, in coherence and harmony.

Merleau-Ponty's own examples include the practice of dancing with a partner and the gesture of shaking hands (Merleau-Ponty [1945] 1995, pp. 142–3; [1960] 1978, p. 168; [1964] 1975, p. 142), but we can easily come up with equally illuminating examples that involve other parts of our operating bodies, for example, swimming together, singing together or working together. Moreover, the experiences of playing football in a team and playing music with an orchestra highlight the fact that body-subjects who operate in concert do not have to perform movements that are physiologically identical or similar, but can by their own movements complement, support and vary the movements of one another. Finally, the bodies operating in concert do not have to belong to one biological species but can also differ grossly by structure, size and/or visual shape. A familiar example is the activity of riding a horse but studies of primates demonstrate that interspecies intercorporeality is not limited by the boundaries of tactile contact or material exchange but allows spatial distance and inclusion of visual and auditory signs.[25]

4 The body-schema, the body-image and the habit-body

As we saw above, intercorporeality is an immediate associative pairing of two, or several, bodies based on their manners of bodily comportment. The association is not established merely between the visual shapes of the bodies or between any of their singular gestures, movements or positions. Rather intercorporeality combines *manners* of moving, that is, continuous *modes* of directed bodily comportment.

Merleau-Ponty uses the term 'body schema' (*scheme corporel*) to denote the invariant that is manifested in the bodily movements, gestures and comportments of an individual person ([1945] 1995, p. 141, cf. 1964, pp. 117–8). Rather than characterizing a static unity of substance, the concept of body schema denotes a dynamic unity of style.[26] It not only combines actual movements but also delineates a range of possible movements. Intercorporeality is to be understood as the communication or correspondence of body schemas.

As such, the concept of *body schema* must be distinguished from that of the *body image*.[27] The difference is not that the former is subconscious or preconscious and the latter is conscious, or that the former is preconceptual and the later is conceptual, as is sometimes claimed.[28] Rather the distinction is in the degree of concreteness that these two phenomena have: whereas the body schema involves all senses and incorporates the synergy of motility, tactility and visibility, the body image is focused on the visual aspects of the experiential body merely. Both structures are preconceptual in Husserl's sense, that is, neither depends on any concept under which individual gestures, postures and movements would be subsumed; both operate simply on partial and overlapping similarities between gestures, postures and movements (Merleau-Ponty [1945] 1995, pp. 233–5).[29]

Merleau-Ponty also argues that the human body is able to extend its motor schema to environing things, to animate them and include them in its own dynamism. The best-known example that he gives of this process is the blind man's cane. The cane is not a proper part of the blind person's lived body, since the person does not sense *in* it, but the cane becomes 'an area of sensitivity' for the person in so far as her kinaesthetic sensations and touch sensations combine systematically with the movements of the cane (Merleau-Ponty [1945] 1995, pp. 143, 152–3).

Similarly, also many other types of things can be incorporated into the lived body, for example, utensils, tools, musical instruments and vehicles. The incorporation of these entities requires large-scale rearrangement and reconstruction of the body schema. Also learning bodily skills and acquiring or unlearning bodily habits demand that we refashion our body schemas. The required change is a change in the manner or style of movement and comportment. This does not compromise the fact that the body schema is invariant, since its changes – evident in these phenomena – manifest the same style that characterizes the motor process itself.

By the analyses of intercorporeality and its experiential foundations in the reflective structures of our own bodies, Merleau-Ponty demonstrates that human consciousness can be comprehended neither as a result of mere mechanical processes nor as an intellectual power of judgement or conceptual articulation. Perceptual consciousness is embodied, its embodiment is intentional and its intentionality is deeply rooted in kinaesthesia and sensibility.

Thus, Merleau-Ponty's philosophy clarifies the experiential ground from which the two dominant paradigms – disembodied mind and mechanical body – emerge by various processes of abstraction and idealization. It shows that these two abstractive models have governed modern philosophy since Descartes and Kant, and it also demonstrates how they guide investigations in behavioural and psychological sciences. Hereby, Merleau-Ponty's discussion serves an important critical function but at the same time it outlines an alternative approach in the investigation of the human mind based on radical phenomenological inquiries into perception and motility. The task at hand is not so much to make use of the results of these investigations but rather to capture their way of questioning and to apply it in new areas of interest.

Notes

1 E.g. Varela, Thompson and Rosch 1991; Dreyfus 2002a, 2002b, 2005; Noë 2004; Gallagher and Zahavi 2005; Gallagher 2009, pp. 368–9; Berendzen 2009; Schear 2012.

2 Marco Iacoboni (2008), for example, uses the results of Merleau-Ponty's phenomenological inquiries to develop his hypotheses concerning mirror neurons.

3 By bodily identities, I mean social-personal identities related the different aspects and dimensions of the lived body, for example, identities related to body size and scale (manifesting, for example, in eating disorders), identities related to bodily skills and capabilities (professional, athletic, etc.), gender identities and identities of sexual orientation. For phenomenology-influenced discussions of eating disorders, see, for example, Turner 1992; Jacobson 2006; Bowden 2012. For phenomenology of gender identities, see Heinämaa 2012.

4 One of the main methodological elements of Husserlian phenomenology is *eidetic analysis*. This is the phase in the analysis that aims at disclosing the essential structural features of the experiences at issue. One example of such structures is the act-object-background structure discussed in note 6 below. Another example is the temporal structure of perceptual experience which includes an indexical present and two-directional references that bind the present to former and subsequent moments of perceiving (Merleau-Ponty [1945] 1995, pp. 68–9).

Husserl called such structures 'the essences' or 'the eide' of intentional experiences, but he argued that one should not confuse his eidetic analysis of experiences with Platonism nor reify or objectify any essences that this analysis may disclose (cf. Merleau-Ponty [1945] 1995, pp. xiv–xv; cf. Heinämaa 1999, 2002). Thus, the still common Rylean line of critique that rejects Husserl's phenomenology as a form of Platonism is based on a misunderstanding (e.g. Ryle [1928] 2009, [1958, 1971] 2009; cf. Ryle [1946] 2009). Cf. O'Connor 2012.

5 For the philosophical-historical starting points of Merleau-Ponty's phenomenological inquiries, see, Moran 2000, especially pp. 23–67.

6 'To intend an object' in this framework means to have an intentional relation to the world or the environment with a focus on a specific thematic object, a thing or an event. Such a relation involves (a) an attentive focus from the part of a conscious subject, human or animal, and (b) an articulation of the world or the environment as consisting of an object and a non-thematic background from which the thematized object stands out (Merleau-Ponty [1945] 1995, pp. 48ff., 68–9, 101–3). Thus understood each intentional relation, each intending of an object, is a dynamic structure with three main elements: the intending act, the intended object and the background from which the object stands out (the corresponding technical terms

are: 'the noetic act', 'the noematic object' and 'the horizon'). Despite the simplicity of its basic structure, such a relation involves structural complexity in terms of temporality and in terms of its conditions.

7 Welton 2000, pp. 53–6; cf. Husserl Hua3: 20–3.

8 Merleau-Ponty uses the concepts soul (*âme*), psyche (*psyché*) and spirit (*esprit*) to thematize different aspects of consciousness as well as different approaches to consciousness. In this, his analysis refers back to the analyses of Sartre, Husserl, Descartes and Aristotle.

9 By 'significative orientation and operation', I mean behaviour that has significance for the subject in question. For example, I raise my arm in order to reach an orange in the tree and then I raise my arm again in order to stretch my muscles. These two movements may look identical for an external observer, but for the moving subject they bear different practical significations or senses. I may also perform a physiologically identical movement while dancing salsa in a club, but here the movement does not have practical sense but bears aesthetic and/or erotic significations. Cf., Merleau-Ponty [1945] 1995, pp. 110ff., 137ff; cf. Heinämaa 2012.

10 This statement is a direct comment on St. Augustine's discourse on 'the inner self' and 'the inner space' but it is targeted at the whole internalist and immanentist tradition that began with his reflections, was rearticulated in the seventeenth century by empiricist such as Locke and Hobbes as the idea of 'the inner theatre' of the mind, reformulated by the eighteenth-century psychologists, Wundt and his followers, as the idea of introspection, and finally demolished by twentieth-century critics such as Gilbert Ryle (1949) and Michel Foucault (1984).

The transcendental self and the transcendental person as sense-giving subjects, disclosed by phenomenological critique, are often wrongly associated with such inner agents but as Merleau-Ponty argues these subjects are essentially relational and connected to the 'outer', intersubjective or objective world by multiple linkages of intentionality. Thus, following Husserl, Merleau-Ponty contends that we should not interpret the thinking ego, discovered by Descartes, as a homunculus but must understand it as a structural feature of experiencing (Husserl Hua1: 100–20, Hua4: 103–83, 324, Hua6: 174–5, Merleau-Ponty [1945] 1995, pp. 398–407).

11 Brentano and Husserl.

12 Here too, Merleau-Ponty's analyses agree with those of Husserl (e.g. Hua3: 78–80; cf. Merleau-Ponty [1945] 1995, pp. 137–9).

13 This structure is called the *horizon*-structure of perception. The phenomenological concept of *horizon* has important systematic and

historical connections to William James' pragmatic concept of *fringe* (e.g. James [1892] 2001, pp. 85ff.). For this connection, see Husserl Hua6: 267.

14 By 'intellectualism', Merleau-Ponty refers to Kantian philosophies.

15 Toadvine 2002, pp. 174–6. On Husserl's influence on Merleau-Ponty, see the articles in the volume *Merleau-Ponty's Reading of Husserl* (2002), edited by Ted Toadvine and Lester Embree.

16 The best explication of Merleau-Ponty's philosophical methods can be found in his own works, *Phenomenology of Perception* and *The Visible and the Invisible*. The preface and the first part of *Phenomenology* together make clear that the method used in this work is phenomenological in the sense that it proceeds by reductions, by first person descriptions (p. 77), by intentional analyses, by eidetic variations and by genetic-phenomenological inquiries (p. xviii, pp. 125–6). Moreover, Merleau-Ponty also operates with a set of analytical concepts developed by Husserl, the concepts of attitude (pp. 39ff.), evidence (p. xvi, p. 23), sedimentation (pp. 136–7, 140, 395), horizon (p. 68, cf. p. 302), inner time-consciousness (pp. 68–9, cf. pp. 410ff.) and expressive relation (p. 160, pp. 174ff.).

17 In this context, experience must not be assimilated with any part or kind of reality, for example, mental state, psychic disposition or social relation. Rather the term 'experience' refers to our basic relationship to reality.

18 For a comprehensive account of the concepts of home-world and alien-world, see Steinbock 1995.

19 Merleau-Ponty's quote here is from Kurt Koffka's *The Growth of the Mind* (Koffka [1924] 2000, p. 320). Koffka was one of the early Gestalt theorists, the results of whom Merleau-Ponty both used and criticized in his *Phenomenology*. For Merleau-Ponty's transcendental-phenomenological critique of Gestalt theories, see his *Phenomenology* ([1945] 1995, pp. 45–51); cf. Heinämaa 2009.

20 Merleau-Ponty introduces the concept of *intercorporeality* in the reading that he gives of Husserl's analysis of embodiment. This discussion is most explicit in the late essay titled 'The philosopher and his shadow' ([1960], 1987, pp. 166–8) but Merleau-Ponty uses Husserl's analyses of embodiment and intersubjectivity extensively already in *Phenomenology* ([1945] 1995, pp. 92–3, 405–9; cf. [1964] 1975, p. 133, pp. 140–8, 254–7). The focus of his interest is in the reflexive relation that living experiencing bodies or body-subjects have to themselves: When a human person (or a primate) touches herself, for example, when she grasps her left wrist with her right

hand fingers, the so-called double sensation – that is, the kinaesthetic sensation of the gesture of touching and the tactile sensation of contact – that characterize each act of touching are doubled. We can consequently distinguish between four sensations that are interconnected in such touchings: (i) the kinaesthetic sensation of movement, (ii) the tactile sensation of encountering a soft smooth surface (resistance), both of which belongs to the right hand, (iii) the kinaesthetic-proprioceptic sensation of rest and (iv) the tactile sensation of being touched by a moving object, both of which belong to the left hand. For a more complete explication, see Heinämaa 2010, 2011a.

In *Phenomenology*, Merleau-Ponty uses this phenomenon as a model for the conceptualization of other types of perceptual relations, most importantly for the conceptualization of the body-thing relation and the body-body relation. In *The Visible and the Invisible*, he takes a step forward and outlines a comprehensive philosophy of nature on the basis of this reflexive way of relating so that he can claim that the human body, or the animal body, is the nature's way of studying itself. Cf. [1960] 1987, pp. 170–1.

21 Merleau-Ponty draws here directly from Husserl: 'The same living body which serves me as means for all my perceptions obstructs me in the perception of itself and is a remarkably imperfectly constituted thing [*Ding*]' (Husserl Hua4: 159; cf. Stein [1917] 1989, pp. 41–9; Merleau-Ponty [1945] 1995, p. 92, 406).

22 Thus, intercorporeality also precedes all process of volitional recognition (in the Hegelian sense) and provides the foundation for such processes.

23 Already in *Phenomenology*, Merleau-Ponty introduces the metaphors of folds and folding to characterize the relationship that the bodily subject has to itself: 'I am not, therefore, in Hegel's phrase, "a hole in being", but a hollow [*creux*], a fold [*pli*], which has been made and which can be unmade' (Merleau-Ponty [1945] 1995, p. 215; cf. [1964] 1975, p. 192). However, this metaphor receives a much more central and general function in his late work *The Visible and the Invisible* in which Merleau-Ponty uses it to develop a complete philosophy of living nature.

24 Diverging from Heidegger, and the pragmatists, Merleau-Ponty does not see Descartes as the proponent of subjectivistic or dualistic metaphysics but discusses him as the forefather of all modern thinking, subjectivistic as well as objectivistic, positivistic as well as radical, rigorously scientific as well as fundamentally ontological. (See Chapter 2). In the introduction to the collection *Signs* (*Signes*, 1960),

he writes: 'Are you or are you not Cartesian? The question does not make much sense, since those who reject this or that in Descartes do so only in terms of reasons which owe a lot to Descartes' ([1960] 1987, p. 11). In *Eye and Mind* (*L'œil et l'esprit*, 1961), he argues that the idea of the embodied subject developed by him in *Phenomenology of Perception* in the line with Husserl has important roots in Descartes' reflections, more precisely in his discourse on the mind-body compound (union) and the so-called third way of knowing that thematizes this compound: 'We *are* the compound of the soul and the body, and so there must be a thought of it. To this knowledge of position and situation Descartes owes what he himself says about it or what he says sometimes . . . about the exterior world "at the end" of our hands. Here the body is not the means of vision and touch but their depository' (Merleau-Ponty 1964, pp. 177–8; cf. [1945] 1995, pp. 198–9; cf. Heinämaa 2003).

25 On the ontogenetic basis of communicative gestures in animals, see, for example, Halina, Rossano and Tomasello 2013.

26 On the Husserlian starting points of Merleau-Ponty's concepts of style and stylistic unity, see his *Phenomenology* and the collection *Signs* ([1945] 1995, pp. 273–4, 280–2, 315–6, 327–30; 403–7, 455; cf. [1960] 1987, pp. 52–5, 65–8; [1964] 1975, pp. 10–13; [1969]1973, pp. 56–7).

27 For Merleau-Ponty, neither the body schema nor the body image is a representation of the body (experienced, thought or observed). Thus, his analysis differs from discussions in which the body schema and the body image are juxtaposed and compared as two different kinds of representations of the objective body (e.g. Vignemont 2009).

28 For example, Gallagher and Cole 1995; Preester and Knockaert (eds) 2005.

29 Merleau-Ponty's concept of *body schema* has important connections to Husserl's phenomenology of types (Husserl [1939] 1985) and to Kant's schematicism. For a more detailed discussion of this background, see Heinämaa 2011b.

References

Berendzen, J. C. (2009), 'Coping with nonconceptualism? On Merleau-Ponty and McDowell'. *Philosophy Today* 53: 161–72.
Bowden, H. (2012), 'A phenomenological study of anorexia nervosa'. *Philosophy, Psychiatry & Psychology* 19: 227–41.

Dreyfus, H. (2002a), 'Intelligence without representation: Merleau-Ponty's critique of mental representation—The relevance of phenomenology to scientific explanation'. *Phenomenology and Cognitive Sciences* 1: 367–83.
— (2002b), 'Refocusing the question: Can there be skilful coping without propositional representations or brain representations'. *Phenomenology and Cognitive Science* 1: 413–25.
— (2005), 'Overcoming the myth of the mental: How philosophers can profit from the phenomenology of everyday'. *Proceedings and Addresses of the American Philosophical Association* 79: 47–65.
Gallagher, S. (2009), 'Neural simulation and social cognition'. In J. A. Pineda (ed.), *Mirror Neuron Systems: The Role of Mirroring Processes in Social Cognition*. New York: Humana Press, pp. 355–71.
Gallagher, S. and Cole J. (1995), 'Body image and body schema in a deafferented subject'. *Journal of Mind and Behavior* 16: 369–90.
Gallagher, S. and Zahavi, D. (2005), *The Phenomenological Mind: An Introduction to Philosophy of Mind and Cognitive Science*. London: Routledge.
Foucault, M. ([1984] 1990), *History of Sexuality, Volume 1: The Introduction*, transl. Robert Hurley. New York: Vintage.
Halina, M., Rossano, F., and Tomasello, M. (forthcoming), 'The ontogenetic ritualization of bonobo gestures', *Animal Cognition*.
Heinämaa, S. (1999), 'Merleau-Ponty's modification of phenomenology: Cognition, passion, and philosophy'. *Synthese* 118: 49–68.
— (2002), 'From decisions to passions: Merleau-Ponty's interpretation of Husserl's reduction'. In T. Toadvine and L. Embree (eds), *Merleau-Ponty's Reading of Husserl*. Dordrecht: Kluwer, pp. 127–46.
— (2003), 'The living body and its position in metaphysics: Merleau-Ponty's dialogue with Descartes'. In D. Zahavi, S. Heinämaa, and H. Ruin (eds), *Metaphysics, Facticity, Interpretation: Phenomenology in the Nordic Countries*. The Hague: Kluwer, pp. 23–48.
— (2009), 'Phenomenological responses to *Gestalt*-psychology.' In S. Heinämaa and M. Reuter (eds), *Psychology and Philosophy: Inquiries into the Soul from Late Scholasticism to Contemporary Thought*. Dordrecht: Springer, pp. 263–84.
— (2010), 'Embodiment and expressivity in Husserl's phenomenology: From *Logical Investigations* to *Cartesian Meditations*'. *SATS–Northern European Journal of Philosophy* 11: 1–15.
— (2011a), 'Body'. In S. Luft and S. Overgaard (eds), *The Routledge Companion to Phenomenology*. London, New York: Routledge.
— (2011b), 'A phenomenology of sexual difference: Types, styles, and persons'. In C. Witt (ed.), *Feminist Metaphysics: Explorations in the Ontology of Sex, Gender and Identity*. Dordrecht: Springer, pp. 131–55.

— (2012), 'Sex, gender and embodiment'. In D. Zahavi (ed.), *Oxford Handbook of Contemporary Phenomenology*. Oxford: Oxford University Press.
Husserl, E. Hua1. *Cartesianische Meditationen und pariser Vorträge*, edited by Stephan Strasser. The Hague: Martinus Nijhoff, 1950. In English *Cartesian Meditations*, translated by Dorion Cairns. Dordrecht: Martinus Nijhoff, 1960.
Husserl, E. Hua3. *Ideen zu einer reinen Phänomenologie und phänomenologischen Philosophie, Erstes Buch: Allgemeine Einführung in die reine Phänomenologie, Husserliana, Band III*, edited by Walter Biemel. The Hague: Martinus Nijhoff, [1913] 1950. In English *Ideas: General Introduction to Pure Phenomenology*, translated by W. R. Boyce Gibson. New York: Collier, 1962.
Husserl, E. Hua4. *Ideen zu einer reinen Phänomenologie und phänomenologischen Philosophie, Zweites Buch: Phänomenologische Untersuchungen zur Konstitution, Husserliana, Band IV*, edited by Marly Bimel. The Hague: Martinus Nijhoff, 1952. In English *Ideas Pertaining to a Pure Phenomenology and to a Phenomenological Philosophy, Second Book: Studies in the Phenomenological Constitution*, translated by R. Rojcewicz and A. Schuwer. Dordrecht: Kluwer Academic Publishers, 1993.
Husserl, E. Hua6. *Die Krisis der europäischen Wissenshaften und die transzendentale Phänomenologie: Eine Einleitung in die phänomenologische Philosophie, Husserliana, Band VI*, edited by Walter Biemel. The Hague: Martinus Nijhoff, [1954] 1962. In English *The Crisis of European Sciences and Transcendental Phenomenology: An Introduction to Phenomenological Philosophy*, translated by David Carr. Evanston, IL: Northwestern University Press, 1988.
Husserl, E. Hua15. *Zur Phänomenologie der Intersubjektivität: Texte aus dem Nachlass, Dritter Teil: 1929–1935, Husserliana, Band XV*, edited by Iso Kern. The Hague: Martinus Nijhoff, 1973.
Husserl, E. ([1939] 1985). *Erfahrung und Urteil: Untersuchungen zur Genealogie der Logik*, revised and edited by Ludwig Landgrebe. Hamburg: Felix Mayer Verlag. In English *Experience and Judgement: Investigations in a Genealogy of Logic*, translated by James S. Churchill and Karl Ameriks. Evanston, IL: Northwestern University Press, 1973.
Iacoboni. M. (2008), *Mirroring People: The New Science of How We Connect with Others*. New York: Picador.
Jacobson, K. (2006), 'The interpersonal expression of human spatiality: A phenomenological interpretation of anorexia nervosa'. *Chiasmi International* 8: 157–73.
James, W. ([1892] 2001), *Psychology, The Briefer Course*. Mineola, NY: Dover.

Koffka, K. ([1924] 2000). *The Growth of the Mind*, translated by Robert Morris Ogden. London: Routledge.

Marratto, S. L. (2013), *The Intercorporeal Self: Merleau-Ponty on Subjectivity*. New York: SUNY Press.

Merleau-Ponty, M. ([1935] 1996), 'Christianity and ressentiment'. In H. Silverman and J. Barry (eds), *Texts and Dialogues: On Philosophy, Politics, and Culture*. New Jersey: Humanities Press. Original 'Christianisme et ressentiment,' *La view intellectuelle* 36 (1935).

— ([1942] 2006), *The Structure of Behavior*, translated by Alden L. Fisher. Pittsburg: Duquesne University Press. Original *La structure du comportment*. Paris: PUF, 1942.

— ([1945] 1995), *Phenomenology of Perception*, translated by Collin Smith. New York: Routledge & Kegan Paul. Original *Phénoménologie de la perception*. Paris: Gallimard, 1964.

— ([1947] 1995), *Sense and Non-Sense*, translated by Hubert Dreyfus and Patricia Dreyfus. Evanston, IL: Northwestern University Press. Original *Sens et non-sens*. Paris: Gallimard, 1947.

— ([1960] 1987), *Signs*, translated by Richard C. McCleary. Evaston, IL: Northwestern University Press. Original *Signes*. Paris: Gallimard, 1960.

— (1964), *The Primacy of Perception and Other Essays on Phenomenological Psychology, the Philosophy of Art, History and Politics*, translated by James M. Edie. Evaston, IL: Northwestern University Press.

— ([1964] 1975), *The Visible and the Invisible*, translated by Alphonso Linguis. Evaston, IL: Northwestern University Press. Original *Le visible et l'invisible*, edited by Claude Lefort. Paris: Gallimard, 1964.

Moran, D. (2000), *Introduction to Phenomenology*. London: Routledge.

Noë, A. (2004), *Action in Perception*. Cambridge, MA: MIT Press.

O'Connor, J. K. (2012), 'Category mistakes and logical grammar: Ryle's Husserlian tutelage'. *Symposium: Canadian Journal of Continental Philosophy/Revue canadienne de philosophie continentale* 16: 235–50.

Preester, H. and Veroniek K, (eds) (2005), *Body Image and Body Schema*. Amsterdam: John Benjamins B. V.

Rorty, R. (1979), *Philosophy and the Mirror of Nature*. Princeton, NJ: Princeton University Press.

Ryle, G. ([1928] 2009), 'Heidegger's "Sein und Zeit"'. In *Collected Papers, Volume 1: Critical Essays*. London: Routledge, pp. 205–22.

— ([1946] 2009), 'Review of Marvin Faber: "The Foundations of Phenomenology" '. In *Collected Papers, Volume 1: Critical Essays*. London: Routledge, pp. 223–32.

— (1949), *The Concept of Mind*. Harmondsworth, Middlesex: Penguin.

— ([1958, 1971] 2009), 'Phenomenology and 'The Concept of Mind''. In *Collected Papers, Volume 1: Critical Essays*. London: Routledge, pp. 186–204.

Schear, J. K., (ed.) (2012), *Mind, Reason and Being-in-the-World: The McDowell-Dreyfus Debate*. London: Routledge.

Stein, E. ([1917] 1989), *The Collected Works of Edith Stein, Volume Three: On the Problem of Empathy*. Washington: ICS Publications.

Steinbock, A. (1995), *Home and Beyond: Generative Phenomenology After Husserl*. Evanston, IL: Northwestern University Press.

Toadvine, T. (2002), 'Merleau-Ponty's reading of Husserl: A chronological overview'. In Toadvine and Embree 2002, pp. 227–86.

Toadvine, T. and Embree, L. (eds) (2002), *Merleau-Ponty's Reading of Husserl*. Dordrecht: Kluwer.

Turner, B. S. (1992), *Regulating Bodies: Essays in Medical Sociology*. London: Routledge.

Varela, F., Thompson, E., and Rosch, E. (1991), *The Embodied Mind: Cognitive Science and Human Experience*. Cambridge, MA: MIT Press.

Vignemont, F. de. (2009), 'Body schema and body image—Pros and cons', *Neuropsychology* 48: 669–80.

Welton, D. (2000), *The Other Husserl: The Horizons of Transcendental Phenomenology*. Bloomington, IN: Indiana University Press.

Wittgenstein, L. ([1953] 2009), *Philosophical Investigations*, revised fourth edition, edited by P. M. S. Hacker and Joachim Schulte, translated by G. E. M. Anscombe, P. M. S. Hacker and Joachime Schulte. Oxford: Blackwell.

CHAPTER FIVE

Gilbert Ryle and logical behaviourism

William Lyons

Gilbert Ryle will always have his name on the honour board of philosophers of mind. But his presence there is liable to be underestimated and misinterpreted. Most often his name will be associated with his clever and ultimately devastating attack on the last remnants of Cartesian substance dualism, namely the view that a human person is made up of two basic substances, matter and spirit (see Chapter 2). Less obvious and less appreciated is his crucial contribution to the way that philosophy of mind subsequently developed in the second half of the twentieth century. It is not too strong a claim to say that Ryle, more than anyone else, was the prime mover in turning philosophy of mind into the analysis of our mental vocabulary and psychological utterances, that is to say, into a branch of philosophy of language. One very important result of this reorientation was that a major focus in the new philosophy of mind after Ryle was the discussion of the status, both logical and ontological, of the main subjects of our psychological descriptions. When we speak of such mental acts as those of intending, believing, willing, feeling and introspecting, and of minds themselves, what is the reference of such descriptions? What is the relation of such descriptions to the descriptions being furnished by the rapid development of the brain sciences? What are the truth conditions for such descriptions? Throughout the second half of the twentieth century and during the first decade of the twenty-first century, philosophers of mind still struggled to answer these questions definitively.

It may be objected that I am inflating Ryle's role in modern philosophy of mind to the neglect of that of Ludwig Wittgenstein. Certainly Wittgenstein's later philosophy, especially as revealed in his posthumously published *Philosophical Investigations*, was indubitably a major influence in philosophy of mind in the second half of the twentieth century. But Ryle was already essaying this new logico-linguistic approach to philosophy of mind in articles published in the 1930s, and his magnum opus, *The Concept of Mind*, the book through which he made his greatest impact in philosophy of mind, was published in 1949, four years before the appearance of the major source for Wittgenstein's philosophy of mind, the *Investigations*.

As with Descartes, so with Ryle, there was an intimate connection between his views about the correct method for engaging in philosophy and his subsequent views about the nature of mind. Indubitably, Ryle's ruminations about the nature of philosophy and its appropriate methods, set out most clearly in his manifesto article 'Systematically Misleading Expressions' (1932), were a major source of his approach to philosophy of mind. But there is also no doubt that one influence on Ryle's view about the nature and methods of philosophy, probably the major influence, was Wittgenstein's views on these matters as set out in the *Tractatus Logico-Philosophicus* (1921). Of course, during the 1930s, Wittgenstein himself was moving away from his logical studies and his earlier notational and pictorial view of language in the *Tractatus*. He was already developing his richer and eventually enormously influential views about language in terms of 'family resemblance' concepts, 'language games', 'meaning as use' and their place in our various 'forms of life'. He was also beginning to apply these new conceptual tools to analysing our talk about our mental life. But, and here is the big difference, in the 1930s Wittgenstein's views on philosophy of mind were known only to those who attended his 'lectures' at Cambridge or were among those privileged few who were permitted to read his manuscripts or samizdat typescripts. So the first public introduction of the new approach to philosophy of mind fell to Ryle. But let us go back and begin at the beginning.

Gilbert Ryle was born in Brighton, England, in 1900, educated at Brighton College on the south coast of England, an educationally progressive school that had banned corporal punishment and introduced the first purpose-built school science laboratory in England. After his school education, Ryle went up to the Queen's College, Oxford, as a Classical Scholar. While he felt that he did not have the requisite skills to become a classicist, he greatly enjoyed the ancient and modern philosophy segments of his BA degree ('Greats'), as well as his brush with logic as it was then taught. He graduated with First Class honours in both halves of the BA, and then, in the space of just one year, sat and gained First Class honours in the then new BA degree of PPE (Philosophy, Politics and Economics – 'Modern Greats'). That same year, 1924, Ryle was appointed to a lectureship (and in the following year to a tutorship) in philosophy at Christ Church, Oxford. Except for some short periods abroad as a much sought after visiting professor, Ryle spent all of his academic life at Oxford, culminating in his appointment to the Waynflete Professorship of Metaphysical Philosophy at Magdalen College. He conformed to the best archetype of a bachelor college don dedicated to his subject, his college and to his students and, as a result, with the exception of his WW2 service in the Welsh Guards, seconded to intelligence, he also spent most of his non-academic life at Oxford.

Despite his prodigious entry into Oxford philosophy, Ryle was initially disappointed and somewhat frustrated with philosophy at Oxford, finding that it was very conservative and lacking in vigour. What was new and exciting seemed to be going on elsewhere, most notably at that other ancient English university in Cambridge. There Moore and Russell had loosened the hold of nineteenth-century Idealism, and Russell had helped to introduce the new mathematical logic and also, arguably more by accident than enterprise, brought in Ludwig Wittgenstein. It fell to Ryle and some others of his generation to import these new ways of engaging in philosophy into the staid and dusty cloisters of Oxford philosophy. Ryle also looked further afield for inspiration. He taught himself German sufficiently well that he could acquaint himself with the work of Meinong, Brentano, Bolzano, Husserl (see Chapter 3) and even some of the work of that new boy on the German-language philosophy block, Martin Heidegger. But more directly than any of the above was the influence on Ryle of the work of the German physicist-philosopher,

Moritz Schlick, one of the founding fathers of the Vienna Circle. With hindsight, there is reason to suppose that the Vienna Circle's adoption of the *Tractatus*, and its emphasis on its positivist themes, was another of the major influences shaping Ryle's views about the role and methods for philosophy in the twentieth century, which in turn shaped his philosophy of mind.

While Ryle himself never became a card-carrying positivist of any sort, he was sympathetic to many of its aims. While, as he put it, 'most of us took fairly untragically its demolition of Metaphysics' (Ryle 1971, p. 10), he was particularly attracted by its uncompromising challenge to existing ideas about the nature and methods of philosophy itself. While he did not subscribe to any form of a Logical Positivists' verification principle, nor ever engage in their incontinent adulation of the sciences, he was eager to incorporate into his own philosophy their new logico-linguistic approach with its 'growing concern with questions of philosophical technique and a growing passion for ratiocinative rigour' that resulted from the use of 'the technicalities of logical theory and scientific method' (Ryle 1956, pp. 3–4).

Chiefly through the influence of the *Tractatus* and the Logical Positivists, Ryle came to see that philosophy was not a science of any sort and so could not be specified in terms of any proprietary subject matter but must be defined in terms of its role and the methods appropriate to it. He came to the conclusion that Wittgenstein was correct in holding that philosophical statements 'are condemned to be uninformative about the world and yet able, in some important way, to be clarificatory of those propositions that are informative about the world, reporting no matters of fact yet correcting our mishandlings of reported matters of fact' (Ryle 1956, p. 5). The task of philosophy was to analyse ordinary language in order to correct its mishandlings when employed for philosophical or cognate purposes. One important aspect of this view of philosophy as linguistic analysis was that a central task of philosophy was to penetrate the surface grammar and surface logical structure of ordinary language statements so as to lay bare their fundamental grammar and true logical form, and so thereby to reveal their real meaning. This approach, of course, echoed Wittgenstein's statement in the *Tractatus* that 'Philosophy aims at the logical clarification of thoughts. Philosophy is not a body of doctrine but an activity' (Wittgenstein 1963, §4.112).

When put into practice, Ryle's linguistic analysis involved bringing to our attention any pseudo-referring expressions, contradictions, infinite regresses, category mistakes as well as any philosophically misleading uses of various words, phrases and statements. After removing these logico-linguistic carbuncles, linguistic analysis then aimed at the positive, rehabilitative tasks of carefully mapping the correct logical geography of a concept which had previously been misdescribed. Mapping the logical geography of a concept amounted to displaying its connections with other related concepts, in particular with those concepts which were basic to any map of this area of discourse and so not in dispute. This employment of certain basic concepts very often amounted, in effect, to a covert appeal to basic indisputable facts. In turn this revealed that, despite Ryle's sometimes saying otherwise, philosophical analysis was not entirely an *a priori* enterprise. However, for Ryle, as for other linguistic analysts, these basic indisputable facts were always held to be ordinary ones readily available to the man or woman on the fifty-nine bus, so there was no need for philosophers to have recourse to the special facts of the specialized empirical sciences. This view of Ryle's was one that definitely did not find favour with the next generation of philosophers of mind.

As early as his essay 'Are there propositions?' (1930), Ryle was choosing philosophy of mind as the source of the majority of his examples illustrating these new methods in philosophy. Thus, for example, in that paper he argued that the true logical form underlying statements of one's beliefs such as 'I believe that X is Y' is 'I believe that if X turns out to be Y, then the statement "X is Y" presents a fact'. In short, statements of belief (as distinct from declarations of knowledge) are disguised hypothetical statements of fact. They are not statements about hypothetical *facts*, for to say that would be to invent unnecessarily an illusory world of subsistent facts.

Likewise, in his essay 'Imaginary objects' (1933), Ryle suggested that because, in the statement 'Mr. Pickwick wore knee breeches', we use the referring expression 'Mr. Pickwick', we may thereby be seduced, at least when philosophizing, into inventing an imaginary object as the real but subsisting entity to which the name 'Mr. Pickwick' refers. More generally, we should always be alive to the fact that pseudo-referring expressions behave *grammatically* in much the same way as genuinely referring expressions, while *logically* they operate very differently. Any mention of Mr. Pickwick is, in effect, shorthand for drawing our attention to the descriptions of Mr. Pickwick in Charles Dickens' work of fiction, *Pickwick Papers*. In more formal logico-linguistic terms, the name 'Mr. Pickwick' is a concealed predicative expression which might amount to our thinking about Mr. Pickwick either in words or in images, the latter perhaps culled from the 1921 silent film, 'The Adventures of Mr. Pickwick', or the illustrations by Phiz to Dickens' classic tale. More generally, in elaborating the nature of 'concealed predicative expressions', Ryle conjured up what he called 'look'-predicates, 'smell'-predicates, 'sound'-predicates and 'taste'-predicates, as well as the more traditional linguistic ones.

Two things are worth noting in regard to these early forays of Ryle into philosophy of mind. The first is that, besides the sources already mentioned, they drew upon an often unnoticed debt to Bertrand Russell's careful unpicking of the fabric of statements (and so of the propositions underlying them) via his work on the 'theory of types' and 'theory of descriptions'. The 'theory of types' (as discussed, for example, in Russell 1908) was generated by Russell when he set out to dissolve certain logical paradoxes in his research in philosophy of mathematics. As part of that endeavour, he pointed out that we need to recognize that classes (or 'types') occur at a number of ascending levels (or 'orders'), and that to confuse these levels often leads to contradictions or paradoxes. Thus, the statement 'My cat is lovely' is at the basic or first-order level, whereas the statement about that former proposition, 'Cat descriptions are often very sentimental', a statement about a class of statements, is at a higher, second-order level, and so on. Russell's 'theory of descriptions' (as discussed, for example, in Russell 1905) depends upon a distinction between 'knowledge by acquaintance' and 'knowledge by description'. The explanation of that distinction included the claim that, ultimately, any 'knowledge by description' gained its purchase on the world, and so its status as knowledge, in so far as it could be analysed into a group of basic sentences that were expressions of 'knowledge by acquaintance' (or expressions of what some observer had actually perceived or could perceive). Of course, Russell's seminal work on the logic of statements (propositions) was also a major influence on his young pupil, Wittgenstein.

The second thing worth noting is that, in these early papers of Ryle, it is already clear how he is going to transform philosophy of mind. By and large, he is going to cut away the host of Cartesian mental entities, events and faculties as conceived by much of the philosophy and psychology of the late nineteenth century and the first decades of the twentieth century, and substitute purely logico-linguistic 'entities'. These early papers already show him borrowing Occam's Razor, giving it a new sharp logico-linguistic blade, and then using it not merely to cut away all the superfluous mental entities posited by theorists but to reshape philosophy of mind.

In *The Concept of Mind*, Ryle's Occamizing zeal and his skilful employment of the logico-linguistic tools he had developed during the 1930s and 1940s were on full display. Written with wit and a rare gift for metaphor and the telling illustration, and uncluttered by footnotes or references, this text became an instant success and reached a much wider audience than philosophy books usually manage. The target in *The Concept of Mind*, as Ryle himself tells us in the Introduction, was 'Descartes [who] left as one of his main philosophical legacies a myth which continues to distort the continental geography of the subject' (Ryle 1949, p. 8.). This myth, or 'official doctrine' as he sometimes called it, states that humans have both a body and a mind. Bodies are in space and time, subject to the mechanical laws governing objects in space-time and detectable by external observers. Minds, on the other hand, are not in space nor subject to mechanical laws nor detectable by external observers. As a Cartesian mind is coextensive with consciousness, Ryle memorably and 'with deliberate abusiveness' described it as 'the dogma of the Ghost in the Machine' (ibid., p. 15).

Ryle began his demolition of this dogma by asserting that 'it is one big mistake and a mistake of a special kind. It is, namely, a category-mistake. It represents the facts of mental life as if they belonged to one logical type or category (or range of types or categories), when they actually belong to another' (ibid., p. 16). So what is a *category mistake*? A category mistake is committed when, describing or employing some concept, one describes or employs it as if it belonged to one logical type or category when in fact it belongs to another. The logical type or category to which a concept belongs is the set of ways in which it is logically legitimate to use that concept. Thus, Ryle sometimes employed the following story to illustrate a category mistake. A foreigner visits Oxford University for the first time and is being given a guided tour of the campus. He is shown the colleges, lecture rooms, libraries, laboratories, administrative buildings and playing fields. However, when the tour has been completed, the visitor says, 'Thank you so much for the tour. I've seen so much beautiful architecture set amid such pleasant surroundings but which building was the university?' The visitor has placed the term 'university' in the category of 'label for a particular building' when in fact it is a complex umbrella term that refers to the buildings, playing fields, streets, students, teachers, researchers, administrators, its education that is designed for the third level, its possessing an official charter that enables it to operate as a university, and so on. Another Rylean illustration was of a foreign visitor being taken to a cricket match for the first time. After having the playing field itself, the wicket, the stumps and bails, bats and balls, the umpires, bowlers, batsmen, wicketkeeper and fieldsmen pointed out to her, she then says, 'But where is the sportsmanship that I hear is so central to the game of cricket?'

Ryle held that a category mistake is often revealed in philosophy by taking a claim or theory at face value and then making a number of logically legitimate inferences from it. If one of these inferences ends up with some absurd conclusion or contradicts common sense, then one can be said to have exposed the mistake inherent in the original claim or theory by means of a *reductio ad absurdum* argument.

However, *The Concept of Mind* is not just a hatchet job on 'the dogma of the Ghost in the Machine'. Ryle is interested in building up a new model of mind to replace the disgraced Cartesian one. The basic structure of this new model involves especially the category of behavioural dispositions. The rebuilding often involves substituting dispositions for the Cartesian conceptual categories of private ghostly faculties and their proprietary activities.

So what are *dispositions*? Ryle describes them as abilities or tendencies or liabilities or pronenesses to act or react, or fail to act or react, in a certain way in certain circumstances. To say, for example, that a person is haemophiliac, is to say that he (and it is almost always a he) is liable to bleed when cut, such that the body's natural coagulant, either missing or in short supply, fails to staunch the flow of blood. To take another example, to say that an animal is a ruminant is to say that the animal chews its cud (i.e. to say that the animal is able to regurgitate food from its short-stay stomach in order to chew it again).

Ryle then set out to develop and refine the logical structure of dispositions and make distinctions with regard to them. Dispositions, he explained, can always be expressed *hypothetically* in a statement of the form 'If circumstances C occur, then X will do or exhibit Y'. Thus, Fred's being a haemophiliac can be expressed as 'If Fred's skin is cut and he bleeds, then Fred will bleed without the body's natural coagulant staunching the flow of blood'. Alternatively, being *lawlike*, dispositions can always be expressed in the form '*Whenever* circumstances C occur, then X will do or exhibit Y'. Thus, Fred's being a haemophiliac can also be expressed as 'Whenever Fred's skin is cut and he bleeds, then Fred will bleed without the body's natural coagulant staunching the flow of blood'. Dispositions also conform to one or other of two basic patterns. They can be *determinate* dispositions or *determinable* ones. Determinate dispositions are pronesses to do or exhibit things of just one unique kind; for example, to say of someone or some thing that it is a ruminant or a cigarette smoker is to attribute a determinate disposition to that person or thing. By contrast, determinable dispositions are 'multi-track' in that they are pronenesses to do or exhibit a wide spectrum of things which however can be grouped under a generic label. Thus to say someone is greedy is to attribute a determinable (yet to be determined) disposition to that person, as it is unclear until the description is filled out in detail what form or 'track' the greediness has taken. Has the greedy person taken more than his fair share of the Thanksgiving turkey, or eaten by himself at a carvery until he becomes sick and vomits, or has she had a huge win on the lottery but failed to share any of it with her family or friends? Then there are *capacity* dispositions and *ability* dispositions. A capacity is merely a proneness to do or exhibit certain things. For example, one might say that Richard has a capacity for being quite undiplomatic in committee meetings or that Miranda has a capacity to drink lots of gin without getting drunk. An ability is a proneness to do something that requires practice and skill, and then achievement. Thus, to say someone is a mathematician is to attribute an ability to that person, because it involves not merely saying that this person frequently does mathematical problems but also saying that he or she frequently does them and *gets them right* most of the time. Finally, *dispositions* must be twinned with *occurrences* where the latter are the publicly observable displays of, and so the evidence for, the existence of the former. We might say someone is greedy, for example, because we frequently observe her taking more than her share of food at the table. Or we might say someone is irascible because we often observe him losing his temper at even the slightest provocation.

Having developed and refined his concept of dispositions, Ryle then set out to use this concept in his campaign against the Cartesian dogma and to find an alternative to it. Ryle first asserted that the basic model behind this dogma was of a mind that had a *cognitive* or knowledge faculty called 'the intellect' that gathered information and processed it into theories or truths about this or that. Working in tandem with this cognitive faculty was a second *conative* or choosing-what-to-do faculty called 'the will' that issued instructions to the body about how best to deploy the theoretical information supplied by the intellect. According to the dogma, those who used their intellect in the right way were called 'intelligent' and those who exerted their will in the right way were said to be 'acting with free will'. Ryle first focused on the dogma's account of 'the intellect'. He suggested that we should first look at how we actually attribute the adjective 'intelligent' to people. When we apply to someone intelligence epithets such as 'shrewd' or 'silly', 'prudent' or 'imprudent', we reveal that 'the description imputes to him not the knowledge, or ignorance, of this or that truth, but the ability, or inability, to do certain sorts of things' (ibid., p. 27). Thus, the shrewd punter is the one who bets on horses and wins, not the one who knows the *Timeform* chart off by heart. The prudent farmer is the one who farms his land in such a way that he survives and prospers in seasons which bankrupt others, not the one who has read and can recall with precision all the facts about farming in the *Farmers' Annual*.

If one wants to characterize it correctly in terms of knowledge, then Ryle suggests that intelligence is a form of *knowing how* (knowing how to do something successfully), not a form of *knowing that* (knowing that something is the case or knowing some fact). What is more, *knowing how* is primary and Ryle reminds us that the 'rules of correct reasoning were first extracted by Aristotle, yet men knew how to avoid and detect fallacies before they learned his lessons' (ibid., p. 30). Ryle chooses the verb 'extracted' with the precision that he always employed in his writing. Ryle is pointing out that Aristotle extracted and formulated his rules after studying the reasoning that his fellow citizens were already using and had used for generations.

More generally, we say someone is intelligent because we have witnessed her successfully *engaging in tasks* we see as requiring some intelligence. Ryle, particularly in his later essays, was at pains to make clear that one can exhibit intelligence in a wide variety of ways, often in tasks that we might not normally thing of as 'intellectual'. A Grand Prix driver may exhibit intelligence by having an ability to anticipate likely trouble ahead and to avoid it by imaginative manoeuvres, so that he is rarely if ever involved in crashes on the race-track. A trout fisherman might exhibit intelligence by regularly catching more trout than his fellow fishermen. In short, we say someone is intelligent when we have observed that person's *behaviour* and decided that this person has an *ability* (a determinable disposition) to accomplish with success tasks which require some understanding of the context, care and attention, an ability to correct mistakes as well as to foresee possible problems. In saying someone is intelligent, we are not attributing to them an internal Cartesian faculty that is in working order, because '[o]vert intelligent performances are not clues to the workings of minds; they are those workings' (ibid., p. 58). More generally, '[t]o find that most people have minds (though idiots and infants in arms do not) is simply to find that they are able and prone to do certain sorts of things, and this we do by witnessing the sorts of things they do' (ibid., p. 61).

Ryle next turned his weapons on the second basic faculty postulated by the Cartesian dogma, namely the will and its proprietary acts, volitions. Employing a typical strategy of his, he first sets out to loosen our adherence to this 'myth of volitions' by suggesting that we first take the myth at face value and then draw some valid logical conclusions from it and see what happens. If, he says, volitions really are small internal ghostly actions initiated by the faculty of the will, then we should be able to say, without philosophical or any other form of embarrassment, that 'he performed five quick and easy volitions and two slow and difficult volitions between midday and lunch-time' (ibid., p. 64). But to say that is risible and so, in effect, is a *reductio ad absurdum* argument against the myth of volitions.

Ryle next aims another type of *reductio argument*, a *dilemma argument*, at the myth. It goes like this. A voluntary human action is defined by the myth as an action (some outward behaviour such as a movement of some limb) caused and so preceded by a volition (an internal act of the will). However, since a volition itself is *ex hypothesi* an action, we can legitimately ask of any volition, Is it voluntary or involuntary? But this leads immediately to a dilemma where, as Ryle asserts, 'Clearly either answer leads to absurdities' (ibid., p. 67). If a volition is *voluntary*, then according to the myth it can only be so because it itself was causally preceded by an act of will, which in turn must have been preceded by another prior act of will, and so on *ad infinitum*. The internal chain of micro mental events preceding the concluding voluntary action or behaviour would be infinite and so impossible. However if, on the other hand, a volition is declared to be *involuntary*, then the basis for the voluntariness of the resulting human action, the outward behaviour, will disappear. It disappears because the behaviour is no longer preceded by a free act of the will but by an involuntary mental event. Wittgenstein clearly had similar doubts about the official doctrine of the will and its volitions and, in his posthumously published *Philosophical Investigations*, he wrote that 'I can't will willing; that is, it makes no sense to speak of willing willing. "Willing" is not the name of an action; and so not the name of any voluntary action either' (Wittgenstein 1958, I, p. 613).

Ryle suggests that we will more readily jettison the myth of volitions if we concentrate more carefully on how we use the words 'voluntary' and 'involuntary' in human discourse. If we do this, we will notice that, in fact, we use the terms 'voluntary' and involuntary' in a quite circumscribed way. They are not words we use in ordinary conversation. In effect, 'voluntary'/'involuntary' are verdict terms that we use when we try to decide who, if anyone, was to blame for something. Did the schoolboy deliberately, *voluntarily*, smash the classroom window, or did his throw of the cricket ball to his pal go astray, so that the upshot, the smashed window, was an *involuntary* act?

But Ryle does not stop there. He gleefully points out that these problems about the myth of volitions are symptoms of an even deeper problem underlying the whole Cartesian dogma of 'the Ghost in the Machine'. Given the way that the Cartesian dogma describes the mental or ghostly aspect of humans and given the way science describes the nature of bodies or, more generally, the physical world, then it becomes impossible to make sense of how the former, the ghostly Cartesian world, could ever have any contact with and so any causal interaction with the physical world. Minds are described by the Cartesian dogma more or less in terms of the negation of the properties of the physical world. Bodies are in space, have dimensions and move according to the accepted mechanical laws of the physical world. Minds are not in space, have no dimensions and are not subject to these mechanical laws. The basic structure of the Cartesian model of humans as inhabiting two worlds, a ghostly Cartesian one and a physical bodily one, makes it impossible to see how humans could ever get their ghostly minds to move their physical bodies into performing any actions. The myth is one vast category mistake.

Ryle continued his attack on the Cartesian dogma with his linguistic analyses of other mental items such as imagination, perception, feelings, emotions and introspection. However, he ran into difficulties, which he always admitted, when he set out to demythologize the Cartesian account of consciousness. Consciousness is ordinarily thought of by ordinary people in much the way that the Cartesian dogma describes it. Humans have inside their heads a private stream of consciousness so that only the person, whose stream it is, has access to it. What is more, since our access is immediate, our reports on it must be more or less infallible. Also the activities of our conscious minds seem to be so circumstance disengaged and behaviour free, that it is hard to see how Rylean dispositional analyses can take hold and so be substituted for the Cartesian account. A disposition is analysed in terms of someone's behaving in manner X, in certain predictable circumstances, C. As we have seen, Ryle's dispositional analysis is a two-place one with no reference to anything inside the behaving subject's head. Those that come after Ryle felt the need to amend his account of dispositions into a three-place one. A disposition, it was argued convincingly by, for example, David Armstrong, is a proneness of some agent (or reagent) to do or react in manner X, in circumstance Y, because inside the agent (or reagent) there is a crucial structural and so 'categorical' (non-hypothetical) factor, F. Fred is a haemophiliac because his blood will flow without staunching (X), if he is wounded (Y), because he lacks any naturally occurring blood coagulant (F). Thus, Fred can be diagnosed by a medical consultant as haemophiliac as soon as he's born, and so before he ever bleeds from any wound, because the consultant might notice that Fred's naturally occurring coagulant is missing. Thus, in insisting on the need to refer to *something inside the body of an agent or reagent* when explaining the nature of dispositions, it is not difficult to see how Ryle's logical behaviourism was developed in ensuing decades into central state materialism and various forms of the identity theory of mind (see Chapters 6 and 7).

Ryle, however, was dedicated to not referring to anything at all that was internal to the human agent, in fear of allowing the Cartesians in by the tradesman's entrance. He first tackled his problem of finding an acceptable alternative to the Cartesian account of consciousness obliquely, by analysing introspection. According to the Cartesian dogma, introspection is described as a person's second-level non-sensuous perception or observation of what is going on in his or her first-level stream of consciousness. He points out that, if we look at how the word 'introspection' is used, we will see that it is a jargon term used only by adherents to the Cartesian dogma. Then he pointed out that, if consciousness really involved attention, as it clearly does, then introspection, as described by the dogma, involves a split in attention that is either impossible or destructive of the purpose of introspection. Either way it makes introspection useless as a tool of psychological enquiry.

Ryle's substitute for the Cartesian account of introspection was borrowed from William James. Everything with which we credit 'introspection' can be explained in terms of the replay in memory of some previous observation of a subject's ordinary behaviour, and so is a sort of 'retrospection'. Famously, or notoriously, Ryle went on to claim that 'the sorts of things I can find out about myself are the same as the sorts of things that I can find out about other people, and the methods of finding them out are much the same' (Ryle 1949, p. 155). Thus, 'I learn that a certain pupil of mine is lazy, ambitious and witty by following his work, noticing his excuses, listening to his conversation and comparing his performances with those of others. Nor does it make any important difference if I happen myself to be that pupil' (ibid., p. 169).

Ryle realized that this attack on the concept of introspection still leaves the concept of a stream of consciousness unmolested, and admitted that his treatment of it in *The Concept of Mind* was inadequate. He spent a great deal of the last 25 years of his life still trying to find a way of giving a behaviourist analysis of such undeniably inner stream-of-consciousness activities as thinking to oneself, doing mental arithmetic and reciting a poem in one's head (Ryle 1979). His preferred way of proceeding was to say that such inner 'activities' are all forms of thinking but that thinking is not really an inner activity at all but an adverbial modification of some outer activity. Thus, paradigm cases of thinking are such things as playing tennis shrewdly (or thinkingly), or playing chess cleverly (or thinkingly), and so on. We say something has been done 'thinkingly' when we note that it was done with care, attention, invention and an ability to self-correct mistakes. But thinking to oneself, doing mental arithmetic and reciting a poem in one's head, activities Rodin's Le Penseur might well be engaged in, look like wholly inner private mental activities with no connections to any outer behaviour nor to anything going on around the thinker. It looks as if one must admit that, when a person is just thinking, something wholly internal and private must be going on in the thinker. But if Ryle had posited *any inner activity* as the bearer of his adverbial modification 'thinkingly', he would have felt that he had capitulated to the Cartesian dogma.

Ryle knew the work of the psychological behaviourists of his time, in particular the work of the founder of psychological behaviourism, J. B. Watson. However, there are important differences between the Ryle's logical behaviourism and Watson's psychological behaviourism. They began in very different ways. Psychological behaviourism was first in the field with Watson's manifesto of 1913, 'Psychology as the Behaviorist Views It'. Watson began life as a student in a laboratory devoted to introspection which was then the chief method for gaining data about the human mind. But he grew disillusioned with the lack of verifiable results. More decisively, after working on animal psychology, he realized that this quite different way of doing psychology involved carefully observing animal behaviour where the results could be checked by other observers. It was a paradigm of objective scientific method compared to the 'self-observations' by subjects in introspectionist laboratories. Human psychology, he felt, should employ the same method and so be the scientific observation of the behaviour of the human animal.

Ryle also adopted a behaviouristic account of human psychology for methodological reasons, but ones concerning philosophy. As we have already seen, in his early academic years he was troubled by the very basic question about what might be the role and appropriate methods for philosophy in the first decades of the twentieth century, a century already dominated by science. Though he gradually softened his approach in practice, in his manifesto article of 1932, 'Systematically Misleading Expressions', Ryle declared that 'Philosophy must then involve the exercise of systematic restatement.... For we can ask what is the real form of the fact recorded when this is concealed or disguised and not duly exhibited by the expression in question. And we can often succeed in stating this fact in a new form of words which does exhibit what the other failed to exhibit. And I am for the present inclined to believe that this is what philosophical analysis is and that this is the sole and whole function of philosophy' (Ryle 1932, p. 61). So naturally enough a lot of his early work amounted to fashioning logico-linguistic tools for engaging in this task of 'restatement' that would then manifest the true logical form underlying our philosophical and psychological claims. The chief weapon that he developed was dispositional analysis which involved substituting behavioural capacities and abilities, and various modifications of them, for alleged Cartesian faculties and activities. His view of philosophy gave birth to what critics called his logical behaviourism. However, as he revealed through his frustrating and ineffectual attempts towards the end of his life to give a behaviourist analysis of inner conscious episodes, logical behaviourism has its limits.

References

Russell, B. (1905), 'On denoting'. *Mind* XIV(4): 479–93.
— (1908), 'Mathematical logic as based on the theory of types'. *American Journal of Mathematics* 30: 222–62.
Ryle, G. (1930), 'Are there propositions?' in Ryle *Collected Papers 1929–1968*. London: Hutchinson, 1971, Vol. II, Collected Essays, pp. 39–62.
— (1932), 'Systematically misleading expressions', in Ryle *Collected Papers 1929–1968*. London: Hutchinson, 1971, Vol. II, Collected Essays, pp. 39–62.
— (1933), 'Imaginary objects', in Ryle *Collected Papers 1929–1968*. London: Hutchinson, 1971, Vol. II, Collected Essays, pp. 39–62.
— (1949), *The Concept of Mind*. London: Hutchinson.
— (1956), 'Introduction', in A. J. Ayer, Kneale, W. C., Paul, G. A., Pears, D. F., Strawson, P. F., Warnock, G. J., and Wollheim, R. A. (eds), *The Revolution in Philosophy, BBC Third Programme Lectures*. London: Macmillan, pp. 1–11.
— (1971) [1970], 'Autobiographical', in O. P. Wood and G. Pitcher (eds), *Ryle, Modern Studies in Philosophy*. London: Macmillan, pp. 1–15.
— (1979). *On Thinking*, ed. K. Kolenda. Oxford: Blackwell.

Watson, J. B. (1913), 'Psychology as the behaviorist views it'. *Psychological Review* 20: 158–77.
Wittgenstein, L. (1958) [1953], *Philosophical Investigations* (second edn), trans. G. E. M. Anscombe. Oxford: Basil Blackwell.
— (1963) [1921], *Tractatus Logico-Philosophicus*, trans. D. F. Pears and B. F. McGuinness. London, Routledge & Kegan Paul.

CHAPTER SIX

The contributions of U. T. Place, H. Feigl and J. J. C. Smart to the identity theory of consciousness

Brian P. McLaughlin and Ronald Planer

In the 1950s, U. T. Place, Herbert Feigl and J. J. C. Smart championed the view that conscious processes are brain processes. The view was revolutionary since behaviourism was dominant at the time both in psychology and in the philosophy of mind (see Chapter 5).

Place, Feigl and Smart did not marshal a full-scale assault on behaviourism.[1] Indeed, Place remarked:

> In the case of cognitive concepts like "knowing," "believing," "understanding," "remembering," and volitional concepts like "wanting" and "intending," there can be little doubt, I think, that an analysis in terms of dispositions to behave is fundamentally sound. (1956, p. 55)[2]

But they rejected behaviourism for consciousness, maintaining that states (events, etc.) of consciousness are states (events, etc.) of the brain, specifically neurophysiological states. Rather than being dispositions to behave, such conscious mental states are internal causes of behaviour.

Thus, in his seminal 1956 article, 'Is Consciousness a Brain Process?', Place answers his title question in the opening sentence, saying

> The thesis that consciousness is a process in the brain is put forward as a reasonable scientific hypothesis, not to be dismissed on logical grounds alone. (1956, p. 55)

And he maintained that the thesis is one we are warranted in accepting.

Feigl, in his masterful 1958 paper, 'The "Mental" and the "Physical"', distinguished two aspects of the mental, the intentional aspect and 'the raw feel' aspect, maintaining the identity theory for the latter. He writes:

> The word "mental" in present day psychology covers . . . not only the events and processes of direct experiences (i.e. the raw feels), but also unconscious events and processes, as well as the "intentional acts" of perception, introspective awareness, expectation, thought, belief, doubt, desire, volition, resolution, etc. . . . [S]ince intentionality as such is to be analyzed in terms of pure semantics . . . it would be a category mistake of the most glaring sort to attempt a neurophysiological identification of this aspect of "mind." But since, on the other hand, intentional acts as occurrents in direct experience are introspectively or phenomenologically describable in something quite like raw feel terms, a neural identification of this aspect of the mind is prima facie not excluded on purely logical grounds. (1958, p. 68)

By 'intentional acts as occurrents in direct experience', he means intentional acts such as consciously thinking something – for example, consciously thinking that the neighbours are home. By saying that such intentional acts are 'phenomenologically describable in something like raw feel terms', he seems to have in mind that they can be described as the having of a mental image (e.g. an auditory image). The content of the image is a matter for semantics, or what is nowadays called 'psychosemantics', not neurophysiology. But the identification of the 'raw feels' (e.g. the feels of aches, pains, itches, tickles and the like) and the 'raw feel' (imagistic) aspects of intentional acts, he tells us, 'is prima facie not excluded on purely logical grounds' (1958, p. 68). Indeed, he goes on to say: 'The crux of the mind-body problem consists in the interpretation of the relation between raw feels and the neural processes' (1958, p. 69). That relationship, he maintains, is identity.

Smart's 1959 article is entitled 'Sensations and Brain Processes', and he argues that sensations are identical to brain processes, specifically neurophysiological processes. He used 'sensations' in a very broad sense to include not only bodily sensations (aches, pains, itches, tickles and the like), but also sense experiences (visual experiences, auditory experiences, etc.), emotional experiences (feelings of anger, sadness, etc.) and experiences of having images (visual, auditory, etc.).

The term 'consciousness' has a number of uses. In one use, to say a being is conscious is just to say that the being is awake. The notion of consciousness that Place, Feigl and Smart were concerned with is nowadays labelled 'phenomenal consciousness'. A being has phenomenal consciousness if and only if it is like something for the being to be the being. States (events, etc.) of phenomenal consciousness are such that it is like something for the subject of the state to be in them (or undergo them) (Nagel 1974). It is, for instance, like something for one as a subject to feel pain, and so pains are states of phenomenal consciousness. The what-it-is-like-for-the-subject quality is what Feigl has in mind by 'the feel' of the state. He called these qualitative feels 'raw feels', because he maintained that they are non-intentional aspects of phenomenal experiences. A more commonly used term for the qualitative feels is 'qualia'. (The singular is 'quale'.) Whether qualia are indeed non-intentional is currently a matter of dispute.[3] And whether it poses a problem for the identity theory if they are intentional (and so not 'raw') is currently an unresolved issue. Due to lack of space, it is not one we will address here.[4] (Hereafter, we will use 'consciousness' as shorthand for 'phenomenal consciousness' in the sense in question.)

Feigl (1958) and Smart (1959) hold the identity theory of consciousness. That is to say, they hold that for any state (event, etc.) of consciousness c, there is a neural state (event, etc.) n such that c is identical with n (i.e. c = n). Although Place held that conscious states are neural states, he was not an identity theorist, for he did not hold that conscious states are identical to neural states. He distinguishes three senses of 'is': the definition, constitution and predication senses (1956, pp. 55–6). And he maintains that a conscious state is a neural state in the constitution sense of 'is', and thus that states of consciousness are constituted by neural states, rather than numerically one and the same as certain neural states. There is, however, also an identity use of 'is'. Leibniz's thesis of the indiscernibility of identicals holds for identity: if A is (is identical to) B, then whatever is true of A is true of B, and whatever is true of B is true of A. But this thesis does not hold for constitution. To use an example that Place does not himself employ, consider the claim that a certain statue is a lump of clay, in the constitution sense of 'is'. That claim does not imply that whatever is true of the statue is true of the lump of clay, and whatever is true of the lump of clay is true of the statue. The lump of clay can, for example, survive being squashed, the statue cannot. Nevertheless, the statue is constituted by the lump of clay (at a time, of course). Our focus is mainly the identity theory of consciousness, not the constitution theory. Feigl and Smart are committed to the view that if a conscious state c is (identical to) a neural state n, then whatever is true of c is true of n, and whatever is true of n is true of c (there being after all just one state).

There is a distinction between types or kinds of states and concrete dated particular states, so-called 'state tokens'; similarly for events and processes. Feigl and Smart are not always as clear as they might have been about the distinction between types and tokens, but they in fact both hold the view that not only are token states of consciousness identical to token neural states, types (or kinds) of states of consciousness are also identical to types (or kinds) of neural states. Feigl and Smart thus hold that for every type of state of phenomenal consciousness C, there is some type of neural state N such that C = N. (Place holds analogous theses, though about constitution, rather than identity (1956, p. 56).) State types are types of properties. Feigl and Smart thus hold that for any conscious property (any quale) C, there is a neural property N such that C = N.

Some philosophers in the nineteenth century maintained that particular mental processes are particular 'neuronal processes', thereby embracing a token identity theory of mental processes (see, e.g. Lewes 1874). Early in the twentieth century, some philosophers embraced the view that token mental states are identical with neural states, but denied that types of mental states are types of physical states of any sort. The British Emergentists Samuel Alexander (1920) and C. D. Broad (1925), for example, were substance monists, maintaining that there are no immaterial souls or immaterial minds or vital élan; and Alexander held and Broad was very sympathetic with the view that token mental states are identical with token neural states. They were, however, property (or type or attribute) dualists: they denied that mental properties are identical to neural properties or indeed physical properties of any sort. They both offered versions of what is nowadays called 'the knowledge argument' to try to show on a priori grounds that conscious properties (qualia) are not identical to physical properties.[5] For example, Broad (1925) maintained that even if one had the computational powers of a mathematical archangel, knew all the physical and chemical facts about a certain chemical and, as well, all the neurophysiological facts about the olfactory system and the brain, one could still not deduce what the chemical smells like.[6] Mental properties, Alexander and Broad maintained, are ontologically emergent from physical properties and relations. Feigl and Smart rejected this emergentism, maintaining, as we noted, that conscious properties are identical with neural properties. (Place's constitution view also entails the falsity of emergentism since emergence, in the sense in question, is a certain kind of fundamental, contingent nomological relation, not constitution).

Smart (1959) credits Feigl with coining the term 'nomological danglers' for conscious properties, as they are conceived on the emergentist view. In the subsequent literature, 'nomological danglers' was also used for the emergent laws that were alleged to link emergent properties with the physical properties from which they emerge. Broad (1925) held that there are contingent, fundamental, irreducible laws of nature linking mental properties with the physical properties and relations from which they emerge. He called such laws 'transordinal laws' since they (are supposed to) bridge properties that emerge at a given level (or order) of complexity of nature from properties and relations among the entities at a lower level (or order) of complexity.[7] Smart held that sensations merely nomologically correlated with brain processes

> would be "nomological danglers," to use Feigl's expression. It is not often realized how odd would be the laws whereby these

nomological danglers would dangle. . . . Certainly we are pretty sure in the future to come across new ultimate laws of a novel type, but I expect them to relate simple constituents; for example, whatever ultimate particulars are then in vogue. I cannot believe that ultimate laws of nature could relate simple constituents to configurations consisting of perhaps billions of neurons (and goodness knows how many billion billions of ultimate particles) all put together for all the world as though their main purpose in life would be a negative feed-back mechanism of a complicated sort. (1959, p. 61)

If states of consciousness are indeed neural states, that is, at best, knowable only a posteriori. Feigl maintained that claims identifying states of consciousness and neural states are 'empirical claims' (1958, p. 69), because mental terms and neural terms always differ in meaning. He also held, however, that although such terms always differ in meaning, it is nevertheless the case that '[t]he "mental" states or events (in the sense of raw feels) are the referents (denotata) of both the phenomenal terms of the language of introspection, as well as of certain terms of the neurophysiological language' (1958, p. 69). He tells us: 'there can be no logical equivalence between the concepts (or statements) in the two languages' (1958, p. 69), but nevertheless terms from the two different languages can be co-referential (i.e. denote the same properties). He in effect insisted that no statement couched solely in physical terms a priori implies any a posteriori statement about a state or states of consciousness, but that that doesn't rule out the possibility that every type of state of consciousness is identical to some type of neural state. Feigl sometimes described his brand of the identity theory as a 'double-language' theory. He preferred, however, talk of 'two-fold access' or 'double knowledge', by which he had in mind that the way we access states of consciousness as such is different from the way we access neural states as such, and that how we know claims about states of consciousness is different from how we know claims about neural states (1958, p. 69). He maintained, however, that the different ways of accessing or knowing were different ways of accessing or knowing the same facts. It seems that his response to the knowledge argument would be that we cannot know what it is like to have a certain conscious state even from knowledge of all the physical facts, because knowing what it is like to have the conscious state requires the kind of access one can have only if one is in the conscious state; and even knowledge of all the physical facts as such won't yield that.[8]

Place likens claims such as 'Pain is brain process such-and-such' to scientific claims such as 'Lightning is a motion of electrical discharge', which he took to be empirical claims of constitution, rather than 'true by definition', as are claims such as 'A square is an equilateral triangle' (1956, p. 56). He emphasized that our talk of consciousness is 'logically independent' of our talk of conscious states and held that we use different kinds of operations for verifying claims of consciousness and for verifying neurophysiological claims (1956, pp. 57–8). But it is, he claims, a mistake to think that 'consciousness and brains processes must be independent entities because the expressions used to refer to them are logically independent' (1956, p. 57).

Smart (1959) maintained that statements asserting that a sensation is identical to a neural state are 'contingent identity statements', like 'The Morning Star is the Evening Star' and 'Lightning is electrical discharge due to ionization of clouds'. He remarked that since 'there can be contingent statements of the form "A is identical with B" . . . a person may well know that something is an A without knowing that it is a B' (1959, p. 63). He points out that 'The Morning Star' and 'The Evening Star' differ in meaning, yet both refer to the same heavenly body, the planet Venus (1959, pp. 62–3). And he points out that 'lightning' and 'electrical discharge due to the ionization of clouds' differ in meaning, but they both refer to the same kind of phenomenon (1959, p. 63). General terms (or concepts) of neurophysiology differ in meaning from general sensation terms (or concepts), but every general sensation term is co-referential with some general term of neurophysiology, some general term of either current neurophysiology or some recognizable descendent of current neurophysiology.

Smart's main contribution to the identity theory of consciousness in 'Sensations and Brain Processes' is his useful replies to a series of objections to the theory. Some of the objections are clearly fallacious, appealing to epistemic considerations to argue for the ontological conclusion that conscious states are not neural states. One of the objections Smart discusses, however, 'objection 3', which he credits to Max Black, is truly formidable. Black's objection begins with the observation that although, for instance, 'The Morning Star' and

'The Evening Star' have the same referent, the descriptions pick out the referent by appeal to different properties, namely, the property of appearing in the morning and the property of appearing in the evening, respectively. Since sensation terms and neural terms have different meanings, they must pick out their referents by appeal to different properties. An issue that arises is thus whether the properties by which the referents of sensation terms are determined are neural properties. Smart puts the concern this way: 'a sensation can be identified with a brain process only if it has some phenomenal property, not possessed by brain processes, whereby one-half of the identification may be, so to speak, pinned down' (1959, p. 64). But that is an incorrect formulation of the objection since the objection is not that the phenomenal property is not possessed by a brain process. The objection is not to token identity theory, but rather to type or property identity theory. Black appears to have been challenging Smart to explain why he rejects a dual aspect theory, according to which brain processes have two kinds of aspects, neurophysiological aspects and conscious or phenomenal aspects (as, we might note, on the British Emergentist view). Indeed, the objection, reformulated as an argument, became dubbed 'the Property Dualism Argument' in the subsequent literature. There have been various attempts to formulate the argument (an argument that is different from the knowledge argument) in the subsequent literature and various responses to it have been given on behalf of the identity theory.[9] Given our limited space here, we will focus on Smart's ingenious reply to the objection, rather than on the objection itself; for Smart's reply, whether successful or unsuccessful, invokes a notion that is his main contribution to the debate over the identity theory.

Smart's reply to Black's objection is that terms (and concepts) for conscious states are 'topic-neutral', by which he means that their reference is determined by a topic-neutral description or property. He illustrates the idea with the example of 'seeing a yellowish-orange after image'. He asserts:

> When a person says, "I see a yellowish-orange after image," he is saying something like "*There is something going on which is like what is going on when* I have my eyes open, am awake, and there is an orange in front of me, that is, when I really see an orange." (64) (Italics his.)

The description 'something is going on which is like what is going on when . . . I really see an orange' is topic-neutral in that it leaves open whether the something in question is a mental occurrence or a physical occurrence. Empirical investigation, Smart maintains, will reveal that it is a physical occurrence, specifically a neural occurrence. This response can be explicated as follows in terms of the connotation/denotation distinction. Terms for states of consciousness connote topic-neutral properties (properties that could be possessed by mental or physical entities), but empirical investigation will reveal that the properties the terms denote are neural properties.

Smart's topic-neutral analysis of 'seeing a yellowish-orange after image' is clearly inadequate. Chalmers (1996, p. 360) notes that there will be a great deal of biochemical activity going on in us when we see a yellowish-orange after image, and asks which of these processes our term (or concept) of seeing a yellowish-orange after image is supposed to pick out as the referent of the term, according to Smart. Thus, one problem is that Smart's topic-neutral characterization isn't specific enough to pick out a unique referent. The description 'the *something going on which is like what is going on when . . .*' is an improper description, like 'the Moon of Jupiter'. One might read 'like' in the description as 'experientially like', which would considerably pare down the candidate referents, but then the description would not be topic-neutral; for only experiences (conscious states and events) can be experientially like experiences. In response to this concern, in a much later work (Smart 2012), Smart suggested revising the analysis by replacing 'what is going on' with 'what typically goes on', thus yielding the description 'there is something going on which is like what typically goes on when . . .', where cases of having an after image are understood to be atypical. But problems remain. One is that one can have a full understanding of the term 'seeing a yellowish-orange after image' without even having the concept of an orange (a kind of fruit). Although the topic neutral analysis he proposes for 'seeing a yellowish-orange after image' is inadequate, his general notion of a topic neutral analysis had a profound influence, inspiring certain later lines of theorizing that are still very widely deployed.

David Armstrong's central state materialism appeals to a refinement of Smart's topic-neutral analysis (1968, 1981; see Chapter 7). Armstrong's topic neutral analysis is given in terms of a state's causal role, its role as cause and role as effect. Armstrong maintains that all mental concepts, those of conscious states included, are inherently *causal* in nature. A description of the form 'the state that is apt to have such-and-such effects and/or apt to be the effect of so-and-so causes' is a topic neutral description of the state in question. If our mental concepts can be given such topic neutral analyses in terms of causal roles, then we can look to science to determine what state types (or properties) occupy the causal roles in question, and so answer to the mental concepts.

David Lewis's (1972, and again Chapter 7) identity theory of mind also employs a refined notion of a topic neutral analysis. He maintained that our mental terms are implicitly defined by the platitudes of folk psychology, which include 'all of the platitudes you can think of regarding the causal relations of mental states, sensory stimuli, and motor responses' as well as 'the platitudes to the effect that one mental state falls under another – "toothache is a type of pain" and the like' (1972, p. 92). One can, in principle, conjoin all of the platitudes of folk psychology and then quantify over the general mental terms in the conjunction. From that quantificational sentence, a Ramsey sentence, one can derive the definitions in questions. The *definiens* of the definitions will be topic neutral descriptions. Thus, the idea is that the platitudes associate a type of mental state with a certain role, one which includes a causal role. And a definition for the mental term is derived by the method of Ramsification, where the *definiens* is a topic neutral definite description. Lewis maintains that the states that answer to the defining topic neutral descriptions in question will be neural states. Lewis's identity theory is often called 'filler functionalism', because the topic neutral descriptions functionally characterize mental state types, and the theory identifies mental state types with the state types that fill the relevant functional roles.

Hilary Putnam (1967; see Chapter 8) raised an objection to the identity theory of consciousness that Place and Smart did not anticipate, though, as we will see later, Feigl anticipated. The objection has been enormously influential. Putnam noted that beings that are very different physically can be in some of the same mental states. For example, it is plausible that octopi feel pain. He pointed out that it may very well be the case the neural state in humans that occupies the role folk psychology associates with pain is different from any state octopi are ever in. If that is indeed the case, and if humans and octopi both feel pain, then the identity theory is false.

Lewis's (1972) response is that mental states are relative to normal members of a species. Thus, there are pains for humans, pains for octopi, pains for dogs and so on. Pain for humans is the state that occupies the appropriate role, call it 'the pain role' (though keep in mind the description must be physical and topic neutral) in normal humans; pain for octopi is the state that occupies the pain role in normal octopi; and so on and so forth.

A number of philosophers objected to this relativization of mental states (see, e.g. Block 1980). They maintained that rather than defining mental states as states that occupy a certain role, functionalists should define mental states as certain second-order states: states of being in some state or other that occupies the relevant role. Thus, continuing to use 'the pain role' as shorthand for a topic neutral description, instead of defining 'pain' as the state that occupies the pain role, 'pain' is properly defined as the state of being in some state or other that occupies the pain role. Both humans and octopi can be in pain – in pain *simpliciter*. For they can both be in the second-order state of being in some state or other that occupies the pain role. It is just that the first-order state that occupies the pain role in humans may very well be different from the first-order state that occupies the pain role in octopi. A notion of 'realization' is invoked in this connection, where realization is to be understood as the relation of role occupancy. Thus, a first-order state realizes a second-order state by occupying the role in question. A given type of mental state (a second-order state) can be realized by more than one first-order state. Thus, mental states can be 'multiply realizable'. This view of mental states, often called 'role functionalism', is also an identity theory, though not one that entails that mental states are neural states. Rather, on this view, mental states are identical to second-order states, ones that can be defined in physical and/or topic neutral terms. And it is taken to be an open empirical question whether, for instance, a silicon-based android could share mental states with us, even though the android lacks any neurophysiology. Whether a silicon-based android can share mental states with us just depends on whether it can be in states that realize the relevant roles.

Because filler-functionalism seems to require relativization of mental states to kinds of beings, most functionalists nowadays reject filler-functionalism, maintaining instead role-functionalism. An insufficiently appreciated drawback of the role-functionalist view in comparison with the filler-functionalist view, however, is that while on the filler-functionalist view the mental states themselves occupy the causal roles that folk psychology associates with them, on the role-functionalist view, they don't. The state of being in some state or other that occupies role R is not itself a state that occupies role R; its first-order realizations are what occupy R. Thus, if role-functionalism is correct, then mental states themselves do not occupy the causal roles that folk psychology associates with them; rather only their realizers occupy those roles. Thus, pains never cause us to wince or cry out, rather physical realizers of pain do.[10]

There are a number of further, truly formidable, concerns about the identity theory of consciousness that Place, Feigl and Smart did not anticipate.

As we noted, Feigl and Smart maintained that it is empirical that conscious states are identical with neural states, by which they meant at least that the relevant identity claims are knowable only a posteriori. But Feigl also seemed to hold that they are contingent, and Smart explicitly claimed they are contingent. Saul Kripke (1971), however, has taught us that there is no contingent identity. Kripke convincingly argued that if A = B, then necessarily A = B. He derived that thesis, the necessity of identity thesis, a priori from two principles that seem themselves to be a priori. The first is that everything is such that it is necessarily identical to itself. (How could something fail to be identical to itself?) The second is Leibniz's indiscernibility of identicals, which is, you will recall, the thesis that if A = B, then whatever is true of A is true of B and whatever is true of B is true of A. Given that everything is such that it is necessarily identical to itself, A is necessarily identical to A. Given the indiscernibility of identicals, if A is identical to B, then B is necessarily identical to A. Thus, if A is identical to B, then necessarily A is identical to B. There is no contingent identity.

That fact, however, may seem at first blush to present no serious problem for Feigl and Smart, for their essential point seems to be that the psychophysical identity claims in question are a posteriori. And Kripke himself noted that although there is no contingent identity, identity claims can be a posteriori. One of his paradigm examples is 'Water is H_2O', which is, as he notes, both necessarily true and yet knowable only a posteriori. So, it may seem that Feigl and Smart can give up the claim that the relevant psychophysical identity claims are contingent and maintain simply that they are a posteriori.

Kripke pointed out, however, that identity theorists face a serious challenge. For, he maintained, when one asserts a claim that is a posteriori yet non-contingent, one incurs a certain dialectical obligation; and if it cannot be discharged, then the statement will not be adequately justifiable. Since the claim is a posteriori, there will be an illusion of contingency; the statement will appear contingent even though it is not in fact contingent (1980, p. 330). The dialectical obligation is to explain away the appearance of contingency of the statement. Kripke provided a model for explaining away the appearance of contingency of an a posteriori necessary claim that he illustrated with the example of 'Water is H_2O'. He noted that that statement seems contingent, because it seems to us that we can imagine (or conceive of) water that is not H_2O. But he argued that we cannot in fact imagine (or conceive of) water that is not H_2O. Although it naively seems to us that we are imagining water that is not H_2O, what we are in fact imagining is an epistemic counterpart of water that is not H_2O. An epistemic counterpart of water is a kind of stuff that looks, smells, tastes, feels and observably behaves (where the observations are unaided) like water. Water is of course an epistemic counterpart of itself. But Kripke noted that an epistemic counterpart of water can fail to be water. What we are in fact imagining is actually possible. It is possible for there to be an epistemic counterpart of water that is not H_2O. And it is that fact, he maintained, that explains away the appearance of contingency of 'Water is H_2O'. Kripke pointed out, however, that this model for explaining away the appearance of contingency of a non-contingent yet a posteriori identity claim is inapplicable to identity claims such as 'Pain is N', where N is a kind of neural state (or indeed any kind of physical state). The reason it is inapplicable is this. An epistemic counterpart of pain is something that feels just like pain. But anything that feels just like pain is pain, for pain is a kind of feeling.

Kripke (1980) himself noted, though, that although the thesis of the necessity of identity holds, there are contingent statements of identity. An example of a contingent statement of identity is 'Benjamin Franklin is the inventor of bifocals'. That statement is contingent since, clearly, Benjamin Franklin might not have been the inventor of bifocals; Newton, for instance, might have been the inventor of bifocals. Kripke maintained that some designating terms are 'rigid' in that they designate the same thing in any possible world in which they designate anything; and some are 'non-rigid' in that they can designate different things in different possible worlds. (Possible worlds can be understood here as ways the world might be.) Proper names, he claimed, are rigid designators, and thus 'Benjamin Franklin' is a rigid designator. But the description 'the inventor of bifocals' is non-rigid since it can designate different individuals in different possible worlds. A statement of identity can be contingent if one of the terms flanking the identity sign is a non-rigid designator. But when the terms flanking the identity sign are both rigid designators, then the identity statement is non-contingent. Kripke (1980) maintains that mental terms such as 'pain' are rigid designators; the term, he maintains, rigidly designates a kind of feeling. And he holds that any candidate theoretical terms of neuroscience will also be rigid designators. Where N is a rigid designator of neurophysiology (or indeed of any physical state type), a statement of the form 'Pain is N' will be non-contingent; if it is true, it is necessarily true, and if it is false, it is necessarily false. He thus claimed that the identity theorist is committed to necessary yet a posteriori identity claims, and so incurs the dialectical obligation of explaining away the appearance of contingency of such statements. And his model, he notes, is unavailable to explain away their appearance of contingency. Thus, identity theorists face the challenge of explaining away the appearance of contingency of the relevant psychophysical identity statements.

Notice that this challenge, 'Kripke's challenge', also arises for role-functionalism about pain. A description such as 'The state of being in some state or other such that . . .' is a rigid designator. It is false that the state of being in some state or other such that *such-and-such* might not have been the state of being in some state or other such that *such-and-such*. The description rigidly picks out a second-order state; that is so, even though the second-order state is multiply realizable. If such a description defines 'pain', then 'pain' too is a rigid designator. Thus, the 'is' of identity will be flanked by rigid designators in the identity statement 'Pain is the state of being in some state or other such that . . .'. It follows that role-functionalism, which asserts that types of mental states are identical to types of second-order states, also faces Kripke's challenge.

Lewis's filler-functionalism, also a kind of identity theory, does not face Kripke's challenge. The reason is that the topic neutral descriptions that he maintains define mental terms are not rigid designators; and if they indeed define mental terms, then mental terms are not rigid designators. In particular, if he is right that 'pain' can be defined by a topical neutral description of the form 'the state such that . . .', where what fills in the blank characterizes a role as explained above, then 'pain' is not a rigid designator. (The state such that such-and-such might not have been the state such that such-and-such.)[11] Moreover, specific type identity statements such as that state type N is pain for normal human beings are not only a posteriori, they are contingent statements of identity since 'pain' is non-rigid. Such statements are a posteriori and contingent. So, Kripke's challenge does not arise for them. As will also now be clear to the alert reader, Kripke's challenge fails to arise for Smart's view. The reason is that his topic neutral descriptions are not rigid designators, and so he is committed to denying that terms such as 'pain' are rigid designators.

The fact that role-functionalism faces Kripke's challenge and Lewis's filler-functionalism doesn't may seem to be a good reason to embrace filler-functionalism instead. One could still hold that all organisms in a certain conscious state share a second-order state, one would just deny that the second-order state is the conscious state. And one could give the following justification for doing so: the conscious state occupies the causal role in question, and the second-order state doesn't. (To repeat: the state of being in a state that has a certain causal role does not itself have that causal role). But one problem with filler-functionalism is the one we mentioned. The occupant of the causal role can vary from species to species. So, filler-functionalism seems required to relativize mental states to kinds of beings. That seems unpalatable. And, unfortunately, it seems unpalatable because terms such as 'pain' and the like seem to be rigid designators. 'Pain' indeed seems to rigidly designate a kind of feeling, one which we are acquainted with in our own case. An organism is in pain if and only if it has that feeling, regardless of the causal role the feeling may have in the organism.

Contemporary identity theorists typically acknowledge that the identity claims they assert are necessary yet a posteriori. Moreover, they acknowledge that Kripke's model for explaining away their appearance of contingency is inapplicable for the very reasons that Kripke gives. They seek an alternative model to Kripke's for explaining away the appearance of contingency of such claims. One such model has been proposed by Christopher Hill (2001); another has been proposed by David Papineau (2002); see also Polger (2004).

(For a discussion of advantages of Hill's model over Kripke's, see McLaughlin (2011)). Let it suffice to note that identity theorists are attempting to meet Kripke's challenge head on, but it remains a topic of dispute whether they can succeed in meeting it.

There is a problem with both filler-functionalism and role-functionalism that seems fatal. And it seems a fatal problem for Smart's view and Armstrong's view as well. Place and Feigl held a 'two language' view, according to which statements about consciousness as such and statements about neurophysiological states as such are 'logically independent', by which they meant there are no analytical implications in either direction from statements of the one sort to statements of the other sort. That point, as Place and Feigl no doubt recognized, generalizes to physical statements of any sort. Moreover, it generalizes as well to topic-neutral statements. There seem to be no relevant analytical connections between mental concepts and physical and/or topic neutral concepts. Jerry Fodor and Ned Block (1975) argued that both inverted-qualia and absent-qualia cases are coherently imaginable.[12] Inverted-qualia cases are cases in which two types of states have exactly the same causal role (specified in physical and/or topic neutral terms) yet one is associated with a quale that is 'inverted' relative to the quale with which the other is associated. For example, one state might be associated with the what-it-is-like-for-the-subject aspect of visual experiences of yellow and the other might be associated with the what-it-is-like-for-the subject aspect of visual experiences of blue (the opponent colour of yellow). In absent-qualia cases, a state has the causal role that folk psychology (or indeed even scientific psychology) associates with a certain quale (e.g. the feel of pain) and yet the state has no associated qualia at all.[13] The fact that such cases are coherently imaginable arguably does not show that they are possible. But it refutes the claim that concepts of consciousness can be analytically defined in physical and/or topic neutral terms. Analytical functionalism, whether the filler version or the role version, is false for phenomenal consciousness. (It is a separate issue whether one or the other version of functionalism is right where intentional mental states such as beliefs, desires, and intentions are concerned).

There can be, however, an a priori connection without an analytical connection. Kripke (1980) noted that there are contingent yet a priori reference-fixing descriptions for certain terms. He noted that the referent of 'meter' was initially fixed as the length of the metre bar in Paris. That was, in 1889, a contingent a priori reference-fixing condition for the term. It is a priori because it is simply stipulated, and it is contingent because it cites an inessential property of a metre. Some philosophers, including Frank Jackson (1998) and David Chalmers (1996), have maintained that even though kind terms such as 'water' do not have analytical definitions, they have contingent a priori reference-fixing descriptions. The a priori reference-fixing description for 'water' would be (very roughly) something like 'the clear, potable, liquid around here that falls from the sky when it rains, that fills much of the oceans and rivers, . . .'. Although 'water' cannot be analytically defined by such a description and the property cited in the description is not an essential property of water, they maintain that such a description nevertheless a priori fixes the reference of 'water', and so is a contingent a priori reference-fixer. So, an identity theorist might look for descriptions couched in physical and topic neutral terms that are contingent a priori reference fixers for terms for states of consciousness, rather than definiens for them.

Such a search would be in vain. The reason is that there are no contingent, a priori reference-fixing descriptions for terms for states of consciousness.[14] Not only are concepts of states of consciousness not analytically definable in terms of physical and/ or topic neutral concepts, there are no relevant a priori connections between concepts of states of consciousness and physical and/or topic neutral concepts.

In roughly the last two decades, some physicalists have maintained that the identity theory of consciousness is defensible, even though there are no physical and/or topic neutral a priori sufficient conditions for being in a conscious state of any sort.[15] Folk psychology yields not analytical definitions of terms for states of consciousness or even a priori sufficient conditions for their application, but rather defeasible criteria for their application. The defeasible criteria can be appealed to in order to help identify what kinds of neural states are correlated with kinds of states of consciousness. But the search for 'neural correlates of consciousness' will also have to deploy the resources of neuroscience, including sophisticated equipment such as fMRIs. Currently, there are in the field of neuroscience various programs for finding the neural correlates of types of states of consciousness. What we will call 'a strict neural correlate' of a type of state of consciousness C (e.g. pain) is a type of neurobiological state N such that it is true and counterfactual supporting that a being is in C if and only if it is in N. It is, of course, an empirical question whether there are strict neural correlates of types of states of consciousness in this sense. And even if such true counterfactual supporting generalizations could be found for every type of state of consciousness (a controversial empirical issue), the question would nevertheless very much remain whether C is (is identical to) N. Appeals to Ockham's razor, such as Smart's (1959) appeal, will by no means decide the issue. It is coherently conceivable that N is a distinct type of state from C, and that N and C are merely strictly correlated as a matter of law. The law might be an emergent law in Broad's sense. It is an open question whether the fundamental laws of nature are small in number and systematically well integrated; perhaps the nomological structure of reality is as grotesquely shaped as the emergentist maintains it is. Moreover, even if we found strict neurobiological correlates for all states of consciousness, it seems that we would still face what Chalmers (1995) calls 'the hard problem of consciousness'. Thus, suppose that one of those strict correlations is that a being is in C if and only if the being is in N. In this instance, the hard problem would be to answer the question, Why does N give rise to C rather than to some other type of state of consciousness or to no state of consciousness at all?

The answer contemporary identity theorists give is that were we to find such a system of strict correlations, then, we would be in a position to maintain that the question is wrong-headed in that its presupposition is false. N does not give rise to C. Rather, N is C. The currently leading type identity strategy is to argue for the following conditional claim: if a system of true, counterfactual supporting generalizations can be found that strictly correlates every type of states of consciousness with a type of neurobiological state, then the best explanation of those generalizations would be that types of states of consciousness are identical to their strict neurobiological correlates. The type identity claims would thus be justified by inference to the best explanation. This justificatory strategy was, to the best of our knowledge, first proposed by Christopher Hill (1992). Jaegwon Kim (2005) has recently attacked the strategy on a number of grounds, including the grounds that identity claims cannot be justified by inference to the best explanation because identity claims are not explanatory. McLaughlin (2010) has responded to all of the strands of Kim's attack on the strategy. As concerns the issue of whether identity claims can be explanatory, McLaughlin argues that Kim ignores the epistemic conditions on explanation and claims that identity claims play a role in meeting those conditions.

There is also, though, you will recall, Putnam's claim that organisms that are very physically different from us may share certain types of states of consciousness with us. Of course, it does not follow from that claim that type identity theory is false for states of consciousness. (Compare the fallacious argument that since coffee, breath and steel can all be hot, there is no (first order) property that they have in common. In fact, they have in common a mean–kinetic energy that exceeds a certain threshold.) Still, though, given the necessity of identity, even if it is merely metaphysically possible for beings to share a type of conscious state with us without sharing a type of neurobiological state with us, then that conscious state type is not identical to a neurobiological state type. So, the issue Putnam raises must be addressed.

Although the issue is too complex to address properly here,[16] several points are worth noting in response to Putnam's concern about type identity theory. A type of state of consciousness might be a highly determinable neurobiological state, one shared by different species. Moreover, it is by no means clear that octopi actually share feelings of pain with us, which is by no means to deny that they are sometimes in states that bear certain functional resemblances to the neural states that occupy the pain role in us. As Feigl (1958) notes, anticipating Putnam's concern, there is good reason to deny that insects, for example, are conscious. Ants engage in escape behaviour when injured, but have very few neurons; and when, for instance, a limb is injured, they don't put any less pressure on the limb. Further, although bees, for example, see, and indeed arguably have visual representations, it is a different matter whether they have visual experiences. It may well not be like anything for a bee as a subject to see something. Bees have only about one million neurons; moreover, most of their visual processing occurs in their eyes. Vision scientists have discovered that vision involves at least two separate streams in our brains: the ventral stream and the dorsal stream.[17] What goes on the ventral stream is associated with our visual consciousness, but what goes on in the dorsal stream is not, though it has direct links to our motor control system. It could well be that animals such as, for example, iguanas, process visual information through a dorsal stream that is not associated with consciousness (McLaughlin 2006b). It may be that only higher animals are phenomenally conscious. Hill (1991) has argued that if we were to find strictly neurobiological correlates of states of consciousness in humans and members of neighbouring species (all mammals, say), we could be in a position to justifiably deny that beings without those neurobiological states have our states of consciousness.[18]

What, however, about the possibility of conscious androids that are silicon based, rather than carbon based, but that have exactly the same behavioural dispositions as a normal conscious human beings? Feigl raised the issue of androids and said: 'As regards the mental life of robots, or . . . "androids", I cannot believe that they could display all (or even most) of the characteristics of human behaviour unless they were made of the proteins that constitute the nervous system—and in that case they would present no puzzle' (1958, p. 71). But silicon-based androids that are behavioural duplicates of human beings certainly seem possible, even if, to the disappointment of AI researchers, they should turn out to be nomologically impossible (to be ruled out by the laws of nature). So, let's grant that such androids are metaphysically possible. The issue is not whether such an android would be intelligent, have beliefs and preferences, and speak a language. The issue is whether such an android would be phenomenally conscious – would have qualia. Given how different such a being would be from us in material composition and structure, the only evidence we would have for its being consciousness is behavioural evidence. Such evidence is defeasible. (Indeed, there are, to repeat, no a priori physical and/ or topic neutral sufficient conditions of any sort for any state of consciousness.) Arguably, when we attribute states of consciousness on the basis of behaviour, we are engaged in a kind of 'same effects/ same cause' reasoning. When we discover that the physical internal states that cause the android's behaviour are very different from the physical internal states that cause the behaviour in us and that are associated with our conscious states,[19] that would defeat the behavioural evidence that the android has conscious states. We would then be left without any (undefeated) evidence that it is phenomenally conscious. One type identity theorist position on such androids is that they may be conscious, but would not have any of our conscious states (Perry 2001, Shoemaker 2007). But some type identity theorists maintain that were we to find strict neurobiological correlates of conscious states in humans and members of neighbouring species (and were we able to answer adequately the objections to the identity theory other than Putnam's objection), then if the android had none of those neurobiological states, we would be in a position to justifiably deny that the android is phenomenally conscious (Hill 1991, McLaughlin 2003a).[20]

Even if both Kripke's and Putnam's challenges can be successfully met (matters of considerable controversy), other truly formidable challenges remain. One deserves special mention since it underlies some of the others (e.g. the objection to the identity theory from the knowledge argument). Thomas Nagel (1974) has pointed out that states of consciousness are subjective states; to fully understand them, we must know what it is like as a subject to be in them; and that requires the ability to successfully empathetically take up a certain kind of experiential point of view. In contrast, physical states such as those of neuroscience and the physical sciences are objective states (or at least much more objective or intersubjective than states of consciousness).[21] How could a subjective state be an objective state? For that matter, how could an objective state be a subjective state? The challenge Nagel poses for identity theorists is to answer those questions.

This challenge too was anticipated by Feigl (1958). And he gestured in the direction of a response:

> The identification of raw feels with neural states, however, crosses what in metaphysical phraseology is sometimes called an "ontological barrier." It connects the "subjective" with the "intersubjective." ... [In] my view, of the matter there is no longer here an unbridgeable gulf, and hence no occasion for metaphysical shudders ... private states known by direct acquaintance and referred to by phenomenal (subjective) terms can be described in a public (at least physical) language and may thus be empirically identifiable with the referents of certain neural terms. (1958, p. 70)

Contemporary identity theorists hold a 'two-language' position, maintaining that our physical terms (both folk and scientific) and our terms for states of consciousness express different kinds of concepts, indeed concepts with conceptual roles so different that there are no a priori links between them. The leading contemporary type identity theory response to Nagel is that the objective/subjective distinction is, in the first instance, an epistemic distinction, a distinction based on ways of understanding. Type identity theorists maintain that a property is subjective or objective only under a conceptualization, that is, only under a concept. And they maintain that a property can be objective under one concept (e.g. a neurobiological concept) and subjective under another (e.g. the concept of pain) (Loar 1990, Sturgeon 1994, McLaughlin 2003a). Conceptual dualism is thus combined with property monism.

It remains an open question whether the identity theory of consciousness is correct. There is, however, no question that Place, Feigl and Smart deservedly occupy an esteemed place in twentieth-century philosophy of mind for their pioneering work.

Notes

1. The revolution in psychology that overthrew behaviourism, the cognitive revolution, began, rather, with Noam Chomsky's 1959 review of Skinner's *Verbal Behavior*.
2. This reference and all of the page references to Place, Feigl, Smart, Armstrong and Kripke in the text are to pages in excerpts reprinted in Chalmers 2002.
3. Gilbert Harman (1990), Fred Dretske (1995) and Michael Tye (1995) maintain that these qualitative aspects of experiences are intentional.
4. It is worth noting, however, that Place, in his discussion of what he called 'the phenomenal fallacy' anticipates some aspects of the contemporary defence of the intentionality of phenomenal consciousness. We also note that we ourselves maintain that the fact that what it is like for a subject to have a visual experience is intentional, in the sense that it is to be as if presented with an environmental scene, is compatible with an identity theory of the qualitative aspects of visual experiences. More generally, we deny that identity theorist must reject the claim that qualia are intentional.
5. The term 'the knowledge argument' comes from Jackson 1984.
6. Here is Bertrand Russell's elegant version of the knowledge argument published two years after Broad, 1925: 'It is obvious that a man who can see knows things which a blind man cannot know; but a blind man can know the whole of physics. Thus, the knowledge which other men have and he has not is not a part of physics' (1927, 389).
7. For a very sympathetic treatment of Broad's emergentist view of conscious properties, see Chalmers 1996.

8   For further discussion of this sort of response to the knowledge argument, see McLaughlin 2012.
9   See, e.g., Loar 1990; Hill 1991; Perry 2003; and Block forthcoming.
10 For further discussion, see Kim 1996 and McLaughlin 2006a. See also Chapter 15.
11 There is a narrow scope reading of that sentence on which it is false, but the relevant reading is the wide-scope reading. It should also be mentioned that although any description can be turned into a rigid designator by inserting 'actual' (e.g. the description 'the actual inventor of bifocals' is rigid), the identity accounts in question do not appeal to rigidified descriptions.
12 They coined the terms 'inverted qualia' and 'absent qualia'.
13 There are also 'absent role' cases (Hill 1991). An example of an absent role case is a case in which someone feels pain, but is not in any state with the causal role (specified in physical and/or topic neutral terms) that folks psychology associates with pain. There are actual absent role cases. People suffering from locked in syndrome can feel pain and have conscious thoughts, feel emotions and so on. Also in horrific cases of anaesthetic awareness, a patient can be fully conscious, consciously thinking and feeling intense pain and emotions, yet be so completely paralysed that even their autonomic system is shut down, so that the patient cannot even breathe on his own.
14 In the terminology of two dimensional semantics, a term (concept) of consciousness will have the same primary and secondary intension (Chalmers 1996).
15 See, e.g., Loar 1990; Hill 1991; Hill and McLaughlin 1999; Papineau 2002; McLaughlin 2001, 2003b, 2006b, 2010, 2011.
16 But see Hill 1991; Perry 2001; Polger 2004; McLaughlin 2006b; and Shoemaker 2007.
17 See, e.g., Goodale and Milner 1992.
18 Such a justification would, of course, require answering all of the other challenges to the type identity theory discussed in this essay (as well as some others).
19 That there is an association between neural states and conscious states is compatible with all of the leading theories of consciousness.
20 For further discussion of the issues raised by certain androids, see Block 2002 and McLaughlin 2003b.
21 The same is true of role-functional states defined in physical and topic neutral terms: they are objective states. So, role functionalism too faces the challenge we are about to raise.

References

Alexander, S. (1920), *Space, Time and Deity*, 2 vols. London: Macmillan.
Armstrong, D. M. (1968), *A Materialist Theory of Mind*. London: Routledge & Kegan Paul.
— (1981), *The Nature of Mind and Other Essays*. Ithaca: Cornell University. Excerpted (pp. 15–31) in Chalmers, 2002, pp. 80–7.
Block, N. (1980), 'What is functionalism?' In N. Block (ed.), *Readings in the Philosophy of Psychology*, vol. 1. Cambridge, MA: MIT Press.
— (2002), 'The Harder Problem of Consciousness'. *Journal of Philosophy* 99: 347–425.
— (forthcoming), 'Max Black's objection to the mind-body identity'.
Broad, C. D. (1925), *The Mind and Its Place in Nature*. London: Routledge & Kegan Paul.
Chalmers, D. M. (1995), 'Facing up to the problem of consciousness'. *Journal of Consciousness Studies* 2: 200–19.
— (1996). *The Conscious Mind*. New York: Oxford University Press.
Chomsky, N. (1959), 'A review of B. F. Skinner's "Verbal Behavior"'. *Language* 35: 26–58.
Dretske, F. (1995), *Naturalizing the Mind*. Cambridge, MA: MIT Press.
Feigl, H. (1958). 'The "mental" and the "physical"'. Excerpted in Chalmers, 2002, pp. 68–72. Original article in H. Feigl, M. Scriven and G. Maxwell (eds), *Concepts, Theories and the Mind-Body Problem* (Minnesota Studies in the Philosophy of Science, Volume 2), Minneapolis: University of Minnesota Press. (The article, with a 1969 Postscript, can be found online).
Goodale, M. A. and Milner, A. D. (1992), 'Separate visual pathways for perception and action'. *Trends in Neuroscience* 15: 20–5.
Harman, G. (1990), 'The intrinsic qualities of experience'. *Philosophical Perspectives* 4: 31–52.
Hill, C. (1992), *Type Materialism*. Cambridge: Cambridge University Press.
— (2001), 'Imaginability, conceivability, possibility, and the mind-body problem'. *Philosophical Studies* 87: 61–85.
Hill, C. and McLaughlin, B. P. (1999), 'There are fewer things in reality than are dreamt of in Chalmer's philosophy'. *Philosophy and Phenomenological Research* 59: 445–54.
Jackson, F. (1982), 'Epiphenomenal qualia'. *Philosophical Quarterly* 32: 127–36.
— (1998), *From Metaphysics to Ethics: A Defense of Conceptual Analysis*. Oxford: Oxford University Press.
Kim, J. (1996). *Mind in a Physical World*. Cambridge: Cambridge University Press.

— (2005), *Physicalism or Something Near Enough*. Princeton, NJ: Princeton University Press.
Kripke, S. (1971), 'Identity and necessity'. In M. K. Muntz (ed.), *Identity and Individuation*. New York: New York University Press.
— (1980), *Naming and Necessity*. Cambridge, MA: Harvard University Press. Excerpted in Chalmers, 2002, pp. 329–34.
Lewes, G. H. (1874), *Problems of Life and Mind*, vols. 1–5. London: Kessinger Publishing, LLC.
Lewis, D. (1972), 'Psychophysical and theoretical identifications'. *Australasian Journal of Philosophy* 50: 249–58.
Loar, B. (1990), 'Phenomenal states'. In J. Tomberlin (ed.), *Philosophical Perspectives 4, Action Theory and Philosophy of Mind*. Medina, NY: Ridgeway Publishing Company, pp. 81–108.
McLaughlin, B. P. (2001), 'In defense of new wave materialism: a response to Horgan and Tienson'. In B. Loewer and C. Gillett (eds), *Physicalism and Its Discontents*, Cambridge: Cambridge University Press, pp. 317–28.
— (2003a), 'Color, consciousness, and color consciousness'. In Q. Smith (ed.), *Consciousness: New Essays*, Oxford: Oxford University Press, pp. 97–154.
— (2003b), 'A naturalist–phenomenal realist response to Block's harder problem'. *Philosophical Issues* 13: 163–204.
— (2006a), 'Is role-functionalism committed to epiphenomenalism?' *Journal of Consciousness Studies* 13: 39–66.
— (2006b), 'Type materialism for phenomenal consciousness'. In S. Schneider (ed.), *The Blackwell Companion to Consciousness*. Malden, MA: Basil Blackwell, pp. 431–44.
— (2010), 'Consciousness, type physicalism, and inference to the best explanation'. *Philosophical Issues* 20: 266–304.
— (2011), 'On justifying neurobiologicalism for consciousness'. In S. Gozzano and C. Hill (eds), *New Perspectives on Type Identity*. Cambridge: Cambridge University Press, pp. 206–28.
— (2012), 'Phenomenal concepts and the defense of materialism'. *Philosophy and Phenomenological Research* 84: 206–14.
Nagel, T. (1974), 'What is it like to be a bat?' *Philosophical Review* 83: 435–50.
Papineau, D. (2002), *Thinking About Consciousness*. Oxford: Clarendon Press.
Perry, J. (2001), *Knowledge, Possibility, and Consciousness*. Cambridge, MA: MIT Press.
Place, U. T. (1956), 'Is consciousness a brain process?' Reprinted in Chalmers, 2002, pp. 55–9. Article originally published in *British Journal of Psychology* 47: 44–50.

Polger, T. (2004), *Natural Minds*. Cambridge, MA: MIT Press.
Putnam, H. (1967), 'The Nature of mental states'. In W. H. Capitan and D. D. Merrill (eds), *Art, Mind, and Religion*. Pittsburgh: Pittsburgh University Press.
Shoemaker, S. (2007), *Physical Realization*. Oxford: Oxford University Press.
Smart, J. J. C. (1959), 'Sensations and brain processes'. Reprinted in Chalmers, 2002, pp. 60–7. Originally published in *Philosophical Review* 68: 141–56.
— (2012), 'The mind/brain identity theory'. *The Stanford Encyclopedia of Philosophy* (Winter 2012 Edition), Edward N. Zalta (ed.), URL: http://plato.stanford.edu/archives/win2012/entries/mind-identity/.
Sturgeon, S. (1994), 'The epistemic basis of subjectivity'. *Journal of Philosophy* 91: 221–35.
Tye, M. (1995), *Ten Problems of Consciousness*. Cambridge, MA: MIT Press.

CHAPTER SEVEN

David Lewis, David Armstrong and the causal theory of the mind

David Braddon-Mitchell

David Lewis and David Armstrong are together responsible for one of the great revolutions in the philosophy of mind in the last century. Prior to this, there were, at one level of abstraction, essentially two accounts of the mind. One was a purely introspective model which takes mental states to expose their entire nature in experience, a conception that is so tacitly imbedded in much of the history of philosophy that it is hard to find it being explicitly put that way. A natural pairing with this model was Cartesian dualism (see Chapter 2), but equally various flavours of idealism are versions of it. The other was the newfangled and allegedly naturalistic doctrine of behaviourism (see Chapter 5). Mental states were of course detectable by perception rather than introspection according to this model. For our purposes, philosophical behaviourism will do as a paradigm of the model, according to which mental states don't cause any behaviour because they just are behaviours or dispositions to behave. In any case, they are not internal states.

The Lewis-Armstrong (and we ought add Smart and Place; see Chapter 6) revolution was to combine the internality of the first model – the claim that mental states are internal – with the naturalism of the second model – that they are detectable by perception and other methods central to the natural sciences. Rather than mental states being understood as behaviours, Lewis and Armstrong both insisted that they are *inter alia* whatever causes behaviour. Since the causes of behaviour are naturalistically investigable, mental states get to be naturalistically investigable. And since, in addition, the causes of behaviour are internal, mental states also get to be internal.

The causal theory and behaviourism

In order to understand what motivated the revolution, and how it happened, it will pay to discuss the connection that the view has with philosophical behaviourism. At the time behaviourism seemed to be the antithesis of the new view; the enemy against which it was defined. At some level, that's probably right: but it's misleading in hindsight, because it disguises the important continuities between the views.

A stumbling block to naturalistic theories of the mind prior to behaviourism was that it was hard to see what the conceptual connexion was between any naturalistic state and mental states. The idea that mental states where what we were acquainted with in experience, on the other hand, seemed conceptually secure. That the connexions had to be conceptual was a background assumption in philosophy that essentially delineated the boundary between philosophy and the natural sciences. Add to that Cartesian arguments that the connexions between the states revealed in experience and naturalistic states could only be contingent, and you get a natural path to dualism.

What made behaviourism exciting is that it seemed to provide the required conceptual connexions between the mental and something naturalistic. The thought was that you are *conceptually* deficient if you fail to see that someone who desires, say, cake, and has no overriding desires, moves towards cake. Of course, the behaviourist programme never produced these conceptual analyses systematically – that was one of its signal failures. But setting that aside it at least seemed as though at last there was a philosophically sound conceptual connection between something naturalistic in the form of behaviour, and our idea of the mental. Behaviourists ridiculed the connexions to experience and introspection as unverifiable and unscientific, and played up the conceptual connexions between mental states and behaviours.

So we can write down a principle which might even be right – and at very least its truth is consistent with the failure of the larger behaviourist goals of providing individual analyses of mental states in terms of particular behaviours.

(1) There is a conceptual connexion between mental states and behaviour.

When David Armstrong was working on perception in the 1950s and writing *A Materialist Theory of the Mind* in the 1960s, this principle seemed – as it still does to many – correct.

But adding further, apparently unobjectionable, principles to it, helps explain one of the most unacceptable claims of behaviourism – that mental states are causally inert.

Adding the principle that conceptual connexions are necessary gives us:

(2) There is a necessary connexion between mental states and behaviour.

Noting that casual connexions are generally understood to be contingent we can get:

(3) The causes of behaviour are only contingently connected to behaviour.

And from (2) and (3), we might conclude:

(4) Mental states are not the causes of behaviour.

Of course, behaviourists had a more straightforward reason to reject the idea that mental states cause behaviours. For their doctrine was more precise than that there is *some* kind of conceptual connexion between mental states and behaviour. They – or at least some of them – held that mental states were behaviours. And since nothing causes itself, mental states don't cause behaviour (and, on more subtle versions, a similar conclusion is reached via the doctrine that dispositions are not the causes of their manifestations).

The more general worry laid the foundation of the problem to be solved. How to accept what is right about (1) while allowing mental states to be causally active parts of the natural order? For Armstrong, Smart and Lewis all held that the conceptual connexion is required to philosophically justify the claim that some naturalistically described states are mental.

The causal theory of the mind

The solution to this problem came from thinking about how its shape changes when we consider the precise version of the necessary connexion that a casual theory proposes. According to a causal theory of the mind, we can be more specific about what the conceptual and hence necessary connections are: they are between mental states and being (inter alia) the causes of behaviour. So we get (2*)

> (2*) There is a necessary connexion between mental states and being the cause of behaviour.

This would look no better if were entitled to use (3) – 'The causes of behaviour are only contingently connected to behaviour' – unambiguously. But there are two ways to read (3). On one is it likely right, the other mistaken. On the correct reading, we understand 'the causes of behaviour' to mean the categorical states which are the causes of behaviour. They, surely, are only contingently connected to their effect. On the other, we mean by 'causes of behaviour' the state of being the cause of behaviour – but that state is trivially necessarily connected to the behaviour which it causes, for where there is no causation the state does not obtain.

A very useful analogy is with the concept of poison. There is a conceptual connexion between poisons and the killing of people (perhaps more accurately between there being some dose such that half the subjects of a certain type die or some such, but let's simplify here). But equally, for each cause of death – arsenic, cyanide, etc. – that kills someone, it surely did so only contingently. The subject could have been more robust, they might have vomited, evolution might have gone differently so that stuff was harmless to people and so on. Thus, a very similar argument could be given to the one above that concludes that poisons don't kill people. There is a conceptual and hence necessary connection between poison and death, causes are contingent, so poisons don't cause death.

But just as in the case of mental states there are two readings of 'the poison only contingently causes death'. On the one hand, we talk about the particular substance that is the poison – say the cyanide. And indeed that only contingently causes death. On the other, we say that something is poison only if it causes death, so it's a necessary connexion. What this shows us is that for each actual poison, *it is only contingently a poison*. The poison – say the arsenic – caused the death. But we can say that the poison only contingently caused the death because there are circumstances in which it wouldn't have (and wouldn't have been a poison[1]). The fact that it wouldn't then have been a poison is what preserves the necessary connexions between death and poison on the other reading.

This insight, applied back to the case of mental states and behaviour, is what solves the problem at hand. There can be a necessary connexion between mental states and the causing of behaviour *even though each mental state only contingently causes the state that it does*. This is because the particular physical (let us suppose) state that is the mental state in question is a mental state only in virtue of what it causes,[2] so if it didn't cause that (or failed in some more indirect way) it wouldn't be a mental state. So mental states are only contingently mental. That's the key insight that opens the way to naturalistic and causal theories of the mind that are compatible with the claim that there is a conceptual connexion between mental states and their causal role.

More complex roles

Described in this way, the casual theory seems to be one which simply replaces behaviour with the causes of behaviour. Understanding its genesis this way is very helpful inasmuch as it draws attention to both its continuity with behaviourism and its break from it. But of course even in the earliest writings of Lewis, Armstrong and Smart, the causing of behaviour is only an example of the kinds of casual roles they have in mind. So while many mental states do indeed cause behaviour, equally what defines them is that they are caused by certain features in the environment as well as having casual effects on each other. So to take the example of pain, it's not only the effect of pain states on causing retreat from damage, or particular gesticulations or sounds that is relevant, but also what it is typically caused by – perhaps bodily damage of certain kinds – as well as other mental states, including for example perhaps the belief that a doctor should be called.

Understood in this way as a theory which defines mental states in terms of more complex causal roles, the theory becomes known as functionalism or causal role functionalism. Earlier the theory was known as the Identity Theory or Central State Materialism.

These are sometimes thought to be quite different theories: indeed some histories of philosophy of mind talk of a change from early identity theories, which posit that mental states and material states are identical, to later functional theories, which identify them with causal roles (see Chapter 1).

This however is a misreading of what Lewis meant by functionalism about the mind, and what Armstrong meant when he later endorsed it. There are, perhaps, doctrines called 'functionalism' about the mind which are distinct – more of that later – but for Lewis, Armstrong, Jackson and others the difference in terminology amounts to a difference in emphasis, not a difference in doctrine.

It has to do, I think, with what seemed controversial and interesting at the time. In 1966, David Lewis writes a paper called 'An Argument for the Identity Theory'. Very roughly, the argument is something like this: mental states are the states that play certain causal roles, material states are those states, so mental states are material states. Similarly, the title of Armstrong's book *A Materialist Theory of the Mind* tells us what the emphasis was. The emphasis is on the conclusion, which is that mental states are, as a matter of contingent fact, material. This was the doctrine that was news, and so was in the headlines.

But the philosophical machinery that lead to this conclusion was pretty much the doctrine that later came to be called 'functionalism'. It was the view that mental states are defined by their roles in a complicated causal theory (the *locus classicus* for this is Lewis' paper 'How to Define Theoretical Terms', though it is to be found more or less explicitly in much of Smart and Armstrong), and that the states that played these roles only contingently played these roles – the lesson of early work on the causal theory of the mind. Thus, we can have a theory that tells you what the conceptual truths about the mind are *without* telling you what kind of entities or states actually play the roles specified in the theory. This aspect of functionalism is centre stage in Smart, where he talks of a 'topic neutral' theory, by which he means a theory that tells you what something needs to do to count as mental, but not what things do it. That the 'topic' of mental state talk is the states that actually do the work tells us that Smart's view (along with Lewis' and Armstrong's) is, in nomenclature which only arose later, a version of functionalism according to which mental states are the occupants of roles, not the states of having the role played.[3]

Materialism, or the Identity theory, is what you get when you combine two claims: 'topic neutral' functional theory and the empirical claim that it is material states that do the required work. Both of these claims are in Armstrong's, Lewis' and Smart's early work. But the emphasis early on is on the materialist conclusion that the combination yields. Later, as materialism becomes more of an orthodoxy in philosophy, the emphasis moves to the conceptual component of the argument, which we might call (with some danger of confusion with other views similarly named) functionalism about the mind. Of course, the functionalist component by itself leaves open the possibility that the casual roles are played by ectoplasmic states, or all sorts of odd things. But the kind of naturalism these authors espoused – naturalism about how things actually are – meant that that didn't concern them. They wanted to know whether *actual* mental states, yours and mine and theirs, were material, and they thought that the functional theory together with plausible assumptions about how things actually are would give us that.

Lewis and the circularity objection

One of the most important early contributions to this theory was David Lewis' 'How to Define Theoretical Terms'. He made it explicit (though again there are traces of this in earlier writings) how to solve what we might call the circularity objection.

This objection has its roots in a problem that bedevilled behaviourism. An important goal for some behaviourists was to say, for each mental state, what behaviour or disposition it was identical with. So we might ask ourselves what behaviour is the desire for ice cream? Of course there can be no answer in general.

The behaviour might be moving to the right, or moving to the left, or flying to Venice, or committing suicide. It all depends on the agent's beliefs: whether, in our example, they believe ice cream is to found to the right, the left, only in Venice or only in Hell (this last coupled with appropriate versions of Theism and a very strong desire for ice cream).

Similarly, the agent's other desires are relevant. For other desires might trump the desire for ice cream (such as a desire for life in the last example of the previous paragraph, or in general desires for good health coupled with beliefs about the pernicious effects of ice cream on health).

So the idea that we can define each mental state in terms of behaviour alone is out of the question. But then so too, it seemed, is the reductive ambition of behaviourism.

The problem can appear to remain in the case of the casual theory and functionalism. For each mental state is defined in terms of its causal relations not just to behaviour and to environmental causes, but also to other mental states. For just as no desire is identical to any particular behaviour, so no desire causes only one behaviour. It only causes behaviours in combination with beliefs and other desires. The desire for ice cream causes different behaviours in combination with the belief that ice cream is to the left, to the right, in Hell and so on. Indeed absent any belief it could cause no behaviour, since there would be encoded opinion about how to change the world to get ice cream.

Thus, a simple model according to which each mental state is defined by what it causes or is caused by (in which we do not mention other mental state terms) is just as out of the question as was the behaviourist ambition to individual analyses.

Lewis points out while individual *definitions* will be unavoidably circular, it is possible in principle to define the entire theory in such a way as the definition consists entirely of 'old terms' – that is terms which are not part of the new theory which is to be defined. This definition can then be used to locate the physical items that play the role. The theory will then look like a long existentially quantified statement that says something like '"There is one state, and another, and another ... such that: X", where X describes the casual relations that must obtain between things in order for them to count as the mental states in question'. Such a sentence is commonly called a *Ramsey sentence*, after Frank Ramsey.

Perhaps this is best explained via an example: consider the outmoded model of the atom and its component particles that is still taught in secondary schools. Nothing about its outmodedness matters for our current purposes. The model says that electrons orbit around nuclei, which are composed of protons and neutrons. The protons repel each other, but a strange force keeps them together. The electrons repel each other, but are attracted to the protons.

Imagine an objector who says: But this theory is useless! It gives no non-circular definitions of the particles! For consider the definition of the electron: it is a particle which is repelled by other instances of it, it is attracted to protons, and it orbits around protons and neutrons. This definitions mentions other 'particle terms' – surely we want to do without those. And worse! when we substitute in the definitions of the particles we get this nonsense: electrons are things which orbit things which are orbited by electrons, and which are attracted to things which are attracted to electrons. It's not just that we have failed to eliminate particle terms, each particle turns out to have its own name in the definition! It's viciously circular!

Lewis' point applied to our example is that we can eliminate the names and describe the structure of the theory by existentially quantifying and saying in effect 'There is one kind of thing, and a second, and a third. The first orbits the second and the third. The first is attracted to the second, but repelled by itself. The second is orbited by the first, and found next to the third. The second is attracted to the first, but repelled by itself'.

Described this way, the whole theory mentions only old properties: orbiting, repulsion, proximity and so forth. But we can now name new properties: being an electron is being the first kind of thing, for example. And we can in principle locate electrons and find how they are realized by finding in the world some system organized in the way described by our existentially quantified theory, and seeing what thing it is in the world which is orbited by two other kinds of thing, which is attracted to one of those and so on. Of course, this requires nature to cooperate in having only one kind of system that answers to this definition, which is likely not so for this particular simple and false theory.

By analogy – so goes this response in the case of mental states – when we have made explicit the right theory of the mind, we'll describe a system which is instantiated in various places, and we'll be able to examine the systems and identify the particular, presumably physical, items which play the roles of being various beliefs and so on.

The causal theory, functionalism and the identity theory

This theory, more or less in common between Armstrong Smart and Lewis, has many of the characteristics of what came to be called 'Functionalism'. But 'Functionalism' is a broad church indeed, and there are many doctrines about mental states that get so labelled. So it will be worthwhile distinguishing the present view from others that go by the same name.

Let's start by stating the two general features that the present view shares with all these other functionalisms.

Like most functionalisms, it defines mental states in virtue of three kinds of causal roles. These are the kinds of things in the environment they are caused by (often called *input clauses*), the roles they play in causally affecting other mental states (often called *internal role clauses*) and the kinds of effects they typically cause in the environment (often called *output clauses*). So the roles are not just the simple ones of what causes the states, as in some accounts of perception, or what the states cause in the world.

In addition, the theory is one according to which mental states are *multiply realizable*. This last phrase is just more or less what Smart and others intended by 'topic neutrality'. It is not part of the functional theory what kinds of entities play the causal roles specified. This is something that is to be investigated empirically, and there is no a priori constraint on what these kinds of entities might be. Thus, in humans we might expect the causal roles to be played by neurobiological states, whereas when general Artificial Intelligence is developed, the roles in those entities might be played by something else: siliconaceous states of some sort.

But that is where the general similarities between doctrines called 'functionalism' end, and very serious differences start. These differences revolve around how to understand the two arenas of broad similarity.

The first is the nature of the three-part theory. For Lewis, Smart and Armstrong, it's an a priori theory. It's a theory which is supposed to just make explicit our mastery of the concept of mental state (or of various types of mental state) that we express when we reliably identify them, explain things via belief-desire psychology and so forth. It needs to be a priori in this way to play the role it inherits from the attempted analysis of mental states in terms of behaviour in behaviourism. It is supposed to analyse the nature of mental states, and this is supposed to give the philosophical basis for making the identity claims that the theory makes. Thus, the theory is a kind of *analytical functionalism*.

Other functionalisms allow that the theory can be discovered a posteriori. So for example, versions of what is called 'psychofunctionalism' characterize the inputs at the periphery of the brain, the outputs similarly, and the internal roles as ones which might be discovered in some ideal future cognitive science.

This shows us that relaxing the requirement that the theory be a priori has a knock on effect: it dramatically widens the scope of the kinds of things that can count as inputs, outputs and so forth. For plausibly we have no a priori grasp of roles described in neuroscientific terms. So specifying these roles must be a matter of a posteriori scientific investigation. So relaxing the a priori constraint allows for these new forms of the theory. But these are in principle independent axes of variation. There could be functionalisms that have a theory that involves the similar kinds of connexions as analytic functionalism between stages, behaviours, and inputs that cause the states, but aims to discover them a posteriori. Or there could, in principle, be ways of characterizing the inputs and so forth which are discoverable a priori yet not be matters of behaviour, inputs and internal role (though this rather unpromising location in logical space is not, to the present author's knowledge, yet occupied).

The second area of difference is around what is meant by 'realise' in multiple realization. For Lewis, Armstrong and Smart, the realizer is the mental state. The role just is the thing it does in virtue of which it gets to count as a mental state. This is just as in the case of the simple atomic model discussed earlier where the electron is the physical object that plays those roles. The electron is not some abstract state brought into being by its being the case that something plays the role, for example. The electron is a concrete role-playing object.

The theory is one which leads, therefore, to an identification of mental states with particular states. Hence the focus of Lewis' 1966 paper 'An Argument for the Identity Theory'. But there is a complication here. In the case of the electron, it is hoped that there will be only one kind of system that will realize the theory; and thus only one kind of physical object which will play the electron role. Thus, it is easy to hope for a general type-type theory. The type electron would be identical to an intrinsically characterizable (in principle) physical type.[4]

But this hope is beyond us in the case of the mind. For in this case, it's explicitly expected that physically very different systems might realize the theory. The things that play the belief role in humans will be very different from beings who are in no way related to us in the rest of the universe, and likely very different in distantly related but intelligent beings like octopuses. Thus it's unlikely that the commonalities between them will be visible at any lower level of abstraction that the functional theory itself.

There are two responses to this. One is that it is in any case possible for there to be a token identity theory. Every belief is identical to a particular physical thing, though contingently so.[5]

The other is to say that the identities are type-type, but domain restricted: pain in dolphins is identical to one physical type, pain in humans another, hunger in Martians another and so on. Such a view is defended by Jackson et al. in 'Functionalism and Type-Type Identity Theories', accepted by Armstrong in *The Mind-Body Problem* and proposed by Lewis (with a rider that states-in-a-domain are identical to what the *typical* realizer is in that domain) in 'Mad Pain and Martian Pain'.

This makes the theory very different from other doctrines called 'functionalism', particularly say Hilary Putnam's version (see Chapter 8) and its successors, which identify the mental states with the role state which is realized. For this class of views, the realizer of the mental state is not the mental state – it's just the thing which is its realizer. Rather the mental state is something like the higher-order state of their being some first-order state that realizes the role.[6]

A slew of counterexamples

Of course, the theory has been subject to a large class of putative counterexamples over the years. The most numerous are ones which simply point to odd looking realizations of the theory and then claim, in virtue of the oddness, that these systems could not evince mentality. Ned Block's China Brain[7] and John Searle's Chinese Room[8] are two such. In the first case, we instantiate the roles specified in a theory by all the people in China in electronic communication. Since no individual has any of the experiences that allegedly would be implemented, we are supposed to conclude that there are none. In the second, we instantiate the theory in one person and a large pile of books and manuscripts, and since the person isn't themselves aware of the mental states allegedly so created, conclude that there are none. Replies are that the locus of experience is the total system in both cases, and it's an illusion of scale and location that it's a little hard to see where the mental states are, in the same way it would be if we looked at our own brain neuron by neuron.

Other objections include ones in which it seems that the functional theory cuts too coarsely: there seem intuitively to be differences in mental state between functionally equivalent systems. The so-called inverted spectrum objection is one such, in which we are asked to imagine two individuals whose colour experience is inverted from birth, so they function in the world in exactly the same way. The thought is that while functionally equivalent, they could have different experiences. Functionalist replies range between biting the bullet and denying the possibility of such a difference, to denying the possibility of such a perfect switch, but explaining the intuition that it is possible by what would happen in imperfect reversals.

The counterexample that has perhaps the most discussion is Frank Jackson's Knowledge Argument, in which we are asked to imagine someone who knows all the physical facts about colour experience, light and vision but has never seen colour, coming to see something red for the first time. The new physical state they come to be in on seeing red is nevertheless one that they knew all the physical facts about in advance. The intuition is supposed to be that, despite this, they come to know something new: what the experience of red is *like*, even though they could have – maybe did – predict in advance everything that they would say and do on having the experience. The reply typically is to deny that there any knowledge of that kind to be had[9] coupled with some move to explain the intuitiveness of it: such as that there is some kind of non-propositional thing that one might call 'knowledge' which is indeed gained, but it is not knowledge of any fact.[10]

The slew of counterexamples and replies is indeed vast, and interesting though they are many perhaps don't raise issues about the structural core of the theory. A reasonably up-to-date account of them can be found in Chapters 4 and 5 of Braddon-Mitchell and Jackson's *Philosophy of Mind and Cognition*.[11]

The a priori status of the causal theory

As we have seen, The Smart-Lewis-Armstrong theory differs from some contemporary philosophy of mind by its insistence that the theory in question is a priori. This has some benefits; it helps to ensure that we have an answer to the claim that we are not changing the subject when we claim that a certain theory is a theory of the mind. It also avoids a potential problem with a posteriori theories when applied to the case of the mind. We might have an a posteriori theory of, say, lightning which allows us to identify it with a certain kind of upwards energy transfer from the ground to the clouds. But ultimately, these kind of observational theories require something close to an a priori that lightning is whatever causes experiences of a certain sort (even if those experiences are of metre readings rather than impressive storms). It's when we discover the nature of whatever it is that seems to cause those experiences we know what lightning is. Such a move in the case of mental states – especially perceptual ones – might be circular in a bad way that no lengthy Ramsey sentence can cure. And not just circular but false: perceptual states are not the cause of perceptual states. They are what is caused by inputs of a certain kind, but that is a priori.

So perhaps the a priori nature of the theory is a benefit as against its functionalist rivals on the one side. Or perhaps not. But if we do accept this, we then have a problem dealing with neo-dualist objections on the left. For they too trade in a priori claims, like experience is that with whose nature is we are wholly acquainted in experience. And from some fairly plausible such principles come versions of David Chalmers' zombie argument, which holds that since it is logically possible that there be a minimal physical duplicate of actuality (i.e. one which is the same in every physical way and has nothing added) which lacks mentality, there must be in actuality some extra, non-physical mental element (see Chapter 14).

Now technically, the Lewis-Armstrong style of theory has no problem with this. For it is a priori that mental states are whatever plays certain causal roles. And it is plausible that whatever is a minimal physical duplicate of reality is a functional duplicate of reality. And thus it is a mental duplicate of reality. And since all of this is a priori, it is of course inconceivable that there could be philosophical zombies (physical duplicates with a conscious difference) as that would be contradictory.

One could just stamp one's foot here: but it then looks like we have something too strong. It turns out that the a priori principles of Lewis and Armstrong rule out arguments for dualism of a certain kind.[12] For it seems that even if it is far-fetched, epiphenomenalist dualism (i.e. where the dualistic states play no causal role) epistemically *could* be true, however unlikely it seems. According to the causal theory of the mind, or analytic functionalism, it is straightforwardly a priori that epiphenomenalism is false.

Defenders and developers of the analytical functionalist approach of Lewis, Armstrong and co. in recent years have suggested modifying what is a priori and analytic to something like a conditional[13]: If there are no non-physical states of a certain kind whose nature is revealed in experience, then mental states are whatever plays certain causal roles; otherwise, the mental states are the occupants of the causal roles. This modification allows independent assessment of the credentials of dualistic theories, but tells us that if they are found wanting, then mental states are the occupants of functional roles in the standard way. But it is no longer straightforwardly analytic that epiphenomenalism is false.[14] The a priori nature of the conditional is justified by the thought that it captures a systematic tendency for agents to form judgements in different circumstances. On the one hand, people who come to believe in non-physical epiphenomenal states whose nature is wholly revealed in experience will generally never conclude that these things cannot be mental in nature, because it is a priori that mental states play causal roles. On the other hand, few that come to believe that there are no such non-physical or epiphenomenal states become error theorists. Instead, they form the judgement that the mental states must be the occupants of functional roles, or perhaps the role states themselves.

Final comments

The suite of views about the mind associated with Armstrong and Lewis are then still with us. And so too are the difficult issues of what part of a theory of the mental will be a priori. At risk of making the kinds of predictions of the success of AI which have been so far overconfident, at some point in the next century we might expect successful implementation of a generalized artificial intelligence acting in the world. At that point it may become, for ethical reasons as much as any other, imperative to decide if it is a conscious mental being. What empirical issues will be relevant? What if it is very different in detail to the way we work at a computational level? It certainly will be at a physical level. The views which are the philosophical successors of Armstrong, Lewis and Smart will give one kind of answer, and it's not clear to the current author that there are any obviously preferable alternatives.

Notes

1. Of course we can modify what it takes to be a poison – say making it probabilistic – so it will still be a poison in some, though not all, of these circumstances.
2. Or is likely to cause, or disposed to cause, or other variations which we will get to.
3. Jackson, Pargetter and Pryor 1982.
4. Of course this is problematic; perhaps at the bottom in physics there are no intrinsically characterizable natures – or if they are, they are forever beyond empirical investigation as that reveals only causal roles.
5. This might involve contingent identity – a controversial but interesting notion – or it might involve the less controversial idea of contingently true identity statements, with identity itself remaining a necessary relation which (uninformatively) holds between things and themselves.
6. See, for example, Lewis 1972.
7. Block 1978.
8. Searle 1980.
9. Lewis 1995.
10. Lewis 1990, Nemirow 1990.
11. Braddon-Mitchell and Jackson 2006.
12. Not every kind: nothing rules out non-actual worlds where there are dualistic mental states playing the roles specified in the theory, or even that we could find our world to be like that.

13 Braddon-Mitchell 2003, Hawthorne 2002.
14 Although it might still be a priori in some other way if various features of it seem logically suspect.

Bibliography

Armstrong, D. M. (1968), *A Materialist Theory of the Mind*. London: Routledge and Kegan Paul.
— (1999), *The Mind-Body Problem: An Opinionated Introduction*. Boulder, CO: Westview Press.
Block, N. (1978), 'Troubles with functionalism'. *Minnesota Studies in The Philosophy of Science* 9: 261–325.
Braddon-Mitchell, D. (2003), 'Qualia and analytical conditionals'. *Journal of Philosophy* 100: 11–135
Braddon-Mitchell, D. and Jackson, F. (2006), *The Philosophy of Mind and Cognition*. Oxford: Blackwell Publishers.
Hawthorne, J. (2002), 'Advice to physicalists'. *Philosophical Studies* 109: 17–52.
Jackson, F. (1982), 'Epiphenomenal qualia'. *Philosophical Quarterly* 32: 127–36.
Jackson, F., Pargetter, R., and Prior, E. (1982), 'Functionalism and type-type identity theories'. *Philosophical Studies* 42: 209–25.
Lewis, D. K. (1966), 'An argument for the identity theory'. *Journal of Philosophy* 63: 17–25.
— (1970), 'How to define theoretical terms'. *Journal of Philosophy* 67: 427–46.
— (1972), 'Psychophysical and theoretical identifications'. *Australasian Journal of Philosophy* 50: 249–58.
— (1983), 'Mad pain and Martian pain'. In *Philosophical Papers*. New York: Oxford University Press, pp. 122–33.
— (1990), 'What experience teaches'. In W. G. Lycan (ed.), *Mind and Cognition: A Reader*. Oxford: Blackwell, pp. 499–519.
— (1994), 'Self-profile'. In S. Guttenplan (ed.), *A Companion to Philosophy of Mind*. Oxford: Blackwell.
— (1995), 'Should a materialist believe in qualia'. *Australasian Journal of Philosophy* 73: 140–4.
Nemirow, L. (1990), 'Physicalism and the cognitive role of acquaintance'. In W. G. Lycan (ed.), *Mind and Cognition: A Reader*. Oxford: Blackwell, pp. 490–9.
Place, U. T.(1956), 'Is consciousness a brain process?'. *British Journal of Psychology* 47: 44–50.

Searle, J. (1980), 'Minds, brains, and programs'. *Behavioral and Brain Sciences* 3: 417–57.
Smart, J. J. C.(1959), 'Sensations and brain processes'. *Philosophical Review* 68: 141–56.
— (1963), 'Materialism'. *Journal of Philosophy* 60: 651–62.
— (2012), 'The mind/brain identity theory'. In E. N. Zalta (ed.), *The Stanford Encyclopedia of Philosophy* (Winter 2012 Edition), URL = http://www.plato.stanford.edu/archives/win2012/entries/mind-identity/.

CHAPTER EIGHT

Hilary Putnam and computational functionalism

Oron Shagrir

For over half a century, Hilary Putnam has been one of the most influential philosophers. He started his career with several seminal papers in mathematical and philosophical logic. His further contributions, published in his numerous books, collections and papers, span the philosophy of mathematics, philosophy of mind, psychology and language, metaphysics and epistemology, ethics and moral philosophy, practical philosophy, Jewish philosophy and more. Our focus here is on Putnam's contributions in the philosophy of mind and psychology (though these are inevitably connected to his work in other domains). In this area, of mind and psychology, Putnam's major impact relates to functionalism. In the 1960s, Putnam promoted a central version of the view, known as computational, or machine, functionalism. The view gained immediate success. One reason why it became so attractive is that functionalism arguably does better as a theory of mind than its two rival views at the time, logical behaviourism and reductive materialism (also known as type-identity theory). Another reason is that computational functionalism aligned with the new science of the mind at the time, namely cognitive science. In the 1980s, however, Putnam became a vocal critic of functionalism; his criticism motivated others to refine and modify the view, or to abandon it altogether.

This chapter will focus on Putnam's arguments for, and then against, functionalism. These arguments will be put in the wider context of the more general discussion about functionalism. We will start with an introduction to functionalism (Part 1), then move to computational functionalism (Part 2) and after that discuss Putnam's main argument for the view (Part 3). Next, we review Putnam's central criticism of the view he once endorsed (Part 4), discussing in more detail his interesting argument against computationalism (Part 5).

1 What is functionalism?

Functionalism is the view that mental states and events – pains, beliefs, desires, thoughts and so forth – are defined by their causal relations to other mental states, stimuli ('inputs') and responses ('outputs'). Thus, being in pain, for example, is defined not only by its relations to stimuli such as certain agitation of nerve cells (caused, say, by stepping on a nail), and responses such as shouting 'Ouch' and moving my hand in the direction of my leg, but also by its relations to other mental states such as the belief that I am in pain, my desire to get rid of the pain, my memory of being in a similar situation a week ago, the hope that removing the nail will reduce the pain and so on.

Functionalism is sometimes traced back to Aristotle's conception of the soul, developed in *De Anima* II, 1 (Levin 2009). Aristotle notes that some things are defined by their purpose or the function they fulfil, and he associates this functional role with their *form* (rather than their matter). Thus, the form of a desk enables it to fulfil its function, which is to support books, laptops, paper and pencil in a way that they can be conveniently used for reading and writing. The form of the heart enables it to fulfil its function, which is, arguably, to pump blood. The human soul, according to Aristotle, is the form of the (human) body, which enables it to fulfil its functions, which are living, perceiving, reasoning and acting in the world. Functionalism follows this view about the mind and mental states, identifying them with their functional roles.

Functionalism associates roles (or forms) with *functional organization*, namely, the way in which mental states are causally related to each other, to sensory inputs and to motor outputs. Rocks, hurricanes and stomachs do not have minds because they do not have the right kind of functional organization. Their functional organization does not appear to be sufficiently complex to render them minds. Other organisms, biological or not, whose brains (or bodies) have the same functional organization as we do, will have minds and mental states as we do, according to functionalism.

Some functionalists think that a functional organization that constitutes mind is likely to be identified with one type of physical state (e.g. Lewis 1966). Most functionalists, however, believe that it is far more likely that minds and their mental states are *multiply realizable*. Multiple realization is the claim that every type of mental state could be realized in different ways in the brains (or bodies) of other biological and even non-biological species. The *realization* part is that every occurrence of a mental property, say being in pain, is instantiated in some sort of physical state, namely, a state with physical properties. The *multiple* part is that different occurrences of pain might be instantiated in different sorts of physical-chemical states, some of which are made, perhaps, of non-biological silicon hardware. Putnam had promoted this multiple realization thesis. He sometimes took this view to the extreme, stating that 'we could be made of Swiss cheese and it wouldn't matter'(1975b, p. 291).

Functionalism comes in different flavours. Analytic or causal-theoretic functionalism provides a functional analysis of our ordinary common-sense psychological concepts (Smart 1959, Armstrong 1968, Lewis 1972, 1980, Shoemaker 1984; see Chapter 7). Psycho-functionalism aims to analyse our scientific psychological concepts, those exhibited in our best scientific theories. Computational functionalism can be seen as a brand of psycho-functionalism: it aims to capture mental states as they are depicted in computational cognitive science (which in many senses is the science of the mind since the end of the 1950s, replacing psychological behaviourism). Putnam, Fodor (1968, 1975) and many others thought of mental states in terms of the computational theories of cognitive science. They viewed mental states and events as computational states of the brain, and, as such, as being defined in terms of 'computational parameters plus relations to biologically characterized inputs and outputs' (Putnam 1988, p. 7).

Computational functionalism can thus be seen as a scientific hypothesis (Block 1979), or as providing conceptual foundations for computational cognitive science (Chalmers 2011), whereas causal-theoretic functionalism is often seen as an *a priori* enterprise.

Much like its two main rivals, logical behaviourism and reductive materialism, functionalism aims to provide a so-called 'naturalistic' specification of types of mental states. This implies specifying mental states in non-mental and non-semantic terms (thus, logical behaviourists specify mental states in behavioural terms, whereas reductive materialists specify them in physical, typically neural, terms). At first sight, this statement looks odd: functionalism does specify mental states by their causal relations to stimuli, to responses and to other *mental* states. Functionalists insist, however, that an adequate specification will get rid of the mental locution, characterizing the relations to 'other mental states' in non-mental and non-semantic terms. The usual way to do this is in terms of Ramsification of the formula describing functional organization (Lewis 1972). We will see below how this strategy works with respect to computational functionalism.

2 Computational functionalism

Putnam developed computational functionalism in two distinct phases (Shagrir 2005). In earlier papers, Putnam (1960, 1964) drew an analogy between minds and machines to show that 'the various issues and puzzles that make up the traditional mind-body problem are wholly linguistic and logical in character . . . all the issues arise in connection with any computing system capable of answering questions about its own structure' (1960, p. 362). Later on, in 1967, Putnam made the additional move of identifying mental states with functional states, suggesting that 'to know for certain that a human being has a particular belief, or preference, or whatever, involves knowing something about the functional organization of the human being' (1967a, p. 424). In 'The nature of mental states', Putnam advances 'the hypothesis that pain, or the state of being in pain, is a functional state of a whole organism' (1967b, p. 433).

Let us first look at the notion of a computing machine, by considering a simple finite-state automaton (FSA) that receives as an input a sequence of 1s; its task is to say whether it has seen

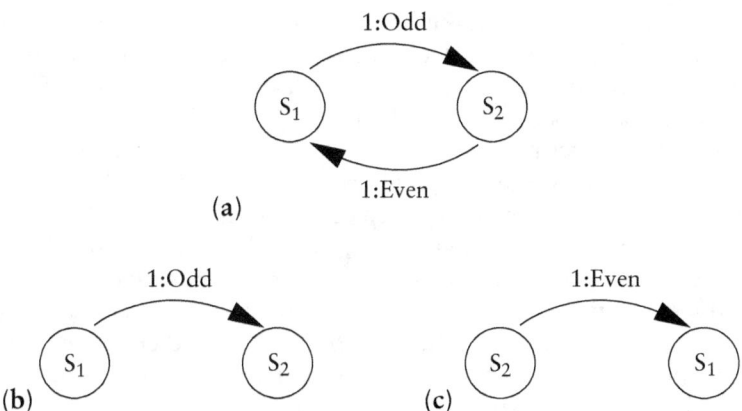

FIGURE 8.1 *A finite-state automaton (fig. 8.1a) that outputs 'Odd' after seeing 1, 3, 5, 7, . . . number of 1s, and 'Even' after seeing 2, 4, 6, . . . number of 1s. It consists of two states S_1 and S_2, and commands associated with each state. The command associated with S_1 is: 'If the input is "1", then produce "Odd" as an output, and move to state S_2,' (fig. 8.1b.). The command associated with S_2 is: 'If the input is "1", then produce "Even" as an output, and move to S_1,' (fig. 8.1c).*

an even or an odd number of 1s (Block 1996). This automaton can be described by a simple flow chart (fig. 8.1). It has two states S_1 and S_2 (as the name suggests, an FSA has a finite number of states). The machine is always in exactly one of these states, though at different times it can be in different states. At each moment, the automaton reads one symbol (in our case the only symbol available is '1'). Each state, S_1 and S_2, is associated with simple operations that are contingent on the read symbol. One command is this: If the machine is in S_1 and it gets '1' as an input, then it produces 'Odd' as an output, and it moves to state S_2. Another is that: If the machine is in S_2 and gets '1' as an input, then it produces 'Even' as an output, and it moves to S_1. It is not hard to see that the automaton outputs 'Odd' after seeing 1, 3, 5, 7,. . . number of 1s, and 'Even' after seeing 2, 4, 6,. . . number of 1s, regardless of the length of the input. This means that the simple two-state automaton can correctly react to any sequence of 1s, even though there is no limit on the number of such sequences (this ability is known as 'productivity').

Putnam noted that the characterization of the computing machine is given in terms of the flow chart, which determines the order in which the states succeed each other, what symbols are read and printed, and when. He referred to these states as the 'logical states' of the machine, states that are described in logical or formal terms, not physical terms (1960, p. 371), and he associated the flow chart description of sequences of logical states with the term 'functional organization' (1960, p. 373). Putnam emphasized that this characterization is expressed in logical-mathematical language, for example, a flow chart description, that makes no reference to the ways the 'machine is physically realized' (1960, p. 371) in copper, platinum, etc. Putnam also noted that logical states are characterized in terms of their *relations* to each other and to [inputs and outputs]' (1960, p. 367). For example, being in S_2 is represented by the following 'maximal' description:

> Being in S_2: being in the second of two states that are related to one another and to inputs and outputs as follows: [Being in one state and getting "1" as an input results in emitting "Odd" and going to the second state. Being in the second state and getting "1" as an input results in emitting "Even" and going to the first state].

The description within the squared brackets captures the functional organization of the automaton.

This parity FSA is a very simple machine. Other FSAs have more states, handle more inputs and include more if-then commands associated with each state. More sophisticated (yet still simple) machines include memory devices that enable the computation of more functions (thus the *addition* function can be computed by an FSA, but not *multiplication*). Putnam himself discusses a *Turing machine*, which is an FSA supplemented with an unbounded memory tape; the FSA flow chart can be then seen as the 'program' of the machine. In his seminal paper, Turing (1936) also introduced the concept of a *universal* Turing machine, which is a machine that can simulate the operations of any Turing machine. This idea of a universal, program-based, machine inspired the developments, since the 1940s, of the digital electronic computers that have subsequently revolutionized our world. Turing (1936, §9) also provided a powerful argument for the claim – known as the *Church-Turing thesis* – that this notion of Turing machine computability captures the notion of algorithmic computability. The Church-Turing thesis asserts that any function that can be computed by means of an algorithm (a finite procedure) can be computed by a universal Turing machine. In 1950, Turing linked his (universal) Turing machine to cognition, proposing a behaviourist test ('The Turing test') for intelligence: Roughly, we would say that a machine passes the Turing test if its behaviour is indistinguishable from that of a human being. Turing further argued that an electronic digital machine (which is, as said, the physical incarnation of a universal Turing machine) will eventually pass the test (Turing 1950). Turing's ingenious ideas gave a major boost in the 1950s to the field known as Artificial Intelligence (see Copeland 2012, for a non-technical presentation of Turing's ideas and their implications).

Putnam took the analogy between minds and machines a step further. He made a comparison between mentality and the *internal* structure of machines (this, as mentioned above, is in accord with the scientific trends of the time, namely, the shift from a behaviourist paradigm to a cognitivist one). At this early stage, Putnam did not advance a theory of the mind. He took the machine analogue to indicate that 'all of the question of "mind-body identity" can be mirrored in terms of the analogue' (1960, p. 362). To take one example, Putnam noted that just as there are two possible descriptions of a computing machine – one in terms of its logical states and another in terms of the realizing hardware – there are two possible descriptions of a human being. There is a description that refers to its physical and chemical structure; this corresponds to the description that refers to the computing machine's hardware. But 'it would also be possible to seek a more abstract description of human mental processes in terms of "mental states"... a description which would specify the laws controlling the order in which the states succeeded one another' (1960, p. 373). This description would be analogous to the machine's functional organization: the flow chart that specifies laws governing the succession of the machine's logical states.

There is thus a striking analogy between humans and machines. The internal make-up and behaviour of both can be described, on the one hand, in terms of physical states governed by physical laws, and on the other, more abstractly, in terms of logical states (machines) or mental states (humans) governed by laws of reasoning. The analogy between minds and machines is important in showing that different descriptions do not imply different entities, states and events. The machine analogue clearly shows that we can have very different descriptions of a machine, in terms of software ('program') and in terms of hardware. Similarly, that mental states and brain states have very different descriptions does not imply that the states themselves are separate. The difference in descriptions is compatible with the idea that brain states realize mental states, much as the physical states of the hardware realize the logical states of the software.

In 1967, Putnam (1967a, 1967b) took the analogy between minds and machines yet another step, arguing that pain, or any other type of mental state, is a functional state: 'Being capable of feeling pain *is* possessing an appropriate kind of Functional Organization' (1967b, p. 434). This further move encompasses two claims: One is computationalism, namely, the claim that organisms with minds are computing systems in the sense that they have functional organization: There is a true 'flow chart' description of the organism in terms of sequences of logical states from inputs and outputs. The other claim, functionalism, is that having a mind just is having the right sort of functional organization, and being a mental state is being in a state of this functional organization. Thus, being in pain is having some property that is characteristic of this functional organization.

We can learn more about the characterization of pain from what we know about the functional organizations of machines. Pain, as a state of the functional organization, is defined by its causal relations to other states (e.g. the belief that I am in pain), inputs (e.g. stepping on a nail) and outputs (e.g. vocalizing 'ouch'). This specification is *naturalistic* in the sense that it is formulated in non-mental and non-semantic terms. The specification of pain in terms of *other mental states* is eliminated in favour of a formula that contains logical terms (e.g. 'there is', 'and'), variables (i.e. x, $S_1, \ldots, S_n$), and biological/physical terms (for the inputs and outputs), but no mental terms.

To see how the elimination (known as 'Ramsification') works, assume that $FO(S_1, \ldots, S_n, i_1, \ldots, i_k, o_1, \ldots o_m)$ is a functional organization of a brain with a mind (this is in parallel to the flow chart description of an automaton). The description of FO consists of the relations between the mental states $S_1, \ldots, S_n$, sensory inputs $i_1, \ldots, i_k$, and motor outputs $o_1, \ldots o_m$. We now quantify over the internal states, treating them as variables. Having a mind, on this specification, is having n states, $S_1, \ldots, S_n$, whose relations to one another and to inputs and outputs are specified by $FO(S_1, \ldots, S_n, i_1, \ldots, i_k, o_1, \ldots o_m)$. Being a bit more formal, we can present the claim as follows:

Having a mind = $\exists X_1 \exists X_2 \ldots \exists X_n [FO(X_1, \ldots, X_n, i_1, \ldots, i_k, o_1, \ldots o_m)]$.

The X_i's in the formula are variables standing for states.

The functionalist's claim is that every organism that satisfies this formula has a mind. Consequently, being in pain is being in a state, say S_5, of this functional organization:

Being in pain = being in X such that $\exists X_1 \exists X_2 \ldots \exists X_n [FO(X_1, \ldots, X_n, i_1, \ldots, i_k, o_1, \ldots o_m)]$, and X is X_5.

Thinking about next summer's vacation is defined by the same formula, except that 'being in state X_5' is replaced with 'being in state X_{87}', and so forth. Again, every organism, or system, that satisfies the functional organization and is in state S_{87} thinks about next summer's vacation.

Putnam and others noted that mental states cannot be literally identified with states of a complex FSA or even a Turing machine. A Turing machine model cannot adequately represent learning and memory (Putnam 1975b, pp. 298–9; see also 1992a, pp. 8–14 and 1997, p. 34). Also, when one is in a state of pain, one is also in many other mental states (e.g. the state of believing that one is in pain), but a Turing machine instantiates only a single state at any given time (Block and Fodor 1972). But these reservations by themselves do not undermine functionalism. Computational functionalism is committed to the claim that mental states are computational states, not to the Turing machine model. It is also not committed to the view that computational states are propositional, symbolic or even digital (this latter view is known as *the computational theory of mind*; see Horst 2009, and Chapter 9). It might well be that the functional organization of cognizing organisms is best represented in terms of neural networks, and not in terms of Turing machines (Churchland and Sejnowski 1992, Churchland 2007, Chalmers 2011; see Chapter 12).

3 Putnam's argument for functionalism

Arguments for functionalism are surprisingly sparse. Putnam's (1967a, 1967b) main argument is that (computational) functionalism avoids the difficulties plaguing its main competitors, logical behaviourism and reductive materialism. Functionalism can even be seen as correcting the deficiencies of behaviourism and reductive materialism.

Logical behaviourism is the view that mental states are kinds of behavioural dispositions (see Chapter 5). Thus, pain, for example, is the disposition to emit certain responses (e.g. 'ouch') under certain stimuli (e.g. stepping on a nail). In a sense, behaviourism welcomes the idea that pain is defined by its functional role, but it explicates this role solely in terms of responses, stimuli and perhaps other observable environmental parameters (plus logical and mathematical vocabularies). The main criticism against behaviourism is that there is no way to redefine mental states one by one; every mental state inevitably is tied to other mental states (Chisholm 1957, Geach 1957). My pain behaviour, for example, is not just a result of my being in pain, but also of my being in *other* mental states, for example, that of believing that uttering the sound 'ouch' is not outrageous behaviour. Putnam dramatized this line of criticism in his 'Brains and behavior' (1963). He asks us to imagine a community of super-Spartans who, though they feel pain, are trained to never utter the sound 'ouch' when stepping a nail. These super-Spartans feel pain though their behavioural dispositions are different from ours. Putnam also asks us to imagine a community of perfect actors who can display the same behavioural dispositions we do, even though their pain fibres have been surgically removed, and, hence, they do not feel pain.

These and other examples demonstrate that my pain behaviour is not just a result of my being in pain, but also of my being in *other* mental states, for example, that of believing that uttering the sound 'ouch' is not an outrageous behaviour. We can correct this deficiency of behaviourism by admitting that pain is not just the disposition to utter the sound 'ouch' when stepping on a nail, but the disposition to utter the sound 'ouch' when stepping on a nail and when in *other mental states*. But this correction is tantamount to endorsing functionalism: pain is identified not just by the relations between stimuli and responses, but also by the relations between stimuli, responses and other mental states. Functionalism avoids the counterexamples easily. The super-Spartans' pain is related to other mental states not held by ordinary humans, and, hence, they react in a manner quite unlike that of ordinary humans. The pain behaviour of the perfect actor results from mental states other than pain.

Reductive materialism is the view that every type of mental state is identical with a type of physical or neural state (see Chapter 6). Thus, pain, for example, is identified with one type of neural state, say C-fibre stimulation. We noted that one difficulty with this view is that mental states need not be identified with specific types of physical or neural states. My pain is perhaps identified with C-fibre stimulation. But, as Putnam argues, the brains of mammals, reptiles and molluscs might be in very different physical-chemical states when these organisms are in pain (Putnam 1967b, p. 436). It is far more likely that types of mental states are multiply realizable, than identical to types of physical states.

Functionalism is consistent with the materialist's intuition that every pain event is a physical event, namely, an event with physical properties (say, C-fibre stimulation). But it is also consistent with *non-reductivism*, namely, the claim that the mental type (property) pain is not the physical type (property), say of C-fibre stimulation. It welcomes the possibility of multiple realization of mental properties, namely the claim that different tokens of pain events might be realized in different types of physical events. In fact, *if* mental states are computational states (as is being assumed in cognitive science), then they could be realized in very different physical make-ups. For we know from the case of machines that 'any Turing machine that can be physically realized at all can be realized in a host of totally different ways' (Putnam 1967a, p. 418). If so, Putnam concludes, 'our mental states, e.g., *thinking about next summer's vacation*, cannot be *identical* with any physical or chemical states. For it is clear from what we already know about computers etc., that whatever the program of the brain may be, it must be physically possible, though not necessarily feasible, to produce something with the same program but quite a different physical and chemical constitution' (1975b, p. 293). The upshot is that if we want to allow multiple realizability, as it seems we should do, then functionalism is more suitable for the job than reductive materialism.

4 Objections to functionalism

Upon its emerging as a central theory about the nature of mental states, many commentators advanced arguments *against* functionalism. Putnam himself introduced several powerful arguments, in the 1980s, against the view he once championed. He introduced a version of the inverted spectra argument, according to which the quality of sensation can be changed, say, from red to blue, though the functional role of the state has not changed (1981, pp. 80–1). Others have argued that even if there are nomologically necessary correlations between functional organization and qualia, there is no identity, as it is metaphysically possible to have the same functional organization but different qualitative properties. It is metaphysically possible, for example, to have zombies, who are just like us in their functional organization but have no consciousness at all (see, e.g. Chalmers 2010; see Chapter 14). Indeed, much of the argumentation against functionalism focuses on the alleged gap between functional organization and the qualitative aspects of (some) mental states. I will not survey these arguments here (for discussion and surveys, see Lycan 1987, Block 1996, Rey 1997, and Levin 2009; see also Chapter 14).

Another objection against functionalism pertains to the holistic nature of the mental (Putnam 1988, 1992b; see also Block and Fodor 1972, Stich 1983, Fodor and LePore 1992). Functionalism is a holistic theory defining each mental state by its causal relations to other mental states. But it is quite plausible that two individuals, John and Mary, can share the same type of belief (say, the belief that water is wet), even if their functional organization is somewhat different (say, Mary believes that water is H_2O, though John does not). In fact, it is plausible that any two individuals somewhat differ in their functional organization. But then we cannot attribute to John and Mary, or any other pair of individuals, the same belief, which is clearly absurd.

One way to tackle this argument is to admit that the same belief can be realized in different functional states. But, then, functionalism is no better than reductive materialism, as the same mental property can be realized in different functional organizations (Putnam 1988, pp. 80–4, 1992b, pp. 448–53). Alternatively, one can aim to find an equivalence relation between the realizing functional organizations.

Yet another route is to adopt a less fine-grained individuation scheme, say in terms of approximation, or subsets of mental states. But it is not easy to express these proposals in non-mental and non-semantic terms. Moreover, these proposals may have recourse to something like the analytic/synthetic distinction that philosophers today find questionable (Putnam 1988, pp. 81–2, 1992b, pp. 450–1; see also Fodor and LePore 1992).

Yet another objection that Putnam raised to functionalism had a huge impact on the philosophical literature. The objection consists of an argument with two main steps. The first involves a philosophical *thought experiment*. Putnam asks us to imagine two individuals, Oscar and his doppelganger Toscar, who are molecule-by-molecule identical. Toscar lives in Twin Earth, which is an environment exactly like Earth, except that our liquid water is replaced with a liquid XYZ, which has the same phenomenological look, taste and sound of our water, yet its chemical structure is very different from H_2O. Let us assume that the year is 1700 or so, before the emergence of modern chemistry, hence before knowledge of the chemical structure of water (we should ignore the fact that our bodies contain water). The second step is the view known as psychological externalism, which can arguably be inferred from the thought experiment. This is the view that the content of mental states is essentially individuated by reference to features in the individual's physical or social environment. In the context of the thought experiment, Oscar's thoughts about water are partly individuated by the fact that they refer to molecules of H_2O, whereas Toscar's thoughts are partly individuated by the fact that they refer to XYZ. Thus, while Oscar and Toscar are physically the same (in the sense that their intrinsic physical properties are identical), their thoughts are different.

Assuming that functional organization ranges over ('supervenes on') internal physical states and bodily inputs and outputs, then externalism conflicts with functionalism. If functionalism is correct, the mental in its entirety – including the content of our beliefs, thoughts, hopes, etc. – is functional. The content of our thoughts, beliefs and so forth is exhaustively specified by their functional properties. These are the functional properties of my thought that water is wet, for instance, that determine that I'm thinking about water and not dogs. In particular, if Oscar and Toscar have exactly the same functional organization, then the content of their thoughts, beliefs, desires, etc., must be the same. They both must be thinking (say) about water and not about dogs. But if externalism is correct, the content of our thoughts is partly determined by features that are in the individual's environment. Thus, two individuals might have the same functional organization, but thoughts with different content.

In 'The meaning of "meaning"', Putnam (1975c) advanced a less ambitious argument. He suggested that content has two factors. One factor determines extension and is associated with 'meaning'. This factor is 'wide', in the sense that some of its identity conditions make an essential reference to the individual's environment. The other factor is associated with features having to do with psychological/phenomenal properties. This factor is 'narrow', in the sense that it is not wide. This factor can still be identified functionally. Later on, Putnam abandoned this view, accepting full-fledged psychological externalism (1992b; see also Burge 1979, 1986 for precursors). Others, however, adhered to some version of the two-factor theory (e.g. Loar 1988). Yet others suggested that inputs and outputs should be understood as extending all the way to the distal environment; this view is known as wide or global functionalism (e.g. Harman 1987). The thoughts of Oscar and Toscar differ in content because they are causally related to different distal inputs and outputs. Oscar's thoughts are related to H_2O, Toscar's to XYZ. Another response is to draw a distinction between the identity conditions of thoughts and the identity conditions of their contents. Oscar and Toscar have mental lives and thoughts at all because they have a certain (same) functional organization. Yet the contents of Oscar's and Toscar's thoughts are different due to the different environments that the thoughts are about (e.g. Fodor 1987, 1990).

In this section, I surveyed objections that target functionalism more generally. In the next section, I discuss another objection by Putnam that aims more directly at the computationalist aspect of (computational) functionalism.

5 Realization reconsidered

Much of the appeal of functionalism has to do with multiple realizability – the claim that each type of mental state is multiply realizable in different types of physical states – and, hence, with non-reductive materialism. Multiple realization, however, has been a topic of an intense discussion in the last decades. I will mention here only very few strands of the debate (for a more comprehensive survey, see Bickle 2009). Kim (1972) notes early on that not every case of multiple realization consists in irreducibility. A higher-order property might be realized in different structures that nevertheless share a lower-level, reductive-base, property. Kim gives as an example the property of being at a certain temperature that can be realized in very different materials, though all the realizers share the lower-level property of a (certain) mean kinetic energy; and, indeed, the paradigm example of reduction is of temperature to mean kinetic energy (see also Churchland 2005). Later on, Kim (1992) further argues that the various physical realizers *must* share such a reductive-base property *if* the realized mental property is a scientific kind (see also Shapiro 2000; for replies see Block 1997, Fodor 1997, Antony and Levine 1997, Gillett 2003, Aizawa and Gillett 2009).

Others have noted that empirical examples of multiple realization, from cognitive neuroscience, are successful only if it is shown that (i) the realized instances belong to the same mental type, and (ii) that the realizing instances belong to different physical types. However, the friends of multiple realization are not careful in every case to show that both conditions are fulfilled (Shagrir 1998). Bechtel and Mundale (1999) further argue that these examples often appeal to different amounts of 'granularity' in individuating mental and neurobiological types. Psychological types are individuated at a coarse-grained level, taking into account loose input-output similarities across species. Neurological types are individuated at a fine-grained level, taking into account small differences across species. Bechtel and Mundale argue that the multiple realization argument is successful only if a common grain is chosen for both mental and neurological types. They further argue that when a common grain is chosen, we can find psycho-physical identities, between mental and neural types, even across species (for replies see Aizawa 2009 and Figdor 2010).

The main argument *for* multiple realization, however, does not rest on examples from the empirical science, but on the assumption (entrenched in computational cognitive science) that mental states are *computational* states, and that computational states can be realized, at least in principle, in many, including non-biological, materials. Ned Block succinctly expressed this inference, saying that 'whatever the merits of physiological reductionism, it is not available to the cognitive science point of view assumed here. According to cognitive science, the essence of the mental is computational, and any computational state is "multiply realizable" by physiological or electronic states that are not identical with one another, and so content cannot be identified with any one of them' (1990, p. 146).

Putnam (1988), once a main proponent of multiple realization, has more recently noted that this realization (or 'implementation' as it is often called when the realized structure is a computational one) is not innocuous. The problem is not that computational structures are *not* multiply realizable. The problem, rather, is that they are realized too easily. Even in the early days, Putnam noted that 'everything is a Probabilistic Automaton under *some* description' (1967b, p. 435). In the appendix to *Representation and Reality* (1988, pp. 121–5), Putnam develops this observation into an argument against functionalism. He proves that every ordinary open system is a realization of every abstract finite automaton. This result, if correct, undermines functionalism for the following reason. It implies that rocks, chairs and hurricanes implement a functional organization that suffices for possessing a mind. Put differently, if a functional organization of a certain complexity is sufficient for having a mind, as the functionalist claims, then rocks too have minds, as they realize this functional organization. In fact, almost everything, given that it realizes this automaton, has a mind. The upshot is that the notion of realization is a double-edged sword. We thought that multiple realization supplies more reasons to believe in functionalism. But it now turns out that multiple realization of an automaton extends to the simultaneous realization of every automaton, which undermines functionalism (Searle 1992, advances a somewhat similar argument).

Putnam's theorem is about finite state automata (FSA) without inputs/outputs (I/O). Here is an outline of the proof. Take the FSA that runs through the state-sequence ABABABA in a given time interval. Here, A and B are the states of the FSA. Assume that a rock can realize this run in a 6-minute interval, say from 12:00 to 12:06. Assume that the rock is in a maximal physical state S_0 at 12:00, S_1 at 12:01 and so forth (a maximal physical state being its total physical make-up specified in complete detail). Also assume that the states differ from each other. Now let us define a physical state **a** as $S_0 \vee S_2 \vee S_4 \vee S_6$ and state **b** as $S_1 \vee S_3 \vee S_5$. The rock implements the FSA in the sense that the causal structure of the rock 'mirrors' the formal structure of the FSA. The physical state a corresponds to the logical state A, the physical b corresponds to the logical B and the causal transitions from a to b correspond to the computational transitions from A to B. A complete proof would require further elaboration and assumptions. But the idea is wonderfully simple and can be extended to any FSA without inputs and outputs.

Putnam observes (p. 124) that the proof cannot be immediately extended to FSA with inputs/outputs (I/O). If the I/O are functionally individuated, then the I/O can be treated much like abstract internal states, and the extension is more natural. But if the I/O are specific kinds of physical or biological organs, then rocks, which lack motor or sensory organs of the required sort, cannot implement a mind because they lack the motor and sensory organs of thinking organisms. Putnam points out, however, that functionalism is in trouble if the difference between rocks and humans is exhausted by I/O. Functionalists argue that the difference between thinking organisms and rocks is rooted in the complexity of functional organization. But if the whole difference between humans and rocks amounts to the kinds of I/O they can handle, then functionalism collapses into behaviourism. Since humans and rocks have the same internal computational arrangements (according to Putnam's theorem), then we can account for the difference between them only in terms of I/O. But this is just behaviourism all over again: 'In short, "functionalism", if it were correct, would imply behaviorism! If it is true that to possess given mental states is simply to possess a certain "functional organization", then it is also true that to possess given mental states is simply to possess certain behavior dispositions!' (pp. 124–5).

Many have responded to Putnam's triviality result (for early responses to Putnam and Searle, see Block 1995, Chrisley 1994, Copeland 1996, and Melnyk 1996; for a recent survey see Piccinini 2010). They accuse Putnam of assuming a much too liberal notion of realization or implementation. They claim that it takes more than Putnam allows to implement the functional organizations that are minds. Chalmers (1996), for example, argues that the state transitions of the implementing machine must be reliable and counterfactual supporting. In addition, the causal structure of the physical object should mirror all the possible formal state transitions of the implemented FSA. Chalmers concludes that when these constraints are taken into account, then rocks might still implement simple FSA, but they do not implement the more complex combinatorial state automata (CSA), which are more likely to be the minds implemented by brains: 'CSAs are much less vulnerable to Putnam-style objections than FSAs. Unlike FSA implementations, CSA implementations are required to have complex internal structure and complex dependencies among their parts. For a complex CSA, the right sort of complex structure will be found in very few physical systems' (1996, p. 325).

It is controversial whether these constraints suffice to completely block triviality arguments (Brown 2012, Scheutz 2001, 2012, Sprevak 2012; see also the replies by Chalmers 2012), or whether these and other not-yet-formulated conditions can be formulated in non-semantic terms, as is required by functionalism (Godfrey-Smith 2009). And even if there are such constraints, it is most likely that they exclude the possibility of our mental life being realized in Swiss cheese, and many other foods and materials. The upshot, then, is that the notion of realization is more intricate that we thought. A successful notion of realization should be, on the one hand, robust enough to block the triviality result, yet, allow, on the other hand, the multiple realizability of mental life.

6 Summary

Computational functionalism continues to play a dominant role as a theory of mind. Since the early days of Putnam and Fodor, others have developed this view by tackling objections and by adjusting it to the more current trends in cognitive and brain sciences. Critics of functionalism have continued to advance more forceful and subtle objections that pertain to issues of causation, introspective and qualitative knowledge, and more. Yet Putnam's early development and arguments for functionalism, and his later arguments against functionalism, are still very much alive and relevant in the philosophy of mind.

References

Aizawa, K. (2009), 'Neuroscience and multiple realization: a reply to Bechtel and Mundale'. *Synthese* 167: 493–510.
Aizawa, K. and Gillett, C. (2009), 'The (multiple) realization of psychological and other properties in the sciences'. *Mind and Language* 24: 181–208.

Antony, L. M. and Levine, J. (1997), 'Reduction with autonomy', in
J. Tomberlin (ed.), *Philosophical Perspectives, Volume 11: Mind,
Causation, and World*. Boston: Blackwell, pp. 83–105.

Armstrong, D. (1968), *A Materialistic Theory of the Mind*. London:
Routledge & Kegan Paul.

Bechtel, W. and Mundale, J. (1999), 'Multiple realizability revisited: linking
cognitive and neural states'. *Philosophy of Science* 66: 175–207.

Bickle, J. (2009), 'Multiple realizability', in E. Zalta (ed.),*The Stanford
Encyclopedia of Philosophy*. http://www.plato.stanford.edu/entries/
multiple-realizability/.

Block, N. (1979), 'Troubles with functionalism', in W. Savage (ed.), *Issues
in the Foundations of Psychology, Minnesota Studies in the Philosophy
of Science: Volume 9*. Minneapolis: University of Minnesota Press,
pp. 261–325.

— (1990), 'Can the mind change the world', in G. Boolos (ed.), *Meaning
and Method: Essays in Honor of Hilary Putnam*. Cambridge:
Cambridge University Press, pp. 137–70.

— (1995), 'The mind as the software of the brain', in D. Osherson,
L. Gleitman, S. Kosslyn, E. Smith, E. and S. Sternberg (eds), *An
Invitation to Cognitive Science, Volume 3: Thinking*,second edition.
Cambridge, MA: The MIT Press, pp. 377–425. Also at http://www.
nyu.edu/gsas/dept/philo/faculty/block/papers/msb.html.

— (1996), 'Functionalism', *The Encyclopedia of Philosophy Supplement*,
Macmillan. Also at http://www.nyu.edu/gsas/dept/philo/faculty/block/
papers/functionalism.html.

— (1997), 'Anti-reductionism slaps back', in J. Tomberlin (ed.),
Philosophical Perspectives, Volume 11: Mind, Causation, and World.
Boston: Blackwell, pp. 107–32.

Block, N. and Fodor, J. A. (1972), 'What psychological states are not'.
Philosophical Review 81: 159–81.

Brown, C. (2012), 'Combinatorial-state automata and models of
computation'. *Journal of Cognitive Science* 13: 51–73.

Burge, T. (1979), 'Individualism and the mental', in P. A. French,T. E.
Uehling, and H. K. Wettstein (eds), *Midwest Studies in Philosophy,
Volume 4: Studies in Metaphysics*. Minneapolis: University of
Minnesota Press, pp. 73–121.

— (1986), 'Individualism and psychology'. *Philosophical Review*
95: 3–45.

Chalmers, D. J. (1996), 'Does a rock implement every finite-state
automaton?' *Synthese* 108: 309–33.

— (2010), 'The two-dimensional argument against materialism', in
D. J. Chalmers (ed.), *The Character of Consciousness*. Oxford:
Oxford University Press, pp. 141–92. Abridged version from 2009

in B. McLaughlin (ed.), *Oxford Handbook of Philosophy of Mind*. Oxford: Oxford University Press, pp. 313–35.
— (2011), 'A computational foundation for the study of cognition'. *Journal of Cognitive Science* 12: 323–57.
— (2012), 'The varieties of computation: a reply'. *Journal of Cognitive Science* 13: 211–48.
Chisholm, R. (1957), *Perceiving: A Philosophical Study*. Ithaca: Cornell University Press.
Chrisley, R. L. (1994), 'Why everything doesn't realize every computation'. *Minds and Machines* 4: 403–20.
Churchland, P. M. (2005), 'Functionalism at forty: a critical retrospective'. *Journal of Philosophy* 102: 33–50.
— (2007), *Neurophilosophy at Work*. Cambridge: Cambridge University Press.
Churchland, P. S. and Sejnowski, J. T. (1992), *The Computational Brain*. Cambridge, MA: The MIT Press.
Copeland, B. J. (1996), 'What is computation?', *Synthese* 108: 335–59.
— (2012), *Turing: Pioneer of the Information Age*. Oxford: Oxford University Press.
Figdor, C. (2010), 'Neuroscience and the multiple realization of cognitive functions'. *Philosophy of Science* 77: 419–56.
Fodor, J. A. (1968), *Psychological Explanation*. New York: Random House.
— (1975), *The Language of Thought*. New York: Thomas Y. Crowell.
— (1987), *Psychosemantics*. Cambridge, MA: The MIT Press.
— (1990), *A Theory of Content and Other Essays*. Cambridge, MA: The MIT Press.
— (1997), 'Special sciences: still autonomous after all these years', in J. Tomberlin (ed.), *Philosophical Perspectives, Volume 11: Mind, Causation, and World*. Boston: Blackwell, pp. 149–64.
Fodor, J. A. and LePore, E. (1992), *Holism: A Shopper's Guide*. Oxford: Blackwell.
Geach, P. (1957), *Mental Acts: Their Content and Their Objects*. London: Routledge & Kegan Paul.
Gillett, C. (2003), 'The metaphysics of realization, multiple realization and the special sciences'. *Journal of Philosophy* 100: 591–603.
Godfrey-Smith, P. (2009), 'Triviality arguments against functionalism', *Philosophical Studies* 145: 273–95.
Harman, G. (1987), '(Nonsolipsistic) conceptual role semantics', in E. LePore (ed.), *New Directions in Semantics*. London: Academic Press, pp. 55–81.
Horst, S. (2009), 'The computational theory of mind', in E. Zalta (ed.), *The Stanford Encyclopedia of Philosophy*. http://www.plato.stanford.edu/entries/computational-mind/.

Kim, J. (1972), 'Phenomenal properties, psychophysical laws, and the identity theory'. *The Monist* 56: 177–92.
— (1992), 'Multiple realization and the metaphysics of reduction'. *Philosophy and Phenomenological Research* 52: 1–26.
Levin, J. (2009), 'Functionalism', in E. Zalta (ed.), *The Stanford Encyclopedia of Philosophy*. http://www.plato.stanford.edu/entries/functionalism/.
Lewis, D. (1966), 'An argument for the identity theory'. *Journal of Philosophy* 63: 17–25.
— (1972), 'Psychophysical and theoretical identifications'. *Australasian Journal of Philosophy* 50: 249–58.
— (1980), 'Mad pain and martian pain', in N. Block (ed.), *Readings in Philosophy of Psychology, Volume I*. Cambridge, MA: Harvard University Press, pp. 216–32.
Loar, B. (1988), 'Social content and psychological content', in R. H. Grimm and D. D. Merrill (eds), *Contents of Thought*. Tucson: University of Arizona Press, pp. 99–109.
Lycan, W. G. (1987), *Consciousness*. Cambridge, MA: The MIT Press.
Melnyk, A. (1996), 'Searle's abstract argument against Strong AI'. *Synthese* 108: 391–419.
Piccinini, G. (2010), 'Computation in physical systems', in E. Zalta (ed.), *The Stanford Encyclopedia of Philosophy*. http://www.plato.stanford.edu/entries/computation-physicalsystems/.
Putnam, H. (1960), 'Minds and machines', in S. Hook (ed.), *Dimensions of Mind*. New York: University of New York Press, pp. 148–80. Reprinted in H. Putnam, 1975a, pp. 362–85.
— (1963), 'Brains and behavior', in R. Butler (ed.), *Analytical Philosophy. Second Series*. Oxford: Basil Blackwell & Mott, pp. 1–19. Reprinted in H. Putnam, 1975a, pp. 325–41.
— (1964), 'Robots: machines or artificially created life?'. *Journal of Philosophy* 61: 668–91. Reprinted in H. Putnam, 1975a, pp. 386–407.
— (1967a), 'The mental life of some machines', in H. N. Castañeda (ed.), *Intentionality, Minds and Perception*. Detroit: Wayne State University Press, pp. 177–200. Reprinted in H. Putnam, 1975a, pp. 408–28.
— (1967b), 'The nature of mental states' (originally published as 'Psychological predicates'), in W. H. Captain and D.D Merrill (eds), *Art, Mind and Religion*. Pittsburgh: University of Pittsburgh Press, pp. 37–48. Reprinted in H. Putnam, 1975a, pp. 429–40.
— (1975a), *Mind, Language and Reality, Philosophical Papers, Volume 2*. Cambridge: Cambridge University Press.
— (1975b), 'Philosophy and our mental life', in H. Putnam, 1975a, pp. 291–303.
— (1975c), 'The meaning of "meaning",' in K. Gunderson (ed.), *Language, Mind and Knowledge, Minnesota Studies in the Philosophy of*

Science, VII, Minneapolis: University of Minnesota Press, pp. 131–93. Reprinted in H. Putnam 1975a, pp. 215–71.
— (1981), *Reason, Truth and History*. New York: Cambridge University Press.
— (1988), *Representation and Reality*. Cambridge, MA: The MIT Press.
— (1992a), *Renewing Philosophy*. Cambridge, MA: Harvard University Press.
— (1992b), 'Why functionalism didn't work', in J. Earman (ed.), *Inference, Explanation and Other Philosophical Frustrations*. Berkeley: University of California Press, pp. 255–70.
— (1997), 'Functionalism: cognitive science or science fiction?', in D. M. Johnson, D. M. and C. E. Erneling (eds), *The Future of the Cognitive Revolution*. Oxford: Oxford University Press, pp. 32–44.
Rey, G. (1997), *Contemporary Philosophy of Mind*. Cambridge, MA: Blackwell.
Scheutz, M. (2001), 'Causal vs. computational complexity?' *Minds and Machines* 11: 534–66.
— (2012), 'What it is not to implement a computation: a critical analysis of Chalmers' notion of implementation'. *Journal of Cognitive Science* 13: 75–106.
Searle, J. (1992), *The Rediscovery of the Mind*. Cambridge, MA: MIT Press.
Shagrir, O. (1998), 'Multiple realization, computation and the taxonomy of psychological states'. *Synthese* 114: 445–61.
— (2005), 'The rise and fall of computational functionalism', in Y. Ben-Menahem (ed.), *Contemporary Philosophy in Focus: Hilary Putnam*. Cambridge, MA: Cambridge University Press, pp. 220–59.
Shapiro, L. (2000), 'Multiple realizations'. *Journal of Philosophy* 97: 635–54.
Shoemaker, S. (1984), *Identity, Cause, and Mind: Philosophical Essays*. Cambridge: Cambridge University Press.
Smart, J. J. C. (1959), 'Sensations and brain processes'. *Philosophical Review* 68: 141–56.
Sprevak, M. (2012), 'Three challenges to Chalmers on computational implementation'. *Journal of Cognitive Science* 13: 107–43.
Stich, S. (1983), *From Folk Psychology to Cognitive Science: The Case Against Belief*. Cambridge, MA: The MIT Press.
Turing, A. M. (1936), 'On computable numbers, with an application to the Entscheidungs problem'. *Proceedings of the London Mathematical Society* 42: 230–65.
— (1950), 'Computing machines and intelligence'. *Mind* 59: 433–60.

CHAPTER NINE

Jerry Fodor and the representational theory of mind

Matthew Katz

Among the most important developments in philosophy of mind in the twentieth century was the introduction of the idea that the mind is a computer; for this idea offers a physicalist theory of the mind that identifies mental states neither with patterns of behaviour, nor with types of brain states. Perhaps more than any other single philosopher, Jerry Fodor has advanced a version of this idea. More specifically, Fodor has described and defended a collection of related hypotheses he refers to as the *Representational Theory of Mind* (RTM). The most famous of these is the *Language of Thought Hypothesis*, which is the idea that thinking takes place within a mental language, though RTM also consists in the idea that the *propositional attitudes* are relations between subjects and mental representations, and in the idea that thinking is a computational process. Fodor is also well known for offering an account of the overall functional architecture of the mind, according to which the mind is partly composed of modules that perform individualized tasks. Ironically, Fodor argues that his modularity thesis suggests limitations on the extent to which cognition can be explained in terms of computation.

Folk psychology, propositional attitudes and functionalism

One way in which questions about the relation between mind and body get expressed is in terms of *folk psychology* and the *propositional attitudes*. Folk psychology, roughly speaking, is the large collection of common-sense laws about the relations between the content of one's mind and one's behaviour, which we often use in the explanation and prediction of behaviour. For example, we might explain Julie's carrying an umbrella with her to work by citing the presence of storm clouds, Julie's subsequent belief that it might rain, her belief that an umbrella will keep her dry in the rain and her desire to stay dry. This explanation relies on, among other things, the common-sense general law that normally functioning people see storm clouds when such clouds are present and form the belief that it might rain.

Such explanations and predictions can make reference to many different sorts of mental phenomena: beliefs, desires, hopes, fears, worries, intuitions and so on. These mental phenomena are often called *propositional attitudes*, because we express the content of a person's mind in terms of their taking an attitude towards some proposition. For instance, 'Julie hopes that it will not rain' claims that Julie holds the attitude of hoping towards the proposition 'It will not rain'.

One major component of Fodor's work has been to defend the reality of the propositional attitudes (and thus the truth, for the most part, of folk psychology) against claims that they do not exist (and thus that folk psychology is a largely false theory). His argument relies on the fact that folk psychological explanation and prediction is ubiquitous, that it has been so for millennia and that it often proves very reliable. Consider one of his examples:

> Someone I don't know phones me at my office in New York from... Arizona. "Would you like to lecture here next Tuesday?" are the words he utters. "Yes, thank you. I'll be at your airport on the 3 p.m. flight" are the words that I reply. That's *all* that happens, but it's more than enough; the rest of the burden of predicting behavior... is routinely taken up by

theory. And the theory works so well that several days later (or weeks later, or months later, or years later...) and several thousand miles away, there I am at the airport, and there he is to meet me. (1987, p. 3).

The theory Fodor mentions here includes general laws such as 'if someone utters the words "I'll be at your airport on the 3 p.m. flight" then all things being equal s/he intends to be at your airport on the 3 p.m. flight' (1987, p. 3), and 'all else being equal, people do what they intend to do', and so on. Since our predictions based on the theory work so well so often, Fodor contends, that theory must be true.

One worry some philosophers have had is that folk psychology, even when predictive, actually fails to provide any explanation at all of much of our mental lives or behaviour. For instance, Paul Churchland asks us to,

consider the nature and dynamics of mental illness, the faculty of creative imagination, or the ground of intelligence differences between individuals. Consider our utter ignorance of the nature and psychological functions of sleep.... Reflect on the common ability to catch an outfield fly ball on the run, or hit a moving car with a snowball.... On these and many other mental phenomena, [folk psychology] sheds negligible light. (1981, p. 73)

Because in his view folk psychology is so woefully inadequate at capturing many of the details of our mental lives, Churchland argues that it must for the most part be false, that it 'must inevitably fail to capture what is going on [in our mental lives], though it may reflect just enough superficial structure to sustain an alchemy-like tradition among folk who lack any better theory (1981, 85).' He maintains, therefore, that folk psychology and its vocabulary will eventually be replaced by neuroscience and its vocabulary. (See Chapter 12 for more on the Churchlands' neurophilosophical project).

Many agree though, that the promise of a psychology that eschews traditional psychological terms in favour of neuroscientific ones is still just that, a promise, which may never come to fruition. Fodor, for one, denies that we will ever make good on that promise, insisting that not only is folk psychology incredibly predictive of human behaviour, but that so far nothing else is. He writes that

> the predictive adequacy [of folk psychology] is beyond rational dispute. . . . If you want to know where my physical body will be next Thursday, mechanics—our best science of middle-sized objects after all, and reputed to be pretty good in its field—*is no use to you at all*. Far the best way to find out (usually, in practice, the *only* way to find out) is: *ask me!* (1987, p. 6)

For a philosopher inclined towards a physicalist account of the mind, though, realism about the propositional attitudes demands an account of their existence in physical terms. Some have argued that when we refer to mental states such as propositional attitudes, we are actually referring to patterns of behaviour or to dispositions to behave in particular ways (see Chapter 5). Others have argued that mental states are identical to types of brain states (see Chapter 6). In contrast, Fodor has argued that propositional attitudes are relations between subjects and mental representations. According to this view, for example, Julie believes that it will rain just in case Julie has tokened a mental representation that means 'it will rain' and Julie bears the relation of belief to that representation. If Julie believes that it will snow, she bears the same relation to a different mental representation (with a different meaning). If Julie hopes that it will rain, she bears a different relation to the same mental representation.

On this account, the difference between propositional attitudes is a difference in the relation one holds towards a given representation. For example, if Julie believes it will snow, she is perhaps likely to wear warm shoes and a warm coat if she goes outside. She is perhaps also likely to affirm, if asked, that it will snow, and she is likely to form other related beliefs such as that the roads may become slippery, that the scenery will be pretty later and so on. If she holds some other attitude towards the proposition that it will snow, she is perhaps likely to behave in different ways and to form different subsequent thoughts. That is, on Fodor's view propositional attitudes are characterized by the kinds of stimuli that cause them and the kinds of effects they cause, where those stimuli and effects include other internal (mental) states. In short, the account is functionalist (see Chapters 7 and 8), and indeed Fodor's early work was devoted to describing and defending a functionalist theory of mind, as a middle ground between dualism and behaviourism (see, e.g. Fodor 1968).

However, if propositional attitudes are defined by what they are caused by and by what they cause, then one needs an account of how they enter into causal relationships with other attitudes, stimuli and behaviour. For example, if Julie's belief that it will snow is a relation between Julie and a mental representation that means 'it will snow', and if this relation consists in part in its causing Julie to also believe that the landscape will be pretty later, which itself is a relation between Julie and a mental representation that means 'the landscape will be pretty later', then there needs to be an account of the processes that take as input the first mental representation and create as output the second. This requirement leads to the idea that thinking is computation, which in turn leads to the Language of Thought Hypothesis.

Computation and the language of thought

In order to understand the idea that thinking is computation, it is useful to begin with a description of Turing machines, the idealized computational devices first described by the British mathematician Alan Turing. Indeed, Turing was the first to argue that thinking is computation (see Turing 1950) and as Fodor notes, his own philosophical project is in large measure an attempt to fit Turing's idea together with the idea that folk psychology is largely true (1994, pp. 1–2).

Turing machines are composed of a string of tape (in theory, infinite in both directions) that is divided into segments, each of which may have a symbol written in it, and a 'write-read' head, which moves along the tape, reading, erasing and writing new symbols in the segments. Strings of symbols on the tape may be interpreted in various ways, for example as numbers or words or logical formulae, and the write-read head follows a set of precise directions that tells it when to erase a symbol, when to leave a symbol alone, when to write a symbol and when to stop. Depending on what directions are given to the write-read head, the machine can solve mathematical problems, perform logical derivations and so on.

The directions Turing machines follow refer to the syntax (roughly, the structure) of the strings of symbols and have no understanding or knowledge of semantic features (roughly, the meaning) of those symbols. For example, a machine that doubles integers might represent those integers with strings of the symbol '*' and have directions that instruct it how to erase each * and replace it with two *s, thus doubling the number represented. Still, even though the machine has no knowledge whatsoever that the strings mean n and $2n$, respectively, the machine will always give the correct answer of $2n$, when asked to double n (provided of course that the directions are correctly written and the machine does not malfunction in some way).

In general, even though Turing machines only pay attention to the structure of the symbols they process, they are able to respect various constraints on the meaning of those symbols such as reliably giving correct answers to mathematical questions. Moreover, because they only pay attention to syntax, they can be implemented as actual physical machines.[1] Indeed, Turing machines are critical progenitors of today's modern digital computer. In today's computing terminology, the tape is the Turing machine's 'memory', the symbols written on the tape are 'data' stored in that memory, the write-read head is its 'central processing unit' and the directions it follows constitute its 'program'.

More importantly for present purposes, the ability of a Turing machine to compute the correct answer to a question, while nevertheless not understanding that it is answering a question, provides a model of how propositional attitudes can cause and be caused by other propositional attitudes. Specifically, mental representations are akin to the strings of symbols on a Turing machine's tape, and the specific attitude a subject takes towards that representation is akin to the set of directions that the Turing machine follows in performing its computations. In other words, the idea that thinking is computation is the idea that propositional attitudes are sets of instructions that determine what mental representations to token, given other previously tokened representations (and that determine what behaviours should be performed, etc.).

Fodor explains that,

> I assume that psychological laws are typically implemented by computational processes.... Computational processes are

defined over syntactically structured objects.... There is a well-known and, in my opinion, completely convincing argument for viewing the implementation of psychological laws in this way: It is characteristic of the mental processes they govern that they tend to preserve semantic properties like truth. Roughly, if you start out with a true thought, and proceed to do some thinking, it is very often the case that the thoughts that the thinking leads you to will also be true. This is, in my view, the most important fact we know about minds.... Well as Turing famously pointed out, if you have a device whose operations are transformations of symbols, and whose state changes are driven by the syntactic properties of the symbols that it transforms, it is possible to arrange things so that, in a pretty striking variety of cases, the device reliably transforms true input symbols into output symbols that are also true. I don't know of any other remotely serious proposal for a mechanism that would explain how the processes that implement psychological laws could reliably preserve truth.... So I assume that Turing was right: the mind is a computer of some sort or other. (1994, pp. 7–9)

In fact, an appeal to a lack of other possibilities is not Fodor's only argument in favour of a computational view of mental processes. In his landmark book *The Language of Thought* (1975), he argued that (at the time) extant accounts of a variety of psychological processes implicitly assumed that thinking is computational. He argued for instance that according to theories of decision-making, subjects settle on a particular course of action by creating a preference ordering over possible consequences of available actions and computing the likelihood of those consequences (1975, pp. 28–31).

An important part of the idea that thinking is computation is that it implies the existence of a system of mental representation and therefore fits well with the account of propositional attitudes as relations between subjects and mental representations, which obviously also implies the existence of mental representations. Consider again Turing machines (and modern digital computers): the very idea of them depends on the idea that there are symbols in at least some of the squares on the tape (i.e. that there are bits of data in memory). Otherwise, there is nothing over which to perform computations. Put another way, the program the machine follows is a set of directions about when to write and erase symbols. So without symbols there can be no program. Or as Fodor writes, 'according to [theories of decision making], deciding is a computational process; the act the agent performs is the consequence of computations defined over representations of possible actions. No representations, no computations' (1975, p. 31).

According to Fodor though, the idea that thinking is computation implies not only the existence of a system of mental representation, but also that that system has certain features. In particular, he argues that the system must be language-like in structure. This then is the famous Language of Thought Hypothesis (LOTH). The idea that mental representations have a language-like structure amounts to the idea that they are composed from a finite store of atomic representations (those that have no meaningful parts, as simple words in English), which may be combined to form compound representations (as sentences are composed of words). The meaning of a compound representation, moreover, is a function of the meaning and arrangement of its component parts (as the meaning of a sentence is determined by the meaning and arrangement of the words in it).[2]

It is no accident, therefore, that LOTH is sometimes described as the view that thoughts are sentences in the head. This can be a useful way of understanding the theory, but it needs to be clarified as well. For one thing, it is important to understand that sentences can be written in many ways in many media. They are written in pen on paper, they are etched in stone, encoded in the dots and dashes of Morse code, and so on. LOTH then is simply the idea that some of the brain's activity can in principle be analysable as the encoding and processing of representations that have a linguistic structure.

Also, it is important to recognize that it is no part of LOTH that these representations are consciously available to thinking subjects. The hypothesis concerns the form of representation employed by the brain, 'beneath and behind' what subjects are aware of when they are thinking. This becomes quite clear when considering one of Fodor's early arguments for LOTH: that explaining how young children acquire a first spoken language requires positing a language of thought.

Fodor argued that language acquisition should be seen as a kind of hypothesis formation and confirmation. The idea was that infants and young children create hypotheses about the extension of the words they hear and test those hypotheses by using those same words to refer to objects around them. These hypotheses are confirmed by affirmation (given by nearby competent speakers) or disconfirmed by correction. Fodor argued, however, that these hypotheses themselves must be cast within an internal representational system with linguistic structure (i.e. a language of thought) and thus, that we cannot explain how human beings acquire natural languages unless we posit a language of thought. And as one would expect, Fodor did not conceive of infants and toddlers as being consciously aware of engaging in hypothesis confirmation (1975, pp. 58–64).

Another reason Fodor gives for thinking that the brain employs a language-like system of representation is that it allows for an infinity of unique representations, a property known as *productivity*. He explains that

> the essential point is the organism's ability to deal with *novel* situations. Thus, we infer the productivity of natural languages from the speaker/hearer's ability to produce/understand sentences on which he was not specifically trained. Precisely the same argument infers the productivity of the internal representational system from the agent's ability to calculate the behavioral options appropriate to a kind of situation he has never before encountered. (1975, pp. 31–2)

But the ability to produce an infinity of unique representations from finite means, argue Fodor and Pylyshyn (1988), demands that arbitrarily complex representations be constructed from a finite store of atomic representations, in which the meaning of any of those complex representations is a function of the meaning and arrangement of the component parts. But that just is a system with linguistic structure.

Similarly, Fodor and Pylyshyn (1988) argued for LOTH from the premise that thought is *systematic*.[3] The idea that thought is systematic is the idea that certain thoughts are related to certain other thoughts in such a way that any thinker who understands the one will also be able to understand the other. For instance, Fodor and Pylyshyn claim that anyone who can entertain the thought *Mary loves John* can also entertain the thought *John loves Mary*. They argue that the best explanation for this is that each is a compound representation, that the compounds share all the same parts and differ only in the arrangement of those parts, and that understanding either implies understanding the component parts. Therefore, if a subject is capable of understanding the one, she will also be capable of understanding the other, since doing so requires all the same abilities as understanding the first. But if this is what explains why the thoughts are systematically related, then LOTH must be true, for the idea that the representations are composed of component parts and have meanings that are dependent on those parts and their arrangements, again, just is the idea that they have a linguistic structure.

Significance and objections

The significance of RTM is often best seen in relation to Descartes' famous claim that a machine could not use reason. He writes that, 'it is not conceivable that . . . a machine should produce different arrangements of words so as to give an appropriately meaningful answer to whatever is said in its presence, as the dullest of men can do' and that it would be impossible for a machine to 'act in all the contingencies of life in the way in which our reason makes us act' (1637/1988, pp. 44–5). Descartes took this line of argument to show that the mind is an immaterial substance that, while joined to the body during life, nevertheless has a 'nature entirely independent of the body' (1637/1988, 46; see Chapter 2).

But Turing's work and the subsequent development of the digital computer suggest that Descartes may be exactly wrong here: by following directions that tell a machine how to manipulate symbols based on the structuring of those symbols, the machine can indeed respond in incredibly complex ways, ways that respect truth and other semantic constraints. If one applies this idea to the human brain, the result is the hypothesis that thinking is computation, and that explaining reason may need no appeal to immaterial substances after all.

The hypothesis that thinking is computation, though, implies a system of mental representation, and according to Fodor, that that system has a linguistic structure. Moreover, the idea that thinking is computing over mental representations allows for the claim that mental states such as propositional attitudes are akin to the programs that ultimately determine the behaviour of a computer. That is, the attitudes determine what stimuli and representations will cause a given representation, and what other representation and behaviour that representation will in turn cause. In short, though dualism is rejected, so too is any identification of mental states with behaviour or with types of brain states.

Still, objections to the above constellation of views, and in particular to Fodor's presentation of them, are legion. It was noted above that some philosophers have argued that folk psychology is a false theory. Moreover, as a version of functionalism, RTM is susceptible to a number of objections facing such theories (see Chapters 7 and 8). Many philosophers have argued that any version of computationalism is bound to fail, or at least, that it faces technical difficulties so challenging they may in fact be insurmountable (see, e.g. Searle 1980 and Dennett 1984). LOTH itself has been widely controversial. Some philosophers and psychologists have argued that, rather than having a linguistic structure, much mental representation has an imagistic format (e.g. Kosslyn 1980). Others have suggested that some mental representation is map-like (e.g. Braddon-Mitchell and Jackson 1996). Still others have wondered whether thought really does have the properties of productivity and systematicity, as Fodor and Pylyshyn claim it does (e.g. Johnson 2004).

Many philosophers initially rejected LOTH because it was seen to be wedded to a particularly strong version of the idea that some concepts are possessed innately. In particular, Fodor's original arguments for LOTH were coupled with an argument that all atomic concepts (i.e. 'words' in the language of thought) are innate. The argument for the latter claim was that if one were to learn an atomic concept, it would have to be by way of hypothesis confirmation (akin to that which explains language acquisition, as discussed above), but that such a process would presuppose knowledge of the concept to be learned and is thus impossible. Fodor argued for instance that if one is to learn the concept RED, then one must be able to form hypotheses about which things are red and which things are not. But such hypotheses must be couched in a system of representation that has resources to express propositions about which things are red and which are not. That is, the system must already possess the concept RED. So one cannot learn the concept RED unless one already possesses it. So learning RED is impossible, and if anyone has the concept they must have possessed it innately.

However, a list of atomic concepts will include many that seem absurd to suppose are possessed innately – CARBURETOR has been a favourite in the literature – and many philosophers took that as argument that Fodor's view is false, or indeed, absurd (e.g. Putnam 1988, Churchland 1986). Fodor himself admits that '[t]his conclusion, according the consensus, was downright loopy' (2008, p. 129), and though he has not abandoned the view he has refined it. While the reasoning in *The Language of Thought* assumed that if a concept is not learned, then it must be innate, Fodor has since distinguished between acquiring a concept and learning one, claiming that learning a concept is just one possible way among many others of acquiring a concept. He writes that,

> *There are all sorts of mind/world interactions that can alter a conceptual repertoire. Concept learning* (if there is such a thing) *is one, but it's certainly not the only one.* Other candidates conceivably include: sensory experience, motor feedback, diet, instruction, first-language acquisition, being hit on the head by a brick, contracting senile dementia, arriving at puberty, moving to California, learning physics, learning Sanskrit, and so forth indefinitely. (2008, pp. 131–2)

He concludes that while the argument that concepts cannot be learned still stands, it does not follow that all concepts are innate. Rather, the question becomes how organisms acquire concepts, since they clearly do so but neither learn them nor possess them innately. He writes,

> The central issue isn't *which concepts are learned*, since . . . none of them are. Nor, however, is it *which concepts are innate*, if an innate concept is one the acquisition of which is independent of experience. Quite likely, there are none of those either. Rather, the problem is to explain how a creature's innate endowment (whether it is described in neurological or in intentional terms) contributes to the acquisition of its conceptual repertoire; that is, how innate endowments contribute to the processes that start with experience and end in concept possession. (2008, p. 145)

One very well-known objection to LOTH stems from the advance in the 1980s of *connectionist networks*. When Fodor wrote *The Language of Thought*, in the early 1970s, the Turing model of computing was the only available model, and as the model demands linguistically structured representations, Fodor argued that viewing the mind as a computer demands positing a language of thought. But in the 1980s, cognitive scientists began to have serious successes modelling various cognitive processes using connectionist networks, computational systems that do not employ linguistically structured representations (see Chapters 12 and 13, and Churchland 1995). Moreover, connectionist networks appear to resemble the brain both in gross architecture and functioning more so than Turing machines and digital computers. They are composed of groups of simple processing units and connections among the units, they lack both dedicated memory and a central processing unit, and activity passes through them in massively parallel fashion, as in the brain, and as opposed to the step-by-step serial processing found in digital models. So some authors have argued that if the brain is a computer, it is one much more akin to such networks than to Turing machines and digital computers.

Much of this debate concerns the possibility that connectionist networks do not offer an alternative to LOTH, but rather suggest a way in which the language of thought might be implemented in the brain. Fodor and Pylyshyn (1988) and Fodor and McLaughlin (1990), for instance, argue that because network architectures lack linguistically structured representations, they cannot account for the productivity and systematicity of thought. Therefore, they argue, they cannot offer a genuine alternative to LOTH. Still others like Smolensky (1988) have tried to show that connectionist networks can indeed explain those phenomena.

One intriguing aspect to debates surrounding the idea that thought is computation is that Fodor himself has argued that it should only be taken to explain the functioning of certain parts of the mind. This argument rests on a view of the overall architecture of the mind that Fodor has defended.

Modularity and the limits of computation

In *The Modularity of Mind* (1983), Fodor argues that a general functional taxonomy of psychological systems would include three kinds of system. This taxonomy would include systems that take in raw data from the environment, called *transducers*, systems that interpret that data, called *input systems*, and systems for everything else, including higher cognitive functions such as belief formation, called *central systems*. Fodor argued that if this taxonomy is correct, it shows that there are significant limits on the explanatory power of the computational aspect of RTM. He writes,

> Over the years, I've written a number of books in praise of the Computational Theory of Mind. . . . It is, in my view, by far the best theory of cognition that we've got. . . . There is . . . every reason to suppose that the Computational Theory is part of the truth about cognition. . . . But it hadn't occurred to me that anyone could think that it's a very large part of the truth; still less that it's within miles of being the whole story about how the mind works. (2000, p. 1)

Fodor's notion of a transducer is that of a system whose output is 'most naturally interpreted as specifying the distribution of stimulations at the "surfaces" (as it were) of the organism' (1983, p. 42) in a format that may then be used by the input systems. For example, it might be the job of a transducer to present patterns of retinal stimulation to the input systems in a format the latter systems employ. The input systems, then, 'deliver representations that are most naturally interpreted as characterizing the arrangement of *things in the world*' (p. 42). Those representations may then be used by the central systems for all manner of higher cognitive functions.

The central claim of *Modularity* is that the input systems, but not the central systems, should be thought of as modules, performing specific tasks that can be more-or-less separated from the rest of the system (roughly like the way a compact disc player might be removed from a stereo system, leaving the rest of the system functioning normally). The argument rests on a list of features that Fodor believes is characteristic of modules, on reasons to believe input systems possess those features and on reasons to believe that central systems do not. For present purposes, the most important of these features are *domain specificity* and *informational encapsulation*.

To say that input systems are domain specific is to say that 'the range of distal properties they can project . . . hypotheses about' is quite narrow (p. 47). For instance, '[c]andidates might include, in the case of vision, mechanisms for color perception, for the analysis of shape, and for the analysis of three-dimensional spatial relations' (p. 47). To say that input systems are informationally encapsulated is to say that their operations are not affected by feedback of 'information that is specified only at relatively high levels of representation' (p. 64). In other words, while the products of input systems are taken as input for computations performed by central systems, the reverse is not true: the products of central systems are not used in computations performed by input systems. Fodor takes perceptual illusions to be evidence of this claim. For example,

> The very same subject who can tell you that the Müller-Lyer arrows are identical in length, who indeed has seen them measured, still finds one looking longer than the other. In such cases it is hard to see an alternative to the view that at least *some* of the background information at the subject's disposal is inaccessible to at least some of his perceptual mechanisms. (p. 66)

Although Fodor describes the function of input systems as characterizing things in the world, he also thinks that their outputs are *shallow*, in the sense that they only employ *basic* categories in doing so, where by 'basic' he means categories that are neither very abstract nor very particular (p. 94). For example, he suggests that input systems might group objects into the category *dog*, but not *poodle* or *thing*. Of course, cognition involves a great deal more than grouping objects into basic categories. Among so many other things, it also involves both more specific and more abstract categorization, belief and hypothesis formation, problem solving and so on. According to Fodor then, the central systems are responsible for all these other functions that neither transducers nor input systems perform.

But if that is true, Fodor argues, then central systems must, in stark contrast to input systems, be both (relatively) domain general and informationally un-encapsulated. To begin with, since input systems are domain specific, for example forming representations of the colour of objects in the environment or of the structure of a rhythm, yet we form beliefs about the relationship between our visual and auditory experiences, the systems responsible for forming those beliefs will have to cross visual and auditory domains. That is, they will have to be relatively domain general as contrasted with input systems. Moreover, Fodor argues that central systems must be un-encapsulated. The line of reasoning here is that we often reason analogically – borrowing information from one domain to use in another – and such reasoning by definition cannot be encapsulated. Here, Fodor looks to the history of scientific discovery as being rich with examples:

> what's known about the flow of water gets borrowed to model the flow of electricity; what's known about the structure of the solar system gets borrowed to model the structure of the atom; what's known about the behavior of the market gets borrowed to model the process of natural selection, which in turn gets borrowed to model the shaping of operant responses.... The point about all this is that "analogical reasoning" would seem to be ... a process which depends precisely upon the transfer of information among cognitive domains previously assumed to be mutually irrelevant. By definition, encapsulated systems do not reason analogically. (1983, p. 107)

Fodor's account of the mental architecture is important in its own right, has been widely influential, and other accounts have been offered in its wake. Some philosophers have argued that there are indeed the modules Fodor says there are, plus other specific ones. Currie and Sterelny (2000), for example, suggest a module for social cognition. Still others have argued that the mind is massively modular, being composed of perhaps hundreds of thousands of domain-specific modules, each one designed by natural selection to perform a function that would have aided our evolutionary ancestors in some way (e.g. Cosmides and Tooby 1994).

Fodor takes his account of modularity to indicate that an appeal to computation is limited in its ability to explain cognition, specifically because the central systems are domain general and un-encapsulated. He argues that the upshot of domain general un-encapsulated central systems is that 'there seems to be no way to delimit the sorts of informational resources which may affect, or be affected by central processes.... We can't, that is to say, plausibly view the fixation of belief as effected by computations over bounded, local information structures' (1983, p. 112). In other words, forming beliefs appears to involve computations that are sensitive to everything the organism knows. Unfortunately, according to Fodor, we have no understanding of and no way to characterize such 'global' sorts of computations. As noted above, his notion of computation is that of processes that are defined over the syntactic structure of representations, and syntactic structure is a local – not global – property. That is, knowing the syntactic structure of a representation does not require knowing anything about other representations. Thus, since Fodor's idea of computation does not fit with his view about how the central systems operate, he concludes that his view of computation cannot be employed in accounts of central cognitive processing. And because he thinks his view of computation is the best available theory to employ in accounts of cognition in general, he takes this result to be 'very bad news for cognitive science' (1983, p. 128).[4]

Conclusion

Regardless of the position one takes with respect to the various parts of RTM, their collective significance is difficult to overstate. Together they comprise answers to some of the oldest and thorniest philosophical problems. Those answers are that our everyday descriptions of our minds and the minds of others are largely true, and that psychological explanation will inevitably rest on mental terms, but that the mind is entirely physical, yet not to be identified with patterns of behaviour or types of brain states. Rather, mental states are functional states – indeed they are computational states – relating subjects with inner mental representations. Those representations, moreover, together form a language.

Still, even if this theory is true, it is merely the sketch of a complete theory of the nature of thought and thinking. The details of the representational structures involved, as well as the details of the processing employed, and a myriad of other aspects of the system all remain to be described. Moreover, if Fodor's account of modularity is correct and his argument concerning central systems is sound, then a computational account may only be possible for those parts of the mind that take in information about the environment and create representations that may then be employed by higher faculties. What happens after that – how those higher faculties process those representations – may remain entirely mysterious.

Notes

1. Strictly speaking, this is not accurate. In theory, a Turing Machine's tape extends infinitely in both directions, and so cannot be built. Nevertheless, the Turing Machine is the basis for the idea of a mechanical device that processes representations syntactically.
2. This description of what linguistic representation amounts to is present in Fodor (1975) and becomes an explicit and central part of the argumentation in Fodor and Pylyshyn (1988).
3. They added an argument from *inferential coherence* as well. Thought is inferentially coherent just in case, given that a subject is capable of drawing some instances of a kind of logical inference, she is able to draw any instance of that kind of logical inference.
4. Of course, these arguments are hotly disputed as well. If the mind is composed entirely of modules, then computationalism may survive. Alternatively, some have argued that the problems Fodor describes here (and similarly in his 2000) do not in fact apply (e.g. Ludwig and Schneider, 2008).

References

Braddon-Mitchell, D., and Jackson. F. (1996), *Philosophy of Mind and Cognition*. Oxford, UK: Blackwell.
Churchland, P. M. (1981), 'Eliminative materialism and the propositional attitudes'. *Journal of Philosophy* 78: 67–90.
— (1995), *The Engine of Reason, the Seat of the Soul*. Cambridge, MA: MIT Press.
Churchland, P. S. (1986), *Neurophilosophy*. Cambridge, MA: MIT Press.
Cosmides, L. and Tooby, J. (1994), 'Origins of domain specificity: the evolution of functional organization', in L. Hirschfeld and S. Gelman (eds), *Mapping the Mind: Domain Specificity in Cognition and Culture*. Cambridge: Cambridge University Press, pp. 85–116.
Currie, G. and Sterelny, K. (2000), 'How to think about the modularity of mind reading'. *Philosophical Quarterly* 50: 145–60.
Dennett, D. (1984), 'Cognitive wheels: the frame problem of AI'. In C. Hookway (ed.), *Minds, Machines, and Evolution: Philosophical Studies*. Cambridge: Cambridge University Press, pp. 129–52.
Descartes, R. (1637/1988), 'Discourse on the method', in J., R. Stoothoff, and D. Murdoch (eds), *Descartes, Selected Philosophical Writings*, trans. Cottingham. Cambridge: Cambridge University Press.

Fodor, J. (1968), *Psychological Explanation: An Introduction to the Philosophy of Psychology*. New York: Random House.
— (1975), *The Language of Thought*. Cambridge, MA: Harvard University Press.
— (1983), *The Modularity of Mind*. Cambridge, MA: MIT Press.
— (1987), *Psychosemantics: The Problem of Meaning in the Philosophy of Mind*. Cambridge, MA: MIT Press.
— (1994), *The Elm and the Expert: Mentalese and its Semantics*. Cambridge, MA: MIT Press.
— (2000), *The Mind Doesn't Work That Way: The Scope and Limits of Computational Psychology*. Cambridge, MA: MIT Press.
— (2008), *LOT 2: The Language of Thought Revisited*. Oxford, UK: Oxford University Press.
Fodor, J. and McLaughlin B. (1990). 'Connectionism and the problem of systematicity: why Smolensky's solution doesn't work'. *Cognition* 35: 183–204.
Fodor, J. and Pylyshyn Z. (1988). 'Connectionism and cognitive architecture: a critical analysis'. *Cognition* 28: 3–71.
Johnson, K. (2004), 'On the systematicity of thought and language'. *Journal of Philosophy* 101: 111–39.
Kosslyn, S. (1980), *Image and Mind*. Cambridge, MA: Harvard University Press.
Ludwig K. and Schneider S. (2008), 'Fodor's critique of the classical computational theory of mind'. *Mind and Language* 23: 123–43.
Putnam, H. (1988), *Representation and Reality*. Cambridge, MA: MIT Press.
Searle, J. (1980), 'Minds, brains, and programs'. *Behavioral and Brain Sciences* 3: 417–57.
Smolensky, P. (1988), 'The constituent structure of mental states'. *Southern Journal of Philosophy* 26: 137–60.
Turing, A. (1950), 'Computing machinery, and intelligence'. *Mind* 59: 433–60.

CHAPTER TEN

Donald Davidson, Daniel Dennett and the origins of the normative model of the mind

Andrew Brook

What has come to be called the normative or interpretationist picture of the mind was launched, at least in its contemporary form, by Donald Davidson and Daniel Dennett at roughly the same time in the late 1960s and early 1970s.[1] The fundamental idea behind the approach is that for an organism (or other entity) to have a mind, its behaviour must satisfy certain norms. Since this is not true of any other complex system, it immediately follows that minds, though natural systems, are very different from other natural systems – including not only brains but also systems of cognitive functioning.

Since the initial launch, the approach has taken a variety of forms in the works of such noted philosophers as John McDowell and Robert Brandom. In the form in which Davidson and Dennett launched it, however, the approach was characterized by two key claims:

1. Psychological explanations, i.e., explanations in terms of a person's reasons for doing what he or she (hereafter "she") did,

are holistic. What is meant by "holistic" here is that a given bit of behaviour can be explained psychologically only by ascribing to the subject of the behaviour a complex of states including some motivation (a desire for something, for example), some beliefs (that doing A is likely to satisfy the desire, for example) and sufficient rational control to be able shape behaviour in a way likely to satisfy the desire, given the actor's beliefs.

Here, it is important to note that, even though psychological explanations are holistic and so quite unlike billiard ball-style causal explanations, both Davidson (especially clear in 1963) and Dennett (especially clear in 1987a) held that they are causal explanations. As Davidson details, in this they both departed from a predominantly British tendency at the time, purportedly following the later Wittgenstein, to argue that they are not.

> 2. Beliefs are and must be mostly accurate (and, therefore, mostly consistent). (As we will see, Davidson's and Dennett's reasons for making this claim are very different.)

These two claims have some big implications. Neither brains nor cognitive systems characterized in any way other than in the psychological language of reasons for action have remotely similar constraints (have remotely similar constitutive elements or constitutive conditions, as Davidson [1970, p. 220, 1974, p. 237] calls them). If so, then there will be good reason to deny that it is possible in any systematic way to relate kinds of states, events, functions, etc., described in psychological language, to – will not be possible to reduce them to – kinds of brain state or, as Dennett once noted but many others have missed, *to kinds of cognitive state either* (1978a, p. xvi).[2] Thus, if Davidson and Dennett are right, not only is reductive physicalism (which tries to identify mental types with brain types; see Chapter 6) wrong but most versions of most people's favoured alternative, functionalism (which tries to identify mental types with cognitive function types; see Chapters 7 and 8), are also wrong.

Davidson called his version of the alternative *anomalous monism*. It is anomalous because psychological kinds cannot be reduced either to brain kinds or to cognitive kinds and it is monist because states described psychologically are still part of the material, natural world.

In the early going, Dennett (1978a, p. xix) tentatively adopted the name *type intentionalism* for his view: "We can clarify, regiment, modify and even sometimes eliminate psychological types" (pp. xix–xx) but we cannot map them onto either cognitive/functional types or brain/physical types in any systematic way.

Whatever one calls the view, its insistence that anything that we'd call a mind must meet two normative standards, namely rationality and accuracy/consistency, and the implication of this that psychological talk cannot be related systematically to any other way of talking about our capacities as information processors, has been thought to entail that cognitive science, that is, a science of the mind, is and will always be impossible. Yet Dennett is a big fan of cognitive science and Davidson was a fan of activities that are at least related, formal decision theory and formal models of syntax and semantics in particular.

In what follows, I will:

- Relate a bit of the history of the development of the picture;
- Summarize first Davidson's, then Dennett's, variants;
- Compare the two;
- Discuss some challenges facing the whole enterprise, including the putative implication that it rules out a science of the mind, and the problems of irrational beliefs and consciousness.

A bit of history

What was the historical relationship between the two bodies of work? Dennett has said that he and Davidson 'pursued strikingly parallel but largely independent courses over the years' (1987b, p. 348). This claim, itself striking, invites the question, 'How independent?' There is probably no way to answer this question in any detail but that does not mean that nothing can be said. Fortunately for us, both Davidson and Dennett have written intellectual autobiographies, three of them in Dennett's case (Davidson 1999, Dennett 1987b, 1998, 2008). Because they discuss Davidson, Dennett's first articles are particularly apposite.

Davidson (b. 1917) was twenty-five years older than Dennett (b. 1942). Thus, one would expect Davidson to have developed anything distinctive in his point of view long before Dennett. However, the gap in the development of their respective variants on the normative model of the mind, if there even was one, was much smaller than that. Davidson was in the US Navy for five years during and after WWII and lost time for other reasons. He did not finish his PhD (under the great American philosopher Willard van Orman Quine on Plato's *Philebus*, remarkably enough) until 1949. He was then 32. He next turned his attention for a decade to decision theory, formal models of indirect discourse ('Peter believed that a is F', where the truth of the whole sentence does not depend on the truth of the embedded clause) and the like. In this work, the Polish logician Tarski was as much his inspiration as Quine and aspects of Tarski's scheme became deeply embedded in Davidson's. Eventually, he applied some of this work to action. The famous paper, 'Actions, Reasons and Causes', the first, partial statement of his new view of the mind, appeared in 1963. The view did not receive full expression until nearly a decade later in 'Mental Events' (1970), 'The Material Mind' (1973) and 'Philosophy as Psychology' (1974).

Meanwhile, Dennett arrived at Harvard as an undergraduate after a year at Wellesley in 1960. Though only 18, he tells us that already 'philosophy of mind and language transfixed my curiosity' (2008, Part 1, p. 23). He graduated from Harvard in 1963, the year in which 'Actions, Reasons, and Causes' was published, and received a doctorate from Oxford in 1965. He was 23! By then many of the ideas that became his first book, *Content and Consciousness* (finished in 1967 and published in 1969), were already well formed. He says (2008, Part 1, p. 22) that the first statement of the view that he came to call the intentional stance was in 'Mechanism and Responsibility', written in 1968 though not published until 1973. His famous 'flagship' paper, as he put it, 'Intentional Systems', was first given to an audience in 1970. It was published in 1971.

As the last two paragraphs make clear, despite the 25-year difference in age, Davidson and Dennett developed their versions of the normative view the mind at about the same time.

Moreover, in the period in which they developed these ideas, they swam in the same philosophical waters. They both studied at Harvard and were both profoundly influenced by Quine. Davidson was there before Dennett – as we saw, he received his PhD in 1949 – but he continued to collaborate with Quine for the rest of Quine's life. As an undergraduate, Dennett went after Quine in his senior thesis (1998a, p. 356) – but choose Quine as one of his examiners. The year he arrived at Harvard, 1960, was the year in which Quine published his immensely influential *Word and Object*. As Dennett (1987b) makes clear, Chapter 6 of that book, 'Flight from Intension', in which Quine introduces the idea that psychological talk is a 'dramatic idiom' (p. 219), indispensable in practical life but useless for doing science of mind, made a deep impression on him (as it did on most philosophers in that period).

Equally, both did the early work on their variants of the normative model in Oxford. Davidson did so during a visit to Oxford in 1960 or 1961 (he does not give the year in his autobiography, but in this period, he read works published only in 1959 and the first paper based on his own work, the famous paper 'Actions, Reasons and Causes', 'eventually emerged' in 1963 [Davidson 1999, p. 37]). In Dennett's case, the crucial period was the year in which he wrote his D.Phil. thesis, 1964–5 (2008, Part 1, pp. 25–6).

Moreover, the two were influenced by many of the same people and themes. Quine's view of psychological discourse, already mentioned, and his closely related views about translation were crucial to both. Both worked on Wittgenstein's views, in particular his view that psychological explanation is quite unlike other forms of explanation, sceptically but intensely. (Dennett says that when he was an undergraduate, Wittgenstein was 'my hero' [1991a, p. 463].) Both discuss Anscombe. As Dennett has made clear (1987c, p. 11), he took Sellars' distinction between the manifest image of people that we use in everyday life and the scientific image of people that animates psychology and human biology to be an important precursor of his own point of view. Though Davidson refers to Sellars very sparingly, Sellars' distinction had to be behind his distinction between psychological and other kinds of explanation, too. More generally, they both cut their philosophical teeth immersed in American Pragmatism, which was centred on Harvard and on Quine in particular. Pragmatism emphasized what works for purposes of prediction and control and was quite sceptical about trying to find out what there is, as philosophers have traditionally done. Both Davidson's and Dennett's models of the mind are firmly in that tradition, as we will see.

Thus, whether or not either directly influenced the other, they had so much in common that in one good sense they did not work entirely independently. Indeed, if they had not developed the normative picture of the mind when they did, probably someone else would have done so soon after. It was in the air. As to direct influence, Dennett must have read 'Actions, Reasons and Causes' while a graduate student in Oxford. It was one of the most widely discussed papers in analytic philosophy of mind and action of the time. However, while Davidson lays out belief/desire holism in the paper, only one paragraph near the end (p. 17) takes up themes that became anomalous monism. Anyway, compared to the influence of Quine, Wittgenstein, Sellars, and even Anscombe (Dennett 2008, Part 1), the impact of one paper of Davidson's would not have been large. Even Aristotle talked about psychological explanation. In the early going, Dennett refers to Davidson (1963) twice, Davidson never refers to Dennett.

Davidson's anomalous monism

Davidson's work on interpreting the mind is always hand-in-glove with his work on interpreting speech, especially speech in a language that the interpreter does not understand. (That is not true of Dennett, who has written relatively little about language.) The underlying principle is Quine's indeterminacy of translation. Quine (1960, Ch. 2) argues that there will always be a possibility of interpreting speech that we do not understand in more than one way. When there is, either translation will be as good as the other(s) and there is no further fact of the matter about what, in our language, the speaker meant in hers. For example, if we hear someone utter 'gavagai' (a word in Nepalese, apparently) while watching and maybe pointing at rabbits, all the behaviour is compatible with the speaker meaning (what we would call in English) rabbits, undetached rabbit-parts, a particularly tasty kind of food, cuteness and so on. While further behaviour may make some of these options implausible, there is no reason to think that it will always or indeed ever eliminate all but one option. (We find the same indeterminacy in building theories to account for a body of facts).

To indeterminacy, Davidson added his well-known (but misnamed) Principle of Charity (which Dennett in turn has treated as a close cousin of his Assumption of Rationality [1987b, p. 343].) Davidson urges that to translate speech in a language that we do not understand, we have to find an interpretation on which most of the speech acts turn out to be true in the speaker's immediate and immediately past environment. (The principle is misnamed because, as Davidson has recognized himself, seeking to find a way to interpret behaviour as reflecting the world accurately is not an act of charity; it is a requirement of finding the behaviour to express beliefs at all, 'since charity is not an option, but a condition of having a workable theory, . . .' (1984a, p. 197)).

Why? Because every speech act expresses not just meanings but also beliefs. If a subject behaves with respect to a speech act in a way that we did not expect, this could be because we have interpreted what she meant incorrectly – or it could be because she has unusual beliefs. In general, we cannot assign meanings without knowing what a subject believes, but we cannot know what a subject believes (since the content of beliefs is linguistic or at least language-like) without knowing what a subject means by her words. The only way to make progress with sorting one side out is to hold the other side roughly constant. And the only way to do that is to assume that the subject has mostly correct beliefs – and then to find a way to assign meanings to the utterances so that they come out to be mostly true (and, therefore, consistent).

From this, of course, the second key claim of the normative approach immediately follows: Beliefs must be mostly true and consistent. Otherwise, no speech could be interpreted as expressing beliefs at all. For Dennett, as we shall see, evolution guarantees general accuracy of belief. Creatures who approached the world with generally mistaken views would soon be some other creature's lunch. Davidson's view is much stronger than this in-fact-mostly-accurate approach. He holds that for us to find some groups of utterances to be expressing beliefs, we must have a way to find them to be mostly accurate.

The requirement that we find beliefs to be mostly true also entails that interpretation of linguistic behaviour is a thoroughly holistic activity. To interpret particular speech acts, we must interpret a whole language or a large part of one.

Indeterminacy of translation and the need for charity that follows in its wake will apply to language of all kinds and beliefs of all kinds. To get anomalous monism about the psychological, we must add one more element, something specific to the psychological (which includes beliefs as vehicles, though not the content of beliefs when content is not psychological). We have already seen what that element is: attributions of psychological states are governed by 'constitutive principles' (1974, p. 237) different from those that govern all other discourse.

Davidson (1970, 1973, 1974) focuses on two: rational coherence and consistency (1974, p. 237). By 'rational coherence' he means that the beliefs and motivators that we ascribe to someone must make her actions 'reasonable' (p. 233). By 'consistency' he means a number of things but the minimal element common to all his discussions is that we cannot ascribe to a subject simple, simultaneous beliefs that contradict one another except on rare occasions. Another is that beliefs and motivators must be responsive to other beliefs and motivators, new evidence and the like (1970, pp. 216–17). Something else he often means is that preferences and beliefs must, for example, be transitive. We cannot find ourselves wanting to ascribe a preference for a over b, b over c, and c over a very often and still be dealing with beliefs and desires (1974, p. 237). And they must in general not be symmetrical: a subject cannot in general prefer a to b and b to a.

If the psychological is constituted by conditions of rationality and consistency, how does it follow that it is anomalous, that is, that smooth, exceptionless laws linking events described psychologically to events described physically will not be possible? Here, Davidson is not very specific. At one point, he says that these constitutive conditions 'have no echo in physical theory, which is why we can look for no more than rough correlations between psychological and physical phenomena'. (He should have said phenomena psychologically and physically described, but let us overlook that.) I think the reason is this. Even if an event described physically is an event described psychologically (one event, two descriptions), there is no reason to expect that the next event having the same psychological properties will have remotely similar physical properties. Hence, *token-token identity* but no *type-type identity*, as the jargon has it.

Nor is this a particularly audacious claim. We find the same pattern all over. Take a patch of colour that has a certain shape. There is no reason to expect that the next patch of the same colour will have the same shape, even though every patch of colour will have some shape. So colour/shape monism and token-token identity but no type-type identity.

Since the development of the basic theory in the early 1970s, Davidson has added some elements. Perhaps the most important two are a form of externalism about content – that the content of belief tracks the world so well because content *consists of* the nearest causes shared by the subject and others (1999, p. 58) – and, related, that interpretation of a subject's speech and actions is a complicated three-way process involving my and the subject's access to a world in such a way that we can 'triangulate' – project lines from ourselves that cross at objects, thereby known by us to be shared (1996), and find in other's and one's own behaviour a pattern of making roughly the same judgements about shared objects and events. Triangulation introduces an entirely new kind of holism into the process of interpretation.

Dennett's intentional system approach

If Davidson starts from the indeterminacy of translation/ascription, Dennett starts from the irreducibility of the psychological to any other 'idiom'. The first 40-odd pages of his first book, *Content and Consciousness*, are devoted to the issue. Now Quine (1960, p. 221) viewed irreducibility as 'of a piece with' indeterminacy but it is not clear that this is so. There could be sources of irreducibility other than indeterminacy; there could be perfectly determinate kinds in two discourses that simply cannot be lined up. Whatever, like Davidson, Dennett thought of psychological discourse as irreducible to other discourses but useful, indeed nigh-indispensible in its own right. And he too thought of it as infected with indeterminacy.

In 'Intentional Systems' and in 'True Believers', which he calls his first and second flagship papers, he starts by distinguishing three explanatory stances that one can take towards a complex organism or system. Consider a simple chess-playing computer (a favourite example of Dennett's).

One stance is to explain its current behaviour and predict its future behaviour by understanding how it is built and what the causal processes in it are like. This would give us an extraordinarily detailed, secure explanation of the system but at a severe price – extreme complexity. Not even the programmers who wrote the chess-playing programme could give this kind of explanation of the system. This stance Dennett calls *the physical stance*.

Another stance is to predict and explain the system's behaviour by understanding the design built into it, in this case the programme controlling its operations. Dennett calls this *the design stance*. This stance will produce an explanation much simpler than the first one – all we need to understand is how the system is designed to behave, not all the details of how and how well it implements this design – but the simplicity comes at a price. For our explanations to be any good, the system has to function as it was designed to function – and we have to assume that it is doing so or the design stance is useless to us. Because of this assumption built into them, explanations from the design stance are less secure than explanations from the physical stance.

A third stance is to predict and explain the system's behaviour by treating it as having goals and some capacity to achieve these goals. We can ask, what is the system trying to do, and what means is it adopting in order to do so? For example, we see it move pawns from in front of its queen. We could adopt the design stance and ask, 'What rules did the programmers build into the programme to cause it to do this?' Or we can ask, 'What is it trying to do? Ah, get its queen out early' and reason, 'It knows that it's got to open a path through its pawns in order to do so'. This Dennett calls *the intentional stance*.

The intentional stance has the advantage of great simplicity. Instead of worrying about thousands of causal relationships (physical stance) or hundreds of rules, qualifiers, etc., built into procedures (design stance), all we have to worry about is one little goal, to get its queen out early, one little belief, that to do it it has to open a path through its pawns, and some fairly simple supplementary beliefs about how to do so in a way that is consistent with the rules of chess and the position of other pieces on the board. A three- or four-line inference and we are there.[3]

Of course, this simplicity comes at a cost: We have to treat the system, not just as having goals and something like beliefs about how to realize its goals, but also as having sufficient rationality to figure out, given what it believes, what it has to do to satisfy its goals. And note: These things have to be assumed or the intentional stance does not work, so we cannot use the intentional stance to test these attributions. Davidson was aware of this trade-off: Using what Dennett calls the intentional stance, he says that 'we can explain behaviour without knowing too much about how it was caused' and the price is that 'we cannot turn this mode of explanation into ... science' (1974, p. 233).

The key point (laid out as early as 1969, Ch. 4) is that we can ascribe psychological states by interpreting relations among environment, history and organic needs. In particular, we can start by ascribing to an organism the beliefs and motivators that it *ought* to have, given its environment, history and nature. So long as we can find a way to treat the target system as sufficiently rational, given its beliefs, to act in ways appropriate to reaching its goals, we are off and running on the road to powerful explanations, predictions and justifications.

Even without indeterminacy or irreducibility, there are important reasons for thinking that we have to pay attention to context if we are to ascribe psychological states. In particular, how a representation is implemented in the brain is not likely to tell you much about what psychological states are implemented in it, if any. Here is an argument (from 1978b, p. 47). Suppose that we devised a brain scanner with sufficient 'resolution' to find the sentence 'America is the world's greatest country!' written in Pedro's brain. Merely from encountering the sentence, we could not tell whether Pedro is jingoistic, ridiculing the idea, using the sentence as an example of a proposition in a philosophy class, just liked the sounds of the words, or what.[4]

If context plays an essential role in psychological ascription, it follows immediately that psychological explanation is massively holistic. We determine a person's psychological states by a complex interpretation of behaviour/brain/environment interactions as a whole. From this, it follows in turn that states described psychologically cannot be systematically reduced to brain states.

Comparison of the two positions

Davidson's and Dennett's picture of the psychological share many features. They agree that psychological explanation is massively holistic, that for a group of states to be beliefs they must be mostly true, that indeterminacy affects all psychological explanation, and that psychological discourse cannot be reduced to any other discourse, discourse about the brain or cognition in particular. Do they disagree about anything important? Various theorists – including

Dennett himself! – have claimed that they disagree about the reality of psychological states. Though both accept Quinean indeterminacy, he says, Davidson is a 'regular strength' realist about the existence of psychological states whereas he is a 'mild realist' (1991b, p. 98). I have doubts about whether there is any real difference in their positions and Dennett himself said later that calling himself a mild realist was at least a tactical mistake (1993, pp. 212–3).

So, for Davidson and Dennett, what status do psychological properties of persons-in-environments attributed under the constraints of rationality and accuracy/consistency have? Quite clearly, they both hold that these properties are real states of some kind. Psychological explanations are causal explanations, they both insist (Davidson 1963, Dennett 1987a). Even if we must redescribe the brain/world state implementing any psychological state in non-psychological language to get a precise statement of the cause and its effect, as both maintain (Davidson 1974, p. 231; Dennett 1987a, p. 57), for X to be a cause, X must exist. So how do they exist?

Much the same way in both pictures, I think. To determine which psychological state someone is in, to the extent to which we can determine this, we have to relate brain and body to the world. A given kind of psychological state can be implemented in many different states of brain/world interaction (the anomalous part of anomalous monism). There will often be some indeterminacy about exactly what psychological state someone is in: The question, Is she jealous or angry? may have no answer. Nonetheless, every psychological state, no matter how indeterminate its exact shape and content may be, will be some brain/world state (the monism part of anomalous monism). And our main access to psychological states of others is via behaviour (we will return to the issue of our access to our own psychological states). Relating behaviour to the world often reveals real patterns in the behaviour that we can see only by positing psychological states as their causes (the irreducibility claim of anomalous monism).

So far as I can see, Davidson and Dennett both believe everything in the previous paragraph. Yet a number of writers – including Dennett – hold Davidson to be more realist than Dennett (Dennett 1998, p. 98; Ross 2000, p. 159, a very important discussion of the issue of realism in Dennett). They tend to rely on what I regard as a slip on Davidson's part. In a few places, he treats indeterminacy as dramatically less radical than what Quine had in mind. For example, in (1991, pp. 214–5), Davidson says that there is no more to the indeterminacy of the psychological than there is to the 'indeterminacy' of whether the heat of something is measured in Celsius or Fahrenheit units. The trouble is, the heat itself is completely determinate. All that is indeterminate is which metric to use to measure it. As I said, I regard this passage as a slip – on a par with Dennett's early mistake of letting himself be called an instrumentalist (1987d, p. 71).[5]

Challenges

Interpretationist views of the mind built on assumptions of rationality and accuracy/consistency face a number of challenges:

1. Both experimentally and via the building of formal models, cognitive research has made a lot of progress with unravelling how the human mind works. This would seem to be just the kind of reductive activity that Davidson and Dennett rule out as impossible.
2. On this approach, how could ascriptions of psychological states be anything more than arbitrary projections of ascribers' beliefs? On what basis could we judge that some ascriptions are better than others?
3. Surely we can ascribe beliefs to subjects who are being massively irrational and who harbour mostly false beliefs, the seriously cognitively disturbed for example?
4. Consciousness is an important part of much of the psychological. It does not seem to be infected with indeterminacy, certainly not as we experience it in ourselves.
5. Related, if free choice requires precise, determinate investigation and selection, as it seems to do, do not Davidson and Dennett rule out free choice?

I am going to dodge (5). Free choice has been a major issue for Dennett, resulting in no less than two big books (1984 and 2003) and many papers. However, Davidson has hardly touched the subject. For reasons of space, I will do the same. Let us look briefly at the other four. (For more on Dennett on these issues, see Brook and Ross 2002).

Challenge 1: Cognitive science is not only possible, it is actual

Many theorists have thought that if anything that we'd call a mind must meet normative standards of rationality and accuracy/consistency, and if psychological talk cannot be related systematically to any other way of talking about our capacities as information processors, cognitive science, that is, a science of the mind, is impossible. Instead, the study of the mind must be a normative study, a study of what norms do and should govern behaviour, and it should be done using methods appropriate for studying norms. (For more on what norms are like and how to study them, see Brook 2009).

This challenge has to be seriously misguided. Davidson did a lot of work in decision theory and the semantics of natural languages that is at least closely comparable to cognitive science. Dennett is a big fan of cognitive science and explicitly introduces cognitive psychology as the approach to which we fall back when the intentional stance ceases to work (1987a).

One way in which the challenge is wrong is this. Cognitive science in its current form does not in fact pay much attention to psychological states described in terms of goals, beliefs and the like. This is because cognitive science in its current form is not much concerned with goals, purposes, or motivation of action. Instead, it is interested in teasing out the mechanisms, the design, by which we process information, reason about it, store it in memory, translate it into action and so on. Since the description of these processes does not carry with it the commitments of the discourse of beliefs and motivators, the constraints that operate on the latter discourse do not operate on the former. The way is open to both empirical theories and formal models of cognition.

A response to this is that cognitive science *should* be interested in psychological processes described psychologically. At present, it may be masking the psychological (the goal-directed, the belief-driven) in the same way that behaviourists did. (Dennett argues this persuasively about behaviourism in 1971 especially Chapter 5, 1978c, and 1978d).

But is cognitive science compatible the normative view of the mind? Yes. Two points. Pylyshyn has argued (e.g. in 1984 and 1999) that the only way to capture many of the similarities in cognitive function of interest to us across differences of subject and brain state is to use psychological language. Even if he is right, however, once kinds of cognitive function have been pinned down using this language with whatever indeterminacies cannot be eliminated, we are then free to explore causality, build models and computational simulations, and so on in any way we choose. Secondly, there is correlational science. As recent brain imaging work has shown, this kind of science can be exciting and revealing even without complete determinacy about the psychological or exceptionless bridging laws.

Challenge 2: Arbitrariness

Here's the challenge. How do we decide that saying a rock has the 'goal' of holding paper in place would be gratuitous, while saying that a bee has the goal of finding honey is not? The intuition seems clear, but we should like to know why. It is not because the bee is capable of formulating its goal to itself; it is not. Davidson did not respond to this challenge, so far as I know, but Dennett certainly has. As early as *Content and Consciousness* (uniquely among philosophers at the time), he had a solution: evolution.

> The principles of evolution proposed to explain learning and discrimination in the brain have the capacity to produce structures that have not only a cause but also a reason for being. That is, we can say of a particular structure that the animal has it because it helps in certain specified ways to maintain the animal's existence. It is a structure for discriminating edible from inedible material, or for finding one's way out of danger. [1969, p. 64]

Given its time, this passage is remarkable. It yields the approach that we have already seen: Start by asking, What goals ought the organism to have, given its evolutionary history and the possibilities presented by its environment? And what beliefs ought it to have, given its evolutionary history, experience, and cognitive apparatus? We then ask what in this repertoire of goals and beliefs would make what it is currently doing rational in its current environment (1987e)?

Challenge 3: False beliefs and irrationality

The challenge: We seem to be able to ascribe beliefs to subjects who are massively irrational and who harbour mostly false beliefs, the seriously cognitively disturbed for example. If so, being mostly accurate/consistent and making behaviour mostly rational are not necessary conditions of being a group of beliefs of someone's.

Dennett has a general strategy for dealing with this problem. Where the intentional stance does not work, back off to the 'design stance', to sub-personal cognitive psychology (1987a) – sub-personal because the subject herself is mostly not aware of the mechanisms in play. There is no requirement of accuracy or rationality here. We do indeed resort to this strategy often but it will not work for the specific problem before us. Sometimes we do not back down to the design stance in the face of massive inaccuracy, etc. We continue to ascribe beliefs.

But is the inaccuracy ever really widespread? Both Davidson and Dennett argue that even in a crazy ideologue, a paranoid conspiracy theorist, or someone suffering delusions and hallucinations, a lot of true beliefs remain (Dennett 1987d; Davidson 1974). These people don't bump into walls, they continue to feed themselves successfully, and, unfortunately, they often have large effects in the social world, effects that require extensive, detailed coordination and planning – and therefore a lot of true beliefs. If we could not find a way to ascribe such quotidian true beliefs as these, it is not clear that we have much reason to ascribe beliefs at all.

Challenge 4: Consciousness

Davidson and Dennett both hold that it is often indeterminate what psychological state we are in. Yet consciousness does not seem to be indeterminate. Much of the content of our conscious mental life seems to be perfectly determinate, or can be made so by redirecting attention to it.

Though most research on consciousness sides with these common intuitions, if they are correct, then Davidson's and Dennett's whole approach to the psychological is doomed. They must conceptualize consciousness in a way that squares with their view of the psychological, and of course with common experience. Davidson rose to this challenge on a number of papers on self-knowledge, Dennett in two books, the huge *Consciousness Explained* (1991a) and a smaller book based on lectures he gave to the Jean Nicod Institute in Paris, *Sweet Dreams* (2005), and many papers going back as far as 1978.

Davidson's papers are subtle and sometimes elusive but the general line is clear. If interpretation of another's speech and actions is a complicated three-way process involving my and the other's access to a world in which we can 'triangulate' – that is, project lines from ourselves that cross at objects, thereby known by us to be shared – my access to the subject, and my access to my own beliefs and the like (1991), so is my view of myself (1984b, 1987 and later papers).

For Dennett, the appropriate method to study consciousness is a special application of the intentional stance. On the new application, we seek to interpret, not what mental states make sense of behaviour, but how things will *seem* to someone given their behaviour. Dennett (1991a, pp. 72–9) calls this *heterophenomenology*, 'hetero' because it is done by another, 'phenomenology' because it seeks to construct how things seem to someone, that is, what their phenomenology is like. When we pay attention to how things seem to ourselves, we are using the same method, interpreting how things must seem to someone given how they are behaving, but, because it is applied to self, not other, and because it uses whatever information is available from the inside, not just behaviour, Dennett calls it *autophenomenology*. However, it is just as much a matter of interpretation and just as much *not* a matter of 'reading off' independently existing features as heterophenomenology.

Dennett has been accused of being an eliminativist, of denying the existence of consciousness. It is hard to see why. Here is his own response to the charge:

> Am I am eliminativist? I am a deflationist. The idea is to chip the phenomena of the mind down to size, undoing the work of inflationists who actively desire to impress upon themselves and everybody else just how supercalifragilisticexpialidocious consciousness is, so that they can maintain, with a straight face, their favourite doctrine: The Mind is a Mystery Beyond All Understanding. [2000, p. 369–70]

As I said, I am dodging challenge (5), free choice.

Summing up

To sum up, though Davidson and Dennett developed their versions of the normative picture of the mind at about the same time (early 1960s) and largely in the same place (Oxford), there is little evidence that either had a substantial influence on the views developed by the other. Moreover, as we saw, the two pictures are more alike on some issues, realism for example, than has been thought. And we saw that both are difficult to reconcile not only with mind/brain identity theory but also with functionalism about the mind. We concluded by examining five challenges to the whole approach. We ducked one of them, agency. Of the other four, the normative picture can handle two quite nicely (the success of cognitive science and the problem of arbitrariness), might have some trouble with a third (beliefs that do not appear to meet the relevant norms) and has laboured mightily to show that a fourth challenge can be met (account for consciousness).

Notes

1 Dennett himself once used the name 'interpretationism' for his view, though reluctantly (1987e, p. 15).

2 It is not clear that Davidson saw this, not at least in (1970, 1973, and 1974). Even Dennett has called himself a functionalism, for example, in (1998, p. 359). However, as he makes clear there, he has psychological function described in psychological language in mind, not cognitive function described mechanistically in what he calls sub-personal language (i.e. we are not aware of the mechanisms so described).

3 Breaking explanation down into a series of nested kinds of explanation, ordered by the size of the basic unit of explanation (beliefs and desires, designed functions, physical components) became a major organizing strategy throughout cognitive studies generally in the 1970s. It is called 'the trilevel hypothesis' – which has the peculiar distinction of not being a hypothesis, not being about levels, and not dealing with a triple of things but more like four or five.

4 In this, Dennett now has some important allies. Dretske urges, for example, that staring at the face of a gauge is not the way to discover what information it provides nor how it provides it (1995, p. 109).

Likewise, peering at a meaningful symbol is not the way to discover its meaning. Wittgenstein had seen the same thing in the 1930s (1967, §612): 'What I called jottings would not be a rendering of the text, not so to speak a translation with another symbolism. The text would not be stored up in the jottings. And why should it be stored up in our nervous system?'

5 Instrumentalism is the view that supposed unobservables such as electrons are really just postulations useful for making predictions. No such things actually exist. For Dennett, by contrast, states like beliefs and desires are real. They are real patterns in behaviour and/or in brain/world interactions. Their reality is like the reality of things such as centres of gravity.

References

Brook, A. and Ross R. (eds), (2002), *Daniel Dennett* (in the series, Contemporary Philosophy in Focus). New York: Cambridge University Press, pp. xii + 302.
Brook, A. (2009), 'Philosophy in and philosophy of cognitive science'. *Topics in Cognitive Science* 1: 216–30.
Davidson, D. (1963), *Actions, Reasons, and Causes*. In Davidson, 1980, pp. 3–20.
— (1970), 'Mental events'. In Davidson, 1980, pp. 207–24.
— (1973), 'The material mind'. In Davidson, 1980, pp. 245–60.
— (1974), 'Psychology as philosophy'. In Davidson, 1980, pp. 229–44.
— (1980), *Actions and Events*. Oxford: Oxford University Press.
— (1984a), 'On the very idea of a conceptual scheme'. Presidential Address, *Proceedings of the Seventieth Annual Eastern Meeting of the American Philosophical Association*, pp. 5–20.
— (1984b), 'First-person authority'. *Dialectica* 38: 102–111.
— (1987), 'Knowing one's own mind'. Presidential Address, *Proceedings of the Sixtieth Annual Pacific Meeting of the American Philosophical Association*, pp. 441–58.
— (1991), 'Three varieties of knowledge'. Reprinted in Davidson, 2001, pp. 205–20.
— (1999), 'Intellectual autobiography of Donald Davidson'. In Hahn, 1999, pp. 3–70.
— (2001), *Subjective, Intersubjective, Objective*. Oxford: Clarendon Press.
Dahlbom, B. (ed.) (1993), *Dennett and his critics: Demystifying mind*. Oxford, UK and Cambridge, MA: Blackwell.

Dennett, D. (1969), *Content and Consciousness*. London: Routledge.
— (1971), 'Intentional systems'. *Journal of Philosophy* 68: 87–106.
— (1978), *Brainstorms*. Montgomery, VT: Bradford Books.
— (1978a), 'Introduction'. In Dennett, 1978, pp. xi–xxii.
— (1978b), 'Brain writing and mind reading'. In Dennett, 1978, pp. 39–52.
— (1978c), 'Skinner skinned'. In Dennett, 1978, pp. 53–70.
— (1978d), 'Why the law of effect will not go away'. In Dennett, 1978, pp. 71–89.
— (1984), *Elbow Room: The Varieties of Free Will Worth Wanting*. Cambridge, MA: MIT Press.
— (1987), *The Intentional Stance*. Cambridge, MA: MIT Press.
— (1987a), 'Three kinds of intentional psychology'. In Dennett, 1987, pp. 43–68.
— (1987b), 'Mid-term examination'. In Dennett, 1987, pp. 339–50.
— (1987c), 'Setting off on the right foot'. In Dennett, 1987, pp. 1–12.
— (1987d), 'Instrumentalism reconsidered'. In Dennett, 1987, pp. 69–82.
— (1987e), 'True believers'. In Dennett, 1987, pp. 13–42.
— (1991a), *Consciousness Explained*. Boston: Little, Brown.
— (1991b), 'Real patterns'. In Dennett, 1998, pp. 95–120.
— (1993), 'Back from the drawing board'. In. B. Dahlbom, 1993, pp. 203–35.
— (1998), *Brainchildren*. Cambridge, MA: MIT Press.
— (1998a), 'Self-portrait'. In Dennett, 1998, pp. 355–66.
— (2000), 'With a little help from my friends'. In Ross et al., 2000, pp. 327–88.
— (2003), *Freedom Evolves*. New York: Viking Press.
— (2005), *Sweet Dreams*. Cambridge, MA: MIT Press.
— (2008), 'Autobiographical essay'. Parts 1–3, *Philosophy Now*, 22–6 July/August; 21–5 September/October; 24–5 November/December.
Dretske, F. (1995). *Naturalizing the Mind*. Cambridge, MA: MIT Press.
Hahn, L. E., (ed.) (1999). *The Philosophy of Donald Davidson*. Chicago: Open Court.
Pylyshyn, Z. (1984),*Computation and Cognition*. Cambridge, MA: MIT Press.
Quine, W. van O. (1960), *Word and Object*. Cambridge, MA: MIT Press.
Ross, D., Thompson, D. and Brook, A., (eds) (2000), *Dennett's Philosophy: A Comprehensive Assessment*, Cambridge, MA: MIT Press.
Ross, D. (2000), 'Rainforest realism'. In Ross et al., pp. 147–68.
Wittgenstein, L. (1967), *Zettel*. Oxford, UK: Basil Blackwell.

CHAPTER ELEVEN

Tracking representationalism: William Lycan, Fred Dretske and Michael Tye

David Bourget and Angela Mendelovici[1]

1 Introduction

There is something that it is like to be you. Perhaps you are currently having a visual experience of something blue, tasting something sweet or feeling a twinge of pain in your foot. These experiences partly characterize the phenomenal, qualitative or subjective aspect of your mental life. This phenomenon of there being something it is like for you to be in certain states is *phenomenal consciousness*.

According to *physicalism*, consciousness is a physical phenomenon. Physicalism offers an attractively simple ontology. The problem is that any putative description of conscious states in physical terms seems to leave out their most crucial feature, their phenomenal character. It seems utterly inexplicable why being in a certain physical state should be like anything at all. As Colin McGinn (1989) puts it, it's hard to see how the technicolour of consciousness can arise from the physical and functional features of soggy grey matter.

This chapter explores a relatively new strategy for understanding consciousness in physical terms, *tracking representationalism*. It's a two-step strategy. The first step accounts for phenomenal consciousness in terms of intentionality, the *aboutness* of mental states. The second step accounts for intentionality in terms of a physical tracking relation to the environment.

We focus on the views of three of the most influential proponents of tracking representationalism: William Lycan, Fred Dretske and Michael Tye. Section 2 describes tracking representationalism. Section 3 explores some of its motivations. Section 4 overviews some of the challenges it faces. Section 5 briefly discusses alternative versions of representationalism.

2 Tracking representationalism

Tracking representationalism is a theory of phenomenal consciousness, the 'what it's like' of being in certain states. Mental states that exhibit phenomenal consciousness are also known as *phenomenal states* or *experiences*. Phenomenal states are said to have *phenomenal properties*.

Tracking representationalism aims to understand consciousness in terms of another mental phenomenon: intentionality. *Intentionality* is the aboutness or directedness of mental states. For example, you can think about your mother, believe that you live on Earth or desire that it rains. These states exhibit a kind of directedness or aboutness. What a mental state is about is its *intentional content* (or just its *content*).

Mental states that exhibit intentionality can be said to have *intentional properties*, for example, the property of representing redness, or the property of representing that you live on Earth. It is useful to distinguish between pure and impure intentional properties. A *pure intentional property* is a property of representing a certain content. An *impure intentional property* is a property of representing a certain content in a certain manner. For example, the property of representing redness is a pure intentional property, while the property of representing redness *in imagination* is an impure intentional property.² We will say more about impure intentional properties shortly.

It is fairly uncontroversial that thoughts, beliefs and desires exhibit intentionality. Many perceptual states seem to exhibit intentionality as well. For example, visual experiences seem to present us with shapes, colours and other features of our environments. It is natural to describe them as having contents involving shapes, colours and other such features. Tracking representationalism claims that all conscious states exhibit intentionality, and that intentionality is the main ingredient in phenomenal consciousness.

More precisely, tracking representationalism combines three doctrines. The first is representationalism:

Representationalism: Every phenomenal property is identical to some (pure or impure) intentional property.³

Intuitively, representationalism is the view that phenomenal consciousness is just a special kind of intentionality. A mental state's representational nature exhausts its phenomenal nature.

Representationalism comes in two main varieties: pure representationalism and impure representationalism. *Pure representationalism* states that phenomenal properties are identical to pure intentional properties. *Impure representationalism* states that phenomenal properties are identical to impure intentional properties.

According to pure representationalism, phenomenal consciousness is a matter of intentional content *alone*. What it is like to be in a mental state is determined solely by what that mental state represents. The challenge facing pure representationalism is that it seems that states that represent the same contents can nonetheless differ in phenomenal character. For example, the following four states arguably involve the same intentional property of representing redness, but involve different corresponding phenomenal properties:

(Perc-red)   Perceptually experiencing unique (pure) red
(Think-red)   Thinking about unique red
(Nonconc-red)   Nonconsciously representing red (e.g. in early visual processing)
(Belief-red)   Having a standing belief about unique red

(Think-red) is an example of an *occurrent conceptual state*. It is *occurrent* in that it is entertained, undergone or active. It is *conceptual* in that it involves concepts. Other occurrent conceptual states include beliefs and desires that you are currently entertaining. (Belief-red) is an example of a *standing conceptual state*, a state that involves concepts but is not occurrent. (Nonconc-red) is an example of an occurrent state that may or may not be conceptual and that we are in no sense aware of.

These cases involve distinct phenomenal characters. (Belief-red) and (Nonconc-red) do not have phenomenal characters. While it is controversial whether (Think-red) has phenomenal character, it is uncontroversial that it has a different phenomenal character than (Perc-red). But if the same intentional properties do not always give rise to the same phenomenal properties, then phenomenal properties cannot be identified with intentional properties and pure representationalism is false. For such reasons, most representationalists endorse impure representationalism, on which the manner in which a mental state represents its content can make a difference to its phenomenal character. Lycan, Dretske and Tye are all impure representationalists.

Impure representationalist views can be further divided into two main types. According to *one-manner impure representationalism*, every phenomenal property is identical to an impure intentional property of the form *representing* C *in manner* M, where M is the *same* manner of representation for all phenomenal states. M demarcates phenomenal from non-phenomenal states, so we will refer to it as the *demarcating manner of representation*. In effect, the one-manner view's appeal to manners of representation serves to preclude certain states, such as (Think-red), (Nonconc-red) and (Belief-red), from having phenomenal properties. Within the class of states exhibiting the demarcating manner, a mental state's phenomenal properties are determined by its intentional properties. Dretske and Tye both endorse one-manner representationalism.

The second type of impure representationalism ascribes a larger role to manners of representation. According to Lycan (1996), each sensory modality has a corresponding manner of representation. Visual experiences represent visually, auditory experiences represent aurally, and so on. Each of these manners of representation factors into the resulting phenomenal character of the experience. On his view, content only determines phenomenal character within a sensory modality. This is *intra-modal representationalism*.[4]

The second component of the tracking representationalism defended by Lycan, Dretske and Tye is reductionism about manners of representation:

> *Reductionism about manners of representation*: Manners of representation are physical or functional properties.

Dretske, Tye and Lycan take the relevant manners of representation to be reducible to physicalistically acceptable entities, such as functional roles or evolutionary histories.

Both Dretske (1995) and Tye (1995, 2000) take the demarcating manner to have two components, one that precludes occurrent and standing conceptual states, like (Think-red) and (Belief-red), from having phenomenal character, and one that precludes states that we are in no sense aware of, like (Nonconc-red), from having phenomenal character.

Dretske (1995) and Tye (1995, 2000) claim that phenomenal states have a certain 'poisedness' to impact on central cognition. They both take poisedness to be part of the demarcating manner, though they understand it slightly differently.[5] According to Dretske and Tye, (Nonconc-red) and other states that we are in no sense aware of do not supply information to conceptual systems, and so they do not have phenomenal properties.

Dretske (1995) and Tye (1995, 2000) also take representing non-conceptually to be part of the demarcating manner of representation. For Dretske, non-conceptual contents are those that are represented by innate (or 'systemic' (Dretske 1995, p. 12)) representations. Tye does not offer a precise account of non-conceptual representation, but he makes some remarks that suggest that it may be a matter of whether the representation allows us to pick out instances of the same property on different occasions (Tye 2000, pp. 62–3). Since (Think-red) and (Belief-red) have purely conceptual contents, they do not represent in the demarcating manner, and so they do not have phenomenal properties.[6]

Lycan (1996) is less committal on how to characterize the relevant manners of representation posited by intra-modal representationalism. He suggests that manners are constituted by functional roles, but he does not specify which roles.

The third component of tracking representationalism is the tracking theory of intentionality:

The tracking theory of intentionality: Intentionality is (or derives from) a tracking relation.

According to the tracking theory, intentionality is a matter of detecting, carrying information about or otherwise correlating with features of the environment. For example, the concept CHAIR might represent chairs because it detects, carries information about or correlates with chairs.[7]

Lycan, Dretske and Tye each has his own favourite refinement of the tracking theory. On Dretske's teleological view, a representational state x represents the property F iff x has the function of indicating F (1995, p. 2). The relevant notion of function is a teleological one; it is a matter of something's 'job' or 'purpose'. In cases of phenomenal states, the relevant functions derive from their evolutionary history. Tye's view is that a state S of creature c represents that P just in case, 'if optimal conditions were to obtain, S would be tokened in c if and only if P were the case; moreover, in these circumstances, S would be tokened in c because P is the case' (2000, p. 136).[8] Lycan (1996) does not settle on a specific version of the tracking theory, but endorses a broadly evolutionary approach.[9]

Recall that tracking representation aims to account for consciousness in physical terms. Together with a physicalistically kosher account of manners of representation, the tracking theory is key to accomplishing this goal. On tracking representationalism, consciousness is a matter of intentionality and manners of representation. Intentionality is a matter of tracking, which is a physical relation, and the manners of representation are functional roles or evolutionary histories.

3 Motivations for tracking representationalism

In this section, we consider motivations for representationalism in general (subsections 3.1–3.3) and motivations specifically for tracking representationalism (subsections 3.4 and 3.5).

3.1 Sensory qualities

Lycan's main consideration in favour of representationalism is that it provides a neat theory of the qualities we are aware of in perception (1987, 1996). When we introspect on our perceptual experiences, we notice various qualities. For example, when you introspect upon a perceptual experience of a blue circle, you notice qualities like *blueness* and *roundness*. One central question about the nature of perception can be put as follows: What are these qualities and where do they fit into our overall theory? Lycan puts the problem in terms of phenomenal objects, where *phenomenal objects* are the bearers of sensory qualities: What are phenomenal objects?

One view of perception, *naive realism*, takes phenomenal objects to be external world objects and the qualities we are aware of in perception to be real properties of those external objects. The circle you experience exists in the external world, and blueness and roundness are properties of this circle. Unfortunately, this view has trouble accounting for the qualities we are aware of in hallucination. In hallucination, we are also aware of sensory qualities, but there needn't be an external object with such qualities. If you are hallucinating a blue circle, there needn't be anything blue and circular before you. So it looks like phenomenal objects can't be external world objects after all.

Another view of perception, the *sense data view*, takes phenomenal objects to be mental objects, or *sense data*, and sensory qualities to be properties of sense data. When you see a blue circle, you have a blue and round sense datum in your mind. Blueness and roundness are properties of the sense datum. This view faces many challenges, but one is particularly relevant for present purposes: It involves a commitment to apparently irreducibly mental particulars, and so it seems incompatible with a physicalist theory of the mind. This leads Lycan (1987) and many other theorists to reject the view.

A third alternative, the *adverbialist* theory of perception, denies the assumption that there are phenomenal objects. Sensory qualities are not properties of *something*. They are not really properties at all. Instead, adverbialism claims that sensory qualities are *ways* of perceiving. When you see something blue, you perceive *bluely*. 'Bluely' is an adverb that modifies the verb 'perceive', which is why the view is called 'adverbialism'. Likewise, when you see a blue circle, you perceive *bluely* and *roundly*. But problems arise in the case of complex experiences. What happens when you perceive a blue circle and a red square? Do you perceive *bluely*, *roundly*, *redly* and *squarely*? The problem is that on this adverbialist treatment this would be indistinguishable from perceiving a blue square and a red circle. This problem is known as the *many properties problem* and was first put forth by Frank Jackson (1977).[10]

Lycan (1987, 1996) argues that representationalism offers the most plausible account of phenomenal objects. It allows us to maintain that sensory qualities are properties of phenomenal objects, but deny that these phenomenal objects are external world objects or sense data. Instead, the representationalist can say that phenomenal objects are *intentional objects*, and sensory qualities are represented properties of these intentional objects.[11] What is an intentional object? On the most general characterization, intentional objects are *represented* objects, or objects that intentional states are about. For example, a fear that the economy is failing has the economy as its intentional object, and a belief that Santa Claus is jolly has Santa Claus as its intentional object. On Lycan's view, then, when you see a blue circle, your experience involves an intentional object that is blue and round. In other words, your experience involves a represented object that is represented as having the properties of blueness and roundness. As the example of believing that Santa Claus is jolly illustrates, intentional objects need not exist. Thus, by taking phenomenal objects to be intentional objects, the representationalist can allow that sometimes phenomenal objects do not exist. In a case of hallucination, you are aware of an intentional object having sensory qualities, but this object happens not to exist.

While this argument for representationalism is best developed in Lycan (1987), echoes of this reasoning are also found in Dretske (1995, 2003), Tye (1995) and Harman (1990). As we will see, the argument from transparency bears some similarities to this argument as well.

3.2 The transparency of experience

Perhaps the best-known argument for representationalism is the argument from transparency. Gilbert Harman (1990) introduces this argument and Tye (1991, 1995, 2000) further develops it.[12]

The argument from transparency is based on introspective observations about what we do and do not notice in experience. In a nutshell, the introspective observations are these:

1. When we pay attention to our experiences, we don't notice qualitative properties attributed to our experiences themselves.
2. When we pay attention to our experiences, the qualitative properties that we notice are attributed to the objects of our experiences.

To borrow Harman's (1990) famous example, when Eloise sees a tree, she notices the greenness of the leaves, the brownness of the trunk and the overall shape of the tree. All the qualities that she notices seem to her to be properties of external objects, not of her experience. Our experiences seem to be characterized by properties of the sorts that external objects have, not properties that sense data or other mental entities have. Moreover, introspection reveals exactly the same properties whether or not corresponding objects exist. All this suggests that the nature of experience is exhausted by represented properties of represented objects.

Though advocates of transparency focus on visual experiences, the transparency observation is supposed to hold for all experiences. When we introspect on our auditory experiences, for example, we notice properties of sounds, such as their loudness and pitch, but we don't notice any qualitative features of our auditory experiences themselves.[13]

The claim that experience is transparent has been challenged on various grounds. Kind (2003) and Loar (2003) suggest that, though we are not *normally* aware of qualitative features of our experiences, with some effort, we can become aware of such features. But perhaps the most common kind of objection comes in the form of examples of experiences in which we do seem to be aware of qualitative features of experience, for example, experiences involved in blurry vision. Since these potential counterexamples to transparency are also potential counterexamples to representationalism, we will discuss them in section 4.

3.3 Co-variation between intentional content and phenomenal character

The intentional properties of experience seem to co-vary with their phenomenal properties. Phenomenal greenness seems to go with represented greenness, phenomenal loudness with represented loudness and so on. Put otherwise, if two experiences differ in their intentional properties, then they also differ in their phenomenal properties, and vice versa. Representationalism can explain this: Phenomenal properties just are a species of intentional properties.

Tye offers a version of this motivation as part of his argument from transparency (2000, p. 48). Suppose your experience of a ripe tomato has a particular intentional property. It also has a particular phenomenal property. If we change the intentional property, say by changing the represented colour of the tomato, then your phenomenal properties change too. Tye claims that this holds for all experiences. If two experiences differ in their intentional contents, then they also differ in their phenomenal characters. In other words, intentional properties supervene on phenomenal properties.

Tye's overall argument for representationalism is an inference to the best explanation: The best explanation of the observed relationship between phenomenal properties and intentional properties *and* the transparency observation is that phenomenal properties are just a species of intentional properties.

Frank Jackson (2004, p. 109) offers the reverse observation in favour of representationalism: If two experiences differ in their phenomenal properties, then they also differ in their intentional properties. For example, your visual experience of a red pen has certain phenomenal properties, and it has certain intentional properties. Suppose we change your experience so that it has different phenomenal properties, say, by switching the red pen with a blue pen. Now your experience also has different intentional properties. Jackson takes similar observations to hold across all experiences. If this is right, then phenomenal properties supervene on intentional properties. But then, Jackson argues, intentional properties suffice for phenomenal properties.[14]

3.4 Providing a physicalist theory of consciousness

As we mentioned at the outset, phenomenal consciousness seems to resist physicalist treatment. By providing a two-step reduction of consciousness to tracking, tracking representationalism offers an attractive physicalist theory of consciousness. The first step reduces consciousness to intentionality and manners of representation. This step relies on the arguments discussed in subsections 3.1–3.3. The second step reduces intentionality to a species of tracking relation, and manners of representations to broadly physical properties. The reduction of intentionality to tracking is somewhat plausible since many of the currently popular theories of intentionality are tracking theories. Combining the two steps, then, offers us a reduction of phenomenal consciousness to broadly physical properties. The technicolour of experience is just a matter of internal states tracking properties in the world in the right way.

3.5 The mapping problem

The *mapping problem* of consciousness is the problem of specifying a model that can predict which phenomenal states accompany which physical states. The mapping problem is independent of the ontological problem of determining the metaphysical nature of phenomenal consciousness, that is, whether it is physical or irreducibly mental. For example, knowing that conscious states are physical would not by itself tell us which physical states are correlated with which phenomenal states. Conversely, knowing which physical states go with which phenomenal states would not tell us whether the correlated states are identical or related in some other way instead. While philosophers have traditionally focused on the ontological problem, solving the mapping problem is crucial for answering various practical questions concerning consciousness; for example, Can comatose patients feel pain? Could electronic circuits ever feel anything? Is there anything it is like to be an ant?

Tracking representationalism underpins all existing theories of consciousness that could provide a solution to the mapping problem, including those that have been advanced by neuroscientists and psychologists (e.g. Crick 1994, Baars et al. 1998, Edelman 1989). These possible solutions share three components corresponding to the three components of the tracking representationalist view. First, phenomenal properties are associated one-to-one with intentional contents (this component is secured by the one-manner representationalist view). The second component is a biological or functional characterization of the property that distinguishes physical states that are associated with phenomenal states from other physical states (e.g. Crick's 40hz hypothesis, or Dretske and Tye's accounts of the demarcating manners). The last component is the identification of the intentional contents of experiences with what their neural vehicles track in the outside world (this is secured by the tracking theory of intentionality). Taken together, these components specify a one-to-one correspondence between phenomenal properties and physical states or physical state types, thereby purporting to solve the mapping problem. All theories of consciousness that come anywhere close to specifying such a correspondence consist in the three above components; they are all forms of tracking representationalism.

Alternative approaches are not merely hard to justify, they are hard to *imagine* or even *formulate*. It is very hard to see how else we could specify a general relation between phenomenal states and physical states than by identifying the intentional contents of the former with the tracked contents of the latter. In our view, this may be the best available motivation for tracking representationalism.[15]

4 Objections

This section considers objections to tracking representationalism. Some are directed specifically at tracking versions of representationalism (subsection 4.1). Others are directed at representationalism in general (subsection 4.2). We close with objections to impure representationalism (subsection 4.3).

4.1 Objections to tracking representationalism

4.1.1 Inverted earth

Ned Block (1990, 1996) argues that the combination of representationalism with a tracking theory of intentionality leads to implausible consequences. Imagine a planet just like the Earth except for two small differences: First, all colours have been inverted. On Inverted Earth, ripe bananas are blue, blueberries are yellow, ripe tomatoes are green and grass is red. Second, colour names are also inverted. For example, inhabitants of Inverted Earth use the word 'yellow' for the colour that we call 'blue'. One night, you are transported to Inverted Earth without your knowledge.

Before you wake up, a spectrum-inverting device is inserted into your optic nerve (again, without your knowledge). As a result, you notice nothing unusual about the colours of things when you wake up. It is highly plausible that you could in principle never figure out that you are now on a planet with inverted colours. You might go on living the rest of your life there without ever noticing anything unusual about the colours of things. This seems to be a perfectly consistent scenario.

This apparent possibility is inconsistent with some forms of tracking representationalism. On Earth, you had a brain state s that tracked the colour red. After you've spent some time on Inverted Earth, this state will come to track the colour green. As a result, tracking representationalism seems to predict that after sufficient time has passed you would experience green when you are in s on Inverted Earth. For example, you should eventually come to experience green when in the presence of ripe tomatoes. But it seems clear that you would not, given the spectrum-inverted device that has been implanted in you.

This argument does not work against all versions of tracking representationalism. In particular, it does not bear on views on which what s represents is the same on Earth and Inverted Earth. This is the case on teleological theories. Take for example Dretske's view that what an experience represents is a matter of what it has the biological function of indicating. Your internal states do not acquire new biological functions on Inverted Earth (those were fixed in the course of evolution on Earth), so this kind of tracking view is compatible with the scenario as described.

4.1.2 Swamp-person

While teleological views easily escape the objection from Inverted Earth, they face another powerful objection: the Swamp-person objection.[16]

Though it is highly unlikely, it seems perfectly possible that a molecule for molecule duplicate of you could suddenly come into existence in a swamp as a result of a lightning strike. Moreover, it seems plausible that this Swamp-person would have conscious experiences. A Swamp-person could see the swamp, feel the mud and have all the other experiences that you would have if you suddenly found yourself in a swamp.

The problem for teleological versions of tracking representationalism is that Swamp-person's mental states have no evolutionarily determined biological functions, since Swamp-person has no evolutionary history. But then they do not have the biological functions relevant to determining intentional content. This means that they cannot represent anything by the lights of teleological accounts of intentionality. Given the kind of representationalist view under consideration, this in turn implies that Swamp-person would have no experiences, which seems implausible. Inverted Earth and Swamp-person together constitute a dilemma for tracking representationalism.[17]

4.1.3 Causal efficacy

Tracking representationalism also faces issues regarding the causal role of experiences. This objection applies to all views on which phenomenal properties are *wide properties*, that is, properties that involve factors outside of one's body at the time of their instantiation. Tracking representationalism implies that phenomenal properties are wide properties because it takes them to involve relational properties involving external objects and/or historical events.

Suppose you are looking for a tomato. You open your refrigerator, lean forward and see a tomato on a shelf. As a result, you extend your arm, grab the tomato and close the door. It seems plausible that your arm movement is caused by the combination of mental states you are in. Simplifying a little, it seems that the movement is caused by (i) your desire to take a tomato out of the refrigerator, (ii) your visual experience of a tomato in the refrigerator and (iii) your belief that you can pick up the tomato thus experienced by making the relevant arm movement. But if the property instantiated in the visual experience in question is a wide property involving such factors as your evolutionary history or a link between your internal brain states and features of your environment, it cannot play an immediate causal role in bringing about your arm movement. Wide properties cannot have immediate effects on one's movements. In principle, it should be possible to fully explain your arm movement in terms of what went on in your head and the rest of your body at the time. If phenomenal properties are a kind of tracking property, they are not *immediately* efficacious in bringing about behaviour.[18]

A typical reply to this objection is to grant the point but try to find some other explanatory role for wide experiences to play. For example, Dretske (1995, p. 161) grants that on his view phenomenal properties cannot be immediate causes of bodily movements. However, he goes on to argue that they can play another kind of explanatory role. For example, the fact that a certain phenomenal state has the function of tracking a certain external property might seem to explain why its tokens tend to occur in the presence of instances of the property. Phenomenal states might well have an explanatory role on Dretske's and similar views. However, this does not erase the fact that tracking representationalism is incompatible with the seemingly obvious fact that instantiations of phenomenal properties have immediate behavioural effects. The objection was not that tracking representationalism makes phenomenal properties explanatorily redundant, but that it is incompatible with their playing an immediate role in bringing about bodily movements.

4.1.4 The mismatch problem

According to Tye's, Dretske's and Lycan's versions of tracking representationalism, the intentional content of a mental state is what it tracks and the phenomenal character of a mental state is its intentional content. In short, the phenomenal character of a mental state is what it tracks.[19] The problem is that the phenomenal characters of some of our experiences are not plausibly identified with the features in our environment that we track. Consider an experience of red. This state plausibly tracks something like the disposition to reflect electromagnetic radiation with a wavelength of approximately 650 nm. The problem is that this does not seem to be plausibly identifiable with the experience's phenomenal character, what it's like to have the experience. The problem is that phenomenal redness and surface reflectance properties seem utterly dissimilar. Many other qualities we are aware of in our experiences seem to have no matching properties in our environment: the painfulness of pain, the sound of a harp and the feeling of heat are not plausibly identified with physical properties of things in our bodies or environment.[20,21]

Tracking representationalists might reply to this worry by appealing to the *phenomenal concepts strategy*. The apparent distinctness between phenomenal redness and surface reflectance properties is an illusion created by the fact that we have two different ways of representing the same property. Somehow, the different operating principles of the two ways of representing are incompatible, making it hard for us to see phenomenal redness is the same thing as some reflectance property. Whether this sort of reply can succeed is a hotly debated topic, but we remain sceptical.[22]

4.1.5 Phenomenal externalism

Many of the above objections to the tracking component of tracking representationalism arise from its commitment to *phenomenal externalism*, the view that the phenomenal character of a mental state is at least partly determined by factors outside the subject's body. According to phenomenal externalism, two intrinsic duplicates (duplicates from the skin in) might differ in their phenomenal properties. The Swamp-person and Inverted Earth objections target specific versions of phenomenal externalism on which phenomenal properties are partly determined by historical or non-historical environmental factors, respectively, while the causal efficacy objection and the mismatch problem are problematic for all versions.[23]

Phenomenal externalism itself might seem outlandish independently of any downstream consequences. Dretske, Lycan and Tye, however, have each offered positive arguments for phenomenal externalism (Dretske 1996, Lycan 2001, Tye forthcoming).

4.2 General objections to representationalism

4.2.1 Perceptual distortion

The objections in the preceding section are targeted specifically at tracking representationalism. Other objections apply to representationalism independently of any commitment to the tracking theory. Most of these objections involve cases of perceptual distortion. These are cases in which what we experience is distorted compared to the way we take the world to be, but we do not tend to regard our experiences as misrepresenting. All objections of this sort aim to show that representationalism is false because some experiences in the same sensory modality can differ in phenomenal character without differing in content. If true, this would imply that there is something more to experience than representing a certain content in the kinds of manners described by Lycan, Dretske and Tye.

Blurry vision is the most widely discussed example of perceptual distortion. When you see blurry, you do not tend to think of your experience as presenting you with some blurry or fuzzy object. This makes it hard to see what intentional contents might characterize blurry vision. This line of argument against representationalism originates from Boghossian and Velleman (1989).

Dretske's (2003) view is that blurry experiences in fact do represent fuzzy objects. Tye (2003) suggests that what characterizes blurry experiences is that their contents leave the contours of objects indeterminate in a certain way. A more recent proposal by Allen (2013) is that blurry experiences represent their objects as having multiple contours.

It is difficult to adjudicate the question of what blurry experiences represent qua blurry experiences. However, we suggest that blurry experiences can easily be seen to differ in representational content compared to non-blurry experiences, because blurry experiences clearly leave out some information about the world. Blurry experiences always involve a deficiency in detail.[24]

Peacocke (1983) presents a set of objections from perceptual distortion against the view that the phenomenal character of an experience is determined by its content. The best known of these objections involves two experiences in which one sees two identical trees from different distances. Tree 1 and Tree 2 do not look different in size, and so the experiences of Tree 1 and Tree 2 do not differ in content. But these experiences differ in phenomenal character corresponding to the different apparent sizes of the trees. So it does not seem that the perspectival aspects of the phenomenal character of visual experiences are captured by their contents.

Lycan (1996), Harman (1990) and Tye (1996) offer accounts of the perspectival aspect of vision. According to Lycan, we need two layers of content to explain perspective: a layer that represents objects in objective three-dimensional space and a layer that represents coloured shapes in a two-dimensional space. In the case of the two trees, the two experiences are alike with respect to the first layer of content but their second layers of content involve different sized shapes. Harman and Tye suggest that the difference in content between the two tree experiences is one in situation-dependent properties such as *being large from here*.

4.2.2 Allegedly contentless phenomenal states

Pains, moods and emotions are challenging for representationalism because it is not at all clear what they represent. Even if they have intentional properties, it is not clear that their phenomenal properties can be identified with any of their intentional properties.

Tye (2008) suggests that pains represent bodily damage at a bodily location, and that they represent the damage as bad. Different pains represent different types of bodily damage. For example, a stabbing pain represents sudden damage at a well-defined location, whereas an ache represents internal damage at a vaguely defined location. These contents determine pain's phenomenal character.

Tye's view attributes two different types of content to pains: bodily damage and badness. Different kinds of worries arise for each content. While bodily damage is plausibly tracked, it is not clear that it captures the phenomenal features of pain. The second component, the representation of badness, does seem to capture an aspect of pain's phenomenal character. However, it is not clear that the tracking representationalist can appeal to this content, since it is not clear that this is a content that we can track. These worries are specific instances of the mismatch problem discussed in subsection 4.1.4.[25]

According to Tye, emotions represent objects as (1) having evaluative features (e.g. as being dangerous, invasive or foul) and (2) causing or being accompanied by a bodily disturbance (e.g. a racing heart or perspiration).[26] As in the case of pain, questions arise as to whether these contents can both be tracked and capture emotions' phenomenal characters.

Moods seem to escape this kind of treatment, since they do not seem to represent external items at all. For example, experiences of sudden elation, free-floating anxiety or pervasive sadness do not seem to qualify any objects. There are several options open to the representationalist. Tye has suggested that moods represent departures from the 'range of physical states constituting functional equilibrium' (1995, p. 129). More recently, Tye (2008) has suggested that at least some moods represent the world in general as having affective properties.[27] Mendelovici (forthcoming) suggests that moods represent the same properties as their corresponding emotions, but that they do not represent any objects as having these properties. Moods represent *mere* properties. Kind (forthcoming) objects that all these views fail to capture the phenomenal character of moods.

4.3 Objections to reductionism about manners of representation

Objections have also been raised against the reductive view of manners of representation that is part of tracking representationalism. The specific proposals put forward by Dretske and Tye have been questioned on a number of grounds. On their view, what distinguishes phenomenal from non-phenomenal representation (beyond differences in content) is that the former, but not the latter, are non-conceptual and relevantly poised to influence cognition. One simple objection to this view is that some subconscious states influence cognition and have non-conceptual content without being phenomenally conscious.[28] The case of blindsight also seems to show that being poised and non-conceptual is not sufficient for a representation to be phenomenally conscious (Block 1995).

The appeal to non-conceptual content might also be questioned on other grounds. According to Dretske and Tye, only non-conceptual contents contribute to phenomenal character. This precludes thoughts from having phenomenal characters, since they are conceptual states. This might seem implausible to some (see Horgan and Tienson (2002), and Pitt (2004)). Relatedly, it is quite plausible that conceptual contents are sometimes involved in perceptual states and are responsible for certain phenomenal features of those states. For example, there is a phenomenal difference between seeing the duck-rabbit as a duck versus seeing it as a rabbit.[29]

It is noteworthy that this approach to demarcating properties is open to general objections to physicalism and functionalism. For example, Chalmers' (1996) zombie argument applies. It is on the face of it conceivable that one has brain states that track features in one's environment while being poised and non-conceptual, but one has no phenomenal experiences. If conceivability is a guide to possibility, this suggests that such a scenario is possible, which is incompatible with the claim that consciousness is a matter of poised, non-conceptual tracking. Jackson's (1982) knowledge argument also applies without modification. See Chapter 14 for more on these debates. That the usual objections to functionalism and physicalism apply suggests that tracking representationalism might not make the ontological problem of consciousness easier after all.

5 Other kinds of representationalism

Most of the objections discussed in previous sections are not effective against representationalism taken on its own. They target representationalism in combination with the tracking theory of intentionality and/or reductionism about manners of representation. This has led several authors to reject the tracking theory and/or the reductionist view of manners of representation while retaining the representationalist component.[30]

One alternative to tracking representationalism is *mere* representationalism. Chalmers (2004) and Pautz (2010a, b) endorse representationalism without endorsing a physicalist view of intentionality or manners of representation. Mere representationalism does not aim to provide a physicalist theory of consciousness or a solution to the mapping problem, but it might still seem to improve our understanding of consciousness. It at least provides us with a better understanding of the internal structure of consciousness, which might help formulate hypotheses regarding its relation to physical structures. Mere representationalism also retains the benefits of reductive representationalism as far as the problem of hallucination discussed earlier goes.

Another alternative to tracking representationalism is the pure representationalist view briefly discussed in section 2, which denies that manners of representation are needed to explain consciousness. On this view, consciousness is simply intentionality: the difference between conscious and nonconscious representations is simply a difference in content. One difference in content that might be relevant is that nonconscious intentional states have less determinate contents than phenomenal experiences. Other differences could be relevant. Bourget (2010a) and Mendelovici (2010) defend pure representationalist theories of consciousness.

6 Conclusion

Tracking representationalism is a relatively new theory of phenomenal consciousness. As our cursory overview shows, it has generated much discussion over the past few years. Whether or not it ultimately succeeds, it has challenged and reshaped the contemporary understanding of the relationship between consciousness and intentionality.

Notes

1. This paper is thoroughly co-authored.
2. We borrow this way of defining intentional properties from Chalmers 2004.
3. Lycan, Dretske and Tye offer slightly different definitions of representationalism. For Lycan, representationalism is the view that 'the mind has no special properties that are not exhausted by its representational properties, along with or in combination with the functional organization of its components' (Lycan 1996, p. 11). Dretske defines representationalism as the view that '[a]ll mental facts are representational facts' (Dretske 1995, p. xiii). Tye takes representationalism to be the view that 'phenomenal character is one and the same as representational content that meets certain further conditions' (2000, p. 45). We believe our working definition captures the core thesis defended by Lycan, Dretske, and Tye.
4. Weaker views are possible. For example, *weak representationalism* merely asserts that phenomenal states are essentially representational.
5. Tye understands it as being a matter of being poised to affect beliefs, desires, and other conceptual states, while Dretske understands it as being a matter of having the function of supplying information to conceptual systems.
6. These accounts of the demarcating manner of representation compete with several accounts of the neural correlate of consciousness found in the scientific literature. Much of the scientific discussion of the problem of consciousness assumes something like the tracking representationalist view (c.f. Crick 1994, Baars et al. 1998, Edelman 1989).
7. Tracking theories need not claim that all intentional states get their content directly from tracking. For instance, a common view is that all atomic representations get their contents from tracking, while composite representations get their contents compositionally from atomic states.
8. See Tye 2000, Chapter 6, for Tye's account of optimal conditions.
9. The teleological approach to intentionality is defended by Millikan (1984), Neander (1995), and Papineau (1993).
10. The problem is further developed by Lycan (1987), who argues that the only available adverbialist solution leads to intentionalism.
11. The view that the objects of perception are intentional objects can be traced back to Anscombe (1965) and Hintikka (1969).

12 The transparency of experience has its historical roots in G. E. Moore (1903), but, as Kind (2003) convincingly argues, the version of the transparency thesis Moore had in mind was considerably weaker than the one Harman and Tye endorse.

13 Harman's (1990) argument from transparency stops there. Tye (2000)'s version of the argument from transparency, however, combines the transparency observations with an additional observation, which we will consider in the next subsection.

It is important to note that Harman only denies that we are aware of any *qualitative* features of our experiences. This is consistent with the possibility of introspecting non-qualitative features of experiences, for example, their representational or temporal features. Some authors take the transparency thesis to rule out such observations. But this makes the transparency thesis stronger than required by Harman's argument.

14 Byrne (2001) also develops an argument along these lines.

15 However, we are sceptical that tracking representationalism succeeds at solving the mapping problem. It is not clear to us that tracking under a physically or functionally specified manner correlates well with phenomenal consciousness. Some of the objections in section 4 speak to this point.

16 This objection was inspired by a thought experiment from Davidson 1987.

17 Tye (2000) attempts to offer an account of the intentionality of phenomenal states that avoids the two horns of the dilemma constituted by these objections. In our opinion, the resulting account seems implausibly *ad hoc*.

18 See Horgan (1991).

19 Tye, Dretske and Lycan endorse an *identity version of representationalism*, on which phenomenal features are identical to intentional features and phenomenal character is identical to intentional content. It is also possible to hold a *mere determination* version of representationalism, on which phenomenal features are not identical to intentional features, but instead are determined by them in some way. The objection in this section applies to this weaker type of view as well. See endnote 21.

20 Since the tracking representationalist wants to be a physicalist, she should not respond to these worries by claiming that there are *non-physical* properties corresponding to redness, painfulness, etc.

21 In endnote 19, we noted that there are possible versions of representationalism on which phenomenal character is not identical to, but is instead merely determined by, intentional content. These views escape the present objection in its current form, since they do not claim that phenomenal characters are identical to tracked contents. However, the apparent dissimilarity between the phenomenal character of experiences of red and what they track poses problems for this view as well. The problem is that there seems to be nothing special about the tracked content that is responsible for its having the phenomenal character of redness, rather than the phenomenal character of greenness or the phenomenal character of pain. In other words, there appears to be no clear connection between the nature of certain surface reflectance properties and the nature of the phenomenal characters that they are supposed to determine, making it baffling how exactly the determination is supposed to take place.

22 See Balog (1999, 2012), Chalmers (2004, 2007), Stoljar (2005) and Alter and Walter (2007).

23 Jackson (2004) combines representationalism with an internalist version of something like the tracking theory. On Jackson's view, intentionality is a matter of our relations to the environment, but intrinsic duplicates are related to the environment in the same ways. This view avoids the Inverted Earth and Swamp-person objections, but it is unclear whether it avoids the causal efficacy objection and the mismatch problem.

24 See Bourget, ms.

25 Bain (2003), Klein (2007), Seager and Bourget (2007), Bourget (2010) and Mendelovici (2010) offer alternative representationalist theories of pain.

26 Seager (2002), Montague (2009) and Mendelovici (forthcoming) also defend representationalist accounts of emotions.

27 Tye describes such states as emotions, but many would classify them as moods.

28 See Seager and Bourget 2007.

29 These objections are discussed in Mendelovici (2010). More objections to Dretske's and Tye's accounts of demarcating properties can be found in Seager (1999, 2003), Kriegel (2002), Byrne (2001, 2003), and Seager and Bourget (2007).

30 Crane (2003), Chalmers (2004, 2006), Seager and Bourget (2007), Pautz (2009, 2010), Mendelovici (2010), Bourget (2010).

Bibliography

Allen, K. (2013), 'Blur'. *Philosophical Studies* 162(2): 257–73.
Anscombe, G. E. M. (1965), 'The intentionality of sensation: A grammatical feature'. In Ronald J. Butler (ed.), *Analytic Philosophy*. Oxford: Blackwell.
Alter, T. and Walter S. (eds) (2007), *Phenomenal Concepts and Phenomenal Knowledge: New Essays on Consciousness and Physicalism*. New York: Oxford University Press.
Austin, J. L. (1962), *Sense and Sensibilia*. Oxford: Oxford University Press.
Baars, B. J., Newman, J. B., and Taylor, J. G. (1998). 'Neuronal mechanisms of consciousness: A relational global workspace approach'. In S. R. Hameroff, A. W. Kaszniak and A. C. Scott (eds), *Toward a Science of Consciousness II*. Cambridge, MA: MIT Press.
Balog, K. (1999), 'Conceivability, possibility, and the mind-body problem'. *Philosophical Review* 108: 497–528.
— (2012), 'In defense of the phenomenal concept strategy'. *Philosophy and Phenomenological Research* 84: 1–23.
Bain, D. (2003), 'Intentionalism and pain'. *Philosophical Quarterly* 53: 502–23.
Block, N. (1990). 'Inverted earth'. *Philosophical Perspectives* 4: 53–79.
— (1995), 'On a confusion about a function of consciousness'. *Brain and Behavioral Sciences* 18: 227–47.
— (1996), 'Mental paint and mental latex'. *Philosophical Issues* 7: 19–49.
Boghossian, P. A. andVelleman, J. D. (1989), 'Color as a secondary quality'. *Mind* 98: 81–103.
Bourget, D. (2010a), 'Consciousness is underived intentionality'. *Noûs* 44: 32–58.
— (2010b), *The Representational Theory of Consciousness*. Dissertation, Australian National University.
— (ms.), 'A general reply to the arguments from blur, double vision, perspective, and other kinds of perceptual distortion against representationalism'.
Byrne, A. (2001). 'Intentionalism defended'. *Philosophical Review* 110: 199–240.
— (2002), 'Don't PANIC: Tye's intentionalist theory of consciousness'. *A Field Guide to the Philosophy of Mind*. URL=http://www.host.uniroma3.it/progetti/kant/field/tyesymp.htm.
— (2003), 'Consciousness and nonconceptual content'. *Philosophical Studies* 113: 261–74.
Byrne, A. and Tye, M. (2006), 'Qualia ain't in the head'. *Noûs* 40: 241–55.
Chalmers, D. J. (2004a), 'The representational character of experience'. In B. Leiter (ed.), *The Future for Philosophy*. New York: Oxford University Press.

— (2004), 'Phenomenal concepts and the knowledge argument'. In
P. Ludlow, Y. Nagasawa and D. Stoljar (eds), *There's Something About
Mary: Essays on Phenomenal Consciousness and Frank Jackson's
Knowledge Argument*. Cambridge, MA: MIT Press.
— (2006), 'Perception and the fall from Eden'. In T. S. Gendler and
J. Hawthorne (eds), *Perceptual Experience*. New York: Oxford
University Press.
— (2007), 'Phenomenal concepts and the explanatory gap'. In T. Alter and
S. Walter (eds), *Phenomenal Concepts and Phenomenal Knowledge:
New Essays on Consciousness and Physicalism*. New York: Oxford
University Press.
Crane, T. (2003), 'The intentional structure of consciousness'. In Quentin
Smith and Aleksandar Jokic (eds), *Consciousness: New Philosophical
Perspectives*. New York: Oxford University Press.
Crick, F. (1994), *The Astonishing Hypothesis: The Scientific Search for the
Soul*. New York: Scribners.
Cutter, B. and Tye, M. (2011), 'Tracking representationalism and the
painfulness of pain'. *Philosophical Issues* 21: 90–109.
Davidson, D. (1987), 'Knowing one's own mind'. *Proceedings and
Addresses of the American Philosophical Association* 60: 441–58.
Dretske, F. (1993), 'Conscious experience'. *Mind*, 102: 263–83.
— (1995), *Naturalizing the Mind*. Cambridge, MA: MIT Press.
— (1996), 'Phenomenal externalism, or if meanings ain't in the head,
where are qualia?' *Philosophical Issues* 7: 143–58.
— (2003), 'Experience as representation'. *Philosophical Issues* 13: 67–82.
Edelman, G. M. (1989), *The Remembered Present: A Biological Theory of
Consciousness*. New York: Basic Books.
Farkas, K. (2008), 'Phenomenal intentionality without compromise'. *The
Monist* 91: 273–93.
Harman, G. (1990), 'The intrinsic quality of experience'. *Philosophical
Perspectives* 4: 31–52.
Hintikka, J. (1969), 'The logic of perception'. In J. Hintikka (ed.), *Models
for Modalities*. Dordrecht: Reidel.
Horgan, T. E. (1991), 'Actions, reasons, and the explanatory role of content'.
In B. P. McLaughlin (ed.), *Dretske and His Critics*. Oxford: Blackwell.
Horgan, T. E. and Tienson, J. L. (2002). 'The intentionality of
phenomenology and the phenomenology of intentionality'. In D. J.
Chalmers (ed.), *Philosophy of Mind: Classical and Contemporary
Readings*. New York: Oxford University Press.
Jackson, F. (1977), *Perception: A Representative Theory*. Cambridge:
Cambridge University Press.
— (2004), 'Representation and experience'. In H. Clapin, P. Staines and
P. Slezak (eds), *Representation in Mind*. Dordrecht: Elsevier.

Kind, A. (2003), 'What's so transparent about transparency?' *Philosophical Studies* 115: 225–44.
Klein, C. (2007), 'An imperative theory of pain'. *Journal of Philosophy* 104:517–32.
Kraut, R. (1982), 'Sensory states and sensory objects'. *Noûs* 16: 277–93.
Kriegel, U. (2002). 'PANIC theory and the prospects for a representational theory of phenomenal consciousness'. *Philosophical Psychology* 15: 55–64.
— (2011), *The Sources of Intentionality*. New York: Oxford University Press.
Lewis, D. (1983), 'Individuation by acquaintance and by stipulation'. *Philosophical Review* 92: 3–32.
Loar, B. (2003), 'Transparent experience and the availability of qualia'. In Q. Smith and A. Jokic (eds), *Consciousness: New Philosophical Perspectives*. New York: Oxford University Press.
Lycan, W. G. (1987a), 'Phenomenal objects: A backhanded defense'. *Philosophical Perspectives* 3: 513–26.
— (1987b). *Consciousness*. Cambridge, MA: MIT Press.
— (1996), *Consciousness and Experience*. Cambridge, MA: MIT Press.
— (1996), 'Layered perceptual representation'. *Philosophical Issues* 7: 81–100.
— (2001a), 'The case for phenomenal externalism'. *Philosophical Perspectives* 15: 17–35.
— (2001b), 'A simple argument for a higher-order representation theory of consciousness'. *Analysis* 61: 3–4.
McGinn, C. (1989), 'Can we solve the mind-body problem?' *Mind* 98: 349–66.
Mendelovici, A. (2010), *Mental Representation and Closely Conflated Topics*. Dissertation, Princeton University.
— (forthcoming), 'Reliable misrepresentation and tracking theories of mental representation'. *Philosophical Studies*.
Millikan, R. G. (1984), *Language, Thought and Other Biological Categories*. Cambridge, MA: MIT Press.
Montague, M. (2009), 'The logic, intentionality, and phenomenology of emotion'. *Philosophical Studies* 145: 171–92.
Moore, G. E. (1903), 'The refutation of idealism'. *Mind* 12: 433–53.
Neander, K. (1995), 'Misrepresenting and malfunctioning'. *Philosophical Studies* 79: 109–41.
Papineau, D. (1993), *Philosophical Naturalism*. Oxford: Blackwell.
Pautz, A. (2009). 'What are the contents of experiences?' *Philosophical Quarterly* 59: 483–507.
— (2010a), 'An argument for the intentional view of visual experience'. In B. Nanay (ed.), *Perceiving the World*. New York: Oxford University Press.

— (2010b), 'Why explain visual experience in terms of content?' In B. Nanay (ed.), *Perceiving the World*. New York: Oxford University Press.
Pitt, D. (2004), 'The phenomenology of cognition, or, what is it like to think that P?' *Philosophy and Phenomenological Research* 69: 1–36.
Seager, W. E. (1999), *Theories of Consciousness: An Introduction and Assessment*. New York: Routledge.
— (2002), 'Emotional introspection'. *Consciousness and Cognition* 11: 666–87.
— (2003), 'Tye on consciousness: Time to panic?' *Philosophical Studies* 113: 237–47.
Seager, W. E. and Bourget, D. (2007), 'Representationalism about consciousness'. In M. Velmans and S. Schneider (eds), *The Blackwell Companion to Consciousness*. Oxford: Blackwell.
Sellars, W. S. (1975), 'The adverbial theory of the objects of sensation'. *Metaphilosophy* 6:144–60.
Stoljar, D. (2005), 'Physicalism and phenomenal concepts'. *Mind and Language* 20: 296–302.
— (2007), 'Consequences of intentionalism'. *Erkenntnis* 66: 247–70.
Tye, M. (1995), *Ten Problems of Consciousness: A Representational Theory of the Phenomenal Mind*. Cambridge, MA: MIT Press.
— (1996), 'Perceptual experience is a many-layered thing'. *Philosophical Issues* 7: 117–26.
— (2000), *Consciousness, Color, and Content*. Cambridge, MA: MIT Press.
— (2003), 'Blurry images, double vision, and other oddities: New problems for representationalism?' In Q. Smith and A. Jokic (eds), *Consciousness: New Philosophical Perspectives*. New York: Oxford University Press.
— (2008), 'The experience of emotion: an intentionalist theory'. *Revue Internationale de Philosophie* 62: 25–50.
— (2009), *Consciousness Revisited: Materialism Without Phenomenal Concepts*. Cambridge, MA: MIT Press.
— (forthcoming), 'Phenomenal externalism, lolita, and the planet xenon'. In T. E. Horgan and D. Sosa (eds), Collection on the Philosophy of Jaegwon Kim. Cambridge, MA: MIT Press.

CHAPTER TWELVE

The neurophilosophies of Patricia and Paul Churchland

John Bickle

Paul M. Churchland and Patricia Smith Churchland are formative figures in late twentieth-century Anglo-American philosophy for bringing approaches and resources from the philosophy of science and neuroscience to bear on philosophy of mind. They are most famous (infamous?) for their *eliminative materialism*. But their more important long-term contributions to philosophy include proposed reformulations of the mind-body problem into first and foremost an intertheoretic reduction question and numerous other traditionally philosophical questions into *neurophilosophical* inquiries, bringing 'connectionist' artificial neural networks to broader philosophical consciousness and importance, and making early groundbreaking strides in neuroepistemology and neuroethics. *Philosophy of neuroscience*, a now-recognized field of academic philosophy, very much began with the Churchlands.

It is common, although mistaken, to think of the Churchlands as a single philosophical entity. Certainly, their concerns, results and *modus operandi* overlap significantly. But there are important differences between the two, especially in philosophical and scientific focus and prose style. Hence the plural, 'neurophilosophies', of my title.

Eliminative materialism

Any critical assessment of the Churchlands' corpus must begin with their eliminative materialism, so prominently a part of 1980s philosophy of mind. Eliminative materialists insist that our common-sense causal explanations of behaviour, in terms of the contents of propositional attitudes like beliefs, desires, perceptions, intentions, hopes, wishes and the like, are radically false and will be replaced by, rather than smoothly reduced to or identified with, developing neuroscientific explanations. Our intellectual history presents precedents of theories, both scientific and commonsensical, subjected to elimination – fluid theories of heat transfer, phlogiston theories of rusting and combustion, the rotating crystal sphere of the night sky, witches, demonic possession and the flat stationary earth. As we did in these cases, the eliminative materialist insists, so we'll do with our common sense or 'folk' psychology: we'll eliminate its postulated kinds and processes from our best scientific ontology. We'll conclude that *there are no such things* as beliefs, desires, perceptions, intentions, wishes and the rest, nor the logic-like mental dynamics operating on their contents. There are only the brain states and dynamics being unravelled by neuroscience and predicted by the eliminativist to end up radically incommensurate with folk-psychological kinds.

The comparisons between folk psychology and historical eliminative theory changes are suggestive, but what arguments backed the Churchlands' specific brand of eliminative materialism? Unfortunately, many philosophers took Paul's argument in his then-popular textbook *Matter and Consciousness* (1983/1987) as canonical.[1] But those arguments were textbook glosses. The detailed early arguments occur in Paul's 1981 and 1985 essays, and in Chapter 9 of Patricia's 1986 book *Neurophilosophy*. Later eliminativist arguments are in Paul's 1989 collection *A Neurocomputational Perspective* and Patricia's 2002 book *Brain-Wise*.

The early arguments focus on the explanatory failures and long-term developmental stagnation of folk psychology, and the explanatory promise of some emerging paradigms in mid-1980s neuroscience. According to the Churchlands, outside of folk psychology's explanatory forte of rational, functioning, adult human behaviour, it suffers massive explanatory failures. Even in its forte, it's explanatorily silent about a lot of clearly psychological phenomena: sleep, memory, learning, intelligence differences, routine psychopathological syndromes, psychological development. The historical examples reveal that this pattern of explanatory failures is a hallmark of theories headed towards elimination.

This first eliminativist argument joins smoothly with a second. Despite its obvious explanatory failures, folk psychology hasn't developed significantly since the time of the ancient Greeks. Ancient Greek folk psychology remains contemporary folk psychology, save for a few bells and whistles slapped on over the centuries (e.g. Freud's unconscious). We read ancient Greek physics or biology, and it takes work for the scientifically trained among us to get our heads around the world picture they were groping towards. But we read ancient Greek drama, tragedy or comedy, and we're at home with the author or playwright. We understand the characters' behaviour and motivations. Why? Because our basic folk psychology is still by and large theirs. Almost nothing else in the ancient Greek worldview is still part of ours. Which explanation of this curious fact seems more reasonable? That the ancient Greeks got everything else so wrong – physics, biology, sociology – and yet got the explanation of human behaviour spot on? Or that, just like their physics, biology and social thought, the ancient Greeks probably also got psychology wrong; only, without yet having a replacement theory in hand, we contemporaries still employ their radically false psychology explanatorily, with continued poor explanatory results? The questions here are rhetorical: of course the second disjunct seems more reasonable.

A third argument was dimly present in the Churchlands' early eliminativist writings. It contains two premises. First, contemporary neuroscience is starting to succeed where folk psychology has failed. Second, neuroscience's developing explanatory resources differ so extensively from folk psychology's, in both conceptual structure and hypothesized dynamics, that future ontological identifications look hopeless. In their early writings, the Churchlands presented few neuroscientific details (aside from some stock neurology examples). This changed significantly in the mid-1980s when they discovered 'connectionist' artificial neural networks.

The Churchlands' connectionist excursion and the numerous philosophical consequences they stressed will be the focus of a later section. But they quickly emphasized its impact on their third early argument for eliminativism, especially towards developing the second premise. Paul writes:

> According to [connectionism], it is activity vectors that form the most important kind of representation within the brain. And it is vector-to-vector transformations that form the most important kinds of computation. This may or may not be correct, but it does give some real substance to the earlier suggestion of the eliminative materialist . . . that the concepts of folk psychology need not capture the empirically significant states and activities of the mind. The elements of cognition, as sketched in the preceding pages, have a character unfamiliar to common sense. (1983/1987 [1987], p. 165)

From this point forward, the historical eliminations and folk psychology's stagnation didn't disappear from the Churchlands' eliminativist arguments; but these took a back seat to the differences the Churchlands noted between connectionist and folk-psychological kinds.

What became of Churchland-style eliminativism? It had its detractors from the outset and no lack of published responses. But like many philosophical fashions, the discipline more lost interest in it, rather than refuted it. Connectionism quickly fell under attack from 'classicists', and exploring its eliminativist consequences became a secondary concern to defending it as cognitive science's best paradigm (more on this below). And by the mid-1990s, philosophers of mind had consciousness as the new hot topic to grapple with, and eliminativism there seemed less plausible from the start. (More on this below, too; also see Chapter 14.) Interestingly, however, neuroscience-inspired eliminativism is making something of a comeback, at least as an argumentative foil (see Jackson, Petit and Smith 2004).

Some readers may have sensed the irony that Churchland-style eliminative materialism began as a *prediction*: about what to expect out of developing neuroscience. One wonders what it might look like if it had remained primarily a methodological recommendation about how best to develop a neuroscience of cognition, and less a metaphysical doctrine about 'the nature of mind' (or lack thereof). In the context of a debate about explaining affect between psychologist Jim Russell and neuroscientist Jaak Panksepp, Bickle (2012b) has speculated about such an 'eliminativism with a little "e"'. Some of the distracting detours the eliminativist debate took throughout the 1980s might have been avoided.

The intertheoretic reduction reformulation of the mind-body problem

One point often lost on critics of Churchland-style eliminativism was that the account was grounded on a complete reformulation of the traditional philosophical mind-body question (see Chapter 2). The details of this reformulation actually constitute the Churchlands' most significant contribution to philosophy of mind.

It has been clear since the heyday of logical positivism that ontological disputes, like the traditional mind-body problem, are philosophical quagmires. But if those disputes can be reformulated, first and foremost into debates with clearer criteria for relevant versus irrelevant evidence and argument, yet ones which still usher in ontological consequences, so much the better. When it comes to questions about ontological relations across distinct theoretical kinds, science resolves such disputes by looking first to intertheoretic relations, principally *reduction*, between the theories postulating the kinds. Electrical and magnetic phenomena aren't identical to strictly mechanical phenomena. That follows because the developed theories of electricity and magnetism turn out not to be reducible to the theory of (classical) mechanics. This kind of strong theory autonomy, where a theory targeted for reduction ends up explaining phenomena that its potential reducing theory can't be developed to explain, implies ontological distinctness. On the other hand, light and other optical phenomena *are* electromagnetic phenomena within specific ranges of wavelengths and frequencies. That follows because optical theory reduces rather smoothly to electromagnetic theory. Temperature in gases is related to mean molecular kinetic energy of the gas's molecular constituents, but the former concept gets revised fairly significantly vis-à-vis the statistical-mechanical kinds. That follows because classical equilibrium thermodynamics reduces to statistical mechanics and the kinetic theory of gases only in mathematical limits never actually realized empirically. And there's simply no such thing as phlogiston, only oxygen, gained and not lost in combustion and rusting. That follows because the theory of phlogiston only very bumpily reduces to the theory of oxygen chemistry. The limiting assumptions and boundary conditions required to capture the former's generalizations within the latter are so wildly counterfactual that we don't even attempt to revise the postulated kinds. We just eliminate them from our best current scientific ontology.

These considerations suggest a general strategy for reformulating the philosophical mind-body problem, into primarily an intertheoretic reduction issue, with folk psychology as the hypothesized theory-to-be-reduced and some developed future neuroscience as the theory-to-accomplish-the-reduction. As in the other scientific examples, the ontological consequences for folk psychology's kinds become secondary to and dependent upon the case's location around the intertheoretic reduction spectrum. Failure to reduce implies ontological autonomy. Smoother reductions imply ontological identities (or close-enough approximations). Bumpier reductions imply revisionary ontological conclusions for the reduced theory's kinds, and bumpier-still reductions finally yield ontological eliminations. So for a case like folk psychology–to–developed neuroscience, whose intertheoretic reduction relation is still at issue, we look to how the reduction seems to be developing. We then locate the case at that appropriate point around the intertheoretic reduction spectrum and predict ontological conclusions for the reduced theory's kinds based upon consequences drawn in historical scientific cases where the intertheoretic reduction relation turned out that way. (See Bickle 1998, Chapter 2, for a pictorial illustration of this intertheoretic reduction reformulation of the mind-body problem.)

What philosophical commitments are required to make this reformulation work? First, we need some kind of scientific realism, to get ontological commitments to science's 'theoretical' postulates. In 1980s Anglo-American philosophy, this wasn't considered problematic. Scientific realism had long replaced logical empiricism in philosophical fashion, and while van Fraassen's (1981) 'constructive empiricism' attracted some followers, it remained a minority view. Second, we need to insist that folk psychology is a theory, in an explicit, robust-enough sense for it to stand in an intertheoretic reduction relationship to developed neuroscience. This too was not problematic at the time. 'Theory' accounts of folk psychology, and of conceptual frameworks generally, dominated Anglo-American epistemology and semantics, although Paul undertook seriously to defend the 'theory' theory (see Chapter 6 of his 1989 and Chapter 2 of Churchland and Churchland 1998). We also need a 'theory' theory of neuroscience, but few in the 1980s doubted that neuroscience was aiming at that. (Few doubt that now, in fact).

Third, and most importantly, the reformulation requires a detailed account of intertheoretic reduction. Here, Anglo-American philosophy of science obliged. Since Ernest Nagel's (1961, Chapter 11) classical account, theories of intertheoretic reduction were commonplace. The Churchlands adopted (and helped develop) Clifford Hooker's (1981) account. Hooker postulated that an 'image' of the reduced theory gets deduced within the reducing framework. His account thus eschews the need for the 'bridge laws' or 'correspondence rules' that plagued Nagel's detailed account, since the deduced image was already specified in the terms of the reducing theory, and so no principles were required to derive the image from the reducing theory. Reducing theories, which typically explain more phenomena than the theory they reduce, get related to the reduced theory with the help of various limiting assumptions and boundary conditions restricting its scope of application. When a reduction involves a false reduced theory, this falsity can be accounted for by counterfactual limiting assumptions and boundary conditions used to derive its image with the reducing theory. Both the logical structure and the explanatory power of the deduced image of the reduced theory could be compared directly to those of the actual reduced theory to obtain at least a qualitative measure of how corrective of the reduced theory a given reduction is. Hooker admitted that he could not provide a fully satisfactory formal account of 'location on the intertheoretic reduction spectrum' from less to more corrective. Construing theories set-theoretically and adapting resources from the structuralist programme in formal philosophy of science, Bickle (1998) sought to provide this missing element in the Churchland-Hooker intertheoretic reduction reformulation of the mind-body problem. The resulting account, along with the spectrum of ontological consequences justified by the scientific realist assumption, was dubbed 'new wave' psychoneural reductionism.

Criticisms followed (see Bickle 2003, Chapter 1, and Bickle 2012a for overviews). The most telling ones challenged the applicability of the general new wave account of reduction to the emerging scientific details. Bickle's response was to move increasingly towards metascience: towards detailed descriptions of the actual experimental practices that distinguished investigations in 'ruthlessly reductionistic' scientific fields (see, e.g. Bickle 2003, 2006, 2009a, 2012a). Is this new approach Churchlandian? Yes and no. Certainly, the Churchlands championed bringing increasingly detailed neuroscience into philosophical discussion. But they always did so through the lens of post–logical empiricist philosophy of science (see especially Patricia's 1986, Chapter 6) – a lens that metascience rejects (see especially Bickle 2009a).

Bechtel (2009) points out that neuroscience itself seems not to speak with one voice about what reductionism is. Cellular and molecular neuroscientists may pursue 'ruthlessly reductionistic' research programmes. But cognitive/systems/behavioural neuroscientists, addressing related cognitive phenomena, instead pursue 'mechanistic' reduction strategies: they seek nested causal mechanisms within mechanisms for the 'complete' mechanistic explanation, and they locate intraneuronal molecular mechanisms within this hierarchy of mechanistic levels, rather than claiming 'ruthless' reductions of cognitive functions exclusively to those molecular mechanisms. For a variety of methodological reasons, Bechtel (2009) sides with the mechanistic reductionists. Bickle (2012a) acknowledges multiple notions of reduction at work within contemporary neuroscience, but sides with the cellular and molecular ruthless reductionists. This ongoing debate about which brand of reductionism will win out in the end – if either – will only be resolved by continued developments in neuroscience. That prescription is certainly Churchlandian, even if their emphasis on *intertheoretic* reduction no longer directs the debate.

Connectionism

Paul Churchland's 1979 book *Scientific Realism and the Plasticity of Mind* ends by longing for a 'new kinematics' for epistemology, to replace the sentence-like representations and logic-like computations of analytic philosophy's classical model. By the early 1980s, inspired by neuroscientific modelling of cerebellar networks, and buoyed by Paul's own tinkerings with a computer-simulated crab-like creature, the Churchlands discovered the power of vectorial representations and transformations. Paul notes that his (1986) essay detailing this work was written 'with some excitement in the spring of 1984' (1989, p. xiv). That autumn, the Churchlands moved to the Department of Philosophy and the interdisciplinary Cognitive Science Ph.D. programme (soon to be the Department of Cognitive Science) at the University of California, San Diego – the home of the Parallel Distributed Processing (PDP) Research Group. There the Churchlands found the missing piece of their philosophical-scientific puzzle. They quickly became strong philosophical advocates for and tutors of this new 'connectionist' paradigm for cognitive science. Patricia published one of the earliest accounts of it in Chapter 10 of her (1986) book, the same year that the landmark two-volume collection by the PDP Research Group first appeared (Rumelhart et al 1986). Paul gave it extended discussion in the revised edition of his textbook (1983/1987, pp. 156–65), where he was quick to suggest its eliminativist consequences (mentioned above).

Explicating connectionism's virtues to philosophers was not the Churchlands' principal goal. Paul soon put the account to work in reformulating issues in the philosophy of science (see especially the essays in Part II of his 1989). He reconceived theories as points in multidimensional weight-error spaces (one dimension for each connection in the network, with the y-axis representing global error of target minus actual output) or as regions in multidimensional unit activation spaces (one dimension for each 'hidden' unit in three-layer networks). He in turn reconceived theory relations – explanation, reduction, conceptual change – as vectorial transitions in these spaces. Theoretical simplicity or parsimony, Kuhnian paradigms, explanatory unification and a variety of distinctions among types of explanations all received novel reconception in Paul's 'neurocomputational perspective'.

Were we really to take these reconceivings at face value? Churchland was explicitly affirmative:

> An individual's overall theory-of-the-world, we might venture, is not a large collection or a long list of stored symbolic items. Rather, it is a specific point in that individual's synaptic weight space. It is a configuration of connection weights, a configuration

that partitions the system's activation-vector space(s) into useful divisions and subdivisions relative to the inputs typically fed the system. "Useful" here means "tends to minimize the error messages". (1989, p. 177)

His reconceivings didn't stop with the philosophy of science. By the time of his more popular 1995 book, *The Engine of Reason, the Seat of the Soul*, Churchland advocated treating consciousness, language, politics, art and neurotechnology's impact on human life all in terms of neurally inspired vectorial representations and transformations in appropriately configured state spaces, with error-reducing 'synaptic' weight-change rules driving network learning.

Unlike the attention philosophers of mind gave to the Churchlands' eliminative materialism, philosophers of science were less interested in engaging Paul's neurocomputational reconceivings. This lesser attention still strikes me as curious. This work wasn't ignored, but it certainly didn't garner the critical attention directed towards the Churchlands' previous work in philosophy of mind. Perhaps philosophers of science are more stubborn about their guiding paradigm? One principled reason for lesser attention may have been the very public fight between Classicists and Connectionists that soon erupted in cognitive science. Interestingly, the Churchlands weren't major contributors to this broader dispute. Principal Classicists included Jerry Fodor (see Chapter 9), Zenon Pylyshyn and Brian McLaughlin; principal connectionist defenders included Paul Smolensky, Terrence Horgan and John Tienson, and, more ecumenically, Andy Clark (see Chapter 13). Anecdotally, my impression is that many philosophers of science judged that the Classicists won this dispute, which could explain the surprisingly limited interest in Paul's neurocomputational reconceivings.

Perhaps more significantly, scientific interest in the kind of connectionism the Churchlands advocated also waned. Worries about biological plausibility, especially of popular and powerful 'supervised' learning algorithms, were much discussed. (Patricia, with neuroscientist co-author Terrence Sejnowski (1992), wrote one of the more vigorous defences of the biological plausibility of many connectionist components.) The advent of compartmental modelling in the mid-1990s, and the development of software that could be run on then-existing desktop computers, allowed computational neuroscientists to model the electrical conductance capacities of patches of neuronal membrane. Individual neurons, including special dendritic, somatic and axonal properties, could be modelled as chains of interacting compartments. Networks could be constructed out of these individually modelled neurons, and so the potential for biologically plausible modelling suddenly increased dramatically. Connectionism didn't die on the vine. Its neural-like architectures, vectorial interpretations and state space geometries continued to find adherents in artificial intelligence and computational modelling. But increasingly their uses were in 'applied' areas of AI, not in the theoretical areas that interested computational neuroscientists. Intriguing and novel as Paul's 'neurocomputational' reconceptions of scientific and other concepts were, computational neuroscience soon left behind the scientific framework that informed them.

Consciousness

Consciousness studies took Anglo-American philosophy of mind by storm in the mid-1990s. The Churchlands participated avidly. Actually, their published discussions of consciousness predated its more popular return. Patricia's (1983) essay argues that neuroscientific discoveries can 'transmutate' our understanding of features of conscious experience. She appeals to neuropsychological and neurological work on phenomena like blindsight and denial syndromes (blindness, paralysis) as case studies. At the same time, Paul was taking on Thomas Nagel's well-known bat argument and Frank Jackson's equally well-known Mary argument (see P. M. Churchland 1985, 1989 Chapter 4). Nagel famously argued that objective science was unsuited to explain the subjective facts about conscious experience, such as 'what it is like to be a bat'. Jackson equally famously argued that Mary, the future vision neuroscientist who knew 'everything there is to know' about activity in the human visual system but who was confined to a room of black, white and variously shaded grey objects, would 'learn something new' with her first visual encounter with a red object, proving that conscious visual qualia (like visually experienced red) can't be identical to any brain state (for then Mary would have already known about it). Against Nagel, Paul posed a dilemma: the bat argument is an instance of the intentional fallacy – it invalidly treats someone's belief about an object as a property of the object itself – or the argument is valid but unsound because it contains a premise about know *ability* to which Nagel could not legitimately help himself. Against Jackson, he insists that 'knows' is equivocated upon, sliding from a kind of 'knowing that' to a kind of 'knowing how'. Patricia (1986) addresses Jackson's insistence that Mary couldn't know red experience based on her 'complete' visual neuroscience, arguing that Jackson was asking us to deliver an intuition that, in our neuroscientific ignorance, we're in no position to deliver confidently. Paul's (1985) reply to Jackson also contains an intriguing precursor of an idea he develops in great detail over the next decade. Mary's knowing what it's like to have a red visual experience while in the black-white-grey room is akin to the ability of a trained musician possessing perfect pitch to use his or her musical knowledge to ruminate on the sound of a bizarre chord (Churchland's example was an F#9th*add*13th; see his 1985) and then to pick out that chord auditorily from a range of similarly structured, equally bizarre, but slightly different chords. He appeals to Edwin Land's (of Polaroid fame) Retinex theory of colour vision, which represents each colour visually discriminable by sighted humans as a distinct ordered triplet of reflectance frequencies at the three critical wavelengths to which the human retina's triune cone system is tuned. Sensations-of-colour get characterized thus as three-element 'chords' in human neural visual processing. So if the trained musician can succeed in his or her analogous task, why not completely-neuroscientifically-knowledgable-but-as-yet-colour-inexperienced Mary in hers? She knows and has experienced the neural states associated with black, white and shades of grey. Why assume she can't ruminate on, and then correctly pick out upon its first presentation, the triplet 'chord' of activations for red in her visual processing system?

By his (1995, Chapter 2) book, Paul develops some details underlying this colour vision example into a connectionism-inspired vector-coding account of all sensory representations. Tastes encode as four-element vectors, with each element representing activation levels reached in the four types of taste receptors populating the human tongue (and projected into the brainstem for further processing and integration). Each taste can thus be represented as a point in a four-dimensional taste space, depending on the activities its chemical components invoke in the four types of human taste receptors and their projection pathways. Subjective aspects of taste experiences so difficult to describe – the experienced similarity of peach and apricot tastes, the experienced difference between quinine and table salt tastes – thus can be assessed and measured geometrically in taste space. Paul (1995) demonstrates the power of neurally realistic vector coding for human visual colour experiences, olfactory experiences (with a nicely illustrated state space comparison to canines) and even simple visually experienced facial recognition features. By his 2005 essay, 'Chimerical Colors', and armed with a more detailed neuroscientific account of colour visual processing, he argues that a vector-coding account yields novel predictions about 'chimerical', 'impossible' colours. He even provides the colour slides so readers can 'savor' these novel colour experiences themselves – experiences predicted directly from the computational neurobiology.

As the consciousness craze swept 1990s philosophy of mind, the Churchlands also challenged philosophers who held out against the reducibility of conscious experience to neuroscience. John Searle's famous insistence, that conscious mental states are 'caused by and realized in' neural states, but not thereby reducible to them, reminds the Churchlands of Betty Crocker's mistaken insistence that microwave ovens agitate water molecules in food causing friction that in turn heats the food (see Churchland and Churchland 1998, Chapter 8). Actually, the increased molecular agitation of water molecules *constitutes* the heated food, with a similar lesson to be urged on Searle for the neural states underlying consciousness. They also insisted that the neurobiologically based vector-coding account of sensory qualia offers an at least empirically motivated (if not yet confirmed) solution to Chalmer's (1996) famous Hard Problem of Consciousness (see Chapter 14). Coupling that account with recurrency (feedback connections) in networks yields a potential account of short-term memory and top-down cognitive effects on sensory conscious experience. 'Inverted experiential spectra' are thus not only conceptually possible, but explicable in detail. (For their arguments for all three of these points, see Churchland and Churchland 1998, Chapter 11). Reflection on some well-known examples from the history of science exposes popular dualist lessons drawn from 'the conceivability of philosophical zombies' (Chalmers 1996) to be nothing more than arguments from ignorance – ones which even ongoing early work in neuroscience already disarm (see P. S. Churchland 1996).

Many (myself included) found the Churchlands' vector-coding account of sensory experiences intriguing. It seemed to offer a plausible story about how sensory experiences within a modality resembled and differed from one another. But more reductive neuroscientific work on consciousness was emerging from cellular and molecular neuroscience (Bickle 2003, Chapter 4). Cortical microstimulation of single cerebral columns throughout primate visual cortex seemed to induce phenomenological experiences (Bickle and Ellis 2005). Genetic engineering of single amino acid residues on various protein subunits of 'fast' $GABA_A$ inhibitory receptors produced mutant mice with quite selective impairments on behavioural measures of various features of phenomenological consciousness (Bickle 2007). It began to look like the Churchlands' account of sensory consciousness was not as reductionistic as ongoing neuroscientific research.

And yet the qualitative features of conscious experience still seemed maddeningly elusive! Why does induced activity in those microstimulated motion-detecting V4 neurons look *like that*? (Like what? Like the way an object moving at a particular speed at a particular angle across my visual field looks). Why not instead *like that* (the colour aquamarine)? Whether one rests content with the Churchlands at the brain's vector-coding level or digs further down into the cellular and molecular mechanisms, answers to these questions about sensory experiences still seemed elusive. Perhaps we still have to be satisfied with neurobiologist William Newsome's answer? Reflecting on his own and others' microstimulation results in rhesus monkeys, Newsome remarks:

> I believe the nature of internal experience matters for our understanding of nervous system function. . . . Even if I could explain a monkey's behavior on our task in its entirety (in neural terms), I would not be satisfied unless I knew whether microstimulation in MT actually causes the monkey to see motion. . . . For the time being . . . I suspect we must feel our way towards these ambitious goals from the bottom up . . . . (1997, pp. 65–7)

It's important to notice that the Churchlands' neurally inspired vector-coding account of sensory consciousness is less reductionistic than is the approach recommended by this prominent neurophysiologist.

Neuroethics and neuroepistemology, up to the present day

Paul's vector-coding work towards a neuroepistemology continues in his latest book, *Plato's Camera* (2012). Here, his emphasis is on neural details of learning, of both dynamically fast and ploddingly slow varieties. Biological plausibility has become more of a concern. He argues that neural mechanisms of Hebbian learning overcome some of the neurobiological implausibility of supervised learning in connectionist networks. The learning brain is groping towards a picture of the landscape of reality. He urges us to take the camera metaphor seriously. Those pictures are composed of high-dimensional maps of regions of reality's landscape. He offers a new defence of scientific realism and increasingly detailed accounts of the semantics of natural language, and the roles of natural language and cultural institutions in shaping the brain's pictures of reality. The basic neurocomputational framework from his studies (1989) and (1995) remains in place.

The Churchlands' contributions to the burgeoning field of neuroethics have also been significant. Paul ended his (1989) collection with a cryptic short essay suggesting a realist view of moral facts and moral knowledge, along similar lines to his scientific realism. The 'neuro' component of his view is nicely summed up the essay's two closing sentences: 'For in fact we do have an organ for understanding and recognizing moral facts. It is called the brain' (1989, p. 303). In his (1995) book, these cryptic remarks get cashed out explicitly in his vector-coding approach. Moral learning is skill learning and moral knowledge is a kind of knowing-how, namely, knowing how to navigate the complex world of human social relationships. Paul does not shy away from normative ethics, comparing his resulting neurocomputational account to Aristotle's virtue ethics (1995, pp. 149–50) and posing an answer to the moral sceptic's 'why be moral?' query: 'because they are easily the most important skills you will ever learn' (1995, p. 294). He even ventures into applied ethics, discussing abortion, criminal policy – including California's then–recently passed 'three strikes' law (1995, pp. 305–14) – and the need to keep public secondary education religiously neutral (2005, Chapter 5).

But it was Patricia who really took up the call to neuroethics. Starting with her discussion of free will in her (2002, Chapter 5) book, Patricia likewise puts to use the familiar vector-coding neurocomputational account. But she also delves deeply into the neurochemistry and molecular biology of motivation and decision-making, especially the neurotransmitters and hormones involved in these neural circuits. These details become increasingly prominent in her (2009) essay, and even more so in her latest book *Braintrust* (2012). Inference to the *best decision*, rather than to the best explanation, becomes her overarching neuroethical theme. Aristotle, pragmaticism and evolutionary theory join with computational neuroscience and cellular and molecular detail, to produce a tour de force about 'what neuroscience tells us about morality'.

The jury of professional opinion is still out on both of the Churchlands' recent books. Patricia's (2012) has seen positive reviews in both *Science* and *Nature*, and numerous reviews in the popular media. Reviews of Paul's (2012) have been mostly in academic journals. One worry has been a lack of updated scientific references, especially for an epistemology that purports to be neurally guided.

Philosophical styles and personalities

One cannot conclude a chapter on the Churchlands without some comment on their philosophical styles and personalities. Both are personally charismatic in different ways, which attract both devoted followers and harsh critics. Their early rhetoric was revolutionary in words and tone – they were leading an effort to transform a tired, old academic discipline, philosophy, with input from one of the hottest young sciences, neuroscience. Nothing in the former would ever be the same again. Paul was particularly gifted at rhetorical flourishes. In one of my personal favourites, he's reflecting on 'new opportunities' offered by maturing neuroscience and the need to leave 'old frameworks' like folk psychology behind:

> Our eyes are little different than a baboon's or a chimpanzee's, but our perceptual knowledge is profoundly superior to theirs. Our motor systems are little different from those of any other primate, but our practical capacities and intentional actions encompass universes quite closed to them. The main difference

lies in the dramatically superior conceptual frameworks we have evolved epigenetically, and not without misadventure, over the course of the last 500,000 years.
 If we have come this far, must the journey end here? Manifestly not. The long awakening is potentially endless. The human spirit will continue its breathtaking adventure of self-reconstruction, and its perceptual and motor capacities will continue to develop as an integral part of its self-reconstruction. But only if we try hard to see new opportunities, and only if we work hard at leaving old frameworks behind. (1989, p. 279)

To which Jerry Fodor, at his curmudgeonly best, replied: 'An endless awakening sounds like not all that much fun, come to think of it. I, for one, am simply unable to self-construct until I've had my morning coffee' (1988, p. 198). For those who think philosophical writing is dull, this full Churchland-Fodor exchange is a panacea: an excellent example of two premier stylists going toe-to-toe, with no philosophical, scientific or rhetorical holds barred.
 Paul's philosophical-cum-scientific creativity is nicely on display towards the end of his (1981) essay, where he takes us 'beyond folk psychology' to a future of distinct brains outfitted with artificial commissures connecting them, with the speed and fluidity with which our own biological corpus callosum connects neurons across our left and right cerebral hemispheres. How will such people understand and conceive of others with whom they share opened channels? 'In roughly the same fashion that your right hemisphere "understands" and "conceives of" your left hemisphere: intimately and efficiently, but not propositionally!' (1989, p. 21) For Paul, linguistic descriptions of philosophical points aren't always sufficient. I've already mentioned the colour slides published with his (2005) essay, allowing readers to experience impossible, chimerical colours predicted directly from the neuroscience. His (1995) book comes equipped with a plastic stereoscope, and stereoscopic photographs of aerial views of the New York City skyline and the planets Jupiter, Saturn and Mars, against the stars of the constellation Virgo, photographed one month apart. These give readers the opportunity to *experience* reality from vastly different visual perspectives. His (1979) book contains simple illustrations of an exercise in perceptual plasticity that enable readers to experience

our solar system with the ecliptic as the horizon – and finally to be 'home in one's universe' visually as well as conceptually.

Patricia's philosophical style is less showy, more direct, but no less effective. She's a master at the unexpected humorous one-liner, inserted into otherwise direct argument. For example, concerning the in-principle possibility for psychology to develop a complete functionalist cognitive theory without help from neuroscience, she writes: 'I don't know whether this is true, and I have no sense of how to assess the claim. My guess is that it shares a flaw with many other philosophical thought-experiments: too much thought and not enough experiment' (1986, pp. 362–3). She can be devastatingly blunt, down to the level of individual word choice (e.g. 'pander'):

> In the mid-seventies I discovered that my patience with most mainstream philosophy had run out. What had instead begun to seem promising was the new wave in philosophical method, which ceased to pander to "ordinary language" and which began in earnest to reverse the anti-scientific bias typical of "linguistic analysis". (1986, p. ix)

Her revolutionary rhetoric can match Paul's, and even routinely employs Kuhnian phrasing:

> Paradigms rarely fall with decisive refutation; rather, they become enfeebled and slowly lose adherents. . . . [M]any of us sense that working within "the grand old paradigm" is not very rewarding. . . . There are remarkable new developments in cognitive neurobiology which encourage us to think that a new and encompassing paradigm is emerging. (1989, p. 546)

The Churchlands' personalities are likewise larger-than-life and come out nicely in a well-written New Yorker profile (Macfarquhar 2007). Paul and Patricia narrate numerous stories about their shared roads to philosophical and scientific stardom. It's salubrious to see that the revolutionary rhetoric that inspired the early days of neurophilosophy still motivates them:

> One afternoon recently, Paul says, he was home making dinner when Pat burst in the door, having come straight from a frustrating faculty meeting. "She said, 'Paul, don't speak to me, my serotonin

levels have hit bottom, my brain is awash in glucocorticoids, my blood vessels are full of adrenaline, and if it weren't for my endogenous opiates I'd have driven the car into a tree on the way home. My dopamine levels need lifting. Pour me a Chardonnay, and I'll be down in a minute.'" Paul and Pat have noticed that it is not just they who talk this way—their students now talk of psychopharmacology as comfortably as of food. (2007, p. 68)

(The ruthless reductionist in me asks, 'What are these "car", "tree", "home", and "Chardonnay" of which you speak, Pat?' But set internal neurophilosophical squabbles aside.)

What will be the legacy of Paul and Patricia Churchland? Historically, their legacy is secure. Their eliminative materialism will continue to be archived in future philosophy textbooks. Their neurocomputational perspective may have been based ultimately on dated computational neuroscience, but the neuroepistemology and neuroethics it spawned in their later work will continue to have impact, both in academic and in popular circles. Few contemporary philosophers can truly be said to have invented an entire field of the discipline. Admittedly, current philosophy of neuroscience looks quite different than the Churchlands' first envisioned: contrast Patricia's (1986) book with the chapters in Bickle's (2009b) edited volume. Much of the early revolutionary rhetoric is now gone. There's little dispute that analytic philosophy's armchair crowd proved far more resistant than the Churchlands expected. But today's philosophers of neuroscience are mostly people who've done graduate work, and even earned graduate degrees, in the neurosciences. And all this work traces directly back to the days when Paul and Patricia Churchland started 'a cautious paddling at the available edges of neuroscience', quickly found themselves 'venturing further and further from shore', and finally setting 'full sail' (P. S. Churchland 1986, p. ix). It was a pied piper's call for a lot of us, and many of us are still trying to kindle that same excitement in the budding philosopher-neuroscientists we encounter.

Note

1 Since I'll emphasize throughout this chapter some differences between the Churchlands' neurophilosophies, I'll sometimes have to resort to less formal first-name usage.

References

Bechtel, W. (2009). 'Molecules, systems, and behavior: Another view of memory consolidation', in J. Bickle (ed.), *The Oxford Handbook of Philosophy and Neuroscience*. New York: Oxford University Press, pp. 13–40.

Bickle, J. (1998). *Psychoneural Reduction: The New Wave*. Cambridge, MA: MIT Press.

— (2003). *Philosophy and Neuroscience: A Ruthlessly Reductive Account*. Dordrecht: Kluwer (now Springer).

— (2007). 'Who says you can't do a molecular biology of consciousness?' in M. K. D. Schouten and H. L. de Jong (eds), *The Matter of Mind*. London: Blackwell, pp. 275–97.

— (2009a). 'Real reductionism in real neuroscience: metascience, not philosophy of science (and certainly not metaphysics!)', in J. Hohway and J. Kallestrup (eds), *Being Reduced*. New York: Oxford University Press, pp. 34–51.

— (2009b). *The Oxford Handbook of Philosophy and Neuroscience*. New York: Oxford University Press.

— (2012a). 'A brief history of neuroscience's actual influences on mind-brain reductionism', in S. Gozzano and C. S. Hill (eds), *New Perspectives on Type Identity*. Cambridge: Cambridge University Press, pp. 88–110.

— (2012b). 'Lessons for affective science from a metascience of 'molecular and cellular cognition', in P. Zacher and R. D. Ellis (eds), *Categorical Versus Dimensional Models of Affect*. Amsterdam: John Benjamins, pp. 173–88.

Bickle, J. and Ellis, R. (2005). 'Phenomenology and cortical microstimulation', in D. W. Smith and A. L. Thomasson (eds), *Phenomenology and the Philosophy of Mind*. New York: Oxford University Press, pp. 140–63.

Chalmers, D. (1996). *The Conscious Mind*. New York: Oxford University Press.

Churchland, P. M. (1979). *Scientific Realism and the Plasticity of Mind*. Cambridge: Cambridge University Press.

— (1981). 'Eliminative materialism and the propositional attitudes'. *Journal of Philosophy* 78: 67–90.

— (1983/1987). *Matter and Consciousness*. Cambridge, MA: MIT Press.

— (1985). 'Reduction, qualia and the direct introspection of brain states'. *Journal of Philosophy* 82: 8–28.

— (1986). 'Some reductive strategies in cognitive neurobiology'. *Mind* 95: 279–309.

— (1989). *A Neurocomputational Perspective*. Cambridge, MA: MIT Press.

— (1995). *The Engine of Reason, the Seat of the Soul.* Cambridge, MA: MIT Press.
— (2005). 'Chimerical colors: some phenomenological predictions from cognitive neuroscience'. *Philosophical Psychology* 18: 527–60.
— (2007). *Neurophilosophy At Work.* Cambridge: Cambridge University Press.
— (2012). *Plato's Camera.* Cambridge, MA: MIT Press.
— (1983). 'Consciousness: the transmutation of a concept'. *Pacific Philosophical Quarterly* 64: 80–95.
— (1986). *Neurophilosophy.* Cambridge, MA: MIT Press.
— (1989). 'Epistemology in the age of neuroscience'. *Journal of Philosophy* 84: 544–53.
— (1996). 'The hornswoggle problem'. *Journal of Consciousness Studies* 3: 5–6.
— (2002). *Brain-Wise.* Cambridge, MA: MIT Press.
— (2009). 'Inference to the best decision', in J. Bickle (ed.), *The Oxford Handbook of Philosophy and Neuroscience.* New York: Oxford University Press, pp. 419–30.
— (2012). *Braintrust.* Princeton, NJ: Princeton University Press.
Churchland, P. S. and Sejnowski, T. J. (1992). *The Computational Brain.* Cambridge, MA: MIT Press.
Churchland, P. M. and Churchland, P. S. (1998). *On the Contrary.* Cambridge, MA: MIT Press.
Fodor, J. A. (1988). 'A reply to Churchland's "Perceptual plasticity and theoretical neutrality" '. *Philosophy of Science* 55: 188–98.
Hooker, C. A. (1981). 'Towards a general theory of reduction' (in three parts). *Dialogue* 20: 38–59, 201–36, 496–529.
Jackson, F., Petit, P., and Smith, M. (2004). *Mind, Morality and Explanation.* New York: Oxford University Press.
Macfarquhar, L. (2007). 'Two heads: a marriage devoted to the mind-body problem'.*The New Yorker* (13 February), pp. 58–69.
Nagel, E. (1961). *The Structure of Science.* New York: Harcourt, Brace, and World.
Newsome, W. (1997). 'Perceptual processes', in M. Gazzaniga (ed.), *Conversations in the Cognitive Neurosciences.* Cambridge, MA: MIT Press, pp. 53–69.
Rumelhart, D. E., McClelland, J. L., and the PDP Research Group (1986). *Parallel Distributed Processing: Explorations in the Microstructure of Cognition, Vols. 1 and 2.* Cambridge, MA: MIT Press.
Van Fraassen, B. (1981). *The Scientific Image.* Oxford: Clarendon Press.

CHAPTER THIRTEEN

Andy Clark, Antonio Damasio and embodied cognition

Monica Cowart

Influenced by the groundbreaking works of Dewey, Merleau-Ponty, Vygotsky, Heidegger and Piaget, Embodied Cognition (EC) emerges as a profoundly interdisciplinary research programme in cognitive science. Despite the diversity of these accounts, they all contend that the specific ways in which an organism is embodied in the environment will directly impact its cognitive processing, its movements and its understanding of the world. Consequently, awareness of an organism's embodiment is viewed as a necessary condition for understanding its cognitive processes since an organism's specific sensorimotor capacities partly determine the options that emerge for it to successfully navigate its environment. Given this theoretical commitment, EC researchers construct cognitive explanations that capture the complexity of the ways in which mind, body and world mutually influence one another to promote the organism's adaptive success.

Embodied cognition theories are often viewed in contrast with long-standing cognitivist/classicist theories that advance a rule-based, information-processing view of cognition. Cognitivist/classicist theories employ a computer metaphor of the mind and assume that (1) problem solving occurs in terms of inputs and outputs, (2) symbolic, encoded representations facilitate computational solutions, and (3) cognition can be properly understood by attending to an organism's internal processes, with an emphasis on those involving computation and representation.

Given the ever-growing list of critiques against the classicist/cognitivist programme(e.g. the symbol grounding problem (Searle 1980, Harnad 1990), the frame problem, the expertise problem (Dreyfus 1992) and the common-sense problem (Horgan and Tienson 1989), etc.), many researchers began to look for viable alternatives that would not fall prey to the same objections.

A further concern was that classicist/cognitivist accounts focused solely on an organism's internal cognitive processes. Some researchers concluded that this resulted in an isolationist flaw since they did not consider how the organism's environment and its bodily instantiation influenced its cognitive development. To avoid this isolationist error, EC theorists favour a relational analysis.

As more and more theorists recognize the challenges of the classicist/cognitivist model, a proliferation of research has occurred that supports the EC thesis. While the verdict is still out on whether or not EC will be able to provide an adequate explanation of cognitive processes, including an explanation of the emergence of cognitive complexity, the goal of this chapter is to articulate the EC framework and to discuss some noteworthy theoretical developments within EC. This chapter will proceed in four parts.

In Part I, I provide an analysis of the common research assumptions adopted by EC theorists.

In Part II, I discuss Andy Clark's work in EC with a particular emphasis on his Extended Cognition theory, which has generated extensive debate in the philosophy of mind in recent years. The central argument results in the provocative conclusion that beliefs can seep into the world.

In Part III, I examine Antonio Damasio's development of the somatic marker hypothesis. This work inspired his more recent views that explore the development of self and consciousness.

In Part IV, I argue that a 'New Frontier' for EC is in trauma studies since body-centred therapeutic interventions, such as EMDR, Mindfulness, and Sensorimotor psychotherapy, are being elevated to evidence-based status due to their efficacy. I maintain that these treatments demonstrate a new frontier where EC assumptions are applied in treatment.

Finally, I conclude by noting that while Embodied Cognition remains an extremely promising research programme, there is still much to be 'ironed out' in terms of (1) fully explaining the notion of coupling and (2) devising interdisciplinary research methodologies that precisely factor in the role of the environment.

Let's turn to an examination of the general EC framework.

I The embodied cognition thesis

EC accounts have been formulated in many of the subfields comprising cognitive science, including developmental psychology, philosophy of mind, linguistics, neuroscience and artificial life/robotics. The diversity of these projects makes it difficult to define Embodied Cognition as a research programme, especially since many of the researchers who self-identify as EC theorists do not agree upon the same theoretical tenets.

Even though these different EC accounts vary significantly in terms of the mechanisms they employ to explain cognition, a few common themes emerge. The goal of this section is to isolate some of the common theoretical assumptions shared by EC views. Let's consider a preliminary definition of Embodied Cognition. Elsewhere I have defined EC as:

> Embodied Cognition is a growing research program in cognitive science that emphasizes the formative role the environment plays in the development of cognitive processes. The general theory contends that cognitive processes develop when a tightly coupled system emerges from real-time, goal-directed interactions between organisms their environment; the nature of these interactions influences the formation and further specifies the nature of the cognitive capacities. (Cowart 2004, p. 1)

Since the research programme itself is still fairly new and certain EC accounts may reject one of the outlined assumptions but endorse others, it is important to note that the following list of theoretical assumptions is not meant to convey the necessary and sufficient conditions for classification as an EC account. Instead, these assumptions will provide the a better understanding of what most EC views generally have in common, despite the fluidity of the research programme. I maintain that the theoretical assumptions most commonly held by Embodied Accounts of Cognition are: (1) the primacy of goal-directed action, (2) embodiment determines cognition, (3) cognition is constructive, (4) faculty psychology is questioned and (5) a traditional, classicist account of representation is denied or viewed as not being the only representational option. Let's consider each theoretical assumption.

Assumption #1: Primacy of goal-directed actions in the 'here and now'

EC theorists contend that thought results from an organism's ability to act in its environment in real time in response to immediate challenges. As the organism learns to control its movements and perform goal-directed actions, it develops an understanding of its own basic abilities/skills, which serve as an essential first step towards acquiring concepts to structure thought and language. Psychologists Thelen and Smith (1994) considered infants who were learning to reach. The challenges each infant had to overcome to learn the new skill was directly related to the physical dynamic of the infant's body. For instance, the extremely active infant, Gabriel, had to learn to slow down his movements so that they would become more focused, while the more sedentary infant, Hannah, had to learn to create enough force to generate a reaching behaviour.

Assumption #2: Embodiment determines cognition

EC theorists believe that the particular way in which an organism is embodied (e.g. a tail, sonar, etc.) will determine how it is able to interact in the world. The types of interactions that are available to the organism based on its physical form further determine the types of categories/concepts it is capable of constructing. This is because EC theorists argue that category and concept formation is made possible and constrained by the organism's particular sensorimotor experiences.

For instance, if a toddler grabs a ball, then she uses her hands, but a dog uses its mouth to grab the ball. Each of these interactions (e.g. grabbing with one's hands, clutching it with one's paws, etc.) has its own corresponding sensorimotor experiences. It is in this sense that embodiment determines cognition; the way in which we are embodied determines the type of action patterns we can perform and these action patterns shape our cognitive processes (i.e. the specific way in which we can conceptualize and categorize).

Lakoff and Johnson (1999) are not the only theorists who argue that the way an organism is embodied will determine its cognitive abilities. Psychologists such as Barsalou and Glenberg (1997, 2005) and Thelen and Smith (1994) also adopt this theoretical assumption even though the specific content of their individual views varies. For instance, Glenberg illustrates how cognition results from embodiment due to 'mesh' which refers to the particular way in which affordances, knowledge and goals combine. In contrast, Barsalou develops a theory of simulation and Thelen and Smith utilize dynamical systems theory. All agree with the theoretical assumption that embodiment determines cognition, but the particular way in which this process occurs varies among these theorists.

Assumption #3: Cognition is constructive

If the way we conceptualize and categorize is based on the way we are embodied, then EC theorists argue that to some extent these concepts and categories are constructed and not merely apprehended wholesale from an observer-independent environment. The point here is that the way in which we are embodied not only constrains the way we interact in the world, but our embodiment directly determines the way the world appears to us.

By 'constructive', EC theorists do not mean to imply that there is no objective external reality and that everything is subjective. Instead, the point is that a type of mutual specification occurs between the organism and its environment, so that the way the world looks and the way in which the organism can interact in the world is primarily determined by the way the organism is embodied. For instance, we view our bodies as having distinct fronts and backs. Due to the characteristics we associate with each of these bodily spatial relations, Lakoff and Johnson (1999) argue that we also characterize objects in the world according to these assignments (e.g. go to the *front* of the house, that is the *back* of her shirt, etc.). This process is considered to be constructive because we project these characteristics onto the world since they reflect the foundational understanding we have of our bodies. Consequently, if we were embodied differently, then we would not see the world in this particular way, but in terms of our new set of defining bodily characteristics.

Taking into account the bodies we do have, our actual projected spatial assignments can be traced back to sensorimotor experience, which enables the formation of spatial schemas that are projected onto a scene to facilitate reasoning without using deductive logic. These schemas are constructive because they do not perfectly mirror what is in the world. Instead, these schemas structure elements within the world in such a way that the organism can understand its environment quickly.

Assumption #4: Faculty psychology is questioned

In *Philosophy In the Flesh*, Lakoff and Johnson maintain that cognitive science has inherited from the Western philosophical tradition a theory of faculty psychology, in which we have a 'faculty' of reason that is separate from and independent of what we do with our bodies. In particular, reason is seen as independent of perception and bodily movement. Yet, an increasing amount of research is bringing into question the claim that any form of reason necessarily must occur in a part of the brain that is completely separate from the sensorimotor regions. However, we must be careful about the type of conclusion that can be drawn from any such findings, assuming that a link between reason and sensorimotor regions is substantiated. Even if we discover that one form of reason depends in some way on the sensorimotor regions, this finding would not rule out the possibility of other forms of reason occurring in parts of the brain that are completely isolated from sensorimotor regions. Given the still primitive state of neuroscience, we cannot argue for a complete rejection of faculty psychology, since such a rejection would require a comprehensive understanding of the brain, which we do not yet have.

In effect, many EC theorists argue that their findings strengthen the claim that sensorimotor experience may underlay some form of reason and reason is not necessarily located in a distinctly separate brain region. In Part III, we will consider to what extent the neurological evidence could support this point when we examine Damasio's formation of the somatic marker hypothesis.

Assumption #5: Traditional account of representation is rejected

Most embodied accounts of cognition reject a traditional account of representation, where representations are defined in terms of arbitrary symbols that are amodal in nature (i.e. Classicist/Cognitivist representations). However, EC theorists differ in the degree to which they are willing to dispense with representation all together as well as how representations should be properly construed. Some argue that cognition is completely non-representational (Varela et al. 1993; Thelen and Smith 1994). Still others (Brooks 1991) maintain that they reject a representational analysis, but a closer examination of their view displays representational undertones. Since different EC theorists define representation in different ways, a detailed understanding of how different EC theorists construe representation is beyond the scope of this chapter. Yet, for those who endorse a representational analysis, the representations are typically multi-modal, action-driven and sensorimotor in nature.

II Clark as EC theorist

Andy Clark has been instrumental in helping to define the EC research programme. His 1997 book, *Being There: Putting Brain, Body, and World Together Again*, serves as one of the first sustained treatments of EC research. Aside from making important contributions of his own (e.g. further defining the coupling relation, noting the importance of scaffolded environments to off-load memory, etc.), this work was instrumental in making other EC theorists aware of the research that was occurring in other disciplines. In *Natural Born Cyborgs: Minds, Technologies, and the Future of Human Intelligence*, Clark

(2003) further argues that the human condition is partly defined by our ability to create complex environments using tools, artefacts and cultural practices that enable us to effortlessly enhance our abilities. With Clark's general research programme in mind, we will now consider a highly controversial argument advanced by Clark that continues to elicit much response in the philosophy of mind literature.

The extended mind thesis

In 'The Extended Mind', Andy Clark and David Chalmers explore the implications of highly coupled systems and reach the ultimate conclusion that in certain tightly coupled systems part of the world is correctly viewed as part of the cognitive process (p. 644). To understand the formation of their view, I will explain active externalism, discuss the Inga/Otto thought experiment and examine potential objections from other theorists.

What is Active Externalism?

Clark and Chalmers formulate a new answer to the question: where does the mind end and the world begin? (p. 643). In contrast to the standard response, that defines the mental as being housed within the barrier of skin and skull so that everything environmentally external to these bodily barriers is automatically excluded from a potential classification as mind, Clark and Chalmers provide a new response that they call 'active externalism', which depicts the environment's active role in facilitating the cognitive process.

So what exactly is active externalism? Clark and Chalmers provide a number of examples in which agents use external environmental features, such as pen and paper, books, nautical slide rule and other cultural props, to support, maximize and enhance cognitive functioning (p. 644). Appealing to Kirsh and Maglio's distinction between epistemic and pragmatic actions, they note that epistemic acts are acts that provide knowledge by altering the environment, such as moving Scrabble tiles in varying combinations to think of words; the information gained facilitates problem solving. In the Scrabble case, the movement itself is not the desired end, but the movement aids the cognitive process so that I am eventually able to play a word that I might not have seen if I had tried to manipulate the tiles only in my head.

Clark and Chalmers argue that when an epistemic act occurs, it makes sense to further state that the *epistemic credit* for the act should also be distributed and viewed as part of the cognitive process. They advance a parity principle that states that:

> If, as we confront some task, a part of the world functions as a process which were it done in the head, we would have no hesitation in recognizing as part of the cognitive process, then that part of the world is (so we claim) part of the cognitive process. Cognitive processes ain't (all) in the head! (p. 644)

Clark and Chalmers note that when an external prop is correctly viewed as part of the cognitive process, then a coupled system exists. This occurs when the agent 'is linked with an external entity in a two-way interaction, creating a coupled system that can be seen as a cognitive system in its own right' (p. 644). Importantly, the external props in these systems are actively providing immediate, in the moment feedback, which has a direct effect upon the agent's mental states and behaviour (p. 645). For instance, they maintain that when an individual manipulates the Scrabble tiles, the tile movement is best classified as 'part of a *thought*' not action (p. 645). Clark and Chalmers conclude that 'this sort of coupled process counts equally well as a cognitive process, whether or not it is wholly in the head' (p. 644).

This thesis of active externalism, with its focus upon the coupling relation, is in line with interdisciplinary research conducted by EC theorists. As noted in Part 1, these theorists also stress, to varying degrees, the crucial role the environment plays in cognition. Clark and Chalmers contend that the acceptance of this claim has real-world implications for how research is conducted and whether certain methodologies are viewed as appropriate for understanding cognition. They further maintain that active externalism provides more explanatory power for a host of actions that could not be adequately explained by theories that only reference internal processes.

One objection that Clark and Chalmers anticipate is a portability concern, in which some might maintain that cognitive processes are limited to the boundary of skin and skull because these processes must be portable and thus exist in the head. The objection states that certain core abilities, resources and operations should always be available to the organism regardless of environmental changes; this portability requirement is seemingly met if one only considers the internal resources of the organism. Clark and Chalmers note that the focus on portability stems from concerns that core cognitive processes should be consistently available and coupled systems involving environmental features could be too easily decoupled (p. 645).

They respond by stating that the concern behind the portability criterion is that reliable coupling must be maintained, especially if the resource is viewed as part of the organism's standard resources. Consequently, a high percentage of reliable coupling occurs internally, but reliable coupling can involve environmental features. For instance, if my iPhone is always with me and I use its various apps as problem-solving opportunities emerge in my daily life, then I am using these resources in a manner that meets reliability concerns. Under such circumstances, my iPhone, or any other object that meets these criteria, can be characterized as being 'part of the basic package of cognitive resources that I bring to bear on the everyday world' (p. 646). Clark and Chalmers state that:

> These systems cannot be impugned simply on the basis of the danger of discrete loss, or malfunction, or because of any occasional decoupling: the biological brain is in similar danger, and occasionally loses capacities temporarily in episodes of sleep, intoxication, and emotion. (p. 646)

Essentially, Clark and Chalmers conclude that there is sufficiently reliable coupling if these resources are present when needed. They stipulate that the brain evolved to take full advantage of altering, exploiting and manipulating environmental resources in order to reduce computational load and enhance cognitive functioning. In effect, these local features, including artefacts and language, become part of the coupled system in a manner that is evolutionarily advantageous. Consequently, from an early age, highly scaffolded environments are created which reinforce the brain's reliance on using coupled systems to learn new skills and off-load memory.

The Inga & Otto thought experiment regarding beliefs

Next, Clark and Chalmers claim that in certain coupled systems the environmental features can partly determine an agent's beliefs so that the mind extends into the environment. To illustrate, they construct the Inga/Otto thought experiment.

We are asked to consider two individuals who each attend a museum exhibition: Inga and Otto. First we consider Inga, whose situation depicts the standard scenario of beliefs accessed through memory. Inga decides to attend an event at the Museum of Modern Art after being told about the event from a friend. After thinking briefly, she remembers that the museum is located on 53rd Street so she travels there and attends the exhibition. Clark and Chalmers note that:

> It seems clear that Inga believes that the museum is on 53rd Street, and that she believed this even before she consulted her memory. It was not previously an occurrent belief, but then neither are most of our beliefs. The belief was sitting somewhere in memory, waiting to be accessed. (p. 647)

In contrast to Inga, Otto uses the environment to help organize his life since he has a mild case of Alzheimer's disease. He does this by carrying a notebook with him wherever he goes. He records new information in the notebook as he learns it and he refers to the notebook when he needs to look up existing information. Clark and Chalmers note that the notebook functions in the same manner as biological memory for Otto. Consequently, when Otto hears about the museum exhibition, he decides to attend. He opens his notebook and sees that the museum is located on 53rd Street, so he travels to 53rd and attends the exhibition.

Both Inga and Otto believed that the museum was located on 53rd Street and both walked there as a result of their respective beliefs. Moreover, both Inga and Otto had the belief that the museum was located at 53rd Street before checking further. The difference is in the exact manner in which they verified the belief; Inga looked internally by consulting her memory and Otto looked externally by consulting his notebook. Yet, Clark and Chalmers maintain that the two cases of Otto and Inga are 'entirely analogous' since Otto's notebook and Inga's memory play the same *functional role* in the system (p. 647). They further state that the informational content of the notebook serves the same role as the informational content of a typical non-occurrent belief, despite the fact that this information is in a notebook in the world.

One might be tempted to conclude that Otto does not have any belief regarding location prior to consulting the notebook or that his belief is that the address in the notebook is the museum's location. However, Clark and Chalmers disagree, since Otto's daily actions and lived experience indicate that he is constantly using his notebook in all types of situations and that this frequent use is parallel to the way that ordinary memory functions in daily life. We would not want to say that Inga must have continued awareness of particular beliefs when those beliefs are no longer required to solve a particular task. Inga may no longer be conscious of a particular belief as the need to be so subsides, but that same belief can be recalled again from memory if needed again. Similarly, Otto should only be required to access the information from his notebook reliably and as needs dictate. Both should be held to the same standard.

Clark and Chalmers clarify the criteria of availability and portability by stating that the environmental resource must be 'reliably available', 'typically invoked', 'easily accessible' and that information retrieved from the resource is not questioned, but instead 'more or less automatically endorsed' by the agent (Clark 2008, p. 46).

A further possible misinterpretation of Otto's situation would be to engage in what Clark later (Clark 2010, p. 46) calls the Otto two-step in which an additional step is added to Otto's processing. This interpretation has Otto thinking in the following manner:

> Step 1: Otto has the belief that information x is in the notebook. (Let x = whatever information Otto needs, such as the address of the museum.)
>
> Step 2: Otto looks in the notebook and then finds the information. At this point, his belief changes and a new belief is formed that reflects the specific content he was needing, such as the exact address. Therefore, Otto's new belief is that the Museum is on 53rd Street.

Clark (2010) notes that the problem inherent in the two-step surfaces when we return to Inga and apply the same two-step reasoning to her.

Step 1: Inga has the belief that information x is in her memory. (Let x = whatever information Inga needs, such as the address of the museum.)

Step 2: Inga consults her memory for information x and acts upon the information. In this case, she accesses the information that the Museum is on 53rd Street.

Clark maintains that to assume that Inga, or Otto, or anyone adds this additional step of needing to consult their memory as a specific step is adding unnecessary complexity to the cognitive process. Moreover, it seems clear that Inga simply refers to her memory just as Otto automatically refers to his notebook. Clark concludes that the two-step 'adds needless and psychologically unreal complexity to introduce additional beliefs about the book or biological memory into the explanatory equations' (p. 47).

Critiques of active externalism/the extended mind thesis

While some theorists side with Clark as he continues to support the extended mind thesis (see Clark 2008, 2010), others have found the view simply untenable. The literature continues to grow as more and more theorists weigh in on the debate, but the responses are too numerous to catalogue here. Yet, I will note three objections. Adams and Aizawa (2001, 2010) argue that Extended Cognition is an untenable view because it suffered from a coupling constitution fallacy and fails to properly address the mark of the cognitive. Sterelny worries that these coupled systems are open to tampering by other agents (see Clark 2008 for a discussion of this critique). Menary (2010) states that many critics of the thesis have a profound misunderstanding of the exact view Clark is advancing. One thing that is clear is that the extended mind thesis continues to be greatly debated with no clear resolution in sight.

III Damasio as EC theorist

Neuroscientist Antonio Damasio argues that emotion and feeling are necessary for individuals to make effective decisions. Moreover, this decision-making process might be construed as a particular form of reason. This reliance of decision-making on a certain amount of emotion, if true, calls into question the canon of analytic philosophy, including the work of Kant and Descartes. This is because these philosophers argue that in order to identify metaphysical truths or recognize moral truths, one must distance oneself from emotion. Put another way, they contend that emotions and bodily perceptions can lead one astray, while pure reason will lead to enlightenment. Due to the influence of analytic philosophy, these Cartesian assumptions have influenced many cognitive scientists to believe that reason must be separate from emotion. Yet, Damasio's research challenges this view of faculty psychology, since he provides neurological support for the claim that emotion and sensorimotor experience are necessary for the adequate performance of at least one form of reasoning: decision-making. In the next section, we will examine the case study that led to the development of Damasio's theory.

Case study: Elliot

While working with patients with prefrontal lobe damage, Damasio discovered the emergence of surprising character traits. Specifically, these individuals (1) had lost the ability to use sound judgement when making decisions, (2) were described as becoming noticeably emotionally detached after the frontal damage occurred and (3) were more likely to deviate from social norms that were formerly respected. In order to understand if these changes were the direct effect of the damage to the prefrontal lobe, Damasio ran a series of tests on one of these patients, Elliot.

Elliot's prefrontal damage was the direct result of a brain tumour, which was subsequently removed. Prior to the removal of the prefrontal region, Elliot was described as a good father, husband, and businessman. After the surgery, family members noted a distinct difference in Elliott's demeanour. Even though Elliott's memory, language skills and bodily movements were the same as before the operation, suddenly Elliott was unable to make certain types of decisions or construct and implement action-plans for specific tasks, whether long term or short term in nature.

Damasio states that Elliott was referred to his care in order to determine if these changes in behaviour were a direct result of the prefrontal lobe damage or if they merely demonstrated deficiencies in Elliot's character that had nothing to do with the removal of the prefrontal region. After initially evaluating Elliott, Damasio describes Elliott's behaviour in the following way:

> The tragedy of this otherwise healthy and intelligent man was that he was neither stupid nor ignorant, and yet he acted often as if he were. The machinery for his decision-making was so flawed that he could no longer be an effective social being. In spite of being confronted with the disastrous results of his decisions, he did not learn from his mistakes. He seemed beyond redemption, like the repeat offender who professes sincere repentance but commits another offence shortly thereafter. It is appropriate to say that his free will had been compromised. . . . (1994, p. 38)

Even though all of Elliott's cognitive abilities (e.g. memory, language, etc.) appeared to be functioning normally, Damasio ran a battery of tests to see if any abilities were impaired. The test results did not indicate any problems. In fact, none of the tests shed any light on why Elliott had such poor judgement when making personal and social decisions. However, Damasio suspected the tests were incapable of simulating the complex personal and social situations with which Elliot struggled; the tests simplified the possible constraints, but in real life these constraints were not so conveniently limited. Still, Damasio struggled to understand why Elliott was struggling.

The beginning of an answer surfaced when Damasio reconsidered the extremely detached way in which Elliott spoke about his own circumstances. This emotional detachment, in conjunction with Elliot's participation in an experiment designed to determine the way emotion-provoking images (e.g. natural disasters, burning houses, injured people) affected individuals, provided an important clue to understanding Elliot's condition. Damasio states:

> As we debriefed Elliott from one of many sessions of his viewing these images, he told me without equivocation that his own feelings had changed from before his illness. He could sense how topics that once had evoked a strong emotion no longer caused any reaction, positive or negative . . . . We might summarize Elliott's predicament as *to know but not to feel*. (1994, p. 45)

Based on this important observation regarding Elliott's inability to feel any emotion, Damasio questioned whether this deficiency could be in some way related to Elliott's inability to make sound judgements concerning personal and social matters. After another battery of tests, Damasio noted that Elliot was unable to make adequate decisions in a timely manner, if at all, due to a defect that was occurring in the late stages of the reasoning process. As a result of this defect, the mere act of choosing became problematic and at times impossible for Elliott. Damasio stipulated that Elliott's inability to make decisions was connected to Elliott's inability to feel emotions. Damasio describes the initial hypothesis in the following manner:

> I began to think that the cold-bloodedness of Elliott's reasoning presented him from assigning different values to different options, and made his decision making landscape hopelessly flat.... [In effect] *reduction in emotion may constitute an equally important source of irrational behavior.* (1994, p. 51)

Therefore, Damasio postulated that the ability to experience emotion was crucial in making sound decisions in a timely manner, since the correct amount of emotion would help to highlight the best choice in a given situation. If this claim is true, then emotion is essential to one form of reasoning (i.e. decision-making), but in the right amount; being too emotional or not experiencing emotion at all, as in the case of Elliot, would lead to either an inability to choose effectively or, in some instances, the inability to choose at all.

In order to demonstrate that Elliott's condition was not anomalous, Damasio studied twelve other patients with similar injuries to the prefrontal cortex. Damasio found impaired decision-making abilities that were accompanied by an inability to experience emotion in each patient. Working from this data, Damasio constructed the somatic-marker hypothesis.

The somatic-marker hypothesis

For Damasio, one way to think of reasoning is in terms of its relation to deciding or choosing between various options in a given situation. Damasio discusses three levels of reasoning involving various degrees of choice. The first two he mentions briefly, since they refer to cases involving either unconscious bodily responses (e.g. regulation of blood sugar) or cases involving learned responses (e.g. avoiding a falling object). Neither involves complex decision-making.

The third level involves complex, deliberate decision-making (e.g. deciding to invest in a stock, choosing a college major, deciding to date someone), which distinguishes it from the other levels. Damasio states that 'the stimulus situations have more parts to them; the response options are more numerous; their respective consequences have more ramifications and those consequences are often different, immediately and in the future, thus posing conflicts between possible advantages and disadvantages over varied time frames' (pp. 167–8). Given this complexity, quick and effective decisions cannot be generated by employing reason alone. This is because a cost/benefit analysis would need to be calculated for every possible action and attending to the long-term consequences for each of these possibilities is too much for the limited capabilities of working memory. Consequently, by appealing to reason alone to determine an action-plan, the individual is overcome by the multiple possible outcomes. They either make an error or choose incorrectly or become paralysed by the possibilities and are not able to choose at all. This is what patients with prefrontal damage experienced. They encountered a computational explosion that was too much for their working memory to handle. Damasio argues that emotion prevents this type of computational explosion from occurring by constraining or limiting the number of options you will consider as deserving of a cost/benefit analysis.

This is because when we consider a complex situation, such as declaring a major, the relevant factors quickly present themselves. Those options, which would clearly result in a negative outcome, such as declaring a math major when you failed algebra, are accompanied by a negative gut feeling. The feeling that accompanies the potential action is called 'a somatic marker', since it conveys to the individual the type of outcome that might be expected by performing that action-option. When a positive action accompanies the somatic marker, the individual views the action favourably and proceeds by conducting a cost/benefit analysis on that option. However, when a negative feeling accompanies the somatic marker, the individual might reject the option immediately and avoid taking the time to conduct the cost/benefit analysis.

Damasio maintains that the somatic marker enables the individual to rule out many unsound options before any kind of cost/benefit analysis occurs. The remaining options are calculated within the capabilities of working memory. Damasio further explains the role of the somatic marker:

> It forces attention on the negative outcome to which a given action might lead and functions as an automated alarm signal which says: Beware of the danger ahead if you choose the option which leads to this outcome. The signal may lead you to reject, immediately, the negative course of action and thus make you choose among other alternatives. The automated signal protects you against future loses, without further ado, and then allows you to choose from among fewer alternatives. There is still room for cost/benefit analysis and proper deductive competence, but only after the automated step drastically reduces the options. (p. 173)

Unfortunately, due to space constraints, we will not have time to discuss the experiments Damasio conducted to support the somatic-marker hypothesis. However, we can see that the neurological evidence suggests that at least one form of reason requires the emotions to operate effectively. Thus, Damasio's work is but one example of why we must question the prevalence of faculty psychology and its influence on how cognitive scientists conduct their research.

Recently, Damasio's somatic marker theory has been applied to economics to show that in certain circumstances emotions that are relevant to the economic analysis can benefit the decision-making process while emotions that are unrelated to the problem set can be detrimental (see Bechara and Damasio 2005). Damasio's most recent work (2010, 2003) applies the somatic marker hypothesis to other domains, including developing an account of self and consciousness.

IV New directions in EC – advancing an 'embodied' psychotherapy

Recent work in trauma studies illustrates how applying an embodied cognition framework can lead to significant advances in treatment success for post-traumatic stress disorder (PTSD) and other trauma-related diagnoses. While many of these clinicians and researchers would not identify as embodied cognition theorists because they are not familiar with that theoretical designation, they would individually state that they adhere to the majority of the EC tenets mentioned in Part I.

This raises the question: why is embodied cognition such a potentially useful framework for understanding new developments in trauma studies? A key reason is that clinical interventions, such as Eye Movement Desensitization Reprocessing (EMDR) (Shapiro 1997), mindfulness-based protocols (Siegel 2007, Germer 2005, Kabat-Zinn 1992) and sensorimotor/somatic psychotherapy (Ogden 2006, Levine 2010), all employ techniques that assume that complex trauma requires an integrated body-focused treatment approach to promote healing. EMDR trainer Grand (2003) explains why, from a neurological perspective, talk therapy will not be as effective as body-based interventions, such as EMDR:

> Talk therapy enters the system through the cortical region of the brain, the seat of logic and thought. But trauma deeply affects the mammalian or emotional brain (which is difficult to access through talking), the reptilian brain, and the body (which is inaccessible to verbal interchange). (p. 100)

He further explains that:

> EMDR appears not only to have access to these regions, but to have the ability to change them. When patients describe *and feel* an image or a negative memory, they're activating the place where it is held in the nervous system—in the body, hindbrain, midbrain, and forebrain. Words can't describe something that happened when we were incapable of speech, but by activating images, sounds, smells and bodily sensations, we gain access to the primitive brain. Evoking the emotions associated with a sensory experience can activate the primitive responses allied with trauma. (p. 101)

Therefore, EMDR is designed to enable the processing of traumatic memories that were not capable of being activated or accessed by the patient through talk therapy. This activation occurs because

EMDR uses body-based techniques to process the trauma, including bilateral stimulation involving eye movements, body scans and cognitive interweaves using embodied metaphors. These clinical techniques require the patient to simultaneously become aware of the primary negative cognition (or self-belief) they associate with the event, their emotions, their bodily responses and any images depicting the event. All of these event-related sensorimotor elements are processed together through a form of bilateral stimulation (e.g. back and forth eye movements, tapping, etc.) until the heightened response associated with the event is diminished.

Grand notes that EMDR processes the traumatic event from the 'bottom-up' since patients are asked to become aware of how their bodies are responding at multiple points during a session. Consequently, EMDR is capable of processing body memories, preverbal somatic feelings and emotions by gaining access to regions of the brain that talk therapy cannot access. This partly explains why patients who were in talk therapy for decades are suddenly reporting significant relief from their trauma-related symptoms, including flashbacks and hyper-vigilance, as a result of EMDR therapy. Finally, Grand (2003) remarks that:

> Healing a patient's trauma is impossible without healing the whole system, physiologically, neurobiologically, and psychologically. The arm does not focus independently from the leg; similarly, emotions and thoughts don't flow in a different system from the body. EMDR is an integrative approach to an integrated system that is centered in the body. (p. 156)

While the discussion thus far has focused on EMDR, it should be noted that mindfulness-based interventions, somatic therapy and sensorimotor techniques have had similar successes in treating trauma. These interventions also employ therapeutic techniques that ask patients to focus upon their bodily experiences. In fact, it is common for therapists who recognize the effectiveness of one of these clinical systems to seek further training in the others since they draw from the same base assumptions, including creating an awareness of how the body is feeling in the present moment.

How can embodied cognition inform these psychotherapies and vice versa? What opportunities are available for interdisciplinary collaborations? What can they learn from each other?

The psychological mechanisms are still in need of isolation for EMDR, mindfulness interventions and sensorimotor psychotherapy. While the clinical trials clearly demonstrate that these techniques are effective, there are only hypotheses regarding exactly how and why these techniques work. Since the techniques themselves often involve coupled systems among the therapist, the client and environmental features, EC theorists might be able to offer new techniques for measuring these relationships. Therefore, it would benefit clinical researchers to become aware of the EC literature. Similarly, EC researchers would benefit from examining the case studies and data behind these clinical successes. Understanding the clinical coupling relation, the importance of the present moment and the role of body scans in releasing traumatic memories might lead to further developments in their own disciplines.

Conclusion

While the verdict is still out on whether EC will be able to live up to the expectations that many EC theorists have for it, it is clear that substantial research developments in understanding cognitive complexity warrant our continued attention. The research programmes of Andy Clark and Antonio Damasio have added much to our understanding of what EC is as a framework as well as its eventual promise. As Clark himself notes, an important next step for EC is whether theorists will be able to develop research methods that are able to capture the complexity of the ways in which mind, body and world mutually influence one another to promote the adaptive success of the organism.

References

Adams, A. and Aizawa, K. (2001), 'The bounds of cognition'. *Philosophical Psychology* 14: 43–64.
— (2010), 'Defending the bounds of the cognitive'. In R. Menary (ed.), *The Extended Mind*. Cambridge: MIT Press.
Bechara, A. and Damasio, A. (2005), 'The somatic marker hypothesis: A neural theory of economic decision'. *Games and Economic Behavior* 52: 336–72.

Block, S. and Block, C. (2010), *Mind-Body Workbook for PTSD*. Oakland: New Harbinger Publications.
Brooks, R. A. (1991), 'Intelligence without representation'. *Artificial Intelligence* 47: 139–59.
Clark, A. (1997), *Being There: Putting Brain, Body, and World Together Again*. Cambridge, MA: MIT Press.
— (1999), 'Embodied, situated and distributed cognition'. In W. Bechtel and G. Graham (eds), *A Companion to Cognitive Science*. Oxford: Blackwell Publishers.
— (2003), *Natural-Born Cyborgs: Minds, Technologies, and the Future of Human Intelligence*. Oxford: Oxford University Press.
— (2008), *Supersizing the Mind: Embodiment, Action & Cognitive Extension*. New York: Oxford University Press.
— (2010a), 'Memento's revenge: The extended mind, extended'. In R. Menary (ed.), *The Extended Mind*. Cambridge: MIT Press.
— (2010b), 'Coupling, constitution, and the cognitive kind: A reply to Adams and Aizawa'. In R. Menary (ed.), *The Extended Mind*. Cambridge: MIT Press.
Clark, A. and Chalmers, D. (2002), 'The extended mind'. In D. Chalmers (ed.), *Philosophy of Mind: Classical and Contemporary Readings*, New York: Oxford University Press. Reprinted from *Analysis* 58: 10–23.
Cowart, M. (2005), 'Embodied cognition'. In Internet Encyclopedia of Philosophy, www.iep.utm.edu/embodcog/.
— (2011), 'EMDR and embodied cognition: The search for theoretical mechanisms and increased explanatory power'. Poster presented at the annual conference of the EMDR International Association, Orange County, CA.
Damasio, A. (1994), *Descartes' Error: Emotions, Reason, and the Human Brain*. New York: Avon Books.
— (1996), 'The somatic marker hypothesis and the possible functions of prefrontal cortex'. *Philosophical Transactions Royal Society of London B* 351: 1413–20.
— (1999), *The Feeling of What Happens: Body and Emotion in the Making of Consciousness*. New York: Harcourt Brace.
— (2003), 'Feelings of emotion and the self'. *Annals of the New York Academy of Sciences* 1001: 253–61.
— (2012), *Self Comes to Mind: Constructing the Conscious Brain*. New York: Vintage Books Edition.
Dreyfus, H. (1972/92), *What Computers Can't Do: A Critique of Artificial Reason*. New York: Harper and Row. (1992), *What Computers Still Can't Do*, Third edition Cambridge, MA:MIT Press.
Germer, C., Siegel, R., and Fulton, P. (2005), *Mindfulness and Psychotherapy*. New York: Guilford Press.

Glenberg, A. (1997), 'What memory is for: Creating meaning in the service of action'. *Behavioral and Brain Sciences* 20: 1–55.

Glenberg, A. M., David, H., Raymond, B. and Mike R. (2005), 'Grounding language in bodily states: The case for emotion'. In Diane, P. and Rolf A. Zwaan (eds), *The Grounding of Cognition: The Role of Perception and Action in Memory, Language & Thinking*. Cambridge: Cambridge University Press, pp. 115–28.

Grand, D. (2003), *Emotional Healing at Warp Speed: The Power of EMDR*. New York: Present Tents Publishing.

Harnad, S. (1990), 'The symbol grounding problem'. *Physica D* 42: 335–46.

Hogan, T. and Tienson, J. (1989), 'Representations without rules'. *Philosophical Topics* 17: 147–74.

Kabat-Zinn, J., Maission, A., Kristeller, J. Peterson, L., Fletcher, K., Pbert, L., Lenderking, W. and Santorelli, S. (1992), 'Effectiveness of a meditation-based stress reduction program in the treatment of anxiety disorders'. *American Journal of Psychiatry* 149: 936–43.

Kirsh, D. and Maglio, P. (1994), 'On distinguishing epistemic from pragmatic action'. *Cognitive Science* 18: 513–49.

Lakoff, G. and Johnson, M. (1999), *Philosophy in the Flesh: The Embodied Mind and Its Challenge to Western Thought*. New York: Basic Books.

Levine, A. (2010), *In an Unspoken Voice: How the Body Releases Trauma and Restores Goodness*. Berkeley, CA: North Atlantic Books.

Menary, R. (2010), 'Introduction: The Extended Mind in Focus'. In R. Menary (ed.), *The Extended Mind*. Cambridge: MIT Press.

Ogden, P., Minton, K., and Pain, C. (2006), *Trauma and the Body: A Sensorimotor Approach to Psychotherapy*. New York: Norton & Company.

Searle, J. (1980), 'Minds, brains, and programs'. *Behavioral and Brain Sciences* 1: 417–24.

Shapiro, F. and Forrest, M. (2004), *EMDR: Eye Movement Desensitization & Reprocessing*, Updated edition. New York: Basic Books.

Siegel, D. (2007), *The Mindful Brain: Reflections and Attunement in the Cultivation of Well-Being*. New York: Norton Company.

Sutton, J. (2010), 'Exograms and interdisciplinarity: History, the extended mind, and the civilizing process'. In R. Menary (ed.), *The Extended Mind*. Cambridge: MIT Press.

Thelen, E. and Smith, L. (1994), *A Dynamic Systems Approach to the Development of Cognition and Action*. Cambridge, MA: MIT Press.

Varela, F., Thompson, R., and Rosch, E. (1991), *The Embodied Mind*. Cambridge, MA: MIT Press.

CHAPTER FOURTEEN

David Chalmers on mind and consciousness

Richard Brown

David Chalmers is perhaps best known for his argument against physicalism in the philosophy of mind (Chalmers 1996). But this is not his only contribution. He is a highly systematic philosopher who has offered important theories and insights in many areas of philosophy.

In what follows, we will separate Chalmers' views into two broad projects. On the one hand, we will look at what we might call the negative project where he aims to show that physicalism about consciousness cannot work. On the other hand, we will look at what we can call his positive project, which consists in giving a theoretical account of consciousness and mind that is consistent with his anti-physicalism.

The case against physicalism

Chalmers starts with his distinction between what he calls the easy and hard problems of consciousness. The easy problems of consciousness all involve those things that straightforwardly involve functioning. This includes such things as discriminating, categorizing and reacting to the environment, the integration of information, reporting on our mental states, accessing our own internal states, focusing attention, controlling behaviour in a deliberate way and discovering the neural basis of sleep and wakefulness (Chalmers 2010, p. 4). The hard problem of consciousness involves explaining why it is that any of that stuff gives rise to consciousness.

The sense of consciousness invoked in the hard problem is that of phenomenal consciousness or there being something that it is like for one to undergo various mental processes and instantiating various mental states. Thus, the hard problem is that of explaining why it is that any of the functioning mentioned above feels the way it does from the inside. In particular, it seems that any of the functioning could have occurred in the absence of any conscious experience whatsoever. So take, for instance, my seeing a red tomato while hearing someone say 'that's a tomato'. It is one thing to explain how it is that light reflected from the tomato affects my eye and how that produces activity in the brain, which results in various utterances and the grouping of that physical object with fire trucks and oxygenated blood. But none of that seems to explain what it is like for me to see red, or why there should be anything that it is like for me to see red in the first place. So too, it is one thing to explain how sound waves lead to certain kinds of brain activity but that doesn't seem to explain how I consciously hear the words or understand their meaning. Why does any of that information-processing happen consciously? Why isn't it all done in the dark?

One intuitive response at this point is to insist that at some point in the future we will be able to see how the hard problem is not really all that hard after all. Sometimes people use examples like life itself. It was once thought that we could not explain life in purely physical terms and that we would need to posit some mysterious non-physical essence to account for the difference between living and non-living things. We now think this isn't true, and that we can give a physical account of what it means to be alive. So too, perhaps, the same will be true for consciousness in 1,000 years. But this response is not promising according to Chalmers (2010, p. 16). In the case of life, it does in fact seem that what needs explaining are functional ideas. What is so striking about consciousness, from his perspective, is that it is totally unique in that it seems to be something more than function. When one has a conscious experience of pain, or seeing blue, or listening to jazz, or thinking about the philosophy of mind, one is in various states that differ from each other in what it is like for one to have them. Explaining why this is the case doesn't seem to be a matter of merely explaining functions. This is what makes the hard problem so hard.

So far, this is just a puzzle. Given that we know we have conscious experience how do we explain how it arises from structure and function? It is not yet an argument. But an argument immediately presents itself. Following Chalmers (Chalmers 2010, p. 106), we can call this the explanatory argument.

1. Physical accounts explain at most structure and function.
2. Explaining structure and function does not suffice to explain consciousness.
3. No physical account can explain consciousness.

This argument captures the case against physicalism in its essence. It is intuitively plausible that if no physical account can explain consciousness, then there is more in the world than what our physical sciences tell us. But the argument leaves much to be desired. One could insist that explaining structure and function is enough to explain consciousness, thereby denying that there is a hard problem of consciousness, or one could insist that failure to explain does not mean that there is more to our world than the physical.

Chalmers argues that when one looks at the various *a priori* arguments against physicalism, one can see a pattern emerge (2010, p. 107, pp. 193–203). These arguments start from an epistemic or conceptual gap between consciousness and physical properties and move to there being an ontological gap. That is exactly what was going on in the above explanatory argument. An explanatory gap, as Joe Levine (1983) calls it, leads us to infer that there is more in the world that what is merely physical.

To take another example, we can look at the Knowledge Argument advanced originally by Frank Jackson (1986). We imagine a super scientist who has been kept in a black and white room but who nonetheless has access to all of the physical theory about the world. Mary, as she is called, has never seen colours until one day she is released and sees a red ripe apple. She says 'ah! *that's* what it is like for one to see red!' Given that Mary cannot know what it is like to see red in her black and white room (i.e. that there is an epistemic gap), but yet she knows all of the facts that can be captured by structure and function, the argument concludes that knowing what it is like to see red is knowing something beyond the physical facts. We cannot deduce one from the other.

Or, finally, take Kripke's (1980) well-known modal argument. In its basic form, the modal argument goes as follows. Identity statements are necessarily true, if true at all. Those who think otherwise, like the early identity theorists (see Chapter 6), are actually confused. When we think we can imagine lightning, say, without electrical discharge, what we really imagine is something that superficially presents the same appearance as electrical discharge (i.e. lightning) does to us, but which is not lightning. It is essentially fool's lightning, or something which resembles our lightning but is not. So if mind/brain identity statements were true, then it would be impossible to have one without the other. But in the case of, say, 'pain is identical to some neural activity' it seems easy to imagine the pain without the neural activity and the neural activity without the pain. But if so, then how can we explain the fact that the identity is necessary? It seems we cannot appeal to the previous strategy since it doesn't seem to make sense to say that there is something that presents itself in the same way that our pain does but is not really pain.

Though the arguments against physicalism all have a similar structure, the one that is most well worked out, and which makes all of the issues maximally clear, is the two-dimensional conceivability argument (2010, p. 142), which has the following form:

1. P&~Q is conceivable.
2. If P&~Q is conceivable then it is metaphysically possible.
3. If P&~Q is metaphysically possible then physicalism is false.

The 'P' above is a placeholder that can be filled in with whatever physical theory you like. It is meant to be a total description of the world in physical terms. The 'Q' is a claim about phenomenal consciousness, like that I see blue or that someone feels pain. Each premise needs to be clarified and defended.

Premise one says that we can conceive of all of the physical facts holding without any consciousness at all. This is what Chalmers calls a zombie world. This premise relies on what Chalmers calls *ideal negative* conceivability. The notion of ideal conceivability is meant to capture what an ideal reasoner would be able to conceive under ideal conditions as opposed to what merely seems conceivable under certain impoverished reasoning conditions to a less than ideal reasoner. Something is negatively conceivable just when it cannot be ruled out on *a priori* grounds. Something is positively conceivable when we are able to form some positive conception of the thing in question. It goes beyond merely not noticing any contradictions. In addition, we are able to form some conception of how the thing in question could be true. Given this, premise one says that it is ideally negatively conceivable that there be a zombie world. This in turn means that this world is not ruled out *a priori* or that there is nothing contradictory that follows from this description of the world. A common way to make the point is to say that there are no 'conceptual hooks' that allow us to move from talking about physical things to talking about phenomenal consciousness.

Premise two makes the claim that the right kind of conceivability is a reliable guide to what is metaphysically possible. These terms get used in many different ways and Chalmers is careful to distinguish various kinds of conceivability and the corresponding notions of possibility. We have already seen that he is interested, in the most part, in ideal negative conceivability but we must introduce the two-dimensional framework to make the rest of the distinctions.

The fundamental idea of two-dimensional semantics is that there are two different aspects of the meaning of statements, which roughly captures something like a Fregean distinction between meaning and reference. Chalmers calls these primary and secondary intensions. These intensions can be thought of as the contents of statements, where what it means for something to be a content is roughly that it divides up the space of possible worlds in a particular way. So corresponding to the two kinds of intensions will be two different ways of carving up the space of possible worlds, which he calls primary and secondary possibility.

It is perhaps easiest to start with the notion of possibility. We can think of the space of possible worlds as containing every coherent description of the way things could be. We can, if we like, metaphorically think of it as knowing all the ways that God could make the world if He so chose. Among that vast set of worlds will be one that describes the world that we actually live in, the real world. Once we know which one that is, we then think of all of the other worlds as 'counterfactual' worlds. That is, we think of them as describing what could have been the case. But while it is the case that one of those descriptions corresponds to or captures the way the world actually is, we can in principle see that any of those descriptions could be the actual world and so we can then think about this space in two different ways. One way of thinking about these worlds is, so to speak, from their point of view. To do this, we think 'what if this world were the actual world? What would be true then?' Another way of thinking about these worlds is, again so to speak, from our point of view. To do this, we ask 'given that we know that our world is the actual world, and that as a result this, that and the other facts hold true, what could have been the case?' The first is the notion of primary possibility, the second the notion of secondary possibility.

Now we can introduce the primary and secondary intensions of a statement. Let's take as our statement the old standby 'water is H_2O'. The primary intension of the statement is a function from a description of a possible world, considered as the actual world, to a truth-value. The secondary intension of the statement is a function from a description of a possible world, considered as a counterfactual world, to a truth-value. To make this concrete, consider the possible world made famous from debates about meaning and reference of terms like 'water' (Putnam 1973). This is the famous Twin Earth, which is just like Earth except that there water is not H_2O but is rather some other chemical substance, dubbed XYZ. XYZ acts and looks in every way like water, and the people on Twin Earth even call it 'water'! Twin Earth is strange but nothing about it is contradictory. It seems entirely coherent that our world could be that way. But given that our world contains in fact H_2O it doesn't seem like it could have been the case that it was otherwise.

So, 'water is H_2O' is true when we consider any possible world as counterfactual. It has a secondary intension that is necessary, which we can call '2-necessity'. This is because 'water is H_2O' is an *a posteriori* necessity, as Kripke pointed out. There are no worlds, considered as counterfactual, where water isn't H_2O. What this means is that when we consider Twin Earth as a counterfactual world it turns out that there is no water on Twin Earth and that it is still true that water is H_2O. This is because it is 2-necessary that water is H_2O. This is exactly what Kripke argued. On Twin Earth, there is only fool's water. It is something that looks the way H_2O does to us but since it is not H_2O it is not water.

But even so, Twin Earth can be coherently described. If we consider Twin Earth as actual instead of counterfactual, 'water is

H$_2$O' comes out false. On Twin Earth 'water is XYZ' is true and so, when we consider Twin Earth as actual, 'water is H$_2$O' is false. That is to say that if Twin Earth were the actual world, 'water is not H$_2$O' would be true (because 'water is XYZ' is true there). Whether or not our world could have been one where water was not H$_2$O, Twin Earth is possible in some sense.

Now, Chalmers continues, the zombie argument relies only on primary conceivability, not secondary conceivability. We are to think of the zombie world as if that world were the actual world. But if the zombie world were the actual world, then consciousness is not physical, since everything physical is there but without consciousness. This can be put a bit more technically by saying that if the zombie world were the actual world then any proposed physicalist theory of consciousness would be false. But since we can (ideally and negatively) conceive of a zombie world, it is a way our world could be. So, the way our world is physically is not enough for consciousness. Which is just to say that the thesis of physicalism is false.

Categorizing the responses

How should one respond to this argument? Chalmers categorizes the responses according to the way in which one reacts to the conceivability argument.

One way to react is to deny the first premise. Those who take this route Chalmers calls type-A physicalists. According to the type-A camp, we can see now that zombies are inconceivable. Or to put it another way, they deny that there is an epistemic gap or a hard problem of consciousness. Chalmers sees many physicalists' views falling into this category. He cites analytic functionalism of the kind David Lewis held (see Chapter 7), and eliminativism, which includes theories like those of Ryle (see Chapter 5), and Dennett (see Chapter 10), as examples (Chalmers 2010, p. 111). According to analytic functionalism, it is *a priori* that mental states are connected to functioning and so anything that was functionally like us would have consciousness. According to the eliminativist, consciousness doesn't exist in the way that gives rise to the hard problem.

The problem with the type-A view, for Chalmers, is that it seems not to take the data seriously. This marks a fundamental divide in the philosophy of mind. There are those who take it as a sort of starting point that there is more to explain than functioning. There is that to explain, of course; those problems make up the so-called easy problems of consciousness. But certainly it is the case we are conscious and it seems to be a further question as to why any of the functioning is done consciously.

A second way to react is to deny the second premise, which Chalmers labels the type-B response. The type-B camp accepts that there is an epistemic gap but then goes on to deny that this amounts to an ontological gap, thereby denying the link between conceivability and possibility. Many philosophers have defended the type-B approach. It is widely accepted that conceivability is in general not a good guide to what is metaphysically possible and this is precisely the type-B strategy. On these kinds of views, it is metaphysically necessary that pain, say, is identical to a certain kind of physical state even though it is conceivable that you have that physical state without it being a pain state (this is the zombie world).

Putting this into the two-dimensional framework, the type-B response is that 'consciousness' has a necessary primary and secondary intension, which Chalmers calls a 'strong necessity'. It has a necessary primary intension because there are no possible worlds that falsify it. So, take the identity between pain and some brain state or other. According to the type-B camp, we can imagine a world with that brain state and no pain but there is no corresponding metaphysically possible world. Since the space of metaphysically possible worlds does not have one where the identity is false, it is necessarily true, or true in all possible worlds. Chalmers goes on to argue that these strong necessities are deeply strange and inelegant.

Ultimately the dispute here is a local instance of the more general dispute about rationalism and empiricism. In particular, we can see the dispute as an instance of the general debate about the principle of sufficient reason. Roughly put, this principle states that every positive fact must have an explanation. Thus, if one accepts that it is a positive fact that pain, say, is identical to some physical state, then we should be able to give an explanation for why that identity claim holds true. On Chalmers' view, identities are in principle knowable *a priori* in the sense that an ideal reasoner who knew the relevant facts could come to know that the identity is true. So, in the case of water and H_2O, if an ideal reasoner knew all of the facts about H_2O

and about the way that 'water' is used, they would be in a position to know that water was H_2O. But the type-B response is to deny that this is true for 'consciousness', which would seem to make it very different from other concepts like 'water' and 'gold'.

There are a couple of ways that type-B folks have responded. One way has been championed by Ned Block (Block and Stalnaker 1999, Block 2007, Block, forthcoming), a well-known type-B physicalist. Identities in general, and between mind and brain in particular, are brute facts about the world. Identities, on his view, do not get explained. Rather, they get stipulated in order to license greater explanatory power. In the case of water and H_2O, stipulating that they are identical allows us to explain the way water behaves in terms of the way H_2O behaves. We can, for instance, explain why water freezes when it does in terms of the way H_2O behaves. But even this identity is not knowable *a priori* on Block's account.

Another type-B strategy is to appeal to the special nature of phenomenal concepts to try to explain why there is a hard problem of consciousness but not of water, in a way that is consistent with physicalism (Balog 2012). This has come to be known as the 'phenomenal concepts strategy'. Very roughly put, the idea is that we know about our own conscious experience in a unique way. Echoing Russell (1912) they say that we are acquainted with our own experience whereas we know everything else in a secondary kind of way. Some spell this out in terms of appeals to indexicals like 'I' and 'now' or demonstratives like 'this' and 'that'. Others argue that the phenomenal experiences actually constitute part of our beliefs about them.

As we will see later in this chapter, Chalmers holds a version of this kind of view as well, but he argues against the physicalist appealing to it by developing what he calls his Master argument (Chalmers 2010, p. 312). The basic idea behind this master argument is that any kind of explanation that is going to be given by someone who wants to invoke the phenomenal concept strategy has to be tested by conceivability. In particular the claim is that we need to know whether it is conceivable that we have a physical duplicate that has the feature in question or not but that lacks consciousness. If this is conceivable, then the concept is not explainable in physical terms and so is a form of dualism, or it is not conceivable in which case we have not succeeded in explaining the actual relationship that we have with our conscious experience. The reason for this second claim is roughly that if it isn't conceivable then that means that zombies could have this property, but zombies are stipulated not to share our epistemic situation (i.e. they are not conscious).

In general there are only two alternatives, on Chalmers' view. We either start off with a conception of consciousness that builds in special epistemic relations, like acquaintance, or we don't. If we do, then we have the problems from conceivability arguments all over again. If we don't, then we haven't captured the way our consciousness is to us. In the sections that follow, we will look at the way that Chalmers develops his account of acquaintance.

The type-C response holds that there is a *prima facie* epistemic gap but that this gap will eventually be closed. With respect to zombies, the claim is that they are *prima facie* conceivable, or conceivable given what we know now, but that they are not ideally conceivable. Paul Churchland (see Chapter 12) is often cited as a type-C physicalist. Thomas Nagel (1974) has used the analogy of a contemporary physicist trying to explain to Socrates $e=mc^2$. Socrates just doesn't have the concepts to understand it. So, too, Nagel suggests, we may be like Socrates with respect to consciousness. Chalmers responds to this move by constructing a dilemma. Either we will discover more structure and function or we will expand science to go beyond structure and function. If we do the first, then it seems we haven't answered the argument. We can still ask why *that* structure and function result in consciousness. If we take the second, then it looks like we have admitted that dualism of some sort is true. So, let's look at the various dualist responses.

The type-D response is the traditional interactive substance dualism familiar from Descartes (see Chapter 2). It is often claimed that this kind of dualism is at odds with science but Chalmers argues that this is not the case (Chalmers 2010, pp. 126–30).

Type-E responses are the epiphenomenal property dualist responses. Epiphenomenalism is the view that physical states cause or produce mental effects, but these mental effects are themselves unable to cause anything in the physical world. Pain, on this view, is a non-physical property of the brain, which is produced by the workings of the brain, but which has no effect on the way the brain functions. Epiphenomenalism has the theoretical cost of denying that conscious experiences are causally involved in the production of action. This is a severe theoretical cost but it is not a knock down argument against the view.

Type-F monism is the view that there are phenomenal or at least protophenomenal properties that underlie physical properties like mass and charge. This is a version of panpsychism. One way of getting to this kind of theory is by way of the zombie argument. We have so far been assuming that the primary and secondary intension for terms like 'mass', 'charge', and other terms that appear in physical theory, are the same. But it is possible that they come apart. This is often called 'Russellian Monism' since Russell (1927) suggested it at one point. This is the view that science as we know it only describes the relational properties of reality. Mass, for instance, is defined in terms of its causes and effects. We are not told what it is that has mass, or what the fundamental nature of mass is. If this is so, then it may be the case that the fundamental stuff is consciousness.

Chalmers has remained in principle neutral on these dualist positions and claims that any of them could turn out to be true; but he seems most attracted to type-F views. This is because it seems to have the best of all worlds. It preserves the spirit of physicalism in that the fundamental phenomenal properties can be thought of as an extension of fundamental posits of physical theory. Zombie worlds are conceivable, because those worlds do not have the fundamental natures of our world – they lack consciousness. But we can also say that consciousness is causally efficacious. If it is the fundamental base of mass and charge, then it has a fundamental role to play in the causal structure of our world.[1]

Another way to respond is by denying the whole apparatus that sets these arguments up, which Chalmers labels the type-Q response. In the spirit of Quine, this response denies that there is any sense in modal talk (for a defence of this view see Mandik and Weisberg 2008). One way to defend this view is by developing the claim that what is conceivable depends on what theories one (tacitly) holds. If this were the case, then finding zombies conceivable might be evidence that one (tacitly) holds a dualist theory or some kind of identity theory, rather than showing us what is possible.

Another challenge that cuts across these distinctions has come from the appeal to the conceivability of physical creatures that have consciousness but no non-physical properties (Brown 2010, Frankish 2007). Brown has called these creatures 'shombies', Frankish calls them 'anti-zombies'. Assuming we are committed to the two-dimensional framework, it cannot be the case that both zombies and shombies are ideally conceivable. This could be used to defend a type-A position, or a type-B position, or a type-Q position, depending on how one proceeds. In its most general form, the claim is simply that it is conceivable that consciousness be physical. Even if we have no clue how it could be physical, there does not seem to be anything contradictory in the idea. Chalmers himself has expressed sympathy with the claim that shombies are at least *prima facie* negatively conceivable (Chalmers 2010, p. 180), though he denies that this is enough to ground a premise in an anti-dualist argument.

We can now turn to examining Chalmers' positive project.

The science of consciousness

It would be a mistake to conclude from the foregoing discussion that Chalmers is not optimistic about the chances for a science of consciousness. He is very much in favour of a science of consciousness but, in his view, it must be one that transcends physical science as we know it now. In particular, as we have seen, he thinks it must include facts about consciousness as basic irreducible facets of reality. Doing this will broaden one's conception of what counts as science, rather than precluding a science of consciousness. So what does the science of consciousness look like according to Chalmers?

He begins by identifying two sources of data for a science of consciousness. The first is the third-person data that we derive in the pursuit of answering the easy questions of consciousness. The other is first-person data, which are the experiences that one has. The science of consciousness then consists in gathering both sorts of data and finding out the ways in which they are linked. Since Chalmers is convinced that first-person data is irreducible to third-person data, the science of consciousness will be in the business of finding the fundamental laws which link these two sorts of data.

Chalmers has speculated about what some of these fundamental laws might look like. One of these he calls the 'principle of structural coherence', the other 'the principle of organizational invariance'. The principle of structural coherence tells us that there is a lawful correlation between the structure of our experience and the structure of what he calls 'awareness', which is one of the easy problems of consciousness. This principle boils down to the idea that we can see law-like regularities between brain activity and conscious experience. Chalmers can then happily accept that psychological theories give us important insights into the structure of conscious experience on the basis of facts about awareness, without positing a reduction.

The principle of organizational invariance tells us that it is the functional organization of the brain that matters for consciousness and mind rather than the specific material of the brain. This brings out the role that computation plays in the science of mind and consciousness for Chalmers. He has defended the claim that reality is in principle computable and that there are a set of computations that suffice for having a mind. This is because mind and consciousness are examples of what Chalmers has called 'organizational invariants'. Something is organizationally invariant when, roughly, a simulation of that thing counts as the real thing. So, being a hurricane doesn't count because a simulation of it is not the real thing. A very good example of something that is organizationally invariant is being a computer. A simulation of a computer is indeed a computer. His claim is that the consciousness and mind are also organizational invariants.

This underscores the central place of the notion of computation in Chalmers' thinking about consciousness and mind. A computation, for Chalmers, is specified relative to some formal system (Chalmers 2011). So, take the classic notion of Turing Machine. A computation for this kind of system involves a reader detecting symbols on a tape and moving the tape and printing new symbols as a result. A physical system implements a computation when the transitions between the states of the physical system reflect or mirror the abstract computation in question. Chalmers has argued that there is a set of computations which, when implemented, are necessary and sufficient for the existence of consciousness (i.e. holding the relevant laws in place). Consciousness and mind are organizational invariants on his view.

The argument for this comes from *a priori* reflection on cases of what Chalmers calls fading and dancing qualia. The basic idea is to imagine having one's brain replaced bit by bit, say by replacing individual neurons one by one with a functional duplicate. Either one's conscious experience would change over the course of doing this or it would not. If it changes, we seem committed to the claim that one cannot notice or report this change, since one is functionally exactly the same from moment to moment. To make this vivid, we can imagine that you are eating your favourite food as the process is being carried out. You will go on saying that you don't notice any change and that the ice cream is delicious, etc. If this were the case, then we would be radically out of touch with our own conscious experience. This gives us good reason to reject the claim that our conscious experience will change as this is happening. If so, then the basic laws which relate the physical to the phenomenal depend on functional organization rather than the material of the brain. Thus, if we were to build a robot that had a functional analogue of availability, it would have consciousness. And if we were to somehow upload the computational structure that our brain implements, we would have uploaded our mind into a computer.

It is important to be clear that Chalmers is not endorsing a functionalist account of consciousness. He has rejected physicalism and all physicalist theories and is thinking of these computations as involving fundamental non-physical phenomenal properties.

Acquaintance with consciousness

Concepts, on Chalmers' account, are mental entities and are the constituents of thought. So when we think about our own experience, we do so by employing some kind of phenomenal concept. Chalmers distinguishes at least two types of phenomenal concepts. There are concepts that pick phenomenal properties out by some relation, and those that pick out phenomenal properties directly. The relational concepts are the concepts we use in our public language community, the concepts that I have individually, and indexical concepts. In each case, the referent of the term is picked out by some relation. So, in the case of the public language concept, 'red' picks out whatever in my community typically causes red experiences. This may be the same or different from what 'red' picks out for me individually. In the same way when I am having a visual experience of green and I think 'this experience is pleasant', the concept 'this experience' picks out the phenomenal experience I am currently having and so its content is determined relationally.

The other kind of concept picks out phenomenal properties directly via their intrinsic natures. These he calls 'pure phenomenal concepts'. One natural way to see the difference here is to think about pre-release Mary in her black and white room. She will be able to use the word 'red', as she will know that people often talk about red outside the room. So pre-release Mary has the public language community concept. The reference of this term is determined by whatever it is that actually produces red experiences.

When Mary is let out of her room and sees red for the first time, she will be able to form a concept that picks red out as such. She can think 'ah *this* is what they meant when they called things "red"'. She can also form the thought 'this very experience is red' where she is, so to speak, pointing to the experience and noting that it is red. 'This very experience' is the indexical concept. When Mary has the thought 'this very experience has a red quality', the indexical concept picks out her red experience. The other side of the thought is occupied by the pure phenomenal concept.

Pure phenomenal concepts can become part of our phenomenal beliefs. So when I believe that I am seeing red, the phenomenal property of redness is taken up and becomes part of the belief itself. To see this, Chalmers invokes a thought experiment about inverted Mary. Inverted Mary sees what we would call green in response to the things that we both call red. So Invert Mary will see fire trucks as green and tomatoes as green even though she will call them 'red'. When invert Mary is let out of her black and white room and sees a tomato for the first time, she can think 'this experience is what it is like to see red'. She will have a different thought than the one that non-inverted Mary has (because she is not having an experience that we would recognize as red). What this shows, for Chalmers, is that these kinds of beliefs cannot be reductively accounted for because they have as one of their parts an irreducible phenomenal quality. Pure phenomenal concepts are very close to what Bertrand Russell had in mind by knowledge from acquaintance.

They also serve as the basis of our knowledge about consciousness. A direct phenomenal belief is partially made up out of the phenomenal property it is about. The subject is acquainted with the phenomenal property. This allows Chalmers to respond to various objections to standard forms of property dualism. For instance it is sometimes held that if epiphenomenalism is true, then we cannot know about our own consciousness. But on the acquaintance view, we can know about it, though not via a way that is causal or functional. We have a direct kind of knowledge of our own conscious experiences. It also allows him to give an account of how experiences can justify beliefs. They do so through the relation of acquaintance.

Non-reductive representationalism

So what are these phenomenal properties that form the basis of phenomenal concepts and which are fundamental, non-physical aspects of reality? Chalmers suggests that it is natural to think that they are representations. This is because we can assess them in terms of accuracy and inaccuracy (Chalmers 2010, p 345).

Representationalism is very popular in the philosophy of mind (see Chapter 11) though most, unlike Chalmers, hold a reductive version of it. Chalmers defends what he calls an internal Fregean representationalism. This is the view that phenomenal properties are identical to a certain kind of representation and that there are at least two kinds of content to a visual experience. On the one hand is the representation of the way the world is. So if I am looking at a red circle, then my perceptual experience consists in a representation of the world as containing a red circle. This is what he calls the Russellian content. Then we have the mode that representation is presented under, which is the Fregean content. Here, Chalmers argues that the phenomenal quality is presented as being typically caused by some external objects. The representation also includes what he calls a 'manner of representation'. For instance representing red visually and representing it in belief involve two different manners of representation. This is distinct from the mode of presentation, which is an aspect of the intentional content of the manner of representation. So for Chalmers, phenomenal properties are phenomenal manners of representation that have as their content a Russellian colour property (in the case of colour experience) which is presented in a particular way; in particular it is presented as being typically caused by the external physical property or object.

In virtue of having Russellian contents, our experiences represent the world as instantiating certain phenomenal properties. The natural next question is whether objects in our world actually do have these kinds of properties or not. Chalmers calls worlds where objects do instantiate phenomenal properties an 'Edenic world'. In an Edenic world when an apple looks red it is because the apple itself has the property of being phenomenally red. Chalmers argues that our world is not an Edenic world, which means that we represent the world as having properties that it does not actually have.

The strongest reason for thinking this comes from thinking about colour inverts. Suppose that we have you and your inverted twin looking at an apple. You experience it as what we would call 'red', while your invert twin experiences it as what we would call 'green'. We have no reason to think that either you or the invert is getting it right, yet if both are veridical then we have to say that objects instantiate opposite properties. But this is absurd so Chalmers concludes that it is better to think that the world does not actually instantiate these properties.

If our world is not an Edenic world, then what kind of properties do objects in our world instantiate? Chalmers argues that the objects in our world must have properties that 'match' Edenic properties. To match, roughly speaking, is to play the same role. In Eden, phenomenal properties cause in perceivers perfect experiences. The properties in our world then can be said to match that role in so far as these properties bring about in us experiences with phenomenal properties. Roughly speaking, the properties of objects in our world can be said to be doing the same kind of work that Edenic properties do in Eden, which is just to cause in us experience with phenomenal properties.

One rival camp of representational theory is the higher-order thought theory of consciousness. This kind of theory is often defended by physicalists, but it is possible to hold a non-reductive non-physical version of it. Chalmers has developed a *prima facie* case against these kinds of theories, stemming from considerations about the unity of consciousness, and we will end this section by briefly looking at that argument.

Chalmers distinguishes several kinds of unity but the most philosophically relevant for the present purposes is what he calls 'subsumptive phenomenal unity'. Intuitively this is the idea that all of our conscious mental states at any given time are necessarily bound into a unified whole. He is tentative about endorsing it, but he does say that it has a strong intuitive appeal to him. However, if it is true, there are many theories of consciousness that would not be able to account for it. Higher-Order Thought theories can account for the unity of consciousness but cannot account for the necessity of this unity. The same is true of several versions of reductive representationalism. If it really is a necessary fact about our experience that it is subsumptively unified, then that would be strong evidence against the higher-order thought theory of consciousness.

Other issues in the philosophy of mind

Up until this point, we have focused on issues surrounding consciousness. We will conclude by briefly looking at how the ideas developed here can be applied to other issues in the philosophy of mind.

Recall the Twin Earth thought experiment that we introduced earlier. Many philosophers have taken the moral of that story to be that natives of Twin Earth have thoughts about XYZ (not H_2O) and so the content of their mental states will be different than ours. When they believe that water is wet, they believe something about XYZ. When I believe it, I believe something about H_2O. If I were to be suddenly transported to Twin Earth and thought to myself 'that water is wet', while looking at a glass of (what I didn't realize) was XYZ, my belief would be false. This suggests that the contents of thoughts are broad in the sense that we can have people with the same psychological make-up who nonetheless have beliefs with differing contents. This is counter-intuitive in that it seems that the content of a thought or belief should be narrow in the sense of being determined by mental things rather than environmental things. Given this, we would expect that there should be something that is common to the beliefs that we and the Twin Earthers make.

Chalmers (2012) has argued that we can use the two-dimensional analysis to shed light on this debate. The people on Twin Earth have mental states that have different secondary intensions. But we share our primary intensions with them. If so, then primary intensions can be used to make sense of narrow content. Mental states have both kinds of content on Chalmers' account. Each belief or thought can be associated with both a primary intension that depends on the mental make-up of the subject and a secondary intension that depends on the environment that the thinker is situated in.

This should not be taken to mean that he insists that all mental phenomena must be in the head. Chalmers (Clark and Chalmers 1998; see also Chapter 13) has argued that the mind can extend outside of the skull and into the environment. The mind, for Chalmers, minus that part that involves consciousness, consists in the performance of certain functions like the ones listed at the beginning of this chapter as the easy problems. These functions are performed by the brain but there is no reason in principle that they couldn't be performed by suitable functional devices outside the head. So for instance, if I am currently thinking that 'I am in New York City' and this thought is realized by a certain computational process in my brain, it follows from the principle of organizational invariance that we could replace the neurons performing that computation with functionally equivalent artificial neurons. This would not affect my belief or its content. Nor does it seem to matter whether this process occurs in the brain or not. As long as it is connected to the brain in the right way so as to allow normal functioning and unimpeded computation, the mind will be undisturbed. Thus if you are looking at some H_2O and believe that it is wet, and this belief is realized by a computer outside of your head (functioning and connected in the right way to your brain), and another, psychologically similar, person is on Twin Earth looking at a glass of XYZ but whose belief is realized by computations in the brain, you both have beliefs that have the same narrow content and different broad content. One of them has a belief that is extended beyond the skull, but that is the only difference between them.[2]

Notes

1 There are also a couple of other responses that he lays out. One could accept causal overdetermination, which he labels the type-O response, or one could be an idealist, which he labels the type-I response.
2 Thanks to David Chalmers and Andrew Bailey for comments on an earlier version of this chapter.

References

Balog, K. (2012), 'Acquaintance and the mind-body problem'. In Hill and Gozzano (eds), *New Perspectives on Type Identity: The Mental and the Physical*. Cambridge: Cambridge University Press, pp. 16–43.
Block, N. and Stalnaker, R. (1999), 'Conceptual analysis, dualism and the explanatory gap'. *The Philosophical Review* 108: 1–46.
Block, N. (2007), 'Max Black's objection to the identity theory', in N. Block (ed.), *Consciousness, Function, and Representation*. Cambridge, MA: MIT Press, pp. 435–98.

— (forthcoming), 'Functional Reduction'.
Brown, R. (2010), 'Deprioritizing the *a priori* arguments against physicalism', *Journal of Consciousness Studies* 17: 47–69.
Clark, A. and Chalmers, D. (1998), 'The extended mind'. *Analysis* 58: 10–23.
Chalmers, D. J. (1996), *The Conscious Mind: In Search of a Fundamental Theory*. New York: Oxford University Press.
— (2010), *The Character of Consciousness*. New York: Oxford University Press.
— (2011), 'A computational foundation for the study of cognition'. *Journal of Cognitive Science* 12: 323–57.
— (2012), *Constructing the World*. New York: Oxford University Press.
Frankish, K. (2007), 'The anti-zombie argument'. *Philosophical Quarterly* 57: 650–66.
Jackson, F. (1986), 'What Mary didn't know'. *Journal of Philosophy* 83: 291–5.
Kripke, S. (1980), *Naming and Necessity*, Cambridge, MA: Harvard University Press.
Levine, J. (1983), 'Materialism and qualia: the explanatory gap'. *Pacific Philosophical Quarterly* 64: 354–61.
Mandik, P. and Weisberg, J. (2008). 'Type-Q materialism', in C. Wrenn (ed.), *Naturalism, Reference and Ontology: Essays in Honor of Roger F. Gibson*. New York: Peter Lang Publishing Group, pp. 223–45.
Nagel, T. (1974), 'What is it like to be a bat?' *The Philosophical Review* 83: 435–50.
Putnam, H. (1973), 'Meaning and reference'. *Journal of Philosophy* 70: 699–711.
Russell, B. (1912). *The Problems of Philosophy*. Oxford: Oxford University Press.
— (1927), *The Analysis of Matter*. London: Kegan Paul, Trench, Trubner.

CHAPTER FIFTEEN

Postscript: Philosophy of mind – the next ten years

Andrew Bailey

One conveniently rough-and-ready way of demarcating the three lobes of the philosophy of mind is by the three 'c's: content, consciousness and causality. That is, how are mental states intentional (i.e. *about* things, in a way that non-mental states are not, e.g. in a non-derived fashion)? How are mental states phenomenal (i.e. how is it that, unlike any other kind of states, there is *something it is like to be* conscious)? And how are mental states the appropriate causes of our actions (where, traditionally, the contrast is with 'merely causal' physical states, but more recently it is with (other?) higher-level states that are non-reducible to the physical)?

In this brief postscript, I will indicate what I believe is afoot, and driving some key work of the next few years, in each of these three areas, with a view to – in a very partial way – linking the figures discussed in the main body of this book with current and near-future philosophical activity.

Content

Is there a cognitively viable notion of narrow mental content and a psychologically plausible notion of wide mental content?

These issues are made pressing by *semantic externalism*. Semantic externalism holds that what a thought is about is partially fixed by factors outside the head of the thinker (see, e.g. Putnam 1975 and Burge 1979). For example, my thoughts about titanium are directed at that particular metallic element, atomic number 22, and even if I have few or faulty beliefs about titanium, or could not tell titanium apart from vanadium, it is nevertheless *that* substance that I am thinking of; the nature of the element itself, over and above my beliefs about it, is what determines what my thought is about. Similarly, my statements about actuarial analysts have their content fixed by the linguistic community of which I am a part, even though I myself may have only the vaguest notion of what I am talking about. These kinds of consideration have firmly established the position that thoughts have *wide content*, content that is not idiosyncratic to individuals or fixed by factors inside their heads.[1]

But this raises deep problems, which are as yet unresolved, for mental content. If our actions are to be appropriately caused by our thoughts (i.e. by the contents of our thoughts), and if our deliberate actions are proximally caused entirely by factors inside our heads, then it seems there must be some sort of *narrow* mental content as well: contents that are determined entirely by individualist, rather than externalist, factors and that are of the right type to explain our actions.[2] What, then, is the nature of narrow mental content and how is it related to wide content?

This is currently an active, and controversial, area of the philosophy of mind, comprised of several debates. One dispute concerns the kind of mental content that is necessary for the causal explanation of behaviour. Fodor, for example (the subject of Chapter 9), has moved from being a key proponent of the position that narrow content is psychologically crucial because causal powers must be local, intrinsic properties (1987), to a considerably more complex, and tentative, view in which content is wide and mental causes are strictly syntactic (1994).

At the furthest end of this spectrum, tendencies within the embodied cognition movement (see Monica Cowart's Chapter 13) call into question whether key areas of mental life, especially related to perception and action, are composed of contentful mental representations at all. The enactivist paradigm, for example, denies that organisms internally represent the world (at least to the extent assumed by classical cognitive science) and proposes instead that their behaviour arises out of a dynamical, real-time interplay between the embodied organism and its environment. Colour vision for example, on this view, is not a matter of encoding colour sensations but of enacting a certain kind of patterned sensorimotor dependence on the surfaces surrounding one. (See Noë 2004; Varela, Thompson and Rosch 1991.)

Another ongoing dispute centres on our introspective access to our own mental states: it is apparently part of the very notion of wide content that I may not have complete access to the meaning of my own thoughts, and this seems *prima facie* to be in tension with some strong intuitions about our ability to know our own minds. Well-known Twin Earth–type thought experiments illustrate the limitations of my knowledge of my thoughts, for the externalist. Here on Earth I might be having thoughts about titanium (i.e. the element with atomic number 22). However, suppose there is a parallel world, Twin Earth, identical to this world in every way except that there the stuff that looks and behaves just like titanium, and is labelled 'titanium' in Twin English, is not an element at all but some sort of metallic compound. My twin's thoughts on Twin Earth will not be about titanium, but about the different stuff in his environment (we might call it, in English, twintanium). But, since my twin is *ex hypothesi* intrinsically identical to me, there will be no introspectable difference between my titanium thoughts and my twin's twintanium thoughts – although they have different contents, our thoughts will seem exactly the same to us. Yet, it seems, I *do* know what I am thinking, in at least some important sense. So what do I know when I know that, for example, I'd like the frames of my spectacles to be made of titanium? There is a large and growing literature on these issues. (See Nuccetelli 2003, Ludlow and Martin 1998.)

Finally, a third important debate about narrow mental content, that has recently become very active, concerns the relationship between phenomenology and intentionality. Horgan, Tienson and Graham (2002, 2004, 2007; see also Searle 1992 and Siewert 1998) have argued that there is an important and pervasive species of mental content that constitutively depends on phenomenology – on how things seem to us consciously and qualitatively. Since, it might seem safe to say, phenomenology is determined or constituted entirely by intrinsic features of the thinker, then this kind of content (often called 'phenomenal intentionality') must be narrow. Indeed, Horgan et al. hold that phenomenal intentionality is 'the *fundamental* kind of intentionality: the narrow, phenomenal kind that is a prerequisite for wide content and wide truth conditions' (2002, p. 529).[3]

This development is significant, not only because of its relevance to the debate over narrow mental content, but because it marks an important shift away from what Lycan has called 'the standard attitude among [analytic] philosophers of mind between the 1950s and the 1980s' (2008, p. 240), which was that phenomenal and intentional properties are quite separate from, and independent of, each other. (This was far less true of philosophers working in the tradition of Husserl and Merleau-Ponty, as Dermot Moran and Sara Heinämaa's chapters have illustrated). On this view, some mental states have content, some have qualitative 'feel' and some may have both, but the two kinds of property are unrelated to each other and each will require separate theoretical explanations. (Sellars 1956, is one important expression of this kind of view, which can also be found in, for example, Davidson 1982, and Putnam 1981).

The new interest in 'phenomenal intentionality', by contrast, suggests both that the problems of consciousness and content may be deeply linked together in ways that have not been properly appreciated in recent mainstream philosophy of mind, and also that the standard modern way of approaching mental content as independent of phenomenology may be wrong-headed. (See Chalmers 2004, Kriegel 2013.)

Finally, 'phenomenal intentionality' is one avenue into the active current debate about non-conceptual mental content (see Gunther 2003). One might ask, for example, is there a form of sensory intentionality that is both contentful – rather than merely a brute play of sensations – and non-conceptual? (Again, this has resonances in the work of continental theorists such as Husserl ('pre-predicative' experience) and Merleau-Ponty (his notion of active perception); see Kelly 2000, and Chapters 3 and 4.) And could, perhaps, this putatively special variety of non-conceptual content shed light on the nature of conscious perceptual experience (as in Tye's PANIC theory, for example; see Tye 2002, and Chapter 11)?

Causation

The problem of mental causation has always been a philosophical issue; it is related, for example, to the hallowed problem of free will and to the philosophy of action. But it is probably fair to say that the issue of mental causation re-emerged in a new guise in the closing decades of the twentieth century, and in this form it remains a centrally unsolved problem in the philosophy of mind.

Jaegwon Kim identifies three sources for the problem of mental causation (Kim 1998, p. 32): the anomalism of the mental, computationalism and content externalism, and 'causal exclusion'. The first of these is discussed in Andrew Brook's chapter on Davidson and Dennett (Chapter 10); the second is related to the issues summarized above (and also see Chapter 8); so let's look at the third.

Causal exclusion is a problem for any account of the mental that resists reducing mental types to low-level physical types. Thus, it is a problem for property dualism and for most types of functionalism, but (arguably) not for mind-brain identity theory (see Chapters 6–8). The problem arises, in essence, because we are committed, qua naturalistic philosophers, to the presumption that all physical events have sufficient physical causes.[4] Thus, all our actions (which are physical movements in space) have complete physical (presumably neural) causes. These physical causes pre-empt, or exclude, mental causes: if all the causal work is being done by brain event p, then what is left over for some associated mental event m, that is either realized by p or correlated with it, to do? As Kim puts it: 'Given that every physical event that has a cause has a physical cause, how is a mental cause also possible?' (1999, p. 38).

This is a worry for functionalism, and other varieties of non-reductive physicalism, because the functionalist identifies the mental with functional *roles* and not with the *fillers* of those roles (see the discussion in Chapters 6 and 7). Pain is a causal role, and in virtue of that we get to say that any organism – human, octopus or android – that instantiates a state *that plays that role* is genuinely in pain. But that means that pain is not the same property as whatever it is that plays that role in humans and androids: it can't be, because humans and androids have quite *different* physical properties despite the postulated sameness of their mental properties. Yet it is the physical realizations of pain – the various fillers of the role – that do all the causal work in bringing about pain behaviour. The upshot, if the exclusion argument is sound, is that pain does not cause pain behaviour.

Among those who find this argument compelling, this conclusion is often taken as tantamount to a *reductio*; and one response to this is to revisit the prospects for some form of mind-brain identity theory and to abandon non-reductive physicalism. (This is Kim's own response; see Kim 2005.) Given the dominance of functionalism for much of the past few decades, this can seem a fairly startling change of direction. Another possible response is to embrace a kind of eliminativism about the mental: to concede that mental properties, if such there were, would be epiphenomenal, mere danglers on the real causally operative structure of the world, and to treat mental predicates as merely a sort of shorthand way of talking (albeit a very important way of talking), or a way of picking out non-causal patterns (see Chapters 10 and 12). But these options, of course, are far from risk-free: the price of identity theory includes, to a first approximation, abandoning the generality of cross-species and possibly even cross-individual psychology, and sacrificing the 'autonomy' of the mental; the cost of eliminativism is, on the face of it, some flavour of anti-realism about the mind.[5] These are difficult choices that, arguably, are still sinking in in the mainstream and certainly have yet to be fully played out.

Consciousness

The difficulty of providing a naturalistic, physicalist account of phenomenal consciousness rose to particular prominence in the 1990s and remains a deeply contested area of the philosophy of mind: few would confidently assert that the problem of conscious has been solved, and many worry that we are far from seeing even the shape of a solution (if indeed a solution is available). (See Richard Brown's discussion of the work of David Chalmers in Chapter 14.)

The issue, then, is: is consciousness ontologically emergent from the physical? Is the phenomenal 'over and above' physics? The debate has been pursued primarily through competing accounts of the phenomenal (Dennett's multiple drafts, Higher-Order Thought/Perception theories, global workspace theories, first-order representationalism, biological theories and so on[6]) and extensive discussion of putative objections to physicalism (zombies, the knowledge argument, the explanatory gap, etc.). However, a persistent stumbling block has been the opaqueness, or indeterminacy, of the futuristic physics with respect to which the phenomenal may or may not be emergent. For example, Patricia Churchland has labelled the apparent argumentative slide from the claim that consciousness is *conceivably* more than physical to the conclusion that it is *actually* more than physical 'the Hornswoggle Problem' (Churchland 1996), on the basis that we do not yet know enough about what a future neuroscience will look like to make these judgements.

In the face of this, in my view, we are seeing a subtle but significant reorientation of the problem of consciousness. The focus of the question is becoming, not so much, what would it be for consciousness to be respectably 'physical' (whatever exactly that means) but what would it be for consciousness to be naturalistically *explained* – what do we require of an adequate theory of phenomenal consciousness. This latter question has the virtue of being more directly oriented towards what is actually at stake in the debate about consciousness. We care much more, I suggest, about being able to *understand* consciousness, and link it in satisfying ways to the rest of the natural world, than we do about the putative universality of, say, mathematical physics. The impetus to physicalism about consciousness came, in the first place, from the recognition that substance dualism left consciousness metaphysically isolated from the rest of reality and completely impervious to any form of naturalistic study.

The recent small vogue for various forms of panpsychism is instructive in this respect (see, e.g. Strawson 2006, Rosenberg 2005). Panpsychism is the theory that phenomenality – some sort of consciousness or proto-consciousness – is a fundamental feature of the world and present throughout the universe. One of the recent drivers of this supposition has been the observation that physics, and the natural sciences more generally, are suited only to describing the *extrinsic* nature of things – the ways in which things are related. An electron, for example, is individuated entirely in terms of its possible relations with other particles and fields; similarly, the property of mass is defined extrinsically with respect to the interaction of objects in gravitational fields (or under acceleration). This apparently leaves unaddressed the *intrinsic* nature of reality. And this seems to dovetail nicely with the problem of consciousness: the problem is, arguably, that phenomenal consciousness seems to be made up of intrinsic qualities, such as sensed pinkness, felt tickles and experienced pain, that are *prima facie* irreducible to the structure and function of physics. Well then: suppose the intrinsic nature of matter, including the matter of the brain, is qualitative – after all, what other acquaintance do we have with anything genuinely intrinsic? – and perhaps the problem is solved.

Note that the issues that are raised by panpsychism do not seem to be, most centrally, questions about whether this is *physicalism*. That is pretty much a sideshow. The real question is whether panpsychism would be, if true, *explanatory* of consciousness: would it, if true, help us to understand better how consciousness fits into the rest of the natural world? (And it is far from clear that it would: e.g. How would the intrinsic nature of matter sum to personal consciousness of the sort that human beings have? Would it so sum in other objects, and if not why not? Does the putatively qualitative intrinsic nature of brain states contribute to their causal efficacy, and if so how? and so on.)

Along similar lines, a disputed question about physicalism which turns out to be of key importance is whether physicalist – or, more generally, naturalistic; or more generally still, thoroughly satisfying – explanations must be a priori. One stance on this question (a stance which Block and Stalnaker 1999, call the *conceptual analysis thesis*) is that an ideal reasoner in possession of all the microphysical facts (plus relevant logical and linguistic facts) could figure out *all* the facts, including phenomenal facts as well as sociological facts, aesthetic facts, biological facts and so on. The key intuition here is that, for it to be the case that physics *fully explains* (not merely fully determines) everything that is empirically true, it must be the case that grasp of the physics (plus grasp of relevant concepts) is in principle *sufficient* for grasp of all those truths. Conversely, for the conceptual analyst, failure of physics to be explanatory suggests the falsity of physicalism: it seems to indicate that consciousness (say) is over and above the physical facts.[7]

Raising the question in this way reveals that there is a middle ground: it might be that, for some reason, physics metaphysically determines the phenomenal facts but fails to *explain* those facts, in the sense that a grasp of the physical (plus conceptual) facts alone is not sufficient to understand how and why the phenomenal facts obtain as they do. That is, even if physicalism is true, we might be left without any satisfactory story as to why or how the properties (states, etc.) picked out by phenomenal concepts are realized/constituted by properties (states, etc.) picked out by physical concepts.

The interesting question, then, is not so much: is physicalism true? It is: is the physical explanatory of the phenomenal?[8] Is the demand for conceptual analysis unreasonably strong, and if it is unattainable what can replace it? Is there a stable form of non–a priori physicalism that can fill the explanatory bill, or alternatively is there perhaps something that does not resemble the physicalism we were expecting (such as perhaps panpsychism) that, if true, would discharge the task of explaining consciousness?

The past 90 years in philosophy of mind have been exciting, intellectually fast-moving times, and a great deal of progress has been made since the early days of the transition from Cartesian dualism to behaviourist or central-state materialist philosophical psychology. I hope the preceding chapters have provided an engaging and thought-provoking grounding in many of the key movements and figures in that history, and that you feel as excited as do I and my fellow authors as we move forward into the next developments in the philosophy of mind; we hope that this book has given you the desire, and some of the conceptual tools, to join us on that journey.

Notes

1 This view is not unanimously held, however: see, for example, Crane 1991, and Segal 2000.

2 Again, there is an active minority of 'extreme externalists' who oppose this view: for example, Wilson 1995, Stalnaker 2008, and Burge 2010.

3 One view, probably that of Horgan, Tienson and Graham, is that phenomenal character is sufficient for a certain kind of intentional content. A stronger position would hold that the phenomenal character of experience is not only sufficient for various forms of intentionality but also necessary for it (Flanagan 1992, calls this 'consciousness essentialism').

The converse view, that phenomenology is entirely constituted by intentionality, is the view explored in Chapter 11. Some proponents of this view argue that aspects of phenomenology are *not* determined internally but instead are essentially determined by causal environmental connections (Dretske 1995, Tye 2002, Lycan 2008).

4 This is known as the principle of the causal closure of the physical. Another assumption operative in this version of the argument is that physical events are not systematically overdetermined: that is, they typically have only one sufficient cause.

5   It is worth noting that exclusion-type considerations apply to any non-reductive naturalistic theory, not just to the mind, and so similar worries can be raised about, say, economic causation, biological causation or geological causation.
6   For representative examples: Dennett 1991, Rosenthal 2005, Baars 1997, Tye 2002, Edelman and Tononi 2000.
7   This is arguably the driver for key anti-physicalist thought experiments, such as the zombie and knowledge arguments.
8   In some of his recent work, Chalmers (2012) asks a question very much like this, though his focus is not (exclusively) on the phenomenal: is the natural world, in some sense, what he calls *scrutable*? That is, given some basic truths, are the rest of the truths comprehensible and derivable (at least by an ideal reasoner)? Furthermore, can all the truths be derived, in principle, a priori from the basic set (what Chalmers calls *a priori scrutability*)?

References

Baars, B. J. (1997), *In the Theater of Consciousness*. New York: Oxford University Press.
Bailey, A. and Richard, T. B. (in press). 'Horgan and Tienson on phenomenal intentionality'. *Philosophical Studies*. (DOI 10.1007/s11098-013-0089-7).
Block, N. and Stalnaker, R. (1999), 'Conceptual analysis, dualism, and the explanatory gap'. *Philosophical Review* 108: 1–46.
Burge, T. (1979), 'Individualism and the mental'. *Midwest Studies in Philosophy* 4: 73–121.
— (2010), *Origins of Objectivity*. Oxford: Oxford University Press.
Chalmers, D. J. (2004), 'The representational character of experience'. In Leiter, 2004, pp. 153–80.
— (2012), *Constructing the World*. Oxford: Oxford University Press.
Churchland, P. S. (1996), 'The hornswoggle problem'. *Journal of Consciousness Studies* 3: 402–8.
Crane, T. (1991), 'All the difference in the world'. *Philosophical Quarterly* 41: 1–25.
Davidson, D. (1982), 'Empirical content'. *Grazer Philosophische Studien* 16/17: 471–89.
Dahlbom, B. (ed.) (1993), *Dennett and His Critics: Demystifying Mind*. Oxford: Blackwell.
Dennett, D. C. (1991), *Consciousness Explained*. Boston: Little, Brown.
Dretske, F. (1995), *Naturalizing the Mind*. Cambridge, MA: MIT Press.

Edelman, G. and Tononi, G. (2000), *A Universe of Consciousness: How Matter Becomes Imagination*. New York: Basic Books.
Flanagan, O. (1992), *Consciousness Reconsidered*. Cambridge, MA: MIT Press.
Fodor, J. (1987), *Psychosemantics*. Cambridge, MA: MIT Press.
— (1994), *The Elm and the Expert: Mentalese and its Semantics*. Cambridge, MA: MIT Press.
Graham, G., Horgan, T., and Tienson, J. (2007), 'Consciousness and intentionality'. In M. Velmans and S. Schneider (eds), *The Blackwell Companion to Consciousness*. Oxford: Blackwell, pp. 468–84.
Gunther, Y. H. (2003), *Essays on Nonconceptual Content*. Cambridge, MA: MIT Press.
Horgan, T. and Tienson, J. (2002), 'The intentionality of phenomenology and the phenomenology of intentionality'. In D. J. Chalmers (ed.), *Philosophy of Mind: Classical and Contemporary Readings*. Oxford: Oxford University Press, pp. 520–32.
Horgan, T., Tienson, J., and Graham, G. (2005), 'Phenomenal intentionality and the brain in a vat'. In R. Schantz (ed.), *The Externalist Challenge: New Studies in Cognition and Intentionality*. Berlin: De Gruyter, pp. 297–317.
Kelly, S. (2000), *The Relevance of Phenomenology to the Philosophy of Language and Mind*. London: Routledge.
Kim, J. (1999), *Mind in a Physical World*. Cambridge, MA: MIT Press.
— (2004), 'The mind-body problem at century's turn'. In Leiter, 2004, pp. 129–52.
— (2005), *Physicalism, or Something Near Enough*. Princeton, NJ: Princeton University Press.
Kriegel, U., (ed.) (2013), *Phenomenal Intentionality*. Oxford: Oxford University Press.
Leiter, B., (ed.) (2004), *The Future for Philosophy*. Oxford: Oxford University Press.
Levine, J. (1983), 'Materialism and qualia: The explanatory gap'. *Pacific Philosophical Quarterly* 64: 354–61.
Ludlow, P. and Martin, N., (eds) (1998), *Externalism and Self-Knowledge*. Stanford: CSLI Publications.
Lycan, W. G. (2008), 'Phenomenal intentionalities'. *American Philosophical Quarterly* 45: 233–52.
McLaughlin, B. P. and Cohen, J. (2007), *Contemporary Debates in Philosophy of Mind*. Oxford: Blackwell.
Noë, A. (2004), *Action in Perception*. Cambridge, MA: MIT Press.
Noordhof, P. (2011), 'Current issues in the philosophy of mind'. In J. Garvey (ed.), *The Continuum Companion to Philosophy of Mind*. London: Continuum, pp. 239–79.

Nuccetelli, S., (ed.) (2003), *New Essays on Semantic Externalism and Self-Knowledge*. Cambridge, MA: MIT Press.
Putnam, H. (1975), 'The meaning of "meaning"'. In K. Gunderson (ed.), *Language, Mind, and Knowledge*. Minneapolis: University of Minnesota Press, pp. 131–93.
— (1981), *Reason, Truth and History*. Cambridge: Cambridge University Press.
Rosenberg, G. (2005), *A Place for Consciousness: Probing the Deep Structure of the Natural World*. Oxford: Oxford University Press.
Rosenthal, D. (2005), *Consciousness and Mind*. Oxford: Oxford University Press.
Searle, J. R. (1992), *The Rediscovery of the Mind*. Cambridge, MA: MIT Press.
Segal, G. (2000), *A Slim Book about Narrow Content*. Cambridge, MA: MIT Press.
Sellars, W. (1956), 'Empiricism and the philosophy of mind'. *Minnesota Studies in The Philosophy of Science* 1: 253–329.
Siewert, C. (1998), *The Significance of Consciousness*. Princeton, NJ: Princeton University Press.
Stalnaker, R. C. (2008), *Our Knowledge of the Internal World*. Oxford: Oxford University Press.
Strawson, G. (2006), 'Realistic monism: Why physicalism entails panpsychism'. *Journal of Consciousness Studies* 13: 3–31.
Tye, M. (2002), *Consciousness, Color and Content*. Cambridge, MA: MIT Press.
Varela, F. J., Thompson, E., Rosch, E. (1991), *The Embodied Mind*. Cambridge, MA: MIT Press.
Wilson, R. A. (1995), *Cartesian Psychology and Physical Minds: Individualism and the Sciences of Mind*. New York: Cambridge University Press.

INDEX

adverbialism 99, 215–16, 229n. 10
after-images/hallucinations 110–11, 215–16, 228
Alexander, Samuel (1859–1938) 107
aliens 6–7, 70, 140
angels 6, 22, 107
Anscombe, G. E. M. (1919–2001) 193, 229n. 11
Aquinas, Thomas (1225–1274) 4, 44
Aristotle (374–322 BCE) 4, 44, 55, 76n. 8, 94, 148, 194, 251–2
Armstrong, David M. (1926–) 8, 97, 111–12, 118, 129–46, 149
artificial intelligence 122, 138, 144, 153, 247

bats, mental life of 247–8
bees, mental life of 2–3, 121, 203
Bechtel, William 9, 12, 161, 244
Bergson, Henri (1859–1941) 39
Black, Max (1909–1988) 109–10
blindsight 227, 247
Block, Ned (1942–) 113, 118, 141, 150–1, 161–2, 220–1, 227, 291, 310
Brentano, Franz (1838–1817) 14n. 8, 40–3, 60, 87
British Emergentism 107, 110

Broad, Charles Dunbar (1887–1971) 107, 120
Brooks, Rodney (1954–) 265

category mistake 91–2
c-fibres 6, 14n. 5, 157
Chalmers, David (1966–) 10, 12–13, 111, 119–20, 142, 150, 155, 158, 163, 227–8, 229n. 2, 249, 266–71, 283–302, 306, 308, 312n. 8
chess 98–9, 197–8
Chinese room 18–19, 141
Churchland, Patricia (1943–) 8, 12, 18, 155, 180, 237–58, 308–9
Churchland, Paul (1942–) 8, 12, 155, 171, 181, 237–58, 292
Clark, Andy 13, 246, 259–82, 300
computation 7, 9, 150–3, 155, 161–4, 173–6, 184–5, 295
  connectionist 9, 155, 180–1, 237, 239–40, 244–8, 251–2, 255
  embodied/extended 259–60, 263, 265, 304–5
Crocker, Betty 249

Damasio, Antonio (1944–) 13, 18, 259–82

Davidson, Donald
(1917–2003) 11–12,
14n. 4, 32n. 9, 189–208,
230n. 16, 306–7
Dennett, Daniel C. (1942–) 11–12,
18, 179, 189–208, 289,
307–8
Descartes, René (1596–1650) 4–5,
17–36, 38–40, 42, 52, 67,
72, 74, 76n. 8, 76n. 10,
78n. 24, 85–6, 90–3,
95–8, 100, 129–30, 178,
272, 292, 311
Desgabets, Robert (1610–1678)
26–7, 33n. 12
dichromacy 1
  unilateral 2
dispositions 92–3, 97, 100,
103–4, 131, 156
Dretske, Fred I. (1932–) 9, 47,
58n. 18, 206n. 4, 209–36,
311n. 3
dropsy 28
embodied/extended mind 13, 19,
31, 39–40, 54, 59, 62–3,
69–74, 259–82, 300–1,
304

emotion 3, 10, 12–13, 18–19,
21, 28, 31, 38–9, 41, 55,
97, 226, 231n. 26, 268,
271–8
epiphenomenalism 18, 29, 31,
96–7, 113–14, 129, 131,
143, 222–3, 292–3, 297,
307–8
explanatory gap 158, 285,
289–90, 292, 308
eye movement desensitization
reprocessing 277–8

Feigl, Herbert (1902–1988) 6,
103–28

functional magnetic resonance
imaging (fMRI) 119, 203
Fodor, Jerry A. (1935–) 7, 9, 18,
118, 149, 158–60, 164,
169–88, 246, 253–4, 304
folk psychology 8, 112, 118–19,
139, 170–3, 179, 238–40,
242–3, 252
frame problem 260

Garber, Daniel 24
gavagai 124
Grand, David 277–8

haemophilia 92–3, 97
Harman, Gilbert (1938–) 124n. 3,
160, 216–17, 225,
230n. 12–13
heat 5, 121, 161, 201, 241–2
Heidegger, Martin (1889–1976) 47,
65, 78n. 24, 87, 259
Hill, Christopher 117–18, 120, 123
holism of the mental 10–11, 42,
158–9, 189–90, 195, 197,
199
Hooker, Clifford 243
hornswoggle problem 309
Hume, David (1711–1776) 39–40,
46
Husserl, Edmund (1859–1938)
12, 37–58, 60–3, 65–9,
72–3, 75n. 4, 77n. 20,
79n. 29, 87, 306

immortality 24–5, 28
Inga/Otto 266, 269–71
innateness 12, 18, 179–80, 213
intersubjectivity 38–9, 52–5, 61,
71–2, 123, 197, 273
introspection 5, 12, 65, 76n. 10,
85, 97–9, 104, 108, 129,
131, 164, 215, 217,
230n. 13, 305

INDEX

Inverted Earth 220–1, 224
iPhone 268

Jackson, Frank (1943–) 107, 119, 134, 140–2, 216, 218, 227, 231n. 23, 247–8, 285
James, William (1842–1910) 39, 44, 76n. 13, 98
Johnson, Mark (1949–) 263–4

Kant, Immanuel (1724–1804) 4, 39–40, 54, 74, 79n. 29, 272
Kim, Jaegwon (1934–) 120–1, 161, 307
knowing how and knowing that 94, 248, 251
knowledge argument 107, 124n. 6, 141, 227, 247–8, 285, 296–7, 308, 312n. 7
  Inverted Mary 297
Kripke, Saul (1940–) 114–19, 123, 286, 288

Lakoff, George (1941–) 263–4
Land, Edwin (1909–91) 248
language of thought 169, 173–9, 185, 238, 254
Leibniz, Gottfried Wilhelm (1646–1716) 106, 114, 290
levels of description/descriptive stances 153–4, 197–9, 204–5, 206n. 3
Lewis, David (1941–2001) 8, 112–13, 116–17, 129–146, 149–50, 289
Locke, John (1632–1704) 4, 46, 76n. 10
Lycan, William G. (1945–) 9, 209–36, 306, 311n. 3

McGinn, Colin (1950–) 210
Malebranche, Nicolas (1638–1715) 29
Meinong, Alexius (1853–1920) 87
memory 38, 41–2, 50–1, 98, 155, 239, 269–71, 275
Merleau-Ponty, Maurice (1908–1961) 12, 46, 59–84, 259, 306
mirror neurons 59
modularity of mind 169, 181–5, 186n. 4
Moore, G. E. (1873–1958) 49, 87, 230n. 12
multiple realizability 6, 113, 117, 121, 138–40, 149, 157, 160–4

Nagel Ernest (1901–1985) 243
Nagel, Thomas (1937–) 55, 123, 247, 292
Newsome, William 250
nomological danglers 107, 308
normativity of the mental 10–11, 189–208

octopus, mental life of 6, 14n. 6, 112–13, 121, 140, 307

pain 5–6, 10, 24, 105, 109, 112–13, 115–19, 121, 134, 140, 148–50, 154–7, 209, 219, 226, 231n. 25, 286, 290, 292, 307, 309
panpsychism 293, 309–11
Peacocke, Christopher (1950–) 225
Piaget, Jean (1896–1980) 259
Pickwick 89–90
Place, Ullin T. (1924–2000) 6, 103–28
Plato (429–347 BCE) 4, 55, 192, 251

poison 132–3, 144n. 1
Price, H. H. (1899–1984) 49
Putnam, Hilary (1926–) 6, 11, 14n. 4, 18, 112, 121, 123, 140, 147–68, 180, 288, 304, 306

qualia/phenomenal properties 10, 46–7, 104–10, 118, 122, 209–10, 215–8, 223, 226, 247–50, 284–5, 293, 296–9
  absent 118, 141
  fading/dancing 295–6
  inverted 118, 141, 158, 249, 297, 299
Quine, Willard van O. (1908–2000) 192–4, 197, 200, 293

Ramsification 112, 136, 142, 150, 154–5
Reid, Thomas (1710–1796) 4, 49
representation, pure and impure 211–13, 228
retina 1, 14n. 1, 182, 248
Richardson, R. C. 30
rigid designation 115–17, 125n. 11
robots 6, 13, 113, 122–3, 261, 296, 307
Russell, Bertrand (1872–1970) 87, 90, 291, 293, 297–8
Ryle, Gilbert (1900–1976) 4, 5, 17–19, 29, 31, 75n. 4, 76n. 10, 85–102, 289

Scrabble® 266–7
Searle, John (1932–) 18–19, 32n. 2, 55, 179, 249, 260, 305
Sellars, Wilfrid (1912–89) 55, 58n. 18, 193–4, 306

Smart, Jack (J. J. C.) (1920–2012) 6, 103–28, 132–9, 142, 144, 149
super-spartans 156–7
swamp-person 221–2, 224

Tarski, Alfred (1901–1983) 192
Thelen, Esther (1941–2004) 262–3, 265
tetrachromacy 2–3
transparency of experience 216–18, 230n. 12–13
trauma 260, 276–9
trialism 26, 32n. 11
trichromacy 1–2
Turing machine 152–3, 155, 173–5, 181, 186n. 1, 295
Turing test 153
Twin Earth 159–60, 288–9, 300–1, 305
two-dimensionalism 286–90, 293, 300
Tye, Michael 9, 209–236, 306, 311n. 3

van Fraassen, Bas (1941–) 242
venus 109–10

Watson, John B. (1878–1958) 99
William of Ockham (1287–1347) 4, 91, 120
Williams, Bernard (1929–2003) 20
Wittgenstein, Ludwig (1889–1951) 66, 86–8, 90, 96, 190, 193–4, 206n. 4
Wollheim, Richard (1923–2003) 51

Yablo, Stephen 18

zombies 142–3, 158, 227, 249, 286–7, 289–90, 292–3, 308, 312n. 7
  anti-zombies/shombies 293–4

www.ingramcontent.com/pod-product-compliance
Lightning Source LLC
Chambersburg PA
CBHW050135240426
43673CB00043B/1674